AN INDISPENSABLE LIBERTY

AN INDISPENSABLE LIBERTY

THE FIGHT FOR FREE SPEECH IN NINETEENTH-CENTURY AMERICA

EDITED BY MARY M. CRONIN

Southern Illinois University Press
Carbondale

Southern Illiois University Press
www.siupress.com

Printed in the United States of America

19 18 17 16 4 3 2 1

Cover illustration: Protesters of free speech burned Pennsylvania Hall on May 17, 1838, after abolitionists spoke there to racially mixed audiences. This fire was one of many extralegal restrictions on freedom of speech that occurred in nineteenth-century America. Lithograph by Swiss-born artist John Caspar Wild (1804–46); The Library Company of Philadelphia.

Cover design by Mary Rohrer

Library of Congress Cataloging-in-Publication Data
An indispensable liberty : the fight for free speech in nineteenth-century America / edited by Mary M. Cronin ; contributions by David W. Bulla, Jon Bekken, Sandra Davidson, Nancy McKenzie Dupont, Joseph Hayden, Lee Jolliffe, Paulette D. Kilmer, Erika Jean Pribanic-Smith, Debra Reddin van Tuyll, Janice R. Wood.
pages cm
Summary: "This collection of eleven essays examines nineteenth-century legal and extralegal attempts to restrict freedom of speech and the press as well as the efforts of others to push back against those restrictions"— Provided by publisher.
Includes bibliographical references and index.
ISBN 978-0-8093-3472-8 (paperback) — ISBN 978-0-8093-3473-5 (e-book) 1. Freedom of speech—United States—History. I. Cronin, Mary M. (Mary Margaret) editor.
KF4772.I53 2016
323.44'3097309034—dc23 2015030165

Printed on recycled paper. ♻

To my husband, Keith Lamonica, who loves the law

CONTENTS

ILLUSTRATIONS

ACKNOWLEDGMENTS

This project began with an e-mail from Professor Christian G. Samito of Boston University's School of Law asking if I would like to helm an edited volume on First Amendment press and speech issues for Southern Illinois University Press. Although a number of excellent works on nineteenth-century media law had already appeared, I agreed with Dr. Samito that a number of gaps still existed in the literature. The idea of a volume that took a broad approach to the legal issues of the 1800s was very appealing. With the permission of Dr. David Sachsman of the University of Tennessee–Chattanooga, the holder of the George R. West Jr. Chair of Excellence in Communication and Public Affairs and cofounder of the annual Symposium on the 19th Century Press, the Civil War, and Free Expression (held annually at UT-Chattanooga), I rounded up most of the authors for the present volume during the 2013 symposium. Thank you, Chris and David, for helping me get the ball rolling on this project.

I'd also like to thank all of those authors for their incredibly hard work and their ability to meet the project's many deadlines. Each did so, which made my work that much easier. Three of this volume's chapter authors in particular have been invaluable for their help (not to mention for their longtime friendship): Professor Paulette D. Kilmer of the University of Toledo, Professor Lee Jolliffe of Drake University, and Professor Sandra Davidson of the University of Missouri. Paulette and Lee helped me complete the lengthy marketing research survey for SIU Press, undertook proofreading duties, and provided lots of moral support.

Sandra helped write part of the introduction to this volume, explaining how and why current legal concerns relate to their historic antecedents. In addition, thanks are due to several important people from SIU Press who have been invaluable to this process: Sylvia Frank Rodrigue, Judy Verdich, Karl Kageff, Linda Buhman, Lola Starck, and Wayne Larsen. We'd also like to thank our copy editor, Julie Bush.

A number of librarians at universities and research collections across the country have provided the chapter authors with invaluable assistance. From all of this book's contributors, I would personally like to express our many thanks to these unsung librarians. Finally, I thank my husband, Keith Lamonica, and my daughter, Emily Lamonica, for putting up with the many hours of writing, library work, and time spent contacting the chapter authors. I owe both of you a really nice vacation somewhere now that this is done.

AN INDISPENSABLE LIBERTY

INTRODUCTION

MARY M. CRONIN AND SANDRA DAVIDSON

Americans are used to voicing the claim that freedom of expression is part of their birthright. Many people locate the legal basis for such freedom within the wording of the First Amendment. Other individuals have long believed that freedom of expression is a natural right. Despite these differences, most citizens perceive this right as a positive one. They recognize that such freedom is prized and must be protected because of its importance to individuals, to broader social concerns (including self-governance), or to both. U.S. Supreme Court justice Benjamin Cardozo acknowledged this in a 1937 decision when he said freedom of speech "is the matrix, the indispensable condition, of nearly every other freedom."[1]

Cardozo's statement reflected a tremendous shift in Americans' legal, political, and social views concerning the role of free expression in society. Prior to the 1920s and 1930s, the nation embraced a republican democratic system that was much more restrictive of free expression rights. Justices frequently upheld politicians' broad use of police powers, even when such laws constrained speech, if such restrictions were aimed at ensuring the communal goal of protecting the general public's welfare. The U.S. Supreme Court's shift toward protecting freedom of expression in the decades following World War I reflected the Court's recognition that the First Amendment is an evolutionary document. As social, economic, and cultural pressures transformed the nation from a republican democracy into a pluralistic democratic system, the Court helped position freedom of expression into a central role in the political process.[2]

Despite the Court's importance, it is just one institution that has assisted in shaping and interpreting legal doctrine throughout the nation's history. Congress, state legislators, local politicians, and public opinion have all helped forge the meaning of the First Amendment in America. And all have aided in defining the boundaries of free expression. Equally important, the rise of the tradition of pluralistic democracy has not resolved the related issues of dissent and the limits of suppression that continue to this day.

The present book provides context for current First Amendment battles by examining how the dueling traditions of dissent and suppression during the nineteenth century gave rise to the civil libertarian interpretations of the First Amendment that many Americans embrace today. The volume explores the legal and extralegal attempts to restrict freedom of speech and freedom of the press and the subsequent pushback against such restrictions by a disparate group of individuals, including members of labor unions, suffragists, authors, editors, doctors, lawyers, and religious figures. The chapters' authors collectively argue that despite judicial, political, and public proclamations of support for freedom of expression, a host of factors, including laws, traditions, superstitions, convenience, gender stereotypes, customs, religion, and fear of social unrest often led to closed minds and narrow judicial and political protection for freedom of expression by individuals and groups whose fresh insights and diverse views upset the status quo.

The contributors to the present work blend legal, social, cultural, and intellectual history approaches and make liberal use of primary sources to untangle the complicated strands of nineteenth-century legal thought. They also demonstrate that while some free expression controversies were decided in the courtroom, others were ultimately decided outside of the judicial arena by federal and state politicians or by the will of the public. This book builds upon and expands on the work of a number of well-regarded legal history scholars, including David M. Rabban, Donna Lee Dickerson, Michael Kent Curtis, Stephen M. Feldman, Mark A. Graber, Paul Murphy, Timothy W. Gleason, and Mark E. Neely Jr. Although these scholars (and others) have developed an excellent body of research on nineteenth-century jurisprudence and legal thought, their studies are narrower in focus than is the present volume. This book examines the changing legal and extralegal attitudes and restrictions on freedom of expression throughout the entire century. The book's original essays provide fresh insights on some already-trodden ground, such as restrictions on the U.S. Civil War press, both North and South, and examine relatively understudied topics on nineteenth-century freedom of expression, including the struggles that laborers faced to gain their right to assemble and express their views and the public outcry for free speech when abolitionists were murdered in Southern states simply for voicing their views.

The arguments for and against restrictions on free expression that developed out of the republican democratic practices inform the majority of the book's chapters. During the 1700s and 1800s, politicians, judges, and members of the public embraced differing, and often conflicting, views regarding speech and press freedoms, viewpoints based on dueling political and legal mindsets. As Jeffery Smith and Michael Kent Curtis have noted, English radical Whig ideology permeated political thought in early America. "This set of perceptions and prescriptions portrayed freedom and power as constantly at odds and maintained that liberty would be preserved only where independent, public-spirited individuals were practicing classical republican virtues of honesty, frugality, industry, and vigilance," Smith has stated.[3] Whig ideology, grounded largely in libertarian doctrine, viewed freedom of expression not only as a necessary right to promote popular sovereignty but also as a reason to justify and support a watchdog function of the press.[4]

This English libertarian tradition, which dated to the 1600s, battled with more orthodox legal views of civil liberties. British monarchs and members of the clergy had tremendous discretionary powers to suppress criticism (whether in written or spoken form) of the government and its officials, as well as criticism of religion and the clergy. Curtis has noted that these dueling traditions of dissent and suppression were not only about free speech. "Fundamentally they were also struggles for democratic government," he states. As the libertarian and orthodox legal philosophies spread to America, government officials, judges, and citizens adopted and espoused these opposing viewpoints. "Americans," Curtis says, "had widely divergent ideas about the meaning of freedom of speech and about how literally to take the creed that in the United States 'we the people' rule."[5]

The importation of oppositional legal traditions is but one factor that explains why many politicians and judges, as well as some citizens during the 1800s, developed a legal environment that was far more restrictive of civil liberties than is true today.[6] Eighteenth-century America's embrace of popular sovereignty, with its broad public acceptance of the idea that the "right to criticize government is healthy for the political system," was an anomaly for its time.[7] The development of the First Amendment was sparked by the social, intellectual, and political environment of the era, yet that amendment, which guarantees speech and press freedoms, did not define those freedoms, nor did it define what, if any, boundaries exist, beyond its public pronouncement that Congress should not engage in speech or press suppression.[8] As a result, as Timothy W. Gleason has stated, the ratification of the Bill of Rights was but a "critical first step in the development of the right to freedom of the press." Determining the meaning and scope of free expression was a far more difficult task in an environment where many citizens presumed they had a right to speak either by congressional legislation or by natural law.[9]

As the nation underwent a dramatic transformation from a largely agrarian society to an industrialized nation, the public's views on social, political, economic, legal, and cultural issues evolved and often clashed. The nineteenth century was a "breeding period" for new ideas about the role that the First Amendment held in society.[10] Yet support for expression of unpopular and nonnormative views often was thin to nonexistent during the century, a social and intellectual narrowness that continues to the present day.[11]

Previous scholars have demonstrated nineteenth-century officials' fears concerning freedom of expression and their willingness to engage in often-conservative interpretations of original intent. Thomas I. Emerson argues in his seminal work *Toward a General Theory of the First Amendment* that jurists took a "relatively narrow" approach when deciding cases involving freedom of speech or press.[12] Howard O. Hunter, who examined freedom of expression cases heard by the U.S. Supreme Court from 1791 to 1930, concurs, stating, "The Court's opinions were sketchy and usually hostile to the speech interests that were asserted."[13] Similarly, Curtis has found that both politicians and judges often provided "little protection for freedom of speech" from the late 1700s through the 1860s. Journalists and speakers who criticized the government were jailed under the Sedition Act of 1798. In the early 1800s, legal and extra restrictions and violence occurred against antislavery speakers. During the 1860s, speakers and publishers opposed to war found their views suppressed and punished by both government and military officials.[14]

David M. Rabban also acknowledges that the legal environment of the 1800s was far more restrictive of civil liberties than is true today. But Rabban, like Donna Lee Dickerson, further argues that the century was marked by both judicial hostility and extralegal hostility toward freedom of speech claims.[15] Despite such hostility, Rabban and Curtis persuasively demonstrate that a more popular free speech tradition—one that many citizens, including labor leaders and public preachers, exercised because they assumed they had just such a right—did exist. Intellectuals debated the extent and boundaries of such expression rights in speeches, at meetings, and in the press. These arguments, many of which were a response to more restrictive interpretations put forth by politicians and jurists, existed throughout the nineteenth century but particularly flourished in the period from the mid-1800s to World War I. Such legal thinking became the basis for the twentieth century's emerging libertarian approach to First Amendment law.[16]

Scholars of nineteenth-century American law also have noted that freedom of speech was not a common judicial concern for much of that century. G. Edward White cites two reasons for this limited judicial debate. First, he states that there were no federal laws and few state statutes that directly regulated speech. Second, he demonstrates that freedom of speech was not developed as its own legal doctrine during the century but instead was subsumed in other legal issues, especially economic or property issues.[17] David P. Currie stresses that jurists' willingness to uphold laws that often restricted freedom of speech and press without including discussion of freedom of expression "might also be thought to have cast light upon what the amendment was understood to mean."[18]

Margaret A. Blanchard's examination of speech and press cases in state courts prior to the 1925 *Gitlow v. New York* ruling (the case in which the U.S. Supreme Court held that the First Amendment's protections applied to the states via the Fourteenth Amendment) helps clarify Currie's statement.[19] Blanchard found that although state court decisions were influential in the development of modern judicial thinking about freedom of expression, many state court decisions during the nineteenth century consistently linked such freedom with "a rather rigorous standard of rights and responsibilities."[20] The U.S. Supreme Court, she adds, largely followed state court decisions that weighed free speech claims against the public's needs.[21] Importantly, Blanchard argues that those jurists who heard freedom of speech and press cases made the "conscious decision to make these rights bend to the needs of the public welfare," which subsequently involved holding that individuals and members of the press must exercise their freedoms responsibly.[22]

A number of other First Amendment scholars, including Alexander Meiklejohn, Thomas Emerson, Vincent Blasi, and Lee Bollinger, also have portrayed the First Amendment as a positive right. Although these theorists differ in their rationales as to why broad protection of expression is of paramount importance to individuals and society, their writings, collectively, have influenced both the courts' and society's understanding of the meaning and purpose of freedom of expression.[23]

Today we benefit from the advances of the past yet are still mired in many of the same problems. Freedom of speech and of the press, guaranteed by the First Amendment, looms as an ideal that inched and sometimes lurched forward through the struggles of the 1700s into the early 1900s. This book focuses on the often-overlooked struggles and advances of the nineteenth century. Looking at our current situation through the lens of the nineteenth-century perspective gives more depth of understanding as we continue to question—and test—the boundaries of free expression.

Preservation of peace was a major concern in the 1800s. Language, even truthful language, that arguably disturbed the peace was looked upon as too dangerous to permit. Those were dangerous times as the country struggled with the enormity of the ideological split between the North and South, with the bloodiest conflagration ever on American soil, with territorial expansion, with economic hardships for laborers that would cause increasing doubt about the viability of capitalism, with rising aspirations of women regularly thwarted by convention, and with partisan struggles that too often displayed raw avarice and an unmitigated thirst for power.

Preservation of peace remains a major legal and social concern. Many of the technologies of war and of communication have changed, often amplifying the problem. What kinds of communications are too dangerous or threatening to permit? While truthful expression receives protection today, threatening expression increasingly does not. For example, in 2003 the U.S. Supreme Court addressed the issue of cross burning in the case of *Virginia v. Black*.[24] The Court looked at this country's history and proclaimed, "Burning a cross in the United States is inextricably intertwined with the history of the Ku Klux Klan," the white supremacy cult formed in 1866 in Pulaski, Tennessee.[25] Calling a burning cross a "symbol of hate," the Court said that "when a cross burning is used to intimidate, few if any messages are more powerful."[26] The bottom line: "The First Amendment permits Virginia [or any other state] to outlaw cross burnings done with the intent to intimidate because burning a cross is a particularly virulent form of intimidation."[27]

History informed the Supreme Court concerning cross burning. Freedom of expression is not determined in a vacuum, and the more one understands history, arguably the more one can address the problems of freedom of expression that still simmer and erupt.

Chapter by chapter, this book addresses problems that loom today.

In "A Press Ablaze: Violent Suppression of Abolitionist Speech, Press, Petition, and Assembly," media historian Lee Jolliffe examines both legal and extralegal restrictions on the abolitionist press and abolitionists. This chapter goes beyond the usual studies of free speech martyrs like Elijah Lovejoy to demonstrate both the extent of public and legal hostility toward abolitionists nationwide and their theoretical arguments for freedom of expression. Jolliffe shows that each violent attack on the abolitionist free press engendered more support of that press by formerly neutral newspapers and the general public. Racial problems and human trafficking itself continue to haunt this country. As cries of "Hands up, don't shoot" echoed from the streets of Ferguson, Missouri—and all over this country and the world—the voices of the past that spoke up for racial justice could be heard again. For those who know the history of martyrs like Lovejoy, such voices of the past are not dead but reverberate in our streets today, while human trafficking remains a global plague against which many human rights activists speak out.

In chapter 2, "'Palpable Injury': Abraham Lincoln and Press Suppression in the Civil War North," media historian David W. Bulla examines the issue of Union press suppression and President Lincoln's controversial restrictions on speech and press liberties during the war. Northern politicians and military leaders closed newspapers, seized property of publishers, barred publications from the mail, and arrested journalists. Some reporters were banished from army camps, and telegraph lines were censored. Two other types of constraints, both of which were informal, included mob intimidation and the blocking of potential advertisers. Today, echoes of this suppression arguably resound in President Barack Obama's unprecedented use of the Espionage Act of 1917 against whistle-blowers and journalists who reveal questionable U.S. responses to the "war on terror." While suppression during the Civil War ended after the culmination of the war, the question now is whether the "war on terror" and its resulting suppression will end.

The same uneasiness about whether freedom of expression today can coexist with the war on terror and afterward resonates in other chapters of this book. In "Freedom of the Press in a Slave Society at War: The Confederate Congress and Others Really Did Make No Law," media historian Debra Reddin van Tuyll uncovers political and military press and speech constraints in the Confederacy and the subsequent debate among publishers and the public as to the meaning of freedom of expression. In "Fight, Fold, Flip, or Flee: The Confederate Press and Enemy Occupation, 1861–65," van Tuyll and fellow historians Nancy McKenzie Dupont and Joseph Hayden examine a rarely studied area of Civil War era censorship: military and political censorship of the Southern press in communities occupied by the Union army during the Civil War. And in "Disturbing the Public Peace: Radical and Conservative Editors in the Reconstruction South," media historian Erika J. Pribanic-Smith unpacks the extent to which Federal military officers and politicians censored, threatened, or chilled the speech of Southern editors and their publications during the tense Reconstruction years.

The second part of the book opens with "The Rocky Road to Truth as a Defense: Libel Construction in the Nineteenth Century," in which law professor (and media scholar) Sandra Davidson details the slow legal march toward the use of truth as a defense in libel law during the nineteenth century. Her chapter reveals that the crucial adoption of the truth defense in libel was not linear. A patchwork of state laws—some supportive of truth as a defense and some not—was the norm during the century. The threat of libel suits continues to be a concern today, but this chapter makes clear how far this country has advanced in permitting truthful expression and the importance of preserving truth as a defense, especially in the political arena.

In chapter 7, "Keeping the Light under the Bushel: Laws, Mores, and Reading," media historian Paulette D. Kilmer examines the origins and reason for often heavy-handed book censorship (and the parallel issue of restricting the dissemination of ideas) throughout the century and the work of individuals who fought against such censorship. Book censorship continues today and has arguably increased in schools in the wake of the Supreme Court's 1988 decision in *Hazelwood v. Kuhlmeier*.[28] That decision put more vigor into some public schools' decisions to ban books from school libraries, even including the Harry Potter books because of their witchcraft content.

In "No Rights for the Working Man: Laboring before the First Amendment Had Force," labor historian Jon Bekken examines the legal and extralegal restrictions on labor unions and the labor press that occurred in the century before the pivotal Industrial Workers of the World free speech fights of the early twentieth century. The chapter demonstrates the difficulties that such labor activists faced in expressing themselves and in organizing. Today, problems concerning labor unions erupt constantly, from the difficulties in Wisconsin that embroiled Governor Scott Walker to the continuous battles in states for so-called right to work laws.

But racial, labor, and war issues are not the only matters affecting current American life. Women still battle inequities, such as the wage gap and the ever-present "glass ceiling." But women have made hard-fought gains, as another chapter of the book illustrates. In "Freedom of Expression for Women: The Fight for Suffrage and Personal Liberty," media historians Lee Jolliffe, Paulette D. Kilmer, and Sandra Davidson examine the breadth of suppression against suffragists, detailing how a variety of laws as well as extreme mob violence were used to silence their speech and expressive conduct. The chapter also examines the suffragists' theoretical arguments for freedom of expression, many of which remain viable today.

For anyone wishing to promote social justice, inspiration arguably could come from looking at past attempts to organize and push for social justice. Chapter 10 provides such inspiration. In "The National Defense Association: Liberal Protector of Free Speech," media historian Janice R. Wood analyzes the importance and functions of the National Defense Association, a civil liberties advocate group established decades before the American Civil Liberties Union. The National Defense Association was composed of a diverse group of authors, artists, lawyers, doctors, and free thought advocates who promoted what was, for the time period, a radical civil libertarian approach toward free expression. Almost all of the members of the association had run afoul of anti-vice crusader Anthony Comstock's reign during the Gilded Age.

And inspiration can likewise come from knowing that past restrictions on public forums have now failed. In "*Davis v. Massachusetts*: Expressive Conduct and Regulated Liberty in the Nineteenth Century," media historian Mary M. Cronin examines the 1897 case *Davis v. Massachusetts*, in which the U.S. Supreme Court justices applied property law analysis to deny speakers their right to public forums. The ruling established a four-decades-long precedent that allowed politicians and judges the right to deny individuals the right to expressive conduct if they so chose. Perhaps knowing that such a restriction existed in the past can create both an appreciation of public forums today and an urge to use those forums.

If "knowledge is power," as English philosopher and lawyer Francis Bacon proclaimed, this book is a source of power. It helps to explain the terrain over which the battles for freedom of expression were fought. It covers many aspects of suppression and some triumphs for freedom, but a careful reading of this book also serves as a warning for the pitfalls that still loom. Suppression is not a thing of the past but an ever-present danger. Tensions concerning race, gender, and labor relations persist. And the fear that arguably most inflames the urge to suppress—the fear of danger from conflict between humans that persist in waging war—has not and perhaps never will end.

The root causes of suppression of expression remain in varying degrees, and that is one reason that the need to know our historical roots of freedom and suppression of expression is so important. Recognizing the pitfalls may help us from falling into them again. Knowing how those who preceded us built modern-day notions of free expression might help us preserve or recover rights being chipped away in the current climate of secrecy and never-ending war. And if history teaches anything, it teaches that we do fall, over and over, but also that we sometimes triumph. This book does strike an optimistic note—as well as a warning to remain vigilant.

Notes

1. Palko v. Connecticut, 302 U.S. 319, 327 (1937).

2. Stephen M. Feldman, *Free Expression and Democracy in America: A History* (Chicago: University of Chicago Press, 2008), 3, 316.

3. Jeffery A. Smith, *Printers and Press Freedom: The Ideology of Early American Journalism* (New York: Oxford University Press, 1988), viii; Michael Kent Curtis, *Free Speech, "The People's Darling Privilege": Struggles for Freedom of Expression in American History* (Durham: Duke University Press, 2000), 35–51.

4. Smith, *Printers and Press Freedom*, 41–48.

5. Curtis, *Free Speech*, 3.

6. Ibid.; David M. Rabban, *Free Speech in Its Forgotten Years* (New York: Cambridge University Press, 1997); Mark E. Neely Jr., *The Fate of Liberty: Abraham Lincoln and Civil Liberties* (New York: Oxford University Press, 1991); Mark A. Graber, *Transforming Free Speech: The Ambiguous Legacy of Civil Libertarianism* (Berkeley: University of California Press, 1991); Donna Lee Dickerson, *The Course of Tolerance: Freedom of the Press in Nineteenth-Century America* (New York: Greenwood Press, 1990). For a narrow example of judicial intolerance, see Butler Cain, "Contempt by Publication in the Southwestern United States, 1855–1899," *Southwestern Mass Communication Journal* 26, no. 1 (Fall 2010): 83–98.

7. Smith, *Printers and Press Freedom*, viii.

8. David A. Anderson, "The Origins of the Press Clause," *U.C.L.A. Law Review* 30 (February 1983): 456–62. Anderson argues that the framers intended that the press serve as a watchdog of government power. By contrast, Eugene Volokh has argued that the framers intended the First Amendment to mean that all Americans were entitled to equal speech rights and that the printing technologies should not be restricted. Eugene Volokh, *Freedom for the Press as an Industry or for the Press as a Technology? University of Pennsylvania Law Review* 160 (2012): 459.

9. Timothy W. Gleason, *The Watchdog Concept: The Press and the Courts in Nineteenth-Century America* (Ames: Iowa State University Press, 1990), 19.

10. Dickerson, *Course of Tolerance*, xvii.

11. Hazel Dicken-Garcia and Giovanna Dell'Orto, *Hated Ideas and the American Civil War Press* (Spokane, Wash.: Marquette Books, 2007); Anthony Lewis, *Freedom for the Thought That We Hate: A Biography of the First Amendment* (New York: Basic Books, 2010).

12. Thomas I. Emerson, *Toward a General Theory of the First Amendment* (New York: Vintage Books, 1966), 35–36.

13. Howard O. Hunter, "Problems in Search of Principles: The First Amendment in the Supreme Court from 1791–1930," *Emory Law Journal* 35 (Winter 1986): 127.

14. Curtis, *Free Speech*, 416.

15. Rabban, *Free Speech in Its Forgotten Years*, 14–21. Similarly, Dickerson details both legal and extralegal attempts to stifle expression during the nineteenth century. See Dickerson, *Course of Tolerance*, x.

16. Rabban, *Free Speech in Its Forgotten Years*, 14–21; Curtis, *Free Speech*, 3–13.

17. G. Edward White, "Justice Holmes and the Modernization of Free Speech Jurisprudence: The Human Dimension," *California Law Review* 80 (March 1992): 396.

18. David P. Currie, *The Constitution in the U.S. Supreme Court: The First Hundred Years, 1989–1888* (Chicago: University of Chicago Press, 1992), 116.

19. 268 U.S. 652 (1925).

20. Margaret A. Blanchard, "Filling in the Void: Speech and Press in State Courts Prior to *Gitlow*," in *The First Amendment Reconsidered: New Perspectives on the Meaning of Freedom of Speech and Press*, ed. Bill F. Chamberlin and Charlene J. Brown (New York: Longman, 1982), 42.

21. Ibid.

22. Ibid., 16.

23. Alexander Meiklejohn, *Free Speech and Its Relation to Self-Government* (New York: Harper and Brothers, 1948); Thomas Emerson, *Toward a General Theory of the First Amendment* (New York: Vintage Books, 1966); Vincent Blasi, *Blasi's Ideas of the First Amendment* (Eagan, Minn.: West Academic Publishing, 2011); Lee Bollinger, *The Tolerant Society* (New York: Oxford University Press, 1988).

24. 538 U.S. 343 (2003).

25. Ibid. at 353.

26. Ibid. at 357.

27. Ibid. at 363.

28. 484 U.S. 260 (1988).

PART 1

NATIONAL CONFLICT AND FREEDOM OF EXPRESSION

1. A PRESS ABLAZE

VIOLENT SUPPRESSION OF ABOLITIONIST SPEECH, PRESS, PETITION, AND ASSEMBLY

LEE JOLLIFFE

"[W]e have the wolf by the ear, and we can neither hold him, nor safely let him go."[1] So wrote Thomas Jefferson in 1820 to his friend John Holmes. It was slavery that was the wolf and the young United States that had grabbed the wolf by its ear by permitting slavery within its borders.

Alas, elected officials found it safer to grip the wolf's ear and keep slavery in hand, at least for another forty years after Jefferson's letter was written. And so it was that publisher Cassius Marcellus Clay found it necessary to arm his "emancipation" newspaper office to the teeth. The mouths of two forty-pound brass cannons loaded with minié balls, nails, and scrap metal took aim at visitors as they came through the front door of the *True American* offices of 1845. Also among the accoutrements that Clay deemed necessary for his Lexington, Kentucky, newsroom were two kegs of gunpowder with remote fuses stashed under the editor's desk, walls reinforced with sheet metal, and a trapdoor leading onto the roof. Yet his paper is not even reckoned a serious abolitionist newspaper by historians,[2] since Clay favored gradual emancipation and felt slave owners should be paid by the states to relinquish their claims to slaves.

But Clay was right to be protective of his place of business and his physical safety. The often-incendiary prose of abolitionist editors made their newspapers the most violently opposed reform presses of the nineteenth century. So important were the persistent efforts of the abolitionist press to make its anti-slavery message heard that Michael Kent Curtis's book *Free Speech*, subtitled

Struggles for Freedom of Expression in American History, focuses almost entirely on abolition.[3]

As this chapter shows, abolitionist speakers were persecuted much more frequently than has been previously discovered. And in a way, this is not surprising; the language of this *Franklin Repository* editorial was not as offensive as many abolition texts, yet it called slaveholders "fat, sleek, lazy nabobs who should wish to steep all men in their infamy—living by the unpaid work of slaves, perhaps their own children."[4] The mere accusation by a Southern mob that a visitor from the North was an abolitionist often led to assaults, whippings, and even lynchings. Southern ministers were kidnapped from their pulpits to be ridden on rails, tarred and feathered, and hung until nearly dead before being cut down, all for allowing black people to listen to their sermons through church windows or for offering Sunday schools that black people could attend. Whole congregations were driven from the South for questioning the morality of slavery.

Thus, abolitionists became key figures in building and securing a new legal tradition of freedom of speech and press in the United States in the face of opposition that was often violent and other times merely steeped in financial self-interest. Slavery was indeed a wolf being held by one ear, as Thomas Jefferson so frequently said in his later years.

Opposition to free expression by abolitionists came from presidents and postmasters, Congress, state legislatures, the courts, and individuals ranging from wealthy slaveholders to the lowliest hardscrabble farmer. At risk were First Amendment rights of free press and speech, but also under frequent challenge were rights to assemble freely; to exercise one's religion, which played a large role in abolition; and to petition the government for redress of grievances. All of these rights were precious in the vigorous and highly participatory young democracy of the early nineteenth century, where mass meetings were attended by people willing to camp out rough for a week as they elected officers and drafted resolutions to "be published in the nearest newspapers and sent to the legislature";[5] where churches were primary centers of cultural life and social welfare in most settlements; and where petition drives were treated by their signers as an assertion of their right to be heard.

In 1835, President Andrew Jackson called on Congress to forbid circulation of "incendiary publications" about slavery.[6] Congress obliged, as did state legislatures, allowing Southern postmasters to pile abolitionist mailings in heaps and burn them. Congress's "Pinckney gag rule" of 1836 was only the first of a decade-long series of congressional resolutions to ignore all petitions from constituents when the subject was the abolition of slavery.[7] Both editors and the general public saw this as the thin edge of the wedge, the dangerous beginning of suppression of people's participation in their own government.

Congress itself became a "bear garden" of fistfights and brawling.[8] Fiery Joshua Giddings, Free-Soil U.S. representative from Ohio's Western Reserve, was censured by the House in 1842 for refusing to comply with its self-imposed gag rule against discussion of slavery. In 1843, several abolition newspapers reported an assassination attempt against Giddings on the very floor of the House of Representatives.[9] In 1856, South Carolina representative Preston Brooks used the heavy metal head of his cane to beat Massachusetts senator Charles Sumner to unconsciousness—on the Senate floor.[10]

In the courts, abolitionist publishers were sued for libel by slaveholders and slave traders and even by the U.S. government.[11] Publishers were prosecuted using charges of treason,[12] seditious libel,[13] and group libel,[14] as well as using several causes of action under common law, especially disturbing the public order.[15] Attempts were even made to extradite Northern publishers to Southern states for prosecution for their abolitionist views,[16] and bounties were offered for their capture.[17] The *Augusta Chronicle* of Georgia aptly summarized Southern sentiment about abolitionist free expression: "The cry of the whole South should be DEATH, INSTANT DEATH, to the Abolitionist, wherever he is caught."[18]

Newspaper offices of abolitionists were set ablaze, most memorably John Greenleaf Whittier's *Pennsylvania Freeman* in Philadelphia in 1838[19] and William S. Bailey's *Newport Weekly* in Kentucky in 1857.[20] Abolitionists were publicly whipped, languished in Southern prisons, and were pelted with rotten eggs and even bricks. People who attended antislavery meetings were attacked with clubs and axes.[21] Publisher Elijah Lovejoy was murdered by a proslavery gang that attacked his press office with a hail of bullets in 1837.[22]

Even carrying or reading abolition publications was outlawed in the South. Visitors from the North often found that their baggage had been searched in their hotel rooms and abolition materials removed. Rewards were offered[23] and the bearers of antislavery tidings were beaten, whipped, or carried around on a rail by mobs.[24] When young seminary student Amos Dresser was caught handing out antislavery publications in the South, a local paper said, "He should be hung up . . . to rot upon the gibbet, until the winds whistled through his bones."[25] On August 15, 1835, the *Washington Globe* reported the jailing of a "man named Crandall . . . [who] was taken up in Georgetown . . . under the charge of circulating Tappan, Garrison & Co.'s papers, encouraging the negroes to insurrection." Abolitionist Robert Bell was hung in Clinton, Mississippi, as an "insurrectionist."[26]

Freedom of assembly to hear speakers on abolition was also impeded by ruffians and mobs in both the North and the South, while freedom of religion was violated particularly in the South by prosecution of preachers who dared to suggest slavery was antithetical to Christian teaching and by the dismantling, board by board, of any churches whose congregants believed slavery to be wrong.[27]

Yet the more stringent or violent the repression, the stronger the backlash against it, and the more public sympathies were shifted *toward* the abolitionists. One repercussion that proslavery forces did not expect was that widespread negative publicity about their attacks would create corresponding support for the abolitionists that arose simply because freedom of speech was sacrosanct to people of the young democracy. For example, after James Birney's *Philanthropist* press was thrown into the river in the Cincinnati riots of 1836, twenty-three Northern newspapers printed editorials opposing the dangerous precedent of quelling *any* freedom of speech.[28] The voting public also expressed disapproval: the *Dayton Republican* reported that "the whig mobocrats, who took such an active part in demolishing the office of the *Philanthropist* . . . have been severely and deservedly rebuked by the friends of free discussion and good order."[29] The public expressed its displeasure about the riots and the attack on free speech by ousting mob organizers from public office: "Not a mother's son of the whole batch of whig candidates in Hamilton county is elected."[30]

LAUNCH OF A SERIOUS ABOLITION MOVEMENT

In 1829, a free black Bostonian, David Walker, published *Appeal to the Coloured Citizens of the World.*[31] Walker wrote that slaveholders "are avaricious creatures, . . . whose greatest earthly desires are, to keep us in abject ignorance and wretchedness, and who are of the firm conviction that Heaven has designed us and our children to be slaves and *beasts of burden* to them and their children."[32] Of people who claimed others as slaves, he wrote, "They have no more right to hold us in slavery than we have to hold them, we have just as much right, in the sight of God, to hold them and their children in slavery and wretchedness."[33]

His incendiary pamphlet was widely circulated in the South, and coming on the heels, as it did, of several violent slave revolts, the pamphlet led to arrests and successful prosecutions of people caught with it in the South, namely James Cowan in North Carolina; Robert Smith in New Orleans; Elijah Burritt in Milledgeville, Georgia; Thomas Lewis in Richmond, Virginia; Edward Smith in Charleston; James Smith in Louisiana; and five missionaries to the Cherokees,

Reverend Samuel A. Worcester, John F. Wheeler, Thomas Gann, Isaac Proctor, and Reverend John Thompson.[34]

However, historians date the beginning of "an *enduring* effort for the emancipation of the slaves" to a day some two years later, when William Lloyd Garrison launched his long-lived antislavery periodical, the *Liberator*, on January 1, 1831.[35] Other groups, particularly the Quakers and free black Northerners, had long worked against the holding of people as chattel in the United States but without the effectiveness that would reward Garrison's efforts. Even in the North, Garrison was feared; one Boston mob dragged him around the city with a noose around his neck, threatening to hang him.[36] Ironically, Garrison was then arrested for "causing a riot."[37]

But Garrison's words sometimes fell on fertile soil, thanks to the Second Great Awakening. Usually dated as having begun about 1790 but flourishing during the late 1820s, particularly in the Great Lakes states, this Great Awakening was built on one key premise: that true Christians must not sit idly by, waiting out their time on earth before achieving admittance to heaven. In fact, Christians had an affirmative duty to work on earth to create a world as heaven-like as possible; by their efforts, they could perfect the human world and in doing so could bring about the Millennium, Christ's Second Coming, and the immediate arrival of heaven on earth. Paul E. Johnson argues ably in *A Shopkeeper's Millennium* that an underlying purpose of this wave of fervor was an attempt by the ownership classes to regain social control of workers who, with the rise of industrialism, had slipped out of the restraints of their employers' oversight simply because they now lived apart from their employers.[38] Live-in apprentices had been replaced by factory workers who lived where and as they pleased.

Whatever the usefulness of the Great Awakening to maintenance of social controls, it also spurred a host of reform movements, of which abolition of slavery was but one. Many of the others are detailed in the following chapters of this book. However, agitation for the abolition of slavery was the one political quagmire that might rend the bonds among the states, and thus many public officials felt an imperative to contain it.

ABOLITION STRATEGIES AND RESPONDING SUPPRESSION, 1830–60

Each new abolitionist strategy for converting public opinion led to a quick retaliation by slavery's supporters to quash that particular effort. But each attempt to suppress antislavery speech led to greater and more widespread public awareness both of the antislavery cause and of the dangerous tactics of the slave power and its adherents. For instance, the American Anti-Slavery Society (AASS), launched in 1833, had garnered 250,000 members by 1838. And by 1850, which saw congressional passage of a stringent new Fugitive Slave Act, the Northern public was no longer in the slave power's pocket; in fact, a fugitive slave who managed to get to Northern soil was more likely to be protected and hidden by ordinary citizens than to be rendered up to ostensible "owners."[39]

Mail-Driven Statutes and a Decade-Long Postal Blockade

A key abolitionist strategy of the 1830s was to mail antislavery literature en masse into the South. Garrison suggested more than once that the newly formed AASS should "scatter tracts, like rain-drops, over the land, with startling facts and melting appeals."[40]

Alas, these "melting appeals" landed upon fearful ears. As early as 1804, Georgia had passed a statute outlawing antislavery speech or press.[41] David Walker's 1829 *Appeal to the Coloured Citizens* had already led to panicked lawmaking, like a Georgia statute imposing harsh penalties for "circulation of pamphlets of evil tendency among our domestics."[42] During the 1820s and especially the 1830s, abolitionists' new strategy of mailing antislavery tracts into the South led Alabama, Louisiana, Maryland, Mississippi, North Carolina, South Carolina, Tennessee, and Virginia to pass similar laws.[43] Still, relatively few prosecutions—only fifteen—have been located that stem from these laws.[44]

Statutes notwithstanding, the young AASS was determined to publish. Advances in printing technology made larger press runs affordable, and in 1835 the AASS allotted $30,000 for mailings to public figures and opinion leaders in the South. As a result, between May 1835 and May 1836, abolitionists sent over one million tracts into the Southern states.[45] After receiving one such cargo on July 29, 1835, the Charleston, South Carolina, postmaster discovered his post office had been invaded by a mob and the mail piled up and burned. "Effigies of Arthur Tappan, Dr. Cox, and W. L. Garrison," noted abolitionists, were "publicly suspended."[46] In response, Charleston's city council appointed a committee to screen the mail and prevent any abolition materials from being delivered.[47]

Charleston's postmaster appealed to the postmaster general of the United States to stop such shipments in the first place. The postmaster general agreed that some mail should not be delivered; he wrote, "We owe an obligation to the laws, but a higher one to the communities in which we live." This widely published comment set off a storm of disapproval in general-circulation newspapers.

The *Vermont Chronicle* called it "anarchical" and named the whole business one of "lawless and horrid outrages."[48]

Charleston would be the first of many Southern cities to block arrival of abolitionist tracts mailed to Southern recipients. In Virginia,[49] Alabama,[50] and North Carolina,[51] postmasters returned, destroyed, or handed over to local mobs any abolition materials that arrived in their offices. State legislatures in the South soon passed laws supporting this censorship of the mails. Virginia, for instance, required local authorities to be notified when any post office received "incendiary publications . . . denying the right of masters to property in their slaves and inculcating the duty of resistance to such right." Not only would offending materials be burned, but recipients to whom the publications were addressed were to be arrested.[52] The South cordoned itself off against incoming abolition publications.

Southern postmasters also appealed to their Northern counterparts in major cities and obtained agreement from some, New York City's postmaster among them, that abolition materials would not be shipped to the South in the first place.[53] U.S. postmaster general Amos Kendall, of Kentucky, commended New York City's actions and supported Southern "blockades" against abolitionist publications.[54]

Residents of some Northern cities also took it upon themselves to destroy abolitionist materials they found being shipped. For instance, a box of abolition pamphlets, also containing newspapers, pocket handkerchiefs, and pictures, was discovered on a steamboat that landed in Philadelphia. A "committee of citizens" took it upon themselves to visit the addressee, who, seeing his callers, denied all knowledge of the package. The self-appointed committee dumped the box into the Delaware River.[55]

Andrew Jackson was the first of a series of presidents who permitted—even encouraged—suppression of the rising antislavery press. In response to his postmaster general's support of the "southern blockade," he wrote,

> We can do nothing more than direct that those inflamatory papers be delivered to none but who will demand them as subscribers; and in every instance the Postmaster ought to take the names down, and have them exposed thro the publik journals as subscribers to this wicked plan of exciting the negroes to insurrection and to massacre.[56]

Jackson went further, proposing to Congress on December 7, 1835, a law to forbid circulation of "incendiary publications intended to instigate the slaves to insurrection."[57]

Contrary to Jackson's proposal, Congress reorganized the post office in July 1836, "forbidding any postmaster, under severe penalty, from unlawfully detaining in his office any letter, package, pamphlet, or newspaper and refusing to deliver the same to the person to whom it was addressed."[58] Unfortunately, postmasters ignored this law at will and with impunity. As late as 1853, the *Circleville Religious Telescope* of Ohio was burned at Glenville, Virginia, and many other newspapers with antislavery contents suffered similar fates.[59]

As Clement Eaton wrote, "The fact that a virtual censorship of the mails crossing the Mason and Dixon line was established after 1835 indicates the ascendancy of the Southern group in federal politics during the ante-bellum period."[60] Only after 1859, when publisher Horace Greeley targeted "Post-Office Despotism" from his newspaper editorial page, was there some reform of this practice.[61]

Suppression by Congress under Presidents Jackson and Van Buren

The notoriously inequitable "three-fifths rule," which counted slaves as three-fifths of a voter, gave the South's white votes so much extra weight in elections that many antebellum presidents—and more congressmen than reflected actual voters—came from slavery's power centers in the South.[62] Southern politicians pressed this advantage ruthlessly and strove to leverage it into even greater power as new territories were added to the Union. When Texas and Florida were being considered as new states, for instance, Southern congressmen threatened to break each territory into four new slave states.[63]

Until Abraham Lincoln's presidency, commanders-in-chief worked hand-in-glove with the slave power; Andrew Jackson and Martin Van Buren were notably supportive of the quashing of antislavery press and speech via federal powers. Though some historians write glowingly of "Jacksonian democracy" and the age of literacy that Jackson is supposed to have ushered in,[64] the truth is that Andrew Jackson's life and presidency were marred by his tendency to jump first at military solutions to political problems. Jackson was also a plantation owner, eventually building up an estate where over 150 people were kept as slaves.[65] Jackson was entirely willing to suppress freedom of the press and allow censorship of the U.S. mail if the subject was abolition.

Still, one situation Jackson did not act upon as president was the deluge of petitions that abolitionists sent to Congress, launched by the AASS along with its pamphleteering campaign in 1835.[66] Jackson left it to Congress to deal with the petitions, which it did beginning in 1836, as Martin Van Buren prepared to take office as president.

Van Buren's inaugural address in 1837 made his position on slavery clear:

> I must go into the Presidential chair [as] the inflexible and uncompromising opponent of every attempt on the part of Congress to abolish slavery in the District of Columbia against the wishes of the slaveholding States, and also with a determination equally decided to resist the slightest interference with it in the States where it exists.[67]

Emboldened by a president who had already once voted, when a member of Congress, to support repression of the abolition press via the public mails, Southern members of Congress moved to quash the people's right to petition the government.

A Volatile Congress and "Pinckney's Gag Rule"

Far from being a hallowed hall of solemn disquisitions on public policy, in the period from 1830 to the Civil War, the Capitol Building witnessed brawling, stabbing, shooting, and canings as congressmen "disagreed" about slavery. Spirited debate often degenerated into literal free-for-alls on the floors of both houses. Theodore Weld complained in 1839 that "slaveholders have turned the Congress of the United States into a . . . bear garden," the scene of "gladiatorial shows."[68] The *Liberator* called it a "bull-bating [*sic*] arena."[69] In 1839, Tennessee representative Abram Maury was thrown through a window during congressional session, "but his adversary [Representative William Campbell, also of Tennessee] saved him by clutching the hair of his head with his left hand, while he struck him with his right."[70]

Theodore Weld blamed slaveholders for bringing the U.S. government into disrepute by their quick-tempered resort to violence:

> President Jackson, Senator Benton, the late Gen. Coffee,—it is but a few years since these slaveholders shot at, and stabbed, and stamped upon each other in a tavern broil. General Jackson had previously killed Mr. Dickenson. Senator Clay of Kentucky has immortalized himself by shooting at a near relative of Chief Justice Marshall, and being wounded by him; and not long after[,] by shooting at John Randolph of Virginia. Governor M'Duffie of South Carolina has signalized himself also, both by shooting and being shot,—so has [Mississippi] Governor Poindexter,[71] and [Kentucky] Governor Rowan,[72] and Judge M'Kinley of the U.S. Supreme Court, late senator in Congress from Alabama,—but we desist; a full catalogue would fill pages. We will only add, that a few months since, in the city of London, Governor Hamilton, of South Carolina, went armed with pistols, to the lodgings of Daniel O'Connell, "to stop his wind" in the bullying slang of his own published boast.[73]

In this atmosphere of quick tempers and sudden violence, discussions of slavery were markedly prone to set off fireworks among representatives. The AASS's petition campaign against slavery in general and slavery in the District of Columbia in particular[74] was the source of many a thrown fist and raised voice. Thus, a rule of order approved by Congress in 1836, known as "Pinckney's gag rule," passed handily among the members:

> Resolved, That all petitions, memorials, resolutions, propositions, or papers, relating in any way or to any extent whatever to the subject of slavery, or the abolition of slavery, shall, without being either printed or referred, be laid upon the table, and that no further action whatever shall be had thereon.[75]

The many and varied petitions sent to Congress and to state legislatures show that Americans expected a responsive, participatory government. Petitions to Congress ranged from requests that a new macadamized road be built,[76] to requests that a new state *not* be admitted to the Union,[77] to requests that the Union be dissolved so that free states need not support slave states.[78]

Passage of Pinckney's rule helped the abolitionist cause immensely, because whatever an individual person's views on slavery, his or her expectation of a right to be heard was explicit and emphatic. After a second gag rule was passed in 1837, the Massachusetts legislature protested it, calling it "a virtual denial of the right of petition, . . . an assumption of authority, against the constitution, and against natural right."[79] Each year the House passed a new gag rule, and each year John Quincy Adams denounced it as "a direct violation of the constitution of the United States, the rules of this House, and the rights of my constituents."[80] Nonetheless, Pinckney's rule and others like it persisted.[81] Petitions against slavery were not discussed in Congress until the last gag order was rescinded in 1845.

Prosecutions and Foiled Extraditions of Abolitionist Speakers and Publishers

Abolitionists were prosecuted under state criminal codes as well as in civil suits, particularly with criminal libel charges and threatening the public order. Phillip I. Blumberg has suggested that these prosecutions served two purposes: to silence antislavery speech and to prod the speaker to flee the jurisdiction.[82] A number of cities passed ordinances meant to quell abolition speech and press as well.

In large part, Southern statutes and ordinances were public position statements, rarely enforced even when abolitionists were arrested and convicted.

Generally, harsh sentences were meted out, but the miscreants were permitted to pay high bails and leave the state or city involved.

It may seem surprising that most prosecutions under state laws against antislavery speech involved ministers, rather than the "insurrectionists" or "rebels" in the language of Southern anti-abolition statutes. On the other hand, many of these ministers were members of the American Missionary Association, whose intent was to preach against slavery in the South. Among the cases brought to criminal court were those of Gruber; Barrett; Bacon; and Crooks, McBride, Worth, and Vestal.[83]

Reverend Jacob Gruber was preaching in his own pulpit in Western Maryland in 1819 when arrested; he was acquitted.[84] Reverend Lysander Barrett was prosecuted in Virginia for circulating a petition opposing slavery that he meant to send to Congress; the case was dropped for lack of evidence.[85] Reverend Jarvis Bacon was arrested for the contents of his Christmas homily at his home parish in Virginia; though found guilty and fined $49.255 cents (yes, half a cent), in a new trial the court found insufficient evidence to warrant prosecution, and Bacon was freed.[86] Also prosecuted in the South was a sales agent for *New World*, arrested in Charleston, South Carolina, for selling abolition materials; bail of $1,000 was demanded. "Is this a free country?" asked the *Vermont Chronicle*.[87] Ministers Adam Crooks, Jesse McBride, Daniel Worth, and William Vestal were arrested and, in their cases, convicted and sentenced yet managed to flee the South as their cases awaited appeal, forfeiting exorbitant bails.[88] McBride reported that he had also been "once stoned, poisoned once, choked twice, and mobbed a number of times."[89]

Southern states also wanted to prosecute Northern abolition publishers for their "invasion" with antislavery tracts. North Carolina tried unsuccessfully to extradite William Garrison, Boston publisher of the *Liberator*, in 1831, but the Massachusetts governor would not allow extradition. Northern public opinion was stirred by the attempt and brought new support to the fiery, abrasive Garrison.[90] Alabama, too, tried to extradite *Emancipator* publisher Robert Williams, but New York's governor also refused to comply, and again public opinion in the North was firmly in Williams's favor.[91]

Indeed, the South's efforts to stop the mouths of abolitionist speakers and writers via these prosecution attempts served, instead, as a great help in enlisting support for the abolitionist press and in consolidating Northern opposition to the Southern memorials (laws and requests for prior restraint of publications). Free state editors, jealous of their journalistic prerogatives, were united against Southern petitions.[92]

MOB VIOLENCE AGAINST ABOLITIONIST EXPRESSION: PRESSES, SPEAKERS, AUDIENCES, AND CHURCHES

Mobs seem to have been quite readily assembled and set into motion in antebellum years. A broad look at anti-abolitionist mob violence in the South suggests that this, like statute enforcement, was a particularly violent form of social norming—enforcing support of slavery, quelling any opposition to it by local citizens or by incomers.

In the North, on the other hand, although anti-abolition mobs were roused in early years (the 1830s) by sheer racism, as the antislavery message began to take hold and gain broader support, anti-abolitionist mobs were generally traceable to particular newspapers fomenting discord[93] or to particular proslavery speakers whose message was most often aimed at working-class men who had immigrated recently and feared free black workers' competition in the job world. The Cincinnati riots of 1829, 1836, and 1841, for instance, are blamed on tensions among competing ethnic groups of workers.[94] But of riots in New York City against abolitionists and black neighborhoods in 1834, the *Liberator* declared, "Who are chargeable with all the guilt and injuries of this mobocracy? . . . Newspapers, especially [James Watson] Webb, with his *Courier*, and [William Leete] Stone, with his *Commercial Advertiser*," and the *Vermont Chronicle* echoed this allegation.[95] Attacks on Garrison in Boston were also put down to agitation by a proslavery press, "the venal presses of Homer & Co."[96]

Many mobs were set in motion by the abolitionist strategy of spreading the movement's message via lecturers who traveled a circuit of rented meeting halls around the country. Educated middle-class white and black abolition advocates worked on the speaking circuit, a strategy that very effectively used free black speakers to demonstrate that—contrary to Southern propaganda—African Americans were as intelligent, moral, and personable as members of the audience.

Not always held indoors, the abolitionist gatherings were well attended, as this contemporary description demonstrates: "Our tent is spread on a fine, green pasture. . . . Carriages without number, and of every description, are around the tent, filled with families, and the huge tent is nearly full of persons, on their feet and on seats."[97] Those attending were "generally native born; the log cabin their birth-place and cradle, clearing the land the employment of their childhood."[98] In this instance, the locale in Ohio had been settled by second- and third-generation citizens who expected and enjoyed freedom and resented the notion that some landowners used stolen labor of slaves to do work that Northern homesteaders were doing for themselves. This shift in population from early hunters and fur traders to settled small-tract farmers of the 1830s and 1840s is one reason abolitionism took hold in the Great Lakes states.

Most of the grassroots attempts to quell abolition speech came from "rowdies," often hirelings paid by local proslavery factions to break up meetings. For instance, in "Triumphant Meeting—Disgraceful Proceedings," the *Liberator* attributed mob interruptions to people "probably employed for the purpose by Gray and his police backers."[99] They were a "shameless, debased, lawless set of rogues and ruffians" who "made the most hideous noises, . . . the hiss of the snake, the grunt of the hog, the yell of the wildcat, and the braying of the ass." The author considered them "faithful representatives of 'southern chivalry.'"[100] At any given meeting, only a few such people might attend, but in this era, only ten or twenty interlopers making a racket could prevent speakers from being heard. One clever group of ruffians loosed a flock of doves into the auditorium during an abolition speech; the speaker, Abel Brown, had narrowly escaped lynching by a mob after being thrown through a window in Auburn during an earlier lecture.[101]

Though bothersome, the tactics meant to break up meetings were the least of abolitionists' worries, as presses, speakers, audiences, churches, and schools were physically attacked many times over the period from 1830 to the Civil War. For example, in Cincinnati, James G. Birney's *Philanthropist* was destroyed in 1835. One national newspaper correspondent reported that, at Birney's offices, a mob "commenced breaking and tearing every thing to pieces . . . , stove all the windows out, and scattered his [Birney's] papers and books in the street, and burned a number of them." Next, they "heave[d] out the press . . . , broke it to pieces, and threw it in the bottom [of the Ohio River]." After fruitlessly trying to find Birney to harm him, the mob went to a black neighborhood and began tearing down houses.[102]

Editor Elijah Lovejoy suffered as well. In May 1836, Lovejoy fled from St. Louis across the Mississippi River to Alton, Illinois, where his antislavery articles still enraged mobs from St. Louis. By 1837, Lovejoy had suffered the loss of three different printing presses to mob attacks. Alas, his fourth press was also attacked, this time by a mob that burned down the warehouse where it was kept and shot Lovejoy with "four or five balls to the chest." As the *Liberator* said, "Thus are freedom of speech, freedom of the press, and free discussion of every kind trampled underfoot."[103] Newspapers nationwide began to shift toward the abolitionists' position. Ian C. Friedman notes, "After Lovejoy's murder, public opinion against mob violence directed at those who wrote or spoke out against slavery soared."[104]

The murder of abolitionist publisher Elijah Lovejoy by a mob on the night of November 7, 1837, aroused widespread public anger that his freedom to publish had been so summarily violated. This print memorialized Lovejoy's martyrdom a year after his death and kept alive in public awareness the importance of a free press to American liberty. Scan of public domain image provided by Penn State University.

In a further example, on August 18, 1845, Cassius Clay had cause to deploy the two cannons he kept in his newsroom in Lexington, Kentucky, as the *True American* was attacked that night and his presses destroyed.[105] Interestingly, he was able to recover monetary damages from the attackers, making him one of only five editors or publishers who sued and recovered money or saw their attackers jailed—or even indicted.[106]

Common defenses of using violence against abolitionist presses were claims that "abolition bred violence,"[107] that abolition agents deliberately roused up violent mobs to garner sympathy, and that abolitionists were fanatic reformers who wanted to upset the entire social order, not merely abolish slavery. Fanaticism was seen as a mental disorder, as can be seen in Ohio's 1839 resolution that its General Assembly considered abolitionists "wild, delusive, and fanatical."[108] Indiana's legislature added "highly reprehensible, unpatriotic, and injurious to the peace" to the list of complaints about abolitionists.[109] By the 1850s, Ohio would reverse its position and pass resolutions in support of free speech and press for abolitionists.

Physical attacks on abolitionist speakers and their audiences were also rife after 1830. William Lloyd Garrison described his reception in Zanesville, Ohio, where many Southerners had settled, this way:

> Zanesville was locked up. Could get no place to lecture, not a shanty even. Putnam [across the river] was little better and I could get one public room. Lectured. A mob from Zanesville came, broke the windows, doors, tore off the gate, and attacked me, when I came out, with stones and clubs.[110]

Lucy Stone's biographer describes an incident during which "a furious mob . . . assaulted the speakers and wrecked the platform, with demoniac screams and yells which were heard at the distance of more than a mile."[111] Eggs and rotten fruit were thrown—sometimes even cobblestones. Audience members became accustomed to carrying umbrellas indoors for protection from these missiles. Stone related the story of a fellow abolition speaker whose home was burned, his horse mutilated, and his carriage torn to bits; arriving just the same at his speaking engagement the next day, he found the meetinghouse "in smouldering ruins."[112] Stone continued her abolition speaking tours, even though, at various times, pepper was burned to make meeting halls uninhabitable, a thrown book hit and stunned her, spitballs were continuously lobbed, and a window was broken out and a fire hose aimed at her in the dead of winter.[113] (She wrapped up in a shawl and made her speech.) Lucy Stone's experiences were unfortunately typical—in early years of the movement because the topic was so generally unpopular, and in later years because the Fugitive Slave Act of 1850 had created stronger support for abolition among Northerners so that a sort of desperation colored the actions of the proslavery faction.

Unfortunately, one did not necessarily need to be an abolitionist to be accosted. Simply being a visitor from a Northern state was enough to create suspicion followed by hostile action. A state geologist from New York, Professor James Hall, "narrowly escaped lynching, being mistaken by the people for an abolitionist," while searching for rocks in Kentucky.[114] When attempting to collect a debt owed to him, James Crangale was conveniently accused of being an abolitionist, robbed, arrested, prosecuted by the brother of his debtor, and exiled from the South.[115] Northerner James W. Rivers was picked up by a Vigilance Committee in Charleston, South Carolina, for no particular reason; he was tarred and feathered and the right side of his head was shaved.[116] Frederic Schaller was no abolitionist, but one January night he was dragged from his home in LaGrange, Missouri, and along with his brother and a man named Mattis was hung until he was unconscious; he then came to his senses to discover he was naked and being whipped with cowhides. His colleagues suffered similar abuse and crawled through the winter forest to find help.[117] All required lengthy recuperations.

Attorney James F. Otis was arrested in Lynchburg, Virginia, because fellow passengers on a train had not liked his comments on slavery.[118] John Cornest, an abolitionist, was stripped, tied to a tree, and whipped by a Vigilance Committee in Grayson County, Virginia, until he agreed to sell his land and leave the state.[119] When a young Irish stonecutter was overheard saying slavery undercut the position of white laborers, a Columbia, South Carolina, Vigilance Committee had him arrested, and after six days in jail he was whipped with thirty-nine lashes, covered to the waist with tar and feathers, thrown into the "negro car" of a train, and sent to Charleston, with many stops for renewed mobs to threaten him. He was finally shipped by steamboat to New York City.[120]

Attacks on abolition speakers might be said to have culminated with the vicious assault on Charles Sumner in the Senate chamber in 1856. Sumner had spoken out against the Missouri Compromise and any extension of slavery into the territories, calling to task particular Southern congressmen who had pressed for the Kansas-Nebraska Act. Representative Preston Brooks avenged his Southern colleagues by beating Sumner to unconsciousness with the heavy metal head of a cane.[121] Many historians name this as the "key event in the chain of falling dominoes that led to the Civil War."[122]

In addition to presses, speakers, and audiences, churches where slavery was opposed as immoral were often attacked, their ministers harried, and their buildings destroyed. Prosecutions of ministers have been discussed earlier, but mob violence was also a constant risk. In Dallas, two Methodist Episcopal ministers were driven from the city by mobs, and one, Reverend Solomon McKinney, was whipped with seventy lashes before friends carried him from the state.[123] Southern-born preacher Anthony Bewley was chased down and murdered—lynched—by a Fort Worth, Texas, "vigilante committee," never having preached one word of abolition sentiments; his crime was simply being part of the Northern branch of Methodist churches, after their schism over slavery in the 1840s.[124] His merely being a member of the Northern branch of Methodism led people to assume "that the minister was an abolitionist and was guilty of promoting slave insurrection."[125]

Reverend John Fee, who was indeed an abolitionist, was dragged from his pulpit near Berea, Kentucky, in January 1858; he and his colporteur Robert Jones were taken to the Kentucky River and threatened with dunking until they drowned. Jones was stripped naked and beaten. A week later, Fee's school

So-called promiscuous, or racially mixed, speakers and audiences enraged mobs even in the North. This engraving from *Harper's Weekly* shows a group of "Negroes and abolitionists" being driven from the Tremont Temple stage by Boston police and rioters on December 3, 1860. Library of Congress Prints and Photographs Division, Washington, D.C.

was burned to the ground by a mob, and in following weeks, church members' houses were burned as well.[126]

Reverend Edward Mathews, traveling for the American Baptist Emancipation Society of New York, was seized by a Richmond, Kentucky, mob and dunked eleven times in a horse pond; after his near drowning, he left the state.[127] Preachers George Candee, William Hendrick, and Robert Jones, missionaries from the abolitionist group the American Missionary Association, were kidnapped by a mob outside Laurel, Kentucky, which took them into the forest, shaved their hair and beards, and applied tar to their faces and heads.[128]

A Northern visitor "supposed to be an agent of some Abolition Aid-Society" was taken by a mob in Pulaski County, Virginia, and hung until nearly dead, cut down and hung again, and finally, after five such hangings, released and told to leave the South.[129] In Rochester, Missouri, a visiting Methodist preacher was attacked and tarred and feathered, but his local protector was not so fortunate; the mob murdered Mr. Holland.[130] Accused of being against slavery, James C. Bungings was picked up by a Vigilance Committee mob in Chappel's Depot, South Carolina, and hung to death in front of the town's railroad station.[131]

During the summer of 1851, a mob of 150 men roamed Guilford, Randolph, Forsyth, and Davidson Counties in North Carolina; these "Regulators" harassed and assaulted Wesleyan Methodists and their ministers, threatening to kill them if they did not leave the state.[132] Harriet Beecher Stowe described in her *Key to Uncle Tom's Cabin* how some denominations were outright driven from the South. Among her examples was this North Carolina man's letter to the *True Wesleyan*:

> You may discontinue my paper for the present, as I am inclined to go Westward, where I can enjoy religious liberty. . . . [A] mob came armed . . . and commenced operations on the meeting-house. They knocked all the weather-boarding off, destroying doors, windows, pulpit, and benches; and I have no idea that, if the mob was to kill a Wesleyan, or one of their friends, that they would be hung.
>
> There is more moving this fall to the far West than was ever known in one year. People . . . are determined to go where it is no crime to plead the cause of the poor and oppressed. They have become alarmed at seeing the laws of God trampled under foot with impunity, and that, too, by legislators, sworn officers of the peace, and professors of religion. And even ministers (so called) are justifying mobocracy.[133]

Opposition to free expression of antislavery sentiments led to the most violent of attacks on free speech during the nineteenth century, in the North and the South, via law and mob, with little respect for First Amendment freedoms to petition, publish, speak, assemble, or worship as one chose.

ABOLITION ACCOMPLISHED

In December 1865, four days after U.S. secretary of state William Seward formally announced adoption of the Thirteenth Amendment to the Constitution, abolishing slavery, William Lloyd Garrison was able, finally, after thirty-five years of stalwart advocacy in the *Liberator*, to publish the issue he had dreamed of: he announced the passage of the Thirteenth Amendment, the abolition of slavery, and "the complete triumph as well as utter termination of the Anti-Slavery struggle."[134] Due in large part to the abolitionist press and speakers, "not a slave is left to clank his fetters, of the millions that were lately held in seemingly hopeless bondage," and "not a slaveholder may dare to claim of property in man, or assume the prerogative of trafficking in human flesh and blood."

In this, his final issue, Garrison wrote, "Hail, the Future, with its pregnant hopes, its glorious promise," and "Hail ye ransomed millions, no more to be chained, scourged, mutilated, bought and sold in the market."[135]

Notes

1. The quotation is from a letter Jefferson wrote to his colleague John Holmes, found in *The Writings of Thomas Jefferson*, ed. Paul Leicester Ford (New York: G. P. Putnam's Sons, 1892–99); see the letter itself at memory.loc.gov/master/mss/mtj/mtj1/051/1200/1238.jpg. Jefferson again used this metaphor in letters to his granddaughter Virginia Jefferson Randolph Trist and to Lydia Huntley Sigourney, Monticello, July 18, 1824, in Charles Sigourney Knox, contr., "Original Documents," *Magazine of American History* 21, no. 2 (April 1889): 431. He is considered likely to have first read it in Suetonius's writings, a copy of which was found to have been part of his extensive library at Monticello.

2. See, for example, Russel B. Nye, *Fettered Freedom: Civil Liberties and the Slavery Controversy, 1830–1860* (East Lansing: Michigan State University Press, 1963), 166.

3. Michael Kent Curtis, *Free Speech, "The People's Darling Privilege": Struggles for Freedom of Expression in American History* (Durham: Duke University Press, 2000).

4. "Two Forms of Government," *Chambersburg (Pa.) Franklin Repository*, September 19, 1860.

5. A search of the Gale Nineteenth Century Newspapers database for "mass meetings" produced 51,718 news stories mentioning such meetings, this one representative: "Rockingham County [Republican] Convention," *New-Hampshire Statesman and Concord Register*, February 13, 1830. Upon electing officers, the crowd then adopted this resolution: "Voted, that the proceedings of this convention be . . . published in all the republican newspapers in this council district."

6. Nye, *Fettered Freedom*, 70–75.

7. "Gag Rule/Pinckney Resolution 3," American Memory, Library of Congress, *U.S. Congressional Documents and Debates*, 1774–1875, pp. 882–83, memory.loc.gov/ammem/hlawquery.html.

8. "Awful Scene in Congress, on a Sabbath Morning!," *Liberator*, April 30, 1836.

9. "The Attempt to Assassinate Mr. Giddings," *Emancipator and Free American*, March 16, 1843; "A Scene in Congress," *Vermont Watchman and State Journal*, March 3, 1843.

10. Among the hundreds of accounts of this assault in newspapers nationwide is this one from Sumner's home state, "Outrage on Massachusetts," *Lowell (Mass.) Citizen and News*, May 23, 1856.

11. *Genius of Universal Emancipation*, November 20, 1829; William Lloyd Garrison, *A Brief Sketch of the Trial of William Lloyd Garrison, for an Alleged Libel on Francis Todd, of Newburyport, Mass.* (Boston: Garrison and Knapp, 1834); Reuben Crandall, *The Trial of Reuben Crandall, M.D., Charged with Publishing Seditious Libels, by Circulating the Publications of the American Anti-Slavery Society, before the Circuit Court for the District of Columbia, Held at Washington, in April, 1836, Occupying the Court the Period of Ten Days* (New York: H. R. Piercy, 1836).

12. See William Goodell and John Greenleaf Whittier, *A Full Statement of the Reasons Which Were in Part Offered to the Committee of the Legislature of Massachusetts on the Fourth and Eighth of March Showing Why There Should Be No Penal Laws Enacted, and No Condemnatory Resolutions Passed by the Legislature Respecting Abolitionists and Anti-Slavery Societies* (Boston: Isaac Knapp, 1836), 11. The treason clause provision was also cited by Congressman John Quincy Adams in defending himself against similar charges. See John Quincy Adams, *Letters from John Quincy Adams to His Constituents of the Twelfth Congressional District in Massachusetts* (Boston: Isaac Knapp, 1837), 24. For examples in which abolitionists were accused of treason, see *New York Courier and Enquirer*, July 11, 1834, and December 27, 1834. One must note, in fairness, that the abolitionists were quick to throw back charges of treason at the South for failure to comply with the U.S. Constitution; see, for example, "Lewis Tappan and John Scoble," *Liberator*, August 13, 1852.

13. *The Trial of Reuben Crandall, M.D., Charged with Publishing and Circulating Seditious and Incendiary Papers, etc. in the District of Columbia, with the Intent of Inciting Servile Insurrections*, pamphlet.

14. *Cong. Globe*, 24th Cong., 1st sess., 83, 120 (1836).

15. "History of Calhoun's Sedition Law," *New York Evening Post*, June 18, 1836.

16. *Cong. Globe*, 24th Cong., 1st sess., 123–24 (1836); "Legislature of New York: Requisition of the Governour of Alabama," *New York Evening Post*, January 11, 1836, 2.

17. See, for example, "Senatorial Villainy," *Liberator*, December 24, 1831; and "What!," *Liberator*, March 10, 1832.

18. "The South: Theory vs. Practice or—The Consistency of Slaveholders," *Liberator*, September 26, 1835, reprinting commentary from the *Augusta (Ga.) Chronicle*; *Washington Globe*, August 15, 1835.

19. Patricia O'Donnell, "John Greenleaf Whittier," Friends Historical Library, http://trilogy.brynmawr.edu/speccoll/quakersandslavery/commentary/people/whittier.php.

20. Daniel Foster, "An Appeal for Wm. S. Bailey of Kentucky," *National Era*, April 9, 1857.

21. Samuel Reckard, "More Border Ruffianism—Ohio Invaded by Virginians," *Ironton (Ohio) Register*, March 17, 1856.

22. "Further from Alton—Horrid State of Society—Christians Fleeing for Their Lives!," *Liberator*, December 1, 1837.

23. *Niles Weekly Register*, August 22, 1835, reported Charleston, S.C., offering a $1,000 reward for such information.

24. One example is young Lane Seminary student James A. Thome of Kentucky, who had left school to travel and speak against slavery; Thome was "dreadfully whipped,—having received 39 lashes on his bare back, so heavily laid on that they nearly cost him his life," reported the *Ohio Observer* (Hudson) of October 8, 1835, citing its source as "More Lynch Law," *New York Mercury*. Similar incidents occurred in Nashville, where Amos Dresser was whipped, and in Hillsborough, Georgia, where Princeton theology student Aaron W. Kitchell was sentenced to be tarred and feathered. See *Newport Mercury*, August 29, 1835; and "Slavery at War with Our Liberties! III. Recent Aggressions," *Liberator*, November 22, 1839, citing *The Anti-Slavery Lecturer*.

25. "The South: Theory vs. Practice or—The Consistency of Slaveholders."

26. *Niles Weekly Register*, August 22, 1835. The *Arkansas Advocate* said, "Some of Garrison's disciples declare themselves ready to suffer martyrdom even, in the good cause. If they will travel this way they can be accommodated." Reprinted in *Niles Weekly Register*, October 3, 1835.

27. Harriet Beecher Stowe, *Key to Uncle Tom's Cabin* (Boston: Jewett, 1854), 188.

28. Published October 21, 1836, the issue included editorials from the *Pittsburgh Gazette, Troy (N.Y.) Times, Columbus (Ohio) Argus, Indiana Palladium* (Indianapolis), *Sandusky (Ohio) Clarion, Springfield (Mass.) Pioneer, Pittsburgh Times, Cleveland Advertiser, Lynn (Mass.) Record, Journal and Herald* (Dayton, Ohio), *Lowell Messenger, Ohio Atlas, Carlisle (Pa.) Herald and Expositor, Boston Times, New York Journal of Commerce, New York Evening Post, Greensburgh (Iowa) Repository, Western Christian Advocate* (Cincinnati), *Western Banner* (Carroll Co., Ind.), and *Pennsylvania Sentinel* (Easton).

29. Quoted in "A Sign of the Times," *Liberator*, November 19, 1836.

30. Ibid.

31. David Walker, *Appeal to the Coloured Citizens of the World* (Boston: David Walker, 1829).

32. Ibid., 4.

33. Ibid., 14.

34. Regarding Cowan, see *Farmer's Cabinet* (Amherst, N.H.), August 28, 1830; regarding Robert Smith, see *Baltimore Patriot*, April 1, 1830; regarding Elijah Burritt, see John G. Polhill, "To the People of Georgia," *Augusta (Ga.) Chronicle*, August 14, 1830, reprinted from the *Federal Union*; regarding Thomas Lewis, Edward Smith, and James Smith, see Herbert Aptheker, *Abolitionism: A Revolutionary Movement* (Boston: Twayne, 1989), 98–100; regarding Worcester, Wheeler, Gann, Proctor, and Thompson, see "Arrest of Missionaries among the Cherokees," *Vermont Chronicle*, April 8, 1831, reprinted from the *Cherokee Phoenix*.

35. See, for example, Russell L. Riley, *The Presidency and the Politics of Racial Inequality: Nation-Keeping from 1831 to 1969* (New York: Columbia University Press, 1999), 26.

36. Ian C. Friedman, "Influencing American Society in the 19th Century," *Freedom of Speech and the Press* (New York: Facts on File, 2005), 22–35.

37. "Recollections of Ellis Ames," *Proceedings of the Massachusetts Historical Society* 18 (1881): 340–44.

38. Paul E. Johnson, *A Shopkeeper's Millennium: Society and Revivals in Rochester, New York, 1815–1837* (New York: Hill and Wang, 1978).

39. Lee Jolliffe, "How Ohioans and Their Newspapers Defended African-Americans Who Emancipated Themselves from Slavery," Association for Education in Journalism and Mass Communication, Washington, D.C., August 2013; Lee Jolliffe, "Becoming the Story: When Newspaper Reporters and Editors Rescued Fugitive Slaves," Popular Culture Association/American Culture Association, Chicago, April 18, 2014; Lee Jolliffe, "Why Slavery's Refugees Chose Ohio: Newspapers Show That Ohioans Actively Defended Refugees and Defied the Fugitive Slave Act of 1850," Symposium on the 19th Century Press, the Civil War, and Free Expression, Chattanooga, Tenn., November 13, 2009.

40. William Lloyd Garrison, "Advice," *Liberator*, March 26, 1831. So important was this policy to Garrison that he repeated it in "What Shall Be Done?," *Liberator*, July 30, 1831.

41. Ga. Laws, Act of May 19, 1804 (1804).

42. Aptheker, *Abolitionism*, 98–99.

43. Phillip I. Blumberg, *Repressive Jurisprudence in the Early American Republic: The First Amendment and the Legacy of English Law* (New York: Cambridge University Press, 2010), 338–39.

44. Ibid., 341.

45. *Third Annual Report of the American Anti-Slavery Society*, May 10, 1836 (New York: William S. Dorr, 1836), 3, 35.

46. "Capt. 'Lynch' in South Carolina," *New-Hampshire Sentinel*, August 13, 1835; Jennifer Mercieca, "The Culture of Honor: How Slaveholders Responded to the Abolitionist Mail Crisis," *Rhetoric and Public Affairs* 10, no. 1 (April 2007): 51–76.

47. "The Post Office," *Vermont Chronicle*, August 20, 1835.

48. Ibid.

49. *Richmond (Va.) Enquirer*, August 25, 1835.

50. Henry Watson Jr., to Julius Reed, August 23, 1835, Henry Watson Jr. Manuscripts, Duke University Library.

51. *Raleigh (N.C.) Standard*, August 6, 1835.

52. *Acts of the General Assembly of the Commonwealth of Virginia, 1835–1836* (Richmond, 1836), chap. 66, sec. 3.

53. "The Post Office," *Vermont Chronicle*, August 20, 1835.

54. Report of the Postmaster General, December 1, 1835, to the President of the United States, *Cong. Globe*, 24 Cong., 1st sess. (1836), appendix, 8–9, as cited by Clement Eaton, "Censorship of the Southern Mails," *American Historical Review* 48 (January 1943): 266–80.

55. "Excitement in Philadelphia," *Liberator*, September 26, 1835.

56. Jackson to Amos Kendall, August 9, 1835, in *Correspondence of Andrew Jackson*, ed. John Spencer Bassett, vol. 5 (Washington, D.C.: Carnegie Institute, 1931), 360–61. Misspellings are from the original text.

57. Quoted in Eaton, "Censorship," 269–70, citing *Cong. Globe*, 24 Cong., 1st Sess., 165 (1836).

58. "Laws of the United States of a Public Nature," no. 64, sec. 32, *Register of Debates in Congress*, 12 (Washington, D.C.: Gales and Seaton), part 4, appendix, 32.

59. Nye, *Fettered Freedom*, 82.

60. Eaton, "Censorship," 267.

61. *New York Tribune*, December 28, 1859.

62. William Jay, *Miscellaneous Writings on Slavery* (Boston: Jewett, 1853), 218–20, outlines the exact electoral results of this inequity.

63. "Florida: Sketch of a Debate in the Senate of the United States, January 10, 1840, on the Presentation of Petitions for a Division of the Territory of Florida," *Boston Emancipator*, February 27, 1840; "The Annexation of the [*sic*] Texas to the United States," *Jackson Mississippian*, February 21, 1844.

64. See, for example, "Jacksonian Democracy and Modern America," *U.S. History Online Textbook*, www.ushistory.org/us/23f.asp, 2014.

65. "Slavery," *The Hermitage Is Much More Than a Mansion*, website of The Hermitage: Home of President Andrew Jackson, www.thehermitage.com/mansion-grounds/farm/slavery.

66. Charles W. Denison, "By Peaceable Legislation and Acts of Righteousness," *New York Emancipator and Journal of Public Morals*, January 14, 1834.

67. Martin Van Buren, "Inaugural Address, Saturday, March 4, 1837," *American History: From Revolution to Reconstruction and Beyond*, www.let.rug.nl/usa/presidents/martin-van-buren/inaugural-address-1837.php.

68. Theodore Dwight Weld, *American Slavery, as It Is: Testimony of a Thousand Witnesses* (New York: American Anti-Slavery Society, 1839), 184–86.

69. "Awful Scene in Congress, on a Sabbath Morning!"

70. *Huntsville (Ala.) Democrat*, June 16, 1838.

71. Mississippi politician George Poindexter was widely believed to have shot before the count was completed, during a duel, and killed his opponent.

72. Here, Weld misspeaks. John Rowan was tried and acquitted for a murder he committed during a dispute over a card game. He later became a U.S. representative and a U.S. senator but not a governor.

73. Weld, *American Slavery*, 185. In 1848, Georgia's U.S. representative Alexander Stephens was also attacked and stabbed multiple times; his assailant, Georgia judge Frances Cone, called Stephens a "traitor to the South" for his willingness to discuss compromise during congressional debates on tariffs, states' rights, and slavery in new territories.

74. Denison, "By Peaceable Legislation."

75. "Abolition Debate in Congress," *Liberator*, February 20, 1836; Robert P. Ludlom, "The Antislavery 'Gag-rule': History and Argument," *Journal of Negro History* 26, no. 2 (Spring 1941): 203–43.

76. "House of Representatives, 28th Congress, 1st Sess.," *National Intelligencer*, February 23, 1844.

77. "From the Citizens of Sangamon County, Illinois, Praying that Texas May Not Be Admitted to the Union; In Senate, 28th Congress, First Session," *National Intelligencer*, April 23, 1844.

78. See "Disunion," *Liberator*, April 13, 1849, for example.

79. "Fate of the Massachusetts Resolutions upon the Right of Petition, and the Abolition of Slavery in the District of Columbia," *Boston Atlas*, January 18, 1838.

80. John Quincy Adams, "To the Citizens of the United States," *Cleveland Herald and Gazette*, June 28, 1839; Eve Errickson, "Lincoln's First Amendment Record," *Cottage Courier* 12 (Summer 2011): 2, www.lincolncottage.org; Walter Berns, "Freedom of the Press and the Alien and Sedition Laws: A Reappraisal," *Supreme Court Review* 1970 (January 1970): 149.

81. See, for example, *Cong. Globe*, 25th Cong., 3rd sess., 22.

82. Blumberg, *Repressive Jurisprudence*, 360.

83. Ibid., 343.

84. David Martin, *Trial of the Rev. Jacob Gruber Minister in the Methodist Episcopal Church at the March Term, 1819, in the Frederick County Court for a Misdemeanor (1819)*, reprinted in *Slave Rebels, Abolitionists and Southern Courts: The Pamphlet Literature*, ed. Paul Finkelman, Slavery, Race, and the American Legal System, 1700–1872 (New Jersey: Lawbook Exchange, 2012), n. 80.

85. Commonwealth v. Barrett, 36 Va. (9 Leigh) 665 (1839).

86. Bacon v. Commonwealth, 48 Va. 602 (1850).

87. "The Liberty of the Press," *Vermont Chronicle*, November 30, 1842.

88. Clement Eaton, *The Freedom-of-Thought Struggle in the Old South* (New York: Harper and Row, 1940), 211–12n66.

89. Stanley Harrold, *The Abolitionists and the South, 1831–1861* (Lexington: University Press of Kentucky, 1995), 101; E. W. Crooks, *Life of Rev. A. Crooks, A.M.* (Syracuse: Wesleyan Methodist Publishing House, 1875).

90. "Fugitives from Justice," *New York Evening Post*, October 14, 1835.

91. "Legislature of New York: Requisition of the Governour of Alabama."

92. Nye, *Fettered Freedom*, 141.

93. "Riots in New York," *Liberator*, July 19, 1834; *Vermont Chronicle*, July 25, 1834.
94. For example, see William Cullen Bryant, "The Cincinnati Mob: August 10, 1836," in *Power for Sanity: Selected Editorials of William Cullen Bryant, 1829–1861*, ed. William Cullen Bryant II (Bronx, N.Y.: Fordham University Press, 1994), 49.
95. "Riots in New York"; *Vermont Chronicle*, July 25, 1834.
96. *Liberator*, November 28, 1835.
97. H. C. W. [most likely Henry Clarke Wright], "Great Convention in the West," *Liberator*, October 5, 1849.
98. Ibid.
99. November 4, 1842.
100. Ibid.
101. "Abolition Riot [at Northampton]," *New York Herald*, March 19, 1843; "Great Excitement, almost a Riot—Attempt at Lynching an Abolition Lecturer—Ultimate Escape of the Modern Clarkson," *New York Herald*, October 5, 1842.
102. "Riot at Cincinnati," *New-Hampshire Statesman and State Journal*, August 13, 1836.
103. "Further from Alton—Horrid State of Society—Christians Fleeing for Their Lives!," *Liberator*, December 1, 1837.
104. Friedman, "Influencing American Society."
105. "The Freedom of the Press in Kentucky—C. M. Clay's 'True American' Suspended by Action of a Mob," *Cleveland Herald*, August 25, 1845.
106. Richard H. Kielbowicz, "The Law and Mob Law in Attacks on Antislavery Newspapers, 1833–1860," *Law and History Review* 24, no. 3 (Fall 2006): 569.
107. Nye, *Fettered Freedom*, 13.
108. "Mr. Flood's Resolutions, as Introduced in the House," *Cleveland Herald and Gazette*, January 21, 1839.
109. "Servility Rewarded," *Emancipator*, March 28, 1839, reprinted from the *Kentucky Commonwealth*.
110. Garrison quoted in Marc Egnal, *Clash of Extremes: The Economic Origins of the Civil War* (New York: Hill and Wang, 2010), online source unpaginated.
111. Alice Stone Blackwell, *Lucy Stone: Pioneer of Woman's Rights* (Charlottesville: University of Virginia Press, 1930), 76.
112. Ibid., 78.
113. Ibid., 77–80.
114. "Geology and Abolition," *Boston Atlas*, May 28, 1841.
115. "Another Southern Outrage: A New Way to Pay Old Debts—An Irishman Imprisoned and Banished," *New York Tribune*, January 11, 1860, citing the *Augusta (Ga.) Evening Dispatch*.
116. "Barbarism Rampant," *Annual Report*, American Anti-Slavery Society, May 1, 1860, 186.
117. Ibid., 188–89, citing the *Quincy (Ill.) Whig*.

118. "Excitement," *Washington (D.C.) Globe*, September 7, 1835.
119. "Lynching an Abolitionist," *Boston Atlas*, September 27, 1851.
120. "Barbarism Rampant," 183–84.
121. Hundreds of newspapers reported the incident. For example, "The Sumner Outrage," *Lowell Citizen and News*, May 26, 1856.
122. Williamjames Hull Hoffer, "North and South: A Legal History of the Caning of Charles Sumner," *Rutgers Law Journal* 43 (2013): 515.
123. David B. Chesebrough, *Clergy Dissent in the Old South, 1830–1865* (Carbondale: Southern Illinois University Press, 1996), 34.
124. Ibid., 35–36.
125. Ibid.
126. Harold D. Tallant, *Evil Necessity: Slavery and Political Culture in Antebellum Kentucky* (Lexington: University Press of Kentucky, 2003), 206–7; Harrold, *Abolitionists and the South*, 102.
127. "Lynching an Abolitionist in Kentucky," *Bangor (Maine) Whig and Courier*, March 19, 1851.
128. "Barbarism Rampant," 183.
129. Citing the *Wytheville (Va.) Telegraph*, "The Way Abolition Emissaries Are Treated in Southwestern Virginia," *Liberator*, December 30, 1859.
130. *St. Joseph (Mo.) Gazette*, quoted in "More Mob Law in Missouri," *Vermont Chronicle*, July 8, 1856.
131. "Barbarism Rampant," 187–88.
132. Charles C. Bolton, *Poor Whites of the Antebellum South: Tenants and Laborers in Central North Carolina and Northeast Mississippi* (Durham: Duke University Press, 1994), 56.
133. Stowe, *Key*, 188.
134. William Lloyd Garrison, "Official Proclamation, Declaring 'Liberty Throughout All the Land, unto All the Inhabitants Thereof,'" *Liberator*, December 22, 1865.
135. Ibid.

2. "PALPABLE INJURY"

ABRAHAM LINCOLN AND PRESS SUPPRESSION IN THE CIVIL WAR NORTH

DAVID W. BULLA

No other period in American journalism history produced a more intense degree of press suppression than the Civil War. Suppression was much more extensive than the closing of newspapers and the arrests of journalists. Historian James G. Randall has pointed to specific methods that President Abraham Lincoln's administration and the Union military used to restrain the Northern press in the Civil War: (1) censoring, including messages sent and received over the telegraphic lines (the Lincoln administration took control of the major telegraph line, the American Telegraph Company, in April 1861); (2) trying by military commissions those reporters operating within Union lines as if they were members of the army; (3) excluding certain reporters from camps by generals; (4) suppressing newspapers by the military authorities; (5) arresting journalists, by military officials or U.S. marshals; (6) seizing newspapers; (7) prohibiting journals from the mail; and (8) prohibiting newspapers from federal military districts.[1] A ninth way of constraining the press came when the House Judiciary Committee compelled citizens to turn over evidence in which the committee might have an interest.

President Lincoln ultimately was responsible for much of that intervention. It is worth noting that Congress did review some of these methods of intervention, especially those involving the postal service.[2] However, almost no condemnation of the president came from Capitol Hill, where, of course, Lincoln's Republicans were in the majority.

Yet it is important to note that Civil War constraints occurred in a piecemeal fashion. It was far from systematic or bureaucratized. The most intense suppression came from those officers who for one reason or another believed the government ought to control the press during the war. Furthermore, most suppression acts resulted in only the temporary closing of newspapers, and such squelching of the press often backfired and caused some editors to be even more vituperative. Still, some newspapers did close permanently.

While Lincoln oversaw the greatest governmental censorship in American history, he was not consistent on this issue. Indeed, Lincoln had mixed feelings about suppression and increased his tolerance of the press—including the extreme vitriol aimed at him from both conservative Democrats and radical Republicans—during the war. Secretary of War Edwin M. Stanton had no such qualms, however, and he often pushed Lincoln toward being less lenient with wayward journalists. Author Shelby Foote claims that the Lincoln administration suppressed 300 newspapers in the North and allowed approximately thirteen thousand political arrests by the federal government during the war, although the former figure seems almost certainly too small.[3] (Of the 3,300 newspapers published in the United States in 1860, approximately 800 were produced in the Southern states. Many of those newspapers—perhaps half—were out of business by 1862.) In Indiana and Missouri alone, close to 150 newspapers were suppressed, thus making the claim that only 300 journals were suppressed problematic at best.[4] There are not detailed studies of press suppression for the other Northern states, so accurate assessment of a comprehensive figure is difficult to achieve.

Historian David Herbert Donald and author Robert Penn Warren also employ that 300 figure in depicting the degree of press suppression in the Civil War North.[5] Donald and his colleague James G. Randall observe, "The larger fact, however, is that the government as a general rule refrained from control of the news."[6] Yet Donald and Randall admit that it "is obvious" that the Lincoln administration "swerved from the course of democratic government and departed from the forms of civil liberty . . . ; that it stretched and at times seemed to ignore the Constitution is evident. The arbitrary arrests cannot be passed over lightly."[7] Randall does concede that Lincoln at the outset of the war gave the government "a dictatorial turn."[8] However, he and Donald reject viewing Lincoln as a dictator. The two historians write, "The word 'dictator' in its twentieth-century connotation would be utterly inappropriate if applied to the Civil War President."[9]

Four cases provide typical examples of Civil War censorship: (1) the arrest of *Los Angeles Star* editor Henry Hamilton in 1862; (2) the suppression of Democratic newspapers in Indiana in the spring of 1863; (3) the suppression of

Wilbur F. Storey's pro-Democratic *Chicago Times* by Major General Ambrose E. Burnside in June 1863; and (4) the suppression of two New York newspapers in 1864 after a reporting scandal in which the journalists made up an exaggerated call for troops by President Lincoln in order to make significant profits on the gold market. In the case of Hamilton, the Lincoln administration first excluded his newspaper from the mail and then had the editor arrested in an attempt to silence him. Those newspapers in Indiana that were told to stop publishing led to several permanently closing. The *Chicago Times* was shut down for only a day before public opinion turned on Burnside and the Lincoln administration reinstated the newspaper.[10] The two New York papers were temporarily closed.

Press suppression during the Civil War ranks with that of World War I as the worst wartime period of constraints on American journalism in the nation's history. The degree of suppression, particularly in the first two years of the war and in the border states, was intense and provides a significant paradox for the great triumph of freedom that came out of the war. The U.S. Constitution on this one narrow area of the First Amendment was certainly mangled by the president, a few members of his cabinet, and some military officers in the field. President Lincoln's record as a liberator, entirely deserved for his ending of slavery with both the Emancipation Proclamation and the Thirteenth Amendment, nonetheless suffers for his administration's and the military's handling of the press during the war.

Lincoln admired the Constitution and always couched whatever constraints on press freedom he allowed—and he tended to be wary of anything that would do that document harm in the long run—in terms of being temporary conditions due to the war and its nature. He also thought one part of the Constitution, the assertion about suspending the writ of habeas corpus during a rebellion, covered what he allowed.[11] Yet a strong argument can be made that his acceptance of press constraints or his looking the other way did in fact create a chilling effect and certainly stimulated mob action against the press as well as unofficial boycotts against newspapers whose editors took critical political tones on their editorial pages, especially those who were Democrats. Still, political orientation is the key in all of this. Lincoln and his administration acted as they did because the press of the midcentury was still almost entirely political in nature. For Lincoln, Stanton, and Secretary of State William H. Seward, the curbs on the press were mostly about politics, although the rumblings of what in the twentieth century would be the national security rationale would also come to the fore.

The long list of methods of censorship above shows that press constraints were not insignificant during the Civil War. These, of course, involved some agency of the federal government. There were also nongovernmental intrusions into press freedom, from mob action against newspaper buildings to economic boycotts. For the present chapter, however, official suppression by agents of the federal government is the issue because the American political system includes constitutional protection, in the First Amendment, for press freedom.

The seizing of newspapers and the matter of prohibiting newspaper distribution in some federal districts involved postpublication constraints. In contrast, the suppression of newspapers and the arbitrary arrests of editors—especially of smaller newspapers—were actions that occurred before publication and made it difficult or impossible to put a newspaper into circulation. Such restrictive policy runs counter to the American tradition of no prior restraints on the press.

These are four cases of suppression, yet each has a very different context. In Hamilton's case, his anti-Republican, proslavery Los Angeles newspaper ran afoul of the Lincoln administration and was harassed for several years before going out of business. In the Indiana case, Milo Hascall targeted newspapers in the northern two-thirds of the state and not in the more conservative region along the Ohio River precisely because he was from Goshen in the north and better understood northern Indiana, thus demonstrating that Civil War press restraints tended to be random and not a well-developed national system. In the Chicago case, Storey's consistent criticism of Lincoln compelled Republicans to appeal for governmental restraints against his newspaper. And the New York case deals with the government's initial prosecution of the publishers of two newspapers that printed a hoax rather than of the reporters of the falsehood.

It is worth mentioning that the most intense suppression took place in Maryland and Missouri in the first two years of the war. Why these two border states? Precisely because Lincoln and the military had to convince—coerce—citizens of these two states to remain loyal to the Union. Maryland had barely even noted Lincoln's presence in the election of 1860, giving him just 2 percent of the vote. In Missouri, Lincoln had received only 10 percent of the vote.[12] While newspapers were banned from the mail and editors were arrested in both states, another threat to newspapers was mob action. For example, one year into the war, a crowd of thugs ransacked the *Baltimore Wecker*, a German-language newspaper with pro-abolition sentiments.[13] In Missouri, one historian counted more than sixty cases of suppression in the state from 1861 to 1864, and in all likelihood that number is low.[14] Union brigadier general Nathaniel Lyon closed pro-Confederate newspapers; meanwhile, John C. Frémont, who ran the state for a while as a military dictator, arrested the pro-Lincoln editor of the *Missouri Democrat* (which was pro-Republican) based on criticism the editor had shared with his brother, who just happened to be Montgomery Blair, the postmaster general of the United States. So it went in Civil War Missouri. Major cases of press suppression also occurred in Iowa, Ohio, Pennsylvania, and Wisconsin. Indeed, no state was immune to constraints and intimidation of the minority press.

SUPPRESSION OF THE *LOS ANGELES STAR*

Henry Hamilton's case is significant because it occurred so far from the front of the war—across the continent in California. Here was a man publishing a newspaper not only a long way from Washington but also a very long way from where almost all of the bullets were flying. Yet Hamilton got into hot water with the Lincoln administration and saw his newspaper barred from the mails. Later he was arrested. These were heavy-handed tactics for a government busy prosecuting a war. As was the case in the other examples of press suppression in this chapter, the president, his cabinet, and many Republican politicians believed Democratic editors like Hamilton should hold their tongues until the war was successfully prosecuted. In other words, the special circumstance of civil war meant that the Union needed a united front, not partisan bickering, until the Confederacy could be subdued.

The state of California (with a population just under four hundred thousand at the start of the war) was relatively loyal to the Union. It was easily able to fill its volunteer quotas, and while it was far from the front, it did have Federal soldiers stationed there. Still, it is a large state geographically, and antiwar sentiment occurred there in small pockets, including Los Angeles. Indeed, Lincoln won the state in 1860 by less than a thousand votes, with Stephen A. Douglas a close second. Although Leland Stanford became the first Republican governor of the state, the legislature was in the hands of the Democrats for the first two years of the war.

From the beginning, Hamilton had little enthusiasm for the war. Like Horace Greeley of the *New York Tribune*, Hamilton was content to let the South leave the national political system. Hamilton, of course, had a very different political orientation from Greeley, who was a Republican. "At all events," Hamilton wrote, "if secession spreads, we hope there will be no attempt at coercion."[15] The Los Angeles newspaper also posted stories about the Confederacy, praised Jefferson Davis, defended the right to secession, and even brought up the idea of California seeking its own independence. Hamilton tended to blast Lincoln and pointed the finger at the Republican policy as the cause of the war. The Los Angeles editor called Lincoln's first inaugural address a failure and said his cabinet was weak. Like many Peace Democrats, Hamilton believed in a strict construction of the Constitution and observed that slavery was constitutional. He wanted the war to end as soon as possible and return to the status quo ante. Moreover, Hamilton often printed the oratory of anti-Lincoln Democrats, which certainly did not endear him to the Republicans.

By March 1862, the Lincoln administration decided to act against the *Star*, as well as against some pro-Democratic papers in Oregon.[16] First, it barred Hamilton's newspaper from the mail.[17] Yet Hamilton seemed not to have been too bothered by the order. He continued to "heap verbal abuse on President Lincoln and the Union cause in the war," according to Thomas C. Hanson.[18] On October 17, 1862, Secretary of War Stanton had Hamilton arrested for discouraging volunteer enlistments and general disloyalty. This was the standard rationale for arrests of wayward Democratic journalists.

Hamilton spent ten days in jail. When he returned to the *Star*, Hamilton did not comment on his arrest. Rather, the editor ran a piece from the *New York World*, which often clashed with the Lincoln administration. The *World* lambasted the administration's policy of arbitrary arrests. In future issues of the *Star*, Hamilton derided the Republicans and wrote that the only loyalty they were concerned with was that to the party. He also claimed that most soldiers were Democrats, were only interested in restoring the Union, and had no desire to fight a war of abolition. In December, Hamilton termed Lincoln's annual message to the nation "the sorriest document which has ever emanated from an occupant of the eminent position. It is without merit of any kind."[19]

A month later, the federal government decided to allow the *Star* to circulate freely again in the mails. The vituperative commentary continued, and Hamilton began to have political aspirations. In the fall of 1863, Hamilton won a seat in the California Senate. Perhaps his notoriety from suppression helped his political ambitions. On the other hand, the newspaper's survival would become an issue in 1864.

By August of that year, Hamilton stepped down as editor of the *Star*. At that time, he believed Lincoln would not win reelection. But only a week later, Atlanta fell to William T. Sherman, and the fall elections would turn decidedly in favor of Lincoln and the Republicans. By October 1864, the *Star* no longer existed. It would be unfair to say that it was completely a casualty of the Union's press constraints. After all, newspapers came and went with regularity in the middle of the nineteenth century. Yet it is quite possible that the ordeal of suppression may have done enough financial damage to make it difficult to continue.

HASCALL'S WAR ON THE INDIANA PRESS

Milo Smith Hascall was an unlikely practitioner of press restraints. Before the war, he had been an attorney and town leader in the northern Indiana town of Goshen. His brother, Melvin B. Hascall, actually owned a financially struggling Democratic newspaper in Goshen, and from time to time Milo supplied him with monetary support, even though Hascall was a Republican. There is almost nothing in his background that would suggest he would become an abuser of civil rights. He was a reasonable, civic-minded gentleman who volunteered to fight in the war, helping raise a regiment from Goshen. Hascall ascended steadily through the ranks of the Indiana Volunteers and served in West Virginia and Tennessee on his way to becoming a brigadier general and then being named the commander of the federal district of Indiana by Major General Ambrose E. Burnside. Technically, he was supposed to focus on Union war concerns in the state, but sometimes he went beyond that charge, which infuriated both Democrats and Republican governor Oliver P. Morton, who preferred to have a political friend in Hascall's position.

From April 1861 to the late summer of 1862, the Civil War more or less had unified the press in Indiana, but after Lincoln announced the Emancipation Proclamation on September 22, 1862, Democratic editors became critical of the war. Meanwhile, Republican editors had a second bogeyman—besides the Confederacy—to trash for the next few years, namely the Peace Democrats. Now Republican scribes could frame the war period in terms of loyalty and disloyalty. Furthermore, the somewhat unclear war news of the first two years of the conflict intensified the divide. Democratic journalists voiced concerns about the draft, while Republicans moved more and more toward abolition as the key war aim. In a sense, both Democratic and Republican editors began to dabble in the politics of fear. Hascall's attempt to shutter the Democratic press in Indiana added fuel to the fire. Republican editors cheered Hascall; Democrats skewered him.

When Hascall was hired as commander of the District of Indiana in April 1863, Burnside charged his subordinate with slowing the tide of desertions in the Hoosier State and with making sure Indiana did its part for the Union cause. Early on, Burnside, who headed the Department of the Ohio and was headquartered in Cincinnati, decided to flush out traitors in what now is the heart of the Midwest. He promulgated General Order No. 38, which restricted written and spoken criticism of the war effort and the president. The order also stated, "The habit of declaring sympathies for the enemy will not be allowed in this department."[20] Burnside added, "Treason expressed or implied will not be tolerated."[21] Most famously, it was used against Clement L. Vallandigham, a former Democratic congressman and editor from Dayton, Ohio. Vallandigham would be arrested, tried, convicted, and exiled to the South. His infraction was a speech critical of Lincoln given in Mount Vernon, Ohio, in early May 1863.

In Indiana, Hascall was the man who would be in charge of enforcing this military law that applied to civilians. Appointed to command the federal district of Indiana just as Burnside put General Order No. 38 into effect, Hascall began by focusing on the desertion crisis, as hundreds of Hoosiers headed home after the Battle of Stones River in Tennessee in the winter of 1863. On April 25, 1863, Hascall published General Order No. 9, which stated that he would deal sternly with anyone agitating against the recently passed Conscription Act. He appealed to members of both parties to suspend their partisan feelings and to unite over the war effort. However, from the start, Hascall had to deal with growing resentment of the new draft, mainly from Democrats and working-class immigrants in Indiana's larger cities. Indeed, several southern Indiana towns, including Indianapolis, and Fort Wayne in the north would witness draft riots in 1863. Democratic editors also seized on the bad battle news at Chancellorsville, Virginia, during the first week of May 1863 to savage the president and the war effort.

Hascall countered by arresting Democratic editors and shutting down their newspapers.[22] In about a month, he would suppress nearly a dozen Indiana newspapers, as far north as South Bend and as far south as Franklin (just to the south of Indianapolis). Four of the eleven journals he suppressed never resumed business; some would switch party allegiance. This had a serious chilling effect on Indiana journalism. Indiana historian Stephen E. Towne observes, "Several outspoken [Democratic] editors refrained from their usual vitriolic condemnation of federal war policy and measured their words carefully."[23]

The details of the suppression of the eleven Hoosier newspapers would get overshadowed a bit by a very public debate between Hascall and Fort Wayne's Joseph K. Edgerton, a Democratic congressman. Hascall and Edgerton sparred in the press, with the general taking the stance that press constraints were a war necessity while the legislator stated that, if anything, Hascall's General Order No. 9 disturbed the peace of the state and was an act of despotism. Edgerton, in fact, encouraged Hoosiers to simply ignore General Order No. 9 as an act of civil disobedience. He wrote that Indiana was "not in rebellion, nor in a state of war, nor 'disloyal.' It has a constitution and laws of its own, all accordant with the constitution of the United States."[24]

This lithograph, produced in 1864 by Smith and Swinney of Ohio, portrays the danger that Confederate president Jefferson Davis, his associates, and the so-called Copperheads, or Peace Democrats, posed to Union interests. It made clear that Davis, portrayed as a snake coiled around a Southern palmetto tree, could be dislodged only by Union soldiers and cannons. Library of Congress Prints and Photographs Division, Washington, D.C.

Edgerton was essentially taking a states' rights approach to the situation, which was a widespread view of civil rights at midcentury. Indiana was a sovereign state and had its own protective press law that the congressman thought was inviolate.[25] Edgerton claimed that Hascall's restraints would not survive judicial review and that the general had been able to shutter the press because society was so focused on the war that it gave the military a free pass when it came to such draconian measures. Edgerton added, with no slight sense of irony, that

> the people of Indiana are not slaves—they are freemen. They will read and think; they will assemble and make and hear speeches; they will freely discuss public affairs, and freely resolve and vote upon them, and they organize political parties, some opposed to, some favoring the Administration, and you cannot prevent it.[26]

Hascall countered Edgerton's argument by saying that the Lincoln administration was effectively the government of the United States because it was wartime. "You know as well as I, that practically, during the next two years, there is no difference between the Administration and the Government. You cannot destroy or impair the one without effecting [*sic*] the other similarly."[27] Hascall had come to see the other two branches of government as temporarily suspended, at least in any adversarial sense. He also wanted to protect the families of the soldiers, especially with casualty rates so high. He was basically telling opponents of Lincoln and his war policy to hold their tongues for the remainder of the war—or at least until the next presidential election. He wrote, "I am going to see to it that in Indiana, at least, such [disloyal] men have no abiding place" to aggravate the grieving widows of the state.[28]

While Hascall suppressed only eleven papers during his brief run as commander of the District of Indiana, the brigadier general set a tone. The chilling effect would continue throughout the war, although it would abate a bit in the last year. Those eleven newspapers would face thirty-one specific instances of intimidation during the Civil War. But Lincoln and Secretary of War Stanton decided that stirring up things in Indiana was not the right policy. Stanton believed Hascall had been a bit too industrious in trying to intimidate Democratic editors and had unnecessarily upset the political equilibrium in Indiana.[29] The secretary of war wanted the next leader of the District of Indiana to work more closely with Governor Morton and other state officials.[30] Hascall was thus forced to resign on June 6.

The relatively quick exit from the post in Indianapolis left Hascall vulnerable to public opinion. Indeed, some of the arrested editors would be emboldened by the attention Hascall had given to them and throttled him in their editorials when he was commanded to step down. Ed VanValkenburgh, the editor of the Democratic newspaper in Plymouth, Indiana, and one of the journalists arrested in the spring of 1863, had the last word, saying General Hascall "was a burning disgrace to our State, and has laid up for himself a treasure of infamy."[31]

BURNSIDE AND THE *CHICAGO TIMES*

Under brash editor Wilbur F. Storey, the *Chicago Times* was a successful penny paper. Therefore, when General Burnside decided to suppress Storey's newspaper in early June 1863, it made national headlines. Indeed, the temporary shuttering of the *Times* was the most significant case of press suppression during the Civil War precisely because Storey was the most influential Peace Democrat editor in the country. Hundreds of Democratic editors across the nation clipped what Storey wrote and published his words in their own newspapers—a common journalistic practice at midcentury. Furthermore, Chicago was perhaps the fastest growing city in the country other than New York, the city that had given the country Abraham Lincoln after his victory at the Wigwam during the May 1860 Republican convention.

Storey was a veteran editor, one who had a regional reputation for taking a newspaper to new heights. Before he become the *Times'* editor at the start of the Civil War, Storey had worked in Indiana and Michigan, with his last stop there being editor of the *Detroit Free Press*. Storey, who ran the pro-Democratic *Free Press* for eight years, built a newspaper in the penny-paper mold. He emphasized local news and published foreign news with a strong corps of correspondents living abroad and included sections on finance and religion. His newspaper was not devoid of sensationalism, with one story telling about a bear that had eaten a child. He also ran highly salacious and very bold headlines.

Storey's *Free Press* harped on the inevitability of a civil war as long as the abolitionists' agenda was forced on the nation. He outsold his Detroit competitors, both the *Advertiser* and the *Tribune*. Storey was not just a good journalist; he was also a savvy businessman. By the time he left Detroit in 1861, the newspaper's value had jumped tenfold.

After Storey left Michigan, he made the pro-Democratic *Chicago Times* competitive with the pro-Republican *Chicago Tribune*. He was an unapologetic racist, opposed Lincoln and the war, and thought prohibition irrational. Storey's main complaint against Lincoln was that the president did not have the necessary background for a statesman or for a military officer and thus was unfit for office. The *Times* editor called Joseph Medill's *Tribune* "the poor old morning abolition newspaper concern" and said a "fire in the rear" was necessary to stop Lincoln and the abolitionists.[32]

When he took control of the *Chicago Times* on June 8, 1861, he was at the helm of a newspaper whose owner, Cyrus H. McCormick, had pushed an editorial agenda that supported Southern secession. Readership was declining, so Storey at first supported Lincoln and the war. "Mr. Lincoln is the head of the government, and upon him, as such, devolves the duty of meeting the insurrection and suppressing it if he can," the *Times* editor wrote.[33]

Storey bought a new building for his journalistic operation on Randolph Street and installed a Hoe press that could print ten thousand sides per hour. He added a night edition in December 1861 and continued pushing sensational news in the "City Intelligence" columns. He also established a network of correspondents to cover the war in the South and ran a steady stream of telegraphic news from the front. The quality of the *Times* was such that it was the highest circulated paper west of the Appalachians.

Storey's support for the war ended on September 23, 1862, the day after Lincoln publicized his emancipation plan. Soon thereafter, Storey ran a story that included an interview with a soldier called "Jonathan." The article concluded, "Wouldst thou fight for a Union with Negro slavery in it? There is no other Union to fight for. Why not fight for a new Union? Because the old Union had liberty in it as well as slavery, and the new Union may not have liberty at all."[34]

No single episode of federal constraints on the press caused a bigger stir than General Burnside's suppression of Storey's *Chicago Times* in June 1863. The general from Rhode Island ignored public opinion and listened intently to Republican leaders in the Department of the Ohio. Illinois governor Richard Yates and Indiana governor Oliver P. Morton, both Republicans, encouraged the Lincoln administration to act against the *Times* and Storey.[35]

The *Chicago Times*' war reporting corps rivaled those assembled by the top New York dailies. Storey had correspondents both in the eastern and western fronts.[36] In his editorials, he courted trouble and enemies. Copperhead editors throughout the North looked to Storey's editorials for ideas about how to trade barbs with their Republican counterparts. Storey was appalled when Burnside and Lincoln had Vallandigham exiled. "He has violated no law," Storey wrote of the Ohio Democrat.

> He is punished because of the maledictions of those who do violate the law—of those who daily pollute their souls with perjury in breaking their solemn oaths to "preserve, protect and defend the Constitution of the United States." If a terrible retribution do not fall upon the authors of this foul wrong, then is not God just.[37]

Less than a month after his highly publicized military conviction of former Ohio congressman Vallandigham, Burnside issued General Order No. 84 on June 1, 1863. It proclaimed, "On account of the repeated expression of disloyal and incendiary sentiments, the publishing of the newspaper known as the *Chicago Times* is hereby suppressed."[38] The order also prohibited the circulation of the *New York World* in the Department of the Ohio. *World* editor Manton Marble claimed that Burnside's edict would have the ironic effect of improving the newspaper's prospects. "He has become a voluntary advertising agent for the *New York World*," Marble remarked.[39] "The fascination of things forbidden," he observed, "has always proved too strong for any cordons to control it."[40] Marble said Burnside stifled delivery of the *World* because the journalist had criticized the officer's military record, which was checkered at best—his doomed battle plan at Fredericksburg was only half a year behind him.

Burnside wired Storey the next day announcing the suppression of the *Times*. Although he was warned not to print on June 3, the *Times* editor nonetheless ordered his employees to produce the next day's newspaper while Storey sought an injunction against the general's order. Approximately eight thousand papers were printed, and some were distributed before Union soldiers took possession of the *Times* building. Judge Thomas Drummond granted Storey's temporary injunction until a full hearing could be held.[41] Still, Burnside's men continued their occupation of the *Times*.

That same day, the Illinois legislature passed a resolution censuring Burnside's general order; in their resolution, the Illinois assemblymen asked Burnside to revoke the order. Chicago's mayor and prominent citizens also opposed it.[42] That night a crowd of several thousand—twenty thousand, according to the *Times*—assembled in Chicago to protest the closing of the paper. Democratic operatives considered torching the *Chicago Tribune*, but a local militia prevented that.

On June 4, Lincoln sent Storey a telegram telling him that suspension of the *Times* must end. Marble at the *New York World* also was informed that General Order No. 84 had been rescinded. Suddenly, though, the president had a change of heart. Lincoln instructed Secretary of War Stanton to telegraph Burnside that the suppression order should stand—unless he had already lifted the ban. Indeed, Burnside had already allowed the *Times* to reopen.[43] The president had vacillated because he did not want to overturn an order of a military leader. Lincoln had also listened to Joseph Medill, the publisher of the *Chicago Tribune* and a loyal supporter. Medill thought Burnside had done the right thing in closing the *Chicago Times* and opposed the president's decision to rescind the general's order, calling Lincoln's revocation a "blunder."[44] However, Medill qualified his criticism of the president, maintaining that Lincoln did not read many newspapers and did not understand the harm springing forth from Copperhead journals, especially those as vitriolic as the *Times*.

The editorial in the first edition after the *Times* was reinstated simply said "REVIVED."[45] Indeed, the *Times* did not quiet its tone in the wake of the suppression episode. Storey continued to agitate for peace and even sent a reporter to interview Vallandigham in Canada. Marble's editorial after Burnside's rescinding of the order did not let Lincoln off the hook:

> It is impossible to isolate the case of the *Chicago Times* from the great mass of proceedings to which it stands related; and taken in connection with the numerous, persistent, and wanton aggression on freedom of discussion which have been perpetrated with Mr. Lincoln's sanction, the revocation merely adds trepidation and inconsistency to the catalogue of his failings.[46]

For his part, Lincoln had to confront the fact that generals and federal operatives were silencing journalists. The president said such constraints were necessary to prevent desertions and to maintain the high number of enlistments needed to fight the war but also said the Constitution suffered no permanent damage, because the constraints on the press were temporary.[47]

NEW YORK GOLD HOAX

A year later, the most famous journalistic scandal of the war occurred. While journalism had better days than May 18, 1864, what happed to two newspapers in New York City was at first a miscarriage of justice. The *World* and the *Journal of Commerce* were initially suspended for a false draft report that each paper published when the real perpetrators of the hoax actually worked at the *Brooklyn Eagle*. The *World* and the *Journal of Commerce,* both anti-Lincoln papers, had reported in their morning editions that the president was calling for a draft of four hundred thousand more men into the Union army. The two newspapers' source was the Associated Press.

The news, coming during tightly fought battles in Virginia, caused prices on the New York Stock Exchange to plummet. At the same time, investors saw the price of gold increase and so began buying the metal. Yet readers were perplexed that only the *World* and the *Journal of Commerce* published the report. The AP soon issued a statement saying it had not sent such a dispatch.

Soon thereafter, Secretary of State William H. Seward declared the report of the call for four hundred thousand more men a forgery. As it turned out, the foremen at both newspapers had received the news at 3:30 A.M. from a courier. They thought the dispatch looked legitimate, stopped the presses, and found a place for the story in that day's paper. Other newspapers got the dispatch but were more skeptical. Editors at those papers checked with one another and decided not to run the story.

In fact, it was the city editor of the *Brooklyn Eagle*, Joseph Howard Jr., who had perpetrated the fraud. Fortunately, after the police pieced together the evidence, they arrested Howard, who confessed. He said he purposely sent the dispatch just as night editors had gone home early in the morning on the day of publication, knowing the foremen at the papers would be in control for a period of time with no ability to double-check facts. Guessing negative war news would cause gold prices to rise, he had invested heavily in the metal the previous day. When the news from the *World* and the *Journal of Commerce* made its way around the city, Howard sold his investment.

The first of four harsh anti-Lincoln satires published by Bromley and Company in New York in 1864 depicts President Abraham Lincoln, cabinet members, and supporters as a band of undertakers about to inter the U.S. Constitution. The unnamed artist protested the president's September 24, 1862, proclamation suspending the writ of habeas corpus "directing trial by court martial or military commissions of all persons who impeded the draft, discouraged enlistments or committed other disloyal acts." Thousands of people were arrested, denied the right of habeas corpus, and held in jail until brought to trial. Library of Congress Prints and Photographs Division, Washington, D.C.

The *World* defended its publication of the story because it said there was "no time to be lost" over deliberating Lincoln's call for more men. The paper claimed one of its paperboys had heard concerns about the dispatch but that the boy had no authority to delete the story. The *World* figured out the hoax by late in the morning of May 18 and proclaimed it so on the bulletin board outside the office. The paper promised $500 and the AP $1,000 to anyone who could finger the forger of the bogus AP dispatch.

Lincoln, who had told General John M. Schofield in Missouri to be cautious the year before, overreacted. Spurred on by Secretary of War Stanton, the president ordered Major General John A. Dix of the Union army to send soldiers to seize the offices of both newspapers. The military also arrested the editors of both journals, which were generally critical of Lincoln, and charged them with treason. Those charges were dropped, but the editors could not reenter their offices, which remained under armed guard. The editors of both papers published their side of the story and protested the fact that their buildings were still under lockdown. "We protest against the assumption of our complicity with this shameless forgery," they wrote. "We protest the suppression of our journals."[48]

Stanton wanted them tried by a military commission, but public reaction was against the president. He soon lifted the suppression order. New York governor Horatio Seymour said the suppression of the *World* and the *Journal of Commerce* was part of a pattern of civil liberties abuse that included the exile of Ohio's Vallandigham and Burnside's closing of the *Chicago Times*. Seymour wanted to punish the Lincoln administration, so he asked the New York district attorney to charge Dix and the other officers who had carried out the orders to suppress the newspapers. The judge in the case ruled against Lincoln, Dix, and the other Union army officers, claiming that the Habeas Corpus Act of 1863 was invalid. Yet no action was taken against the president and the military officers.[49] Meanwhile, Howard was jailed for three months. Ironically, that summer Lincoln did call for five hundred thousand more men to serve.

The pro-Democrat *Brooklyn Eagle* had no idea that Howard had perpetrated the fraud. Editor Isaac Van Anden refused to condemn the *World* and the *Journal of Commerce*. He understood that both newspapers "were made the innocent victims of the heartless fraud." Their worst offense was their carelessness. The *Eagle* supported the *New York Tribune* when the latter criticized Lincoln's decision to suppress the *World* and the *Journal of Commerce*, and when the *Eagle* discovered Howard's role in the hoax, it quickly distanced itself from his "transgression." Van Anden wrote that it had not been possible for the *Eagle* to denounce the ruse sooner because he had no prior knowledge of Howard's conceit. He regretted the shame that Howard had brought upon his friends and the "disgrace upon himself."[50]

In the end, the gold hoax was, as historian Ford Risley has observed, "a major embarrassment for the Lincoln administration. Although some blamed Stanton for the arrests and seizures, Lincoln assumed responsibility."[51] Furthermore, the scandal had offered Stanton the opportunity to seize the Independent Telegraph Company, a competitor of the more famous American Telegraph Company—which the Federals had seized at the start of the war. Major General Dix closed the Independent Telegraph offices and took possession of its equipment. But with the fallout of the government's response to the hoax, Lincoln and Stanton decided to throw an olive branch to the company, offering it direct access to government transmissions.

CONSTRAINTS NOT PERMANENT

The Lincoln administration and the military sometimes used measures against the press that were so dramatic that they seemed to encourage public outcry. At best, the press suppression effort by the Union government was a crude attempt to silence the opposition press. Perhaps it was so unsophisticated because the extensive federal government system the United States has today simply did not exist in the 1860s. Yet the administration did cast a temporary chilling effect on the Northern press and added another chapter to the history of the government's resorting to restraints during stressful moments.

But Lincoln would not see the Constitution and the rule of law destroyed by the war. He and his administration argued that the restraints placed on journalists were only temporary. Restraints often were supported by the suspension of the writ of habeas corpus, a legal maneuver that had very questionable legal backing, especially in areas where the war was not being fought. The writ of habeas corpus was enforced by military commissions, which, in *Ex parte Milligan*, were outlawed beyond the military front by the U.S Supreme Court, although not until after the war.[52] During a civil war, balancing the need for security and maintaining the U.S. Constitution were challenging, to say the least. Subsequent wars would again see governmental restraints on the press, particularly in World War I, with Lincoln's policy during the Civil War cited as precedent. Yet, no matter how effective—or ineffective—press censorship was in the Civil War, Lincoln never asked Congress for a sedition law, as John Adams had done and Woodrow Wilson would do. In 1863, he instructed General Schofield to use "great caution, calmness, and forbearance" in shuttering the press. Lincoln told his general to act against journalists only if they were causing "palpable injury" to the military.[53] Nor did Lincoln go after any of the great newspapers on the East Coast, including the *New York Tribune* and the *New York Herald*. Except for troop movements and size, his administration and the military put no topic off limits.

It is important to remember that while the vast majority of press suppression in the Civil War occurred in the North, there were some constraints against journalists in the South, although much of what happened there was either Confederate troops ransacking the offices of newspapers whose editorial policies they disagreed with—which happened to the *Standard* in Raleigh, North Carolina, in September 1863—or the drying up of advertising revenue when local businesses felt an editor had strayed too far from the party line.

President Jefferson Davis did not participate in constraints on the press, and Confederate military officers were much less likely than their Union counterparts to spend time interfering with journalists. Davis and his political allies believed that they had to be as democratic as possible as leaders of the new independent nation, and they wanted free institutions left alone. The Confederate leaders attempted to offer a contrast to Lincoln, whose administration did fetter the press, as we have seen. Davis and his generals were too busy fighting the war. Furthermore, Southern journalism suffered mightily during the war. The South lost perhaps half of its total number of newspapers, so it was deemed practical to let Confederate editors be—and compared to the North, there was far less dissent.

It is also worth noting that well more than half of Canada's newspapers tended to be pro-South during the war. But even if Lincoln and Secretary of State Seward would have wanted to silence those anti-Union newspapers, they had no legal authority to do so.[54] The same was the case with the many British newspapers that took no dim view of the Confederacy, many of which were available to American readers, especially in the larger port cities. In reality, the U.S. federal government could constrain the press only within its own jurisdiction, and in an age of both the clipped newspaper article and the telegraph, already journalism was global in that information and opinion were imported from around the world. This state of affairs showed the sheer folly of suppression.

In *Lincoln's Constitution*, Daniel Farber observes that the relative "infrequency and arbitrariness of cases like *Vallandigham* strongly suggest that these actions were not truly necessary."[55] That is, even Lincoln himself, with his instructions to Schofield being the best evidence, had misgivings about squelching the press. Farber remarks that Lincoln's record on civil rights is mixed because of the nature of the war—fraternal—and the huge number of casualties resulting from it, all of this while the democratic process was not suspended. Farber concludes, "Lincoln's occasional efforts to defend these actions do not bear up under the test of time. Overall, however, given the extremity of the country's situation, Lincoln's record on civil liberties was not at all bad."[56] Let us not forget that the sixteenth president added to the nation's heritage of freedom in a way no other president has, by freeing the slaves—no small feat. History has its paradoxes.

Notes

1. James G. Randall, *Constitutional Problems under Lincoln* (New York: D. Appleton, 1926), 481, 490–92, 500–502.

2. Dorothy Ganfield Fowler, *Unmailable: Congress and the Post Office* (Athens: University of Georgia Press, 1982). Chapter 3 of Fowler's book covers Union postal censorship.

3. Shelby Foote, *The Civil War: A Narrative*, vol. 2, *Fredericksburg to Meridian* (New York: Vintage Books, 1986), 635; Mark E. Neely Jr., *The Fate of Liberty: Abraham Lincoln and Civil Liberties* (New York: Oxford University Press, 1991), 115.

4. Physical actions against editors also occurred, including threats, violence, and arrests. Jon Paul Dilts, "Testing Siebert's Proposition in Civil War Indiana," *Journalism Quarterly* 63, no. 2 (1986): 365–68.

5. David Herbert Donald, *Why the North Won the Civil War* (New York: Touchstone, 1996), 89; Robert Penn Warren, *The Legacy of the Civil War* (Lincoln: University of Nebraska Press, 1961), 37.

6. David Herbert Donald and James G. Randall, *The Civil War and Reconstruction*, 2nd ed. (Lexington, Mass.: D. C. Heath, 1969), 308.

7. Ibid., 308.

8. James G. Randall, "Lincoln in the Role of Dictator," in *Lincoln's American Dream: Clashing Political Perspectives*, ed. Kenneth L. Deutsch and Joseph R. Fornieri (Washington, D.C.: Potomac Books, 2005), 279.

9. Donald and Randall, *Civil War and Reconstruction*, 309.

10. Geoffrey R. Stone, *Perilous Times: Free Speech in Wartime from the Sedition Act of 1798 to the War on Terrorism* (New York: W. W. Norton, 2004), 107–8.

11. Mark E. Neely Jr., *Lincoln and the Triumph of the Nation: Constitutional Conflict in the American Civil War* (Chapel Hill: University of North Carolina Press, 2011), 64–65.

12. Eric Foner, *The Fiery Trial: Abraham Lincoln and American Slavery* (New York: W. W. Norton, 2011), 144.

13. David W. Bulla and Gregory A. Borchard, *Journalism in the Civil War Era* (New York: Peter Lang, 2010), 163.

14. Ibid., 165.

15. *Los Angeles Star*, February 2, 1861.

16. Robert J. Chandler, "Crushing Dissent: The Pacific Coast Tests Lincoln's Policy of Suppression, 1862," *Civil War History* 30, no. 3 (1984): 235–54.

17. The outspoken editor of another California newspaper, the *Visalia Equal Rights Expositor*, also was denied permission to use the mails. Glenna Matthews, *The Golden State in the Civil War: Thomas Starr King, the Republican Party, and the Birth of Modern California* (New York: Cambridge University Press, 2012), 186–87.

18. Thomas C. Hanson, *Abraham Lincoln: Press Freedom and War Restraints from the Documents of that Period* (Greenville, S.C.: Hanson Communications, 2005), 49.

19. *Los Angeles Star*, December 13, 1861.

20. *War of the Rebellion: A Compilation of the Official Records of the Union and Confederate Armies* (Washington, D.C.: Government Printing Office, 1880–1901), series 2, vol. 5, 480.

21. Ibid.

22. Neely states that Lincoln discouraged his generals from arresting journalists. See Neely, *Fate of Liberty*, 28.

23. Stephen E. Towne, "Killing the Serpent Speedily: Governor Morton, General Hascall, and the Suppression of the Democratic Press in Indiana in 1863," *Civil War History* 51, no. 1, (2006): 53.

24. *Indiana Weekly State Sentinel* (Indianapolis), May 18, 1863, 2.

25. David W. Bulla, *Lincoln's Censor: Milo Hascall and Freedom of the Press in Civil War Indiana* (West Lafayette, Ind.: Purdue University Press, 2008), 179–80.

26. *Dawson's Daily Times and Union* (Fort Wayne, Ind.), May 18, 1863.

27. *Indiana Daily State Sentinel* (Indianapolis), May 13, 1863.

28. *Columbia City (Ind.) News*, May 21, 1863.

29. Jeffery A. Smith, *War and Press Freedom: The Problem of Prerogative Power* (New York: Oxford University Press, 1999), 116.

30. Ibid.

31. *Plymouth (Ind.) Democrat*, May 28, 1863.

32. *Detroit Free Press*, February 6, 1861.

33. *Chicago Times*, June 22, 1861.

34. Ibid., September 27, 1862.

35. Robert S. Harper, *Lincoln and the Press* (New York: McGraw-Hill, 1951), 257.

36. Justin E. Walsh, *To Print the News and Raise Hell! A Biography of Wilbur F. Storey* (Chapel Hill: University of North Carolina Press, 1968), 182.

37. *Chicago Times*, May 27, 1863.

38. Ibid., June 3, 1863.

39. *New York World*, June 3, 1863.

40. Ibid.

41. Stone, *Perilous Times*, 108.

42. Ibid.

43. Towne, "Killing the Serpent Speedily," 61.

44. *Chicago Tribune*, 5 June 1863.

45. *Chicago Times*, June 5, 1863.

46. *New York World*, June 6, 1863.

47. Smith, *War and Press Freedom*, 115.

48. *New York World*, May 23, 1864.

49. Smith, *War and Press Freedom*, 118.

50. *Brooklyn Daily Eagle*, May 19, 21, 1864.

51. Ford Risley, *Civil War Journalism* (Santa Barbara: Praeger, 2012), 105.

52. 71 U.S. 2 (1866).

53. *Abraham Lincoln: Speeches and Writings, 1859–1865* (New York: Library of America, 1989), 518, from Roy P. Basler, ed., *The Collected Works of Abraham Lincoln* (New Brunswick, N.J.: Rutgers University Press, 1990), 9:148.

54. John Boyko, *Blood and Daring: How Canada Fought the American Civil War and Forged a Nation* (Toronto: Alfred A. Knopf Canada, 2013), 9. Boyko states that eighty-four Canadian newspapers were pro-Confederate; thirty-three were pro-Union.

55. Daniel Farber, *Lincoln's Constitution* (Chicago: University of Chicago Press, 2003), 174.

56. Ibid., 175.

3. FREEDOM OF THE PRESS IN A SLAVE SOCIETY AT WAR

THE CONFEDERATE CONGRESS AND OTHERS REALLY DID MAKE NO LAW

DEBRA REDDIN VAN TUYLL

Consideration of what a particular concept meant at a particular time to a particular people must start with definitions, but that is not so easy in the case of press freedom. Even so august a body as the U.S. Supreme Court has never explicitly determined what the framers had in mind when they wrote the most famous five words in the Constitution: "Congress shall make no law . . ." Judges, philosophers, and academics have written volumes about the meaning of press freedom without ever coming to complete agreement. Some have argued that press freedom is an absolute, others that it is not an absolute, that it is a social construct, that it is a dependent variable that behaves differently when placed in differing circumstances . . . the list goes on.[1]

This debate is further complicated by the fact that press freedom is not an "either/or," nor is it a matter of concern merely for newsmen. Press freedom is a continuum that is possessed by citizens and societies as well as by journalists. Freedom House, an independent group that is concerned with press freedom globally, contends that press freedom has three components: law, politics, and economics. These are issues that influence entire societies, not just the press.[2]

A typical nineteenth-century American would have agreed that freedom of expression belonged to the citizen as well as to the journalist, but he would have also fully approved of efforts by the government, or by citizens, to constrain "licentiousness" by journalists, and, while he might have agreed that each man was entitled to his own opinion, he would have firmly believed that some opinions were wrong and others right. The press, he would judge, ought to confine itself to presenting proper ideas and opinions—proper because they agreed with his opinions or conformed to social norms.[3]

This attitude was prevalent among Southerners who had learned the value of political unity and the danger of dissent during the sectional conflicts of the antebellum period. The region's response had been to adopt practices and laws limiting expression to the "generally acceptable." When the American Anti-Slavery Society decided in 1835 to flood the South with abolitionist literature, Southern postmasters fought back by banning such publications from their mails. They did so with the blessings of President Andrew Jackson and his postmaster general, Amos Kendall, both of whom were slave owners.

Slavery was at the base of Southern notions about all civil liberties, including freedom of the press. It was also the basis for editorial attitudes on the topic of abolition. Some scholars have argued that elite slave owners used their power to force Southern journalists into silence on the topic of abolition, but this argument ignores the fact that about 35 percent of the South's newspaper editors owned slaves in 1860. That is a rate 10 percent greater than that among the general public.[4] Southern journalists were participants in the slave society, not just detached bystanders. By the same token, Southerners were complex people. While general societal agreement existed on matters of slavery and dissent, public opinion was not monolithic. Southern abolitionists lived side by side with fire-eaters.[5]

Studies of censorship and repression during the Civil War abound. The North's experience was dramatic, highlighted by the frequent and determined suppression of Copperhead newspapers.[6] The South's experience was different and, arguably, even more instructive, for it is the story of a press attempting to function normally in the face of invasion by an enemy army. This sort of situation has occurred only twice in American history—during the Revolutionary War and in the South during the Civil War. How Southerners thought about one particular civil liberty, press freedom, is the topic of this chapter.

CIVIL WAR AND CIVIL LIBERTIES

Nineteenth-century Americans inherited a strongly libertarian ideology from their Revolutionary forebears. This ideology set the stage for national thought about press freedom during the sparring over the first Alien and Sedition Acts in the 1790s.[7] Americans came to see press freedom as a cornerstone of citizen liberties. This early libertarianism did not always translate into a hands-off attitude with regard to the press, however. Southerners in the early Republic and antebellum periods did ban abolitionist publications from the mails in their region, and no one tolerated a licentious press, with "licentious" defined as an opposition press.

Civil War historian Mark Neely Jr. has made extensive studies of civil liberties in both the Confederacy and the Union, and he reached the same conclusion another scholar had predicted many years ago: in times of war or other national crises, governments become more repressive, particularly with regard to free speech. Neely found that both the South and the North took fairly draconian approaches to dealing with political dissenters—with one exception: the South might jail or otherwise persecute an individual dissenter, but as Neely admits, "Freedom of the press was a reality under Jefferson Davis."[8] This was one of the great ironies of the war: the side fighting to free slaves was far more likely to suppress the press than was the side fighting to retain slaves. Neely's research documented more than 13,500 cases of political repression in the North. In the South, he found only 4,108. More important for the topic of this chapter, Lincoln's government and military suppressed more than three hundred newspapers.[9] In the South, not a single newspaper was suppressed by federal authorities.[10] State and local authorities were another matter, as the case involving Parson Brownlow shows.

In December 1861, Tennessee state officials charged William G. Brownlow, editor of the *Knoxville Whig* and an avowed Unionist, with treason. Brownlow agreed to surrender to Confederate authorities in return for safe passage to the Union lines, but before an escort could be arranged, Tennessee district attorney J. C. Ramsay, who loathed Brownlow, rushed in before the safe conduct could be organized and ordered Brownlow's arrest.[11]

Confederate secretary of war Judah P. Benjamin was exasperated by the Tennessee attorney's impertinence, and he firmly defended Brownlow. The war secretary threatened to obtain a presidential pardon for Brownlow if any harm came to him while in state custody. Benjamin warned Ramsay that the precipitous arrest of Brownlow could made it appear that the editor had been entrapped, which, Benjamin feared, could cause even more hard feelings in an area where support for the Confederacy was already shaky.[12] Ramsay and the Tennessee authorities dragged their feet for three more months before actually conveying Brownlow to Union authorities in Nashville, doing so only after Benjamin wrote a terse, one-sentence letter to the military commandant of Knoxville: "You are authorized to send Brownlow out of Tennessee by the Cumberland Gap or any other safe road."[13]

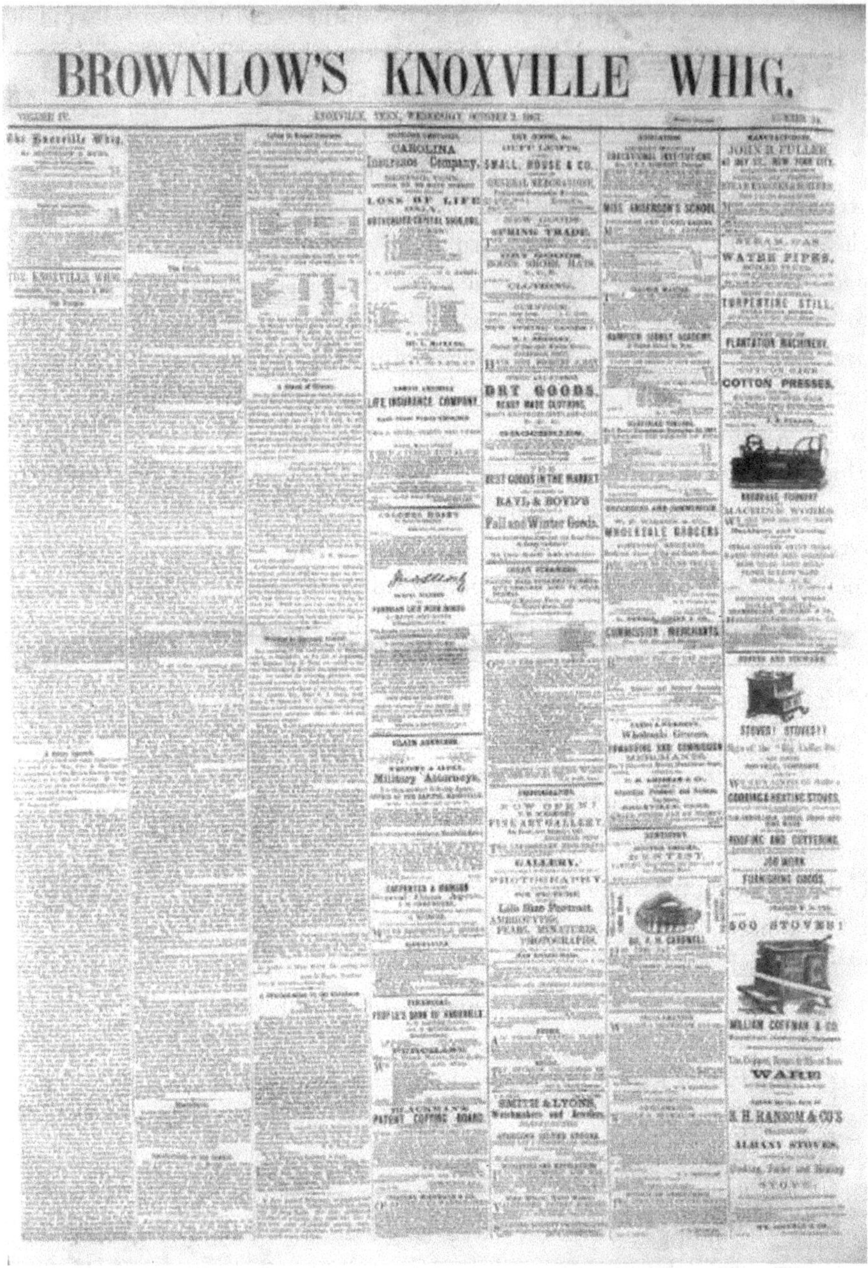

BROWNLOW'S KNOXVILLE WHIG.

CAROLINA Insurance Company.

LOSS OF LIFE

SMALL, HOUSE & CO.

DRY GOODS

LIFE INSURANCE COMPANY

Fall and Winter Goods.

WHOLESALE GROCERS

COMMISSION MERCHANTS

Military Attorneys.

WATER PIPES.

TURPENTINE STILL.

PLANTATION MACHINERY.

COTTON PRESSES.

STOVES! STOVES!!

500 STOVES!

SMITH & LYONS

WILLIAM COFFMAN & CO.

William G. Brownlow, known as Parson Brownlow, was exiled from the Confederacy for anti-Confederate sentiments expressed in his newspaper, the *Knoxville Whig*. The editor and minister, who later served as governor of Tennessee during the Reconstruction era, was one of the South's most controversial figures for his outspoken opposition to secession. Library of Congress Prints and Photographs Division, Washington, D.C.

The Southern national government's response in this instance was outside the predicted norm, and would continue to be so throughout the war, if one accepts Frederick S. Siebert's theory that governments increase restrictions on press freedom in times of instability. Siebert's study of press freedom across three centuries found that as the stability of a state decreases, its constraints on speech increase.[14] And in fact, studies of the Confederacy show that the Southern people were more likely than the national government to want to silence journalists.[15] So the Confederate government's atypical behavior raises a question: why did the South's leaders respond so differently to the pressures of war than the North's?

The literature on press freedom in the South during the Civil War has typically considered actions taken to suppress or to protect journalists. These works have usually concluded that there was less official censorship in the South than in the North but that journalists in both regions had to endure considerable interference from the military. Some studies have speculated that the Southern press had to deal with fewer restrictions because Southern newspapers were just too few in number to pose much of a threat.[16] But the evidence to support this argument is thin. Reading Southern newspapers makes it abundantly clear that Southern journalists were more careful in their publishing choices due to their willingness to balance societal needs with professional freedoms and responsibilities. Southern journalists, as a whole, were willing to cooperate with military authorities so long as they themselves remained in control of their publications.[17]

Confederate journalists' refusal to remain silent when they disagreed with government policy, even if it harmed civilian morale, was an important moment in American press history, and a substantial positive contribution to the country's concept of press freedom, according to Hodding Carter, a Mississippi newspaper editor in the civil rights era. In Carter's perspective, "The rank and file Southern editors produced a largely honorable and courageous estate made up of journalists who were more concerned with press freedom and its expression in time of peril than in individual or professional safety."[18] Carter's work is more public, rather than academic, history, and his estimation of the Confederate press is a bit overstated, but it balances another group of studies that have found press freedom virtually nonexistent in the antebellum and Civil War South.[19]

IDEAS ABOUT PRESS FREEDOM IN THE CONFEDERACY

The key idea in this study is "press freedom," and the starting point for its definition is the First Amendment to the U.S. Constitution. The Confederacy had the same starting point, though its name was not quite so elegant. When Confederates assembled in Montgomery, Alabama, in February 1861 to create their new government, they did so systematically and intentionally, and they began by composing a new constitution. That document was a restatement of the U.S. Constitution in just about every particular, with a few exceptions. The Confederate Constitution guaranteed the continuation of slavery, established presidential term limits (one six-year term), gave speaking privileges to cabinet members on the floor of Congress, and included a few other particulars such as the incorporation of the Bill of Rights into the body of the constitution.[20]

For Confederate journalists, there was no First Amendment, but there was an Article 9, Section 1, and it read, "Congress shall make no law respecting an establishment of religion or prohibiting the free exercise thereof, or abridging the freedom of speech, or of the press, or the right of the people peaceably to assemble and petition the Government for a redress of grievances." Exactly what those words meant and how far they should be taken was a matter of controversy in both the Confederacy and in the Union.[21]

Press freedom and press role have been inextricably linked throughout American history. The country's democratic system of self-government requires that citizens have information in order to make informed decisions. The press has been assigned the task of obtaining and distributing that information.[22] Southern journalists were fully aware of their professional obligations, and they wrote often about both press freedom and journalistic duties during the Civil War. One of their most frequent themes was that the job of journalists was to keep the public informed.

A quotation from the *Memphis Appeal* captured a widely shared idea that the job of the press was to "give the public all the facts on both sides of every important question."[23] The *Richmond Dispatch* in March 1862 was a bit more eloquent in expressing this idea: "The press is regarded as the palladium of liberty," which, according to the *Charleston Mercury*, rendered "the preservation of the press . . . a matter of duty by the Constitution."[24] Journalists in the Old South understood that they had an obligation to keep the public informed and that they should do so in a responsible manner.

They did not, however, always agree on the definition of "responsible." When faced with a congressional bill to allow military censorship, the *Richmond Dispatch* argued a point made frequently in other Confederate papers that the press had every right to report military movements, troop numbers, and locations and to comment on the strategies and tactics of military leaders. It was not wise, the paper argued, "to deprive [the people] of their mouth piece and organ."[25]

The *Dispatch* editors argued, "Better for the enemy to know all of our military movements and plans than that the wholesome dread of exposure through the public journalist should cease to keep in the paths of integrity and purity the business agents of our armies."[26]

Most journalists were not so libertarian in their thinking; they fell more into a category that today might be called "social responsibility." The *Charleston Courier*, for example, argued that the press should adhere to principles of "truth, justice, public virtue . . . and the diffusion of sound conservative principles, law, and morals, and manners and habits."[27] The editor of the *Augusta True Democrat* reflected this ideology when he reminded his readers that "the newspaper press is for good or for evil the most powerful influence that acts on the public mind."[28]

In the South, as in the North, political affiliation had much to do with whether a newsman would argue for or against restraints on publication.[29] The South had no political parties during the Civil War, so political affiliation was by faction, not by party. One Confederate faction consisted of those who supported President Jefferson Davis and his expanded centralized government, a group that historians have referred to as the "nationalists." The *Augusta Chronicle and Sentinel*'s editor summarized the nationalistic perspective well in an August 1863 piece, writing, "In times of peace, a newspaper can say whatever it wishes without doing vital injury to our liberties. Now, however, an indiscreetly conducted newspaper can do us great harm by advocating measures, which if carried out, would deprive us of our liberties all together."[30]

The other faction, the libertarians, favored protection of individual liberties above all else. This group believed winning the war at the cost of civil liberties would produce a hollow victory. The nationalists were willing to accept temporary limitations on liberty in order to secure the longed-for Southern independence. The libertarians were not.[31]

A sterling example of this difference in ideology occurred in the third year of the war and centered on the controversial and powerful editor of the *Raleigh Standard*, William W. Holden. North Carolina was a hotbed of unrest in that summer, particularly in the mountainous western regions. Peace movements had existed throughout the Confederacy from the beginning of the war, although they had been fairly ineffectual.[32] But in North Carolina that summer, peace proponents surged into frenzied activity. They gathered in more than a hundred peace meetings all over the state. Soldiers from the mountain areas deserted in huge numbers, encouraged, it was widely believed, by the work of one man: Holden.[33]

There was reason to be suspicious of Holden. Many of the peace meetings passed a resolution that was remarkably similar to one that had appeared in the *Standard*. A good number of those resolutions added passages that praised Holden and his newspaper.[34] Holden had been shaping public opinion for the past twenty years, so it was not surprising he was considered culpable. One prominent North Carolinian, Jonathan Worth, was convinced that most of the citizens of his state would fight more willingly for Holden than for the Confederacy.[35] If anyone in North Carolina had the power to turn opinion against the war, it was Holden.[36]

Holden's purpose was never to spearhead the secession of North Carolina from the Confederacy, as many supposed. He always considered himself a loyal Confederate who was just upholding his journalistic responsibility to let the government know when it had erred so that political leaders could do a better job of governing. Holden consistently urged North Carolina troops not to desert and to obey all laws.[37] Further, he believed his coverage was simply of the peace movement that summer. North Carolina governor Zebulon B. Vance's assessment was that a "driver sits behind the team and yet may be said to follow his horses."[38]

Confederate servicemen agreed with Vance. More than thirty regiments adopted resolutions that denounced the editor and the North Carolina peace meetings.[39] The controversy so stirred up the public that Governor Vance, after consulting with Holden and a variety of other political leaders, issued a proclamation in early September 1863 urging citizens to stop their agitation. Such unrest was dangerous to public peace. Two days after Vance issued his proclamation, General Henry Benning's brigade of Georgia soldiers arrived in Raleigh on their way to the Virginia front, and someone in the regiment decided it was time for Holden to learn some home truths. The soldiers first marched on the editor's house, but when he was not found there, they headed for the *Standard* office, which they sacked. Holden went straight to Vance for help. Only the governor's prompt intervention kept the newspaper's shop from being completely destroyed. The governor lectured the soldiers on the concept of freedom of the press before sending them off to their camps.[40]

Within a month, Holden began publishing the *Standard* again, and in each issue he defiantly published the text of the North Carolina Constitution's guarantee of press freedom and the Confederate Constitution's Article 9, Section 1: "Congress shall make no law . . . abridging the freedom of speech, or of the press, or the right of the people peaceably to assemble and petition the Government for a redress of grievances."[41]

Journalists as a group had mixed reactions to what was perceived as Holden's bold opposition to the war. Some believed he crossed the boundary between opposition and treason.[42] In neighboring Virginia, for example, John Syme, then editor of a newspaper in Petersburg but formerly editor of the *Raleigh Register*, so fervently believed the Raleigh editor should be silenced that he persuaded a Virginia legislator to introduce a resolution prohibiting the *Standard* from circulating in Virginia. The measure failed, but the Virginia attorney general, John Wooten, agreed to issue an order that prohibited the paper from being distributed in his state either to civilians or to soldiers.[43]

The Raleigh newspaper *Spirit of the Age* was more sympathetic toward Holden and far more condemning of the soldiers and the citizen mob that attacked the *Raleigh Standard*.[44] The editor wrote that the mobbing "was not only an outrage by brute force upon a private citizen, but was a contemptuous insult to the State of North Carolina—such an one as demands at the hands of President Davis that prompt and severe punishment be meted out to all engaged."[45] The editor concluded with an invocation of press liberty that echoed the South's justification for secession: "The liberty of speech and of the press belongs to us.—Let us firmly refrain from using either for mischievous and dangerous purposes, as we contend for their rights and exercise."[46]

Just over a year after Holden's paper was mobbed, the second controversy over the limits of press freedom arose in the Confederacy. By November 1864, the Confederate army had been decimated by desertion and other losses. Jefferson Davis had estimated in a September speech in Macon that as many as two-thirds of the men who should be serving in the army had left their posts.[47] To remedy that problem, Davis proposed legislation to alter the conscription law. In its original form, the law had allowed certain essential professions, including journalism, to be exempt from conscription.[48] Jefferson Davis stepped right into the middle of that controversy in November 1864 when he proposed removing all exemptions, including the ones for journalists, in order to refill the depleted ranks of the Southern army. The manpower situation was so dire that Davis even went so far as to propose offering slaves their freedom in return for military service.[49]

Journalists were appalled not only by the suggestion that slaves be armed and freed for military service—a proposal that seemed to fly in the face of the reason for the long and bloody war—but also by a new power Davis appeared to be seeking for himself: the power to detail drafted soldiers. The Confederate army used details to staff essential jobs with soldiers. Davis's idea was that the South had more newspapers than it actually needed and could make do with only a few that would circulate widely, thereby freeing many editors to serve in the military. The rub was that Davis's proposal called for all editors to be drafted and then allowed him to decide which ones would become soldiers at the front and which ones would be left back home to run the newspapers that would continue to serve Confederate readers.[50]

As the *New Orleans Daily True Delta* noted, journalists, almost to a man, whether Davis supporters or not, were united in their assessment of the measure: it was a bad idea and the worst sort of infringement of press freedom.[51] The *Charleston Mercury* believed such a measure would destroy the press and put the Confederacy on the same suppressive footing as Russia, the United States, and France.[52]

While this protest sounds self-serving, and probably was to some degree, the Confederacy's editors had a point, and one that they all could agree on: a responsible press can never allow the head of state to decide who will run newspapers. Editors assumed that Davis would not be able to resist the all-too-human temptation to send friendly editors to their editorial sanctums and unfriendly ones to serve with General Lee at the front.[53]

Taken together, the Holden issue and the conscription incident show something about the parameters of Confederate journalists' thinking about press freedom. Confederate journalists believed they had an obligation to the people. Where they differed was on what exactly that obligation was, an assessment that depended heavily on whether they were nationalists or libertarians. This nationalist-libertarian debate was widespread in the Confederacy, and it went to the highest levels of government. Even Davis's vice president, Alexander Stephens, came down on the side of the libertarians.[54] Nationalists believed they should be silent on matters that might shake public confidence in Confederate leaders. Nationalist editors, like those at the *Richmond Examiner*, thought that newspapers had a duty to say nothing that ought to be kept secret.[55] The opposing libertarians, on the other hand, believed they had an obligation to tell the public the truth, period.

Even opposition papers, though, treaded carefully when deciding just how much truth to publish. The *Charleston Mercury* experience illustrates the cautious approach of opposition editors. The *Mercury* was never a friend of Jefferson Davis.[56] The paper's Richmond correspondent, Dr. George W. Bagby Jr., "Hermes," shared the *Mercury*'s loathing for and lack of confidence in the Confederate president. He also shared the paper's concern for giving the public as much information about the government as possible,[57] and that included disseminating his opinions of the president, who he found to be "cold, haughty, peevish, narrow-minded, pig-headed, malignant," as he wrote in his diary.[58]

Bagby's impassioned diary entry was far more virulent than the diatribes he wrote about Davis for publication, though even in those pieces he would accuse the president of petty jealously, corruption, and abuse of power. The correspondent argued that the list of Davis's abuses should be published but added that he was using restraint in his stories because they would be too inflammatory in the midst of a war.[59]

Nevertheless, Bagby wrote bitterly enough about what Davis was doing wrong that his handlers at the *Mercury*, perennial Davis opponents themselves, counseled him to moderate his prose. Late in November 1861, Bagby's rhetoric went so overboard that the paper's editor, Robert Barnwell Rhett Jr., ordered him to stop writing diatribes against the president. The correspondent's last three letters had been unusable because of their "despondent and fault-finding tone," the editor wrote, adding that the "*Mercury* is clearly right" in its negative assessment of Davis but that the Confederate people were too weak to deal with such virulent criticism of the president. "People cannot always stand too much truth," Rhett wrote. "Please try and shape your correspondence with these views: the truth, but not all the truth for now."[60]

Jefferson Davis, the president of the Confederate States of America, believed in a hands-off approach to the press. Newspaper suppression was not the norm in the South during wartime. Library of Congress Prints and Photographs Division, Washington, D.C.

In terms of basic principles, the Civil War did not change journalists' ideas about the meaning of press freedom, or the source of its value, though the conflict did lead journalists to consider—and to reach different conclusions—about the limits of press freedom in wartime. The South's journalists disagreed, for example, on whether opposition speech was valuable or treasonable, though they did nearly all agree that the government control of the press was going too far toward a muzzled and censored press.

Southern journalists in both the late antebellum period and the Civil War believed that press freedom was the foundation of a free country because it was the protector of the public's right to know, the conduit of information to the public, and a shaper of public opinion.[61] Collapsed into that right were the freedoms to write, print, and "use any and all channels of circulation," particularly if the subject was government or a political candidate. Southern journalists even advocated, at least in theory, toleration for unorthodox views.[62]

While antebellum Southern newsmen could be said, in modern parlance, to have leaned toward social responsibility in their thinking about press freedom, the exigencies of war pushed some to radicalize their perspective and to become far more libertarian. Taken as a whole, then, the meaning of freedom of the press in the Confederacy, at least as far as journalistic understanding was concerned, had much in common with the way contemporary American journalists understand freedom of the press.

Journalists, however, were not the only occupants of the Confederacy, and their ideas were not the only ones that influenced the South's lived experience with freedom of the press during the Civil War. Other important groups included the Confederate public, the Confederate government, and the Confederate military. It is more difficult to assess what the Confederate citizens thought as an aggregate, for there were no public opinion surveys or other direct measures of public sentiment then. Journals and personal letters reveal little, for then, as now, the press was such a part of the social fabric that it became just another element in the background of daily life. About the only time citizens wrote about the press was to complain about something that had been published that they disagreed with.

That holds as true for generals and legislators, who actually had the formal power and/or weapons to constrain the press, though the public was not entirely powerless, either, Generals and legislators were also in positions that required them to leave a trail of official paperwork, which gives some insight into their ideas about how free, or unfree, the press should be in a country at war. The next sections of this chapter will examine what that trail reveals.

WHAT CONFEDERATE MILITARY LEADERS THOUGHT ABOUT FREEDOM OF THE PRESS

For the first time in history, information moved fast enough during the Civil War for military leaders to be concerned about how its circulation might affect their operations. Telegraph and rail systems in 1860 were extensive enough to make the dissemination of information far quicker than it had been in the past. This, coupled with the fact that the warring sides shared a common language, meant military concerns about the flow of information moved from the abstract and theoretical.[63]

The simple answer to the question of what Confederate military leaders thought about freedom of the press would be "Not much." The social functions assigned to journalists and to soldiers in a democratic society create a tense, but perhaps necessary, dialectic. Journalists have the responsibility for informing the public about government functions and performance. Soldiers have the duty to undertake difficult, dangerous, and deadly operations against national enemies that often require secrecy. Conflict is innate in such a dialectic. The press cannot inform the public if its representatives do not have access to information; the military cannot conduct its operations safely if vital information is handed to the enemy.[64]

Many, perhaps even most, Confederate journalists were willing to accept some limitations on what they published if there was a good enough strategic reason. The *Charleston Courier*, *Savannah Republican*, and *Richmond Dispatch* were among the newspapers that reminded their correspondents and readers at various times in the war that journalistic responsibility required them to avoid publishing articles that revealed too much military information or that might dishearten soldiers or citizens.[65]

Confederate military men viewed the press in three different ways: as a weapon to be wielded against the enemy, as a vehicle with which to build personal fame and reputation, or as a threat to be suppressed. For the most part, they believed secrecy was necessary. Period. Robert E. Lee expressed this when, according to the *Macon Telegraph*, he opined that the Confederacy had made a bad mistake at the beginning of the war by putting the worst generals to work commanding armies in the field and the best editing newspapers. Lee and most of his subalterns were scratchy about press issues, for they understood that newspaper content had value in that it could give away military secrets and could affect public support for the war and civilian morale. Lee and his officers did their best to horde that value for their side.[66]

The Confederate Congress and War Department often functioned as effective buffers for the worst attempted military abuses of press freedom. The case of Major General Earl Van Dorn offers a good example. Van Dorn was commandant of southern Mississippi and eastern Louisiana when he declared martial law there in the summer of 1862. His order included a threat to arrest any journalist who published information about troop movements or anything that might impair public confidence in civilian or military leaders, and it also proscribed the death penalty for anyone who communicated with the enemy. "Disloyalty will not be countenanced. The credit of the government must be sustained," stated the command.[67]

Van Dorn's order evoked a lively debate in Congress and several stinging rebukes.[68] Tennessee congressman Henry S. Foote, a former journalist himself, proclaimed Van Dorn to be a threat to the "great pillars" of freedom in the Confederacy, and Louisiana senator T. J. Semmes introduced legislation to restrain military leaders who tried to exercise unauthorized powers. Both houses passed the bill. Van Dorn bowed to public pressure and revoked his order.[69]

Civilian military leaders seem to have thought differently from the career military personnel they supervised. Secretary of War Leroy Walker relied on a journalist's sense of honor to govern publication decisions and only distributed guidelines on what should or should not be printed. Specifically, he asked newspapers to not report force size, number of weapons, or the condition of the troops. They were also asked not to speculate on possible military plans.[70]

Walker's communication to journalists was in the form of a request, not an order, as was typical of the Confederate War Department through the war. Even when military authorities—including the revered Lee himself—asked for official intervention with journalists, the consistent answer was that there were no laws that would allow for official intervention. Political leaders trusted journalists to be responsible and readers not to demand more information than could be published without harming military objectives. President Davis summed up this philosophy in a letter to his friend General Braxton Bragg. "To preserve the liberty of the press, yet restrain its license, is possible only where it is controlled by a sound taste and sentiment in its patrons," he wrote. "To give information to the enemy is an injury little extenuated by an improper anxiety to satisfy the curiosity of its readers."[71]

Further, Confederate civilians who ran the War Department were firm with generals, insisting that, as military commanders, they had all the tools they needed to deal with the press, or, more properly, to deal with their officers and soldiers. The Confederacy's on-again-off-again secretary of war, Judah P. Benjamin, scolded General Joseph E. Johnston for pursuing censorship measures against the *Richmond Dispatch* in early 1862 when William G. Shepardson, its reporter who used the pen name Bohemian, reported on the winter locations of particular units. Benjamin agreed that the publication was egregious, but he laid the blame for the offense at the general's feet. Johnston was being too lenient with reporters and not properly enforcing the military laws that already existed to deal with the press, the secretary told him.[72] Those rules came from the publication *Army Regulations Adopted for the Use of the Confederate States*, and they constrained not what journalists could write or publish but what soldiers could legally say. This approach—of controlling those who were legally under the control of military authorities and leaving the press alone—is one that has received the approbation of the U.S. Supreme Court in the twentieth century.[73]

Johnston's response was typical of a military man, and one that other Confederate generals, including P. G. T. Beauregard, used throughout the war.[74] He expelled all correspondents from his army and reminded his soldiers that they faced death if they conveyed information that would give aid to the enemy, even if the information was given unwittingly. The general acknowledged that "reserve in correspondence may be a sacrifice," but sacrifices were necessary in order to win the war.[75] The press's reaction was predictable: they either ignored it or they denounced the order.[76] "General Johnston's order is unjust to the press, the army and the country," the *Richmond Examiner*'s editors wrote. "In this war, the people have a right to know all that is transpiring within the limits of prudent mention, and our brave volunteers have the right to expect that the press will perform its mission in going forward to redeem their deeds from oblivion."[77]

Not even Robert E. Lee had sufficient pull to move political leaders to act against the press. In the summer of 1862, Lee complained to the new secretary of war, George W. Randolph, about a *Richmond Dispatch* article that disclosed troop locations. He demanded that Randolph do something to stop such publications. The secretary dutifully sent out copies of the letter to all Richmond newspapers, to which he appended a note stating that he hoped he would not have to intervene further. He added that the War Department desired to end the conflict without ever having to suppress a single newspaper so that the new nation could demonstrate its greater dedication to constitutional principles.[78]

Civilian leaders did take control of communications technology early in the war. Within only a few weeks of the fighting in Charleston Harbor that began the war, the Confederate Congress authorized Davis to seize the telegraph lines and appoint censors to supervise their use. The bill sanctioning this also outlawed transmission over the lines of information that would endanger the success of military operations. This law, however, only slowed down a correspondent's dispatches—it did not stop them completely—for its reach did not include either the mail system or private couriers.[79]

Ultimately, the Confederate military's attempts to control the press were hit-or-miss because each general was left to set his own rules.[80] Had there been a supreme commander, some sort of concerted effort at controlling the press might have been possible, and, of course, that would have given the Confederate military a point man to lobby for censorship legislation. Lee, of course, was eventually named to such a post, but not until the last few months of the war, far too late to be effective.

WHAT CONFEDERATE POLITICAL LEADERS THOUGHT ABOUT FREEDOM OF THE PRESS

The Chief Executive

Like most Southerners, Jefferson Davis had firm notions about the Constitution and the rights and responsibilities it conveyed to citizens. Though he was not a lawyer, he had a lifelong interest in legal theory and gained "a well-deserved reputation as a legalistic hairsplitter" in his twenty years of public service.[81] Davis turned to that legal theory in crafting a justification for the revolution he led, one that raised significant constitutional questions and was the basis for his thinking about how to deal with the press during that revolution.[82]

One particular legal theory shaped Davis's philosophy. He was what today would be called a strict constructionist. That is, he believed the Constitution should be read literally, and if it said that something could be done, it could be done. If the document prohibited something, it could not be done. If the document did not address a matter, it was a matter best left untouched by federal authorities. Davis firmly believed in state sovereignty and limited power for the federal government. Something changed, though, when the Mississippian became president of the Confederacy, and the shift he made in his thinking was significant enough that one historian has referred to it as a "schizophrenic swing" between the opposing ideologies of libertarianism and nationalism.[83]

After becoming president of the Confederacy, Davis "played to win . . . finding powers in the Confederate constitution that he would never have located in the United States document."[84] Before the war ended, he would suspend the writ of habeas corpus, imprison citizens who disagreed with him, and flirt with the idea of suppressing dissenting newspaper editors. But he never could bring himself to silence the men of the press, even when citizens beseeched him and even when he realized journalists could pose a danger to the fledgling republic he led.[85] Where the press was concerned, Davis held true to his faith in the "holy cause of constitutional liberty."[86]

As the war began, Davis and many Southerners believed that the Confederacy was the embodiment of true American democracy, that the new Southern republic was the true heir of the founding fathers and the continuation of the work they began.[87] He used this rhetoric over and over to justify the South's revolution. He proudly boasted that the South had done nothing "to impair personal liberty, or the freedom of speech, of thought or of the press." According to the *Memphis Appeal*, Davis was even willing to endure Parson Brownlow's heated anti-Confederate rhetoric in his *Knoxville Whig*. Editors at the *Appeal* reported that Davis told a man they had interviewed that the Confederate government would preserve press freedom "to the utmost extent compatible with the safety of the government—that no journal should be proscribed for opinion's sake, unless for the utterance of open and avowed treasonable sentiments." Davis was reputed also to have defended the right of the press to criticize government as an "unalienable prerogative," one that would never be suppressed with his consent.[88] Even during the extremities of opposition in North Carolina, the president held back.[89] He did inquire during that period about whether something ought to be done specifically about Holden and his newspaper, but he bowed to Governor Vance's counsel that public opinion would be sufficient to direct the editor's behaviors.[90] In contrast, when he was given the power to impose martial law and to suspend the writ of habeas corpus, he used it.[91]

Davis's basic instincts were that political leaders ought to keep their hands off newspapers. Press criticism was a temporary evil, he told his good friend and noted Confederate spy Rose O'Neal Greenhow before her dramatic death eluding capture by the Union navy. "It is a dangerous thing to interfere with the liberty of the press," she reported the president saying, "for what would it avail us if we gain our independence and lose our liberty."[92]

He had made a similar comment a bit earlier in the war when William M. Brooks of Richmond, Virginia, wrote to him about press criticism of Davis. "I have borne the reproach in silence, because to reply by an exact statement of facts would have exposed our weakness to the enemy," Davis replied. "History, when the case is fully understood, will do justice to the men who have suffered from hasty judgment and unjust censure."[93] The president was able to maintain this attitude even in the wake of personal attacks by Southern newspapers that accused him of not burning his cotton, as other planters had been asked to do to keep it out of the hands of the invading enemy.[94]

Davis was a man who was generally sensitive to criticism, but his years in politics seem to have given him an understanding of the give-and-take of political dogfighting. As a consequence, he was far less offended by criticism than other Confederate leaders, especially those among the military like Braxton Bragg. Davis's attitude was an anomaly for his age. The antebellum period was the heyday of the political press, a time when politicians and journalists often were one and the same thing, yet the Confederate president avoided that sort of relationship. As he explained to one journalist in the days just prior to Lincoln's election,

> In my political career, I have had less than is usual to do with newspapers, not that I have held them in lower consideration than others, but the rather because I have felt we had separate walks which best could be trodden when we kept apart; and also, no doubt because I have always been too busy in my own sphere to encroach upon another.

If any other nineteenth-century politician shared this idea, he would have been one of only a handful.[95]

Congressmen

The Confederate Congress confronted the matter of press freedom, or matters that might impinge on press freedom, several times during the war. Two of those have already been addressed: the Van Dorn martial law order and President Davis's 1864 proposal to conscript editors, which was roundly criticized by congressmen and then consigned to the Judiciary Committee, where it died a quiet death. On other occasions, congressmen considered legislation to restrict press access to the telegraph and direct censorship of journalists. One of Congress's earliest measures gave President Davis control of the Southern telegraph system. This move was not aimed directly at the press, but it did affect how correspondents conveyed information to their newsrooms.[96]

One such bill congressmen considered would have established rules to govern press behavior and to even ban journalists from a particular newspaper from ever covering the Senate. The controversy over Senate coverage arose in late February 1863 when the *Richmond Enquirer* commented on a speech by Senator Albert G. Brown of Mississippi. The Senate quickly put together a Special Committee on the Rights and Privileges of Reporters and on March 12, 1863, considered a resolution to ban all the *Enquirer*'s reporters from the legislative hall. The main argument in favor of the resolution was that access to proceedings was not a right of reporters but a privilege conveyed to them by the legislators themselves. In the end, however, the resolution failed, and the *Enquirer* continued to cover the Congress. Near the end of the war, a similar situation arose with the *Richmond Sentinel*, and that time, senators decided the best way to respond was to ignore the story.[97]

Members would revisit press freedom on several occasions, proposing bills intended to prevent publication of information about troop strength, to regulate access to congressional sessions by reporters, and to prevent sedition. In virtually each of these cases, arguments against the restrictive measures invoked the concepts of press freedom or freedom of expression. Each measure failed.[98]

Other measures the Confederate Congress considered included a sedition law and a bill to allow the suspension of habeas corpus in order to control journalists who might reveal military secrets.[99] Ultimately, each of these debates ended in failure for those who had proposed restrictive measures, and the most common objection was that they would violate the constitutional principles upon which the Confederacy had been founded, including freedom of discussion and freedom of the press.[100] Few explanations have been offered for this congressional course. It could be that Confederate leaders wanted their government to appear stable to the foreign interests they were courting for recognition. Another possibility would be that congressmen had a profound respect for constitutionalism, specifically for freedom of the press.[101]

WHY SOUTHERNERS BELIEVED WHAT THEY DID ABOUT PRESS FREEDOM

Asking what a particular people believed at a certain point necessarily raises the question of why they believed that, a question that presents certain difficulties when the people under scrutiny are Southerners. Scholars have gone around and around for the better part of forty years over the question of Southern exceptionalism. Was the Southerner really different from the Northerner, or was the perceived difference just a figment of the imagination of a "maladjusted outsider" that, in the aggregate, morphed into a sort of mass psychosis?[102]

In most ways, Southerners were no different from their Northern brethren, but one element of their society made them vastly different from other Americans. Daily, they lived with a labor system based on bondage. It is impossible that one could live in such a system and not be influenced by it. Such close proximity to those who had lost all vestiges of freedom could not have helped but give Southerners radical notions about the value of their freedom.

There is ample evidence of the influence. Southerners thought and wrote about slavery and freedom, and, largely, they subscribed to country republicanism political ideology. This ideology taught Southerners to mistrust strong government and that "power is inherently expansionist and that only external popular vigilance could safeguard liberty."[103] Stated differently, country republicanism taught that politics was a power continuum and that what was good for the government was bad for the people.[104] Personal independence was perceived as the bedrock of liberty. That personal independence extended to "a striking individuality . . . subject to no authority," an "absolute independence" that "created naturally a great tenacity of rights and a watchful and resultful jealousy of any outside interference."[105] To antebellum Southerners, personal independence meant having control over "their own persons, property, and family."[106]

The uncompromising nature of these teachings taught Southerners to fear dependence on others—in fact, to see dependence as just another form of slavery. In the Southern mind, to be dependent was to be degraded, an argument made as early as 1777 in a pamphlet that defined slavery as "being wholly under the power and control of another as to our actions and properties."[107] Southerners, from their experience with slavery, knew far better than other Americans what it meant to be dispossessed of individual rights. South Carolina historian Lacy K. Ford Jr. explained the thinking best when he wrote that Southerners' "day-to-day experience of black chattels in their midst served only to intensify their fear of submission and dependence."[108] Black slavery reinforced to Southerners just how fragile their own liberty was and how easily it could be lost without careful, deliberate husbanding.[109]

Southerners had a second fear that would have contributed to their more radical and stringent thinking about certain civil liberties: fear of slave rebellion. That fear intensified throughout the antebellum period until, by the late 1850s, many Southerners came to feel like "they were living under a siege."[110] Even Alexis de Tocqueville noted this during his visit to the United States in the 1830s. He wrote that "the danger of a conflict between the white and the black inhabitants of the Southern states of the Union . . . perpetually haunts the imagination of Americans, like a painful dream."[111] The eighteenth-century slave revolt in Santo Domingo, Denmark Vesey's insurrection in 1822, Nat Turner's in 1831, and John Brown's assault on Harpers Ferry in 1859 stoked those fears.[112] Southerners might publicly attest to the belief that slaves were docile and loyal, as James Henry Hammond boasted in his 1858 "Cotton Is King" speech,[113] but this was a clear case of denial. Southerners might have claimed to have no fears of their bondsmen, yet they went to great lengths to suppress abolitionist publications during the antebellum period, fearing that slaves might be stirred up to revolt if any criticism of the peculiar institution was allowed.[114]

Given their lived experience with slavery and the ideas to which they were exposed, it is entirely understandable that Southerners developed a more radical approach to free speech. It is also understandable that the military took a different perspective, for though its members were steeped in the same cultural traditions, their subsequent training and experiences would have intervened to teach them different values.

It is unwise to generalize too far about so diverse a group of men as the Confederacy's newspaper editors, but this research does indicate that most Confederate journalists and politicians saw press freedom as the foundation of a free society. They believed press freedom was a right they shared with the public and that their freedoms gave them particular obligations to the public, including the duties to disseminate information and opinion and to protect the channels of communication from undue control by the government. Military leaders thought differently. Their more restrictive approach was born of necessity. Information moved swiftly enough in this war that it could be used as a weapon, and that made its dissemination dangerous to the country's war aims and to its armies. That meant, in the military mind, it needed to be harnessed and constrained, even if a few constitutional principles did get a bit mussed in the process.

Taken as a whole, then, the meaning of freedom of the press in the Confederacy comprised a complex set of sometimes contradictory beliefs that flowed from the generally shared political philosophy of the day, libertarianism, and from the shared experience of living within a slave society. Antebellum Southerners understood what it meant to give up individual liberty to government, and they were not about to do so willingly.

Like their communities, antebellum Southern journalists were steeped in the libertarian tradition. They cherished their freedoms, but most were willing to sacrifice some of their liberties temporarily to accomplish shared goals. But there were limits, and allowing direct government involvement in running newspapers was one of those lines that even the most patriotic journalists were unwilling to cross. Journalists were joined in this perspective by a chief executive and a Congress that might have flirted with direct censorship of newspapers but never officially sanctioned it and that even stepped in to stop the worst abuses of press freedom by military leaders.

While the meaning of press freedom in the Confederacy was fashioned from a set of complex and sometimes contradictory beliefs, values, and principles, it is possible to reach a few broad generalizations. It is clear that Southerners valued press freedom as an essential element of free society and as something deserving of protection even during the worst sort of national crisis, despite the possible dangers that could result from that protection. Further, they believed that press freedom was something to be used responsibly, that it was something shared between the press and society, and that it was something to be defended whenever necessary.

Notes

1. Frederick S. Siebert, Theodore Peterson, and Wilber Schramm, *Four Theories of the Press: The Authoritarian, Libertarian, Social Responsibility and Soviet Communist Concepts of What the Press Should Be and Do* (Urbana: University of Illinois Press, 1963); John C. Nerone, ed., *Last Rights: Revisiting Four Theories of the Press* (Urbana: University of Illinois Press, 1995); David H. Weaver, "The Press and Government Restriction: A Cross-National Study over Time," *Gazette* 23, no. 2 (1977): 152; Christina Holtz-Bacha, "What Is 'Good' Press Freedom? The Difficulty of Measuring Freedom of the Press Worldwide," presented at the International Association for Media and Communication Research, Porto Alegre, Brazil, July 25–30, 2004.

2. "Survey Methodology," Freedom of the Press 2009 Survey Release, available from http://www.freedomhouse.org/template.cfm?page=470, accessed August 7, 2009.

3. B. F. Arthur to Dear Sir, October 23, 1861, B. F. Arthur Papers, South Caroliniana Library, University of South Carolina; C. Vann Woodward, *Mary Chesnut's Civil War* (New Haven: Yale University Press, 1982), 50, 80–81, 104, 134, 350, 377.

4. Carl Osthaus, *Partisans of the Southern Press: Editorial Spokesmen of the Nineteenth Century* (Lexington: University of Kentucky Press, 1994); Eugene D. Genovese, *The Slaveholders' Dilemma: Freedom and Progress in Southern Conservative Thought, 1820–1860* (Columbia: University of South Carolina Press, 1992), 64.

5. Stanley Harrold, *The Abolitionists and the South, 1831–1861* (Lexington: University of Kentucky Press, 1995).

6. John Paul Jones, "The Confederate Press and the Government," *Americana* 37 (1943): 10.

7. Hazel Dicken-Garcia, *Journalistic Standards in 19th Century America* (Madison: University of Wisconsin Press, 1989); Leonard W. Levy, *Emergence of a Free Press* (New York: Oxford University Press, 1985), 309.

8. Mark E. Neely Jr., *The Fate of Liberty: Abraham Lincoln and Civil Liberties* (London: Oxford University Press, 1992); Mark E. Neely Jr., *Southern Rights: Political Prisoners and the Myth of Confederate Constitutionalism* (Charlottesville: University of Virginia Press), 173; Robert N. Mathis, "Freedom of the Press in the Confederacy: A Reality," *Historian* 37, no. 4 (1975): 633–48; Richard Reid, "William W. Holden and 'Disloyalty' in the Civil War," *Canadian Journal of History/Annales Canadiennes d'Histoire* 20, no. 1 (1985): 23–44; Frederick S. Siebert, *Freedom of the Press in England, 1476–1776: The Rise and Decline of Government Controls* (Urbana: University of Illinois Press, 1952), 10.

9. Clement Eaton, *A History of the Southern Confederacy* (New York: Macmillan, 1956), 231; Neely, *Fate of Liberty.*

10. J. Cutler Andrews, "The Confederate Press and Public Morale," *Journal of Southern History* 32, no. 4 (1966): 456.

11. "News from the Rebel States; The Arrest of Parson Brownlow at Knoxville on a Charge of Treason Rumored Landing of National Troops in North Carolina Another Call for Arms in Mississippi, Etc.," *New York Times*, December 17, 1861; William G. Brownlow to W. H. Carroll, November 22, 1861, and W. H. Carroll to Judah P. Benjamin, November 28, 1861, *War of the Rebellion: A Compilation of the Official Records of the Union and Confederate Armies* (hereafter *Official Records*) (Washington, D.C.: Government Printing Office, 1880–1901), series 1, vol. 7, 719–20; C. B. Crittenden to Judah P. Benjamin, December 13, 1861, *Official Records*, series 1, vol. 7, 764; J. G. M. Ramsey and William H. Tibbs to Jefferson Davis, December 7, 1861, *Official Records*, series 1, vol. 7, 742–44; J. C. Ramsay to Judah P. Benjamin, December 7, 1861, *Official Records*, series 1, vol. 7, 744–45.

12. Judah P. Benjamin to J. C. Ramsay, December 22, 1861, *Official Records*, series 1, vol. 7, 787.

13. Untitled editorial, *Knoxville Whig*, October 26, 1861, 2; *Harper's Weekly*, "Parson Brownlow, the Exile from Tennessee," April 19, 1862, 253; J. C. Ramsay to Judah P. Benjamin, December 7, 1861, *Official Records*, series 1, vol. 7, 744; G. H. Monsarrat to Judah P. Benjamin, December 29, 1861, *Official Records*, series 1, vol. 7, 803; Judah P. Benjamin to Major Monsarrat, March 1, 1862, *Official Records*, series 1, vol. 7, 913.

14. Siebert, *Freedom of the Press in England*, 10.

15. Donald L. Shaw and Stephen W. Brauer, "Press Freedom and War Constraints: Case Testing Siebert's Proposition II," *Journalism Quarterly* 46, no. 2 (1969): 243–54; Jon Paul Dilts, "Testing Siebert's Proposition in Civil War Indiana," *Journalism Quarterly* 63, no. 1 (1986): 365–68.

16. Hazel Dicken-Garcia and Giovanna Dell'Orto, *Hated Ideas and the American Civil War Press* (Spokane: Marquette Books, 2008), 178–79; James G. Randall, "The Newspaper Problem in Its Bearing upon Military Secrecy during the Civil War," *Journal of Southern History* 23, no. 2 (1918): 313.

17. Neely, *Southern Rights*, 173; J. Cutler Andrews, *The South Reports the Civil War* (Princeton: Princeton University Press, 1970), 529; Mathis, "Freedom of the Press in the Confederacy," 633–48; Randall, "Newspaper Problem," 313; Donna Lee Dickerson, *The Course of Tolerance: Freedom of the Press in Nineteenth-Century America* (New York: Greenwood Press, 1990), 189, 200; Debra Reddin van Tuyll, "The Rebels Yell: Conscription and Freedom of Expression in the Civil War South," *American Journalism* 17, no. 2 (2000): 15–29; Reid, "William W. Holden and 'Disloyalty' in the Civil War," 23–44; Cal M. Logue, Eugene F. Miller, and Christopher J. Schroll, "The Press under Pressure: How Georgia's Newspapers Responded to Civil War Constraints," *American Journalism* 15, no. 1 (1998): 13–34; Jones, "Confederate Press and the Government," 18; Joseph J. Mathews, *Reporting the Wars* (Minneapolis: University of Minnesota Press, 1957), 95; Patricia Towery, "Censorship of South Carolina Newspapers, 1861–1865,"

in *South Carolina Journals and Journalists*, ed. James B. Meriwether (Spartanburg, S.C.: Reprint Co. Publishers, 1975), 147.

18. Hodding Carter, *Their Words Were Bullets: The Southern Press in War, Reconstruction and Peace*, Mercer University Lamar Memorial Lectures No. 12 (Athens: University of Georgia Press, 1969), 27.

19. Phillip Knightley, *The First Casualty: From the Crimea to Vietnam; The War Correspondent as Hero, Propagandist, and Myth Maker* (New York: Harcourt Brace Jovanovich, 1975), 25; Loren B. Thompson, "The Media versus the Military: A Brief History of War Coverage in the United States," in *Defense Beat: The Dilemma of Defense Coverage*, ed. Loren B. Thompson (New York: Lexington Books, 1991), 13–14; Clement Eaton, "The Freedom of the Press in the Upper South," *Mississippi Valley Historical Review* 18, no. 4 (1932): 499; Osthaus, *Partisans of the Southern Press*.

20. *Greeneville Alabama Beacon*, March 22, 1861.

21. Russel B. Nye, *Fettered Freedom: Civil Liberties and the Slavery Controversy, 1830–1860* (East Lansing: Michigan State College Press, 1949), 125; Timothy W. Gleason, "Nineteenth Century Legal Practice and Freedom of the Press: An Introduction to an Unfamiliar Truth," *Journalism History* 14, no. 1 (1987): 27; John Calhoun Ellen Jr., "Political Newspapers in the Piedmont Carolinas in the 1850s" (PhD diss., University of South Carolina, 1958), 121.

22. David Bulla, *Lincoln's Censor: Milo Hascall and the Freedom of the Press in Civil War Indiana* (West Lafayette, Ind.: Purdue University Press, 2008), 60; "The Floridian and Journal," *Tallahassee Floridian and Journal*, January 1, 1859; *Linden (Ala.) Jeffersonian*, September 5, 1862; *Augusta (Ga.) Daily Constitutionalist*, July 3, 1864.

23. "Explanatory," *Memphis Appeal*, June 22, 1863; William H. Johnson, "Dr. Robert Wilson Gibbes: Southern Editor and Publisher, 1852–1864" (unpublished master's thesis, University of South Carolina, 1969), 5.

24. *Richmond Dispatch*, March 13, 1862; "The Freedom of the Press," *Charleston Mercury*, September 27, 1862.

25. *Charleston Mercury*, July 1, 1862; "The Press and the Law," ibid., August 26, 1862; "The Press," ibid., August 13, 1862; *Richmond Dispatch*, January 13, 1863.

26. *Richmond Dispatch*, January 13, 1863.

27. *Charleston Courier*, January 25, 1864.

28. "Personalities," reprinted in the *Alabama Beacon* (Greeneville), October 19, 1860.

29. Bulla, *Lincoln's Censor*, 119.

30. *Augusta Chronicle and Sentinel*, August 14, 1863.

31. Paul D. Escott, *After Secession: Jefferson Davis and the Failure of Confederate Nationalism* (Baton Rouge: Louisiana State University Press, 1978), 91; Marc W. Kruman, *Parties and Politics in North Carolina, 1836–1865* (Baton Rouge: Louisiana State University Press, 1983), 244.

32. Georgia Lee Tatum, *Disloyalty in the Confederacy* (Chapel Hill: University of North Carolina Press, 1934), 25; John Raymond Brumgardt, "Alexander Stephens and

the Peace Issue in the Confederacy, 1863–1865" (PhD diss., University of California at Riverside, 1974), 351; Carleton Beales, *War within a War: The Confederacy against Itself* (Philadelphia: Chilton Books, 1965), 152; Morris Schaff, *Jefferson Davis: His Life and Personality* (Boston: John W. Luce, 1922), 198.

33. Letter from Lt. Col. George W. Lay to Col. J. S. Preston, Superintendent of Conscription, September 2, 1863, *Official Records*, series 4, vol. 2, 783–85.

34. Horace W. Raper, "William W. Holden and the Peace Movement in North Carolina," *North Carolina Historical Review* 31, no. 4 (1954): 497; Richard E. Yates, "Governor Vance and the Peace Movement," pt. 1, *North Carolina Historical Review* 17, no. 2 (1940): 1–25, 89–113; Reid, "William W. Holden and 'Disloyalty' in the Civil War," 24.

35. Reid, "William W. Holden and 'Disloyalty' in the Civil War," 23–44, 34.

36. *Raleigh Daily Progress*, April 3, May 1, and August 10, 1863.

37. Reid, "William W. Holden and 'Disloyalty' in the Civil War," 23–44, 40, 43.

38. *Raleigh Standard*, February 19, 1864; Zebulon B. Vance to Edward J. Hale, Edward J. Hale Papers, State Department of Archives and History, Raleigh, North Carolina.

39. J. G. De R. Hamilton, *Reconstruction in North Carolina* (New York: Columbia University Press, 1914), 52.

40. *Fayetteville Observer*, September 17, 1863; *Savannah Republican*, September 11, 16, 1863; Yates, "Peace Movement" pt. 1, 17; the Confederate Constitution, *Official Records*, series 1, vol. 29, part 2, 710; *Official Records*, series 1, vol. 51, part 2, 763–65; Mathis, "Freedom of the Press in the Confederacy," 642.

41. *Weekly Standard*, October 7, 1863.

42. Yates, "Peace Movement," pt. 1, 8.

43. *Raleigh Standard*, October 16, 30, 1863.

44. "Mob Violence in Raleigh," *Hillsborough Recorder*, September 16, 1863, 2.

45. "Mob Violence," *Raleigh Spirit of the Age*, September 14, 1863.

46. Ibid.

47. *Macon Telegraph and Confederate*, September 23, 1864.

48. *Proceedings of the First Confederate Congress*, second sess. and third sess. in part, Southern Historical Society Papers, n.s. 10, whole 48 (Richmond: Virginia Historical Society, 1925), 21–33, 81; 181–83; *Journal of the Confederate Congress* (Washington: Government Printing Office, 1904), vol. 6, 733–35, 740–41.

49. *Macon Telegraph and Confederate*, September 23, 1864.

50. Van Tuyll, "Rebels Yell."

51. *New Orleans Daily True Delta*, December 17, 1864.

52. "Freedom of the Press," reprinted from the *Charleston Mercury* in *Milledgeville (Ga.) Confederate Union*, December 20, 1864, 2.

53. Van Tuyll, "Rebels Yell."

54. Escott, *After Secession*, 91.

55. *Richmond Examiner*, June 23, 1862.

56. Amy A. Robertson, "Jefferson Davis and Southern Opinion Change, 1861–1865, as Seen through 12 Diaries," *Lincoln Herald* 86, no. 3 (1984): 143–49.
57. Andrews, "Confederate Press and Public Morale," 455.
58. George W. Bagby Jr. Diary, George W. Bagby Jr. Papers, Mss. 1B1463a1636, Virginia Historical Society, Richmond. This entry is hidden in the middle of the diary, among many blank pages.
59. *Charleston Mercury*, November 5, 1861.
60. Robert Barnwell Rhett Jr. to George William Bagby Jr., 25 November 1861, Bagby Papers, Virginia Historical Society.
61. *Chattanooga Daily Rebel*, January 22, 1863; "Exemption of Printers," *New Orleans True Delta*, March 23, 1862; *Richmond Enquirer*, November 10, 1864; untitled article and "The Duty and Privilege of the Press," *Macon Telegraph*, December 2, 1864.
62. "Freedom of the Press in Minnesota," *Charleston Mercury*, April 12, 1858; "The Liberty of the Press," ibid., November 13, 1856; "Freedom of the Press in the North," *Richmond Examiner*, September 7, 1861; "New England Proscription," *Macon Telegraph*, August 31, 1861; "The President and the Press," *Richmond Sentinel*, November 25, 1864; *Augusta Daily Constitutionalist*, July 3, 1863.
63. Richard B. Kielbowicz, "The Telegraph, Censorship, and Politics at the Outset of the Civil War," *Civil War History* 10, no. 2 (1994): 95.
64. Miles Hudson and John Stainer, *War and the Media: A Random Searchlight* (New York: New York University Press, 1998), 309.
65. "Our Duty," *Charleston Courier*, July 16, 1863; "To Correspondents," *Savannah Republican*, July 18, 1862; "Military Movements," *Richmond Dispatch*, July 18, 1861; "From Norfolk," *Richmond Dispatch*, July 23, 1861; Randall, "Newspaper Problem," 323; Quintus C. Wilson, "Voluntary Press Censorship during the Civil War," *Journalism Quarterly* 19 (1940): 251–61.
66. Jurgen Brauer and Hubert P. van Tuyll, *Castles, Battles and Bombs: How Economics Explains Military History* (Chicago: University of Chicago Press, 2008); *Macon Telegraph and Confederate*, December 2, 1864; Robert E. Lee, *Recollections and Letters of General Robert E. Lee* (New York: Doubleday, 1904), 416; General D. H. Hill to General R. C. Gatlin, *Official Records*, series 1, vol. 4, 693–94; F. K. Zollicoffer to S. Cooper, *Official Records*, series 1, vol. 7, 690; J. B. Magruder to George Randolph, April 4, 1862, *Official Records*, series 1, vol. 14, 422; Robert E. Lee to George Randolph, June 11, 1862, *Official Records*, series 1, vol. 14, 590; Sam Jones to George Randolph, *Official Records*, series 1, vol. 16, part 2, 954–55; R. O. Selfridge to W. L. Elliott, July 12, 1862, *Official Records*, series 1, vol. 17, part 1, appendix; S. G. French to Gov. Zebulon B. Vance, October 27, 1862, *Official Records*, series 1, vol. 18; Gen. John Pemberton to Maj. Gen. Stevenson, April 15, 1865, *Official Records*, series 1, vol. 24, part 3, 744; James Seddon to Robert E. Lee, June 29, 1865, *Official Records*, series 1, vol. 40, part 2, 701; P. G. T. Beauregard to L. P. Walker, June 30, 1861, *Official Records*, series 1, vol. 60, part 2, 152.

67. General Order No. 9, *Official Records*, series 1, vol. 15, 771–72; ibid., series 2, vol. 5, 772; Report from District of Middle Florida to General P. G. T. Beauregard, ibid., series 1, vol. 19, 731; Mathis, "Freedom of the Press in the Confederacy," 638; Dickerson, *Course of Tolerance*, 195–96.

68. Louis Turner Griffith and John Erwin Talmadge, *Georgia Journalism, 1763–1950* (Athens: University of Georgia Press, 1951), 71–72.

69. "Martial Law and Gen. Van Dorn," *Charleston Mercury*, September 16, 1862.

70. "Hon. L. P. Walker and the Correspondents of the Southern Press," ibid., July 6, 1861; Donald Reynolds, "Words for War," in *The Press in Times of Crisis*, ed. Lloyd Chiasson Jr. (Westport, Conn: Praeger, 1995), 96.

71. Jefferson Davis to Braxton Bragg, August 5, 1862, cited in Don C. Seitz, *Braxton Bragg: General of the Confederacy* (Columbia: State Co., 1924), 155.

72. Letter from Judah Benjamin, *Official Records*, series 1, vol. 5, 1021; Dickerson, *Course of Tolerance*, 194.

73. *Army Regulations Adopted for the Use of the Confederate States (Revised from Those of the United States, 1857)* (Richmond: West and Johnston, 1861), 21; Nebraska Press Assoc. v. Stuart, 427 U.S. 539 (1976); Jones, "Confederate Press and the Government," 9–10.

74. General Order No. 54, *Official Records*, series 1, vol. 10, part 2, 543.

75. General Order No. 98, ibid., vol. 51, part 2, 428; "Expulsion of Correspondents," *New Orleans Picayune*, June 26, 1862.

76. Mathis, "Freedom of the Press in the Confederacy," 640; James J. Mathews, *Reporting the Wars* (Minneapolis: University of Minnesota Press, 1957), 95.

77. "The Army and the Press," *Richmond Examiner*, January 21, 1862.

78. Letter from Robert E. Lee, *Official Records*, series 1, vol. 11, part 3, 636; Quintus Charles Wilson, "A Study and Evaluation of the Military Censorship in the Civil War" (unpublished master's thesis, University of Minnesota, 1945), 208.

79. James M. Mathews, *The Statutes at Large of the Confederate States of America, 1st Congress, 4th Session* (Richmond: R. M. Smith, Printer to Congress, 1864), 106; Andrews, *South Reports the Civil War*, 52; Kielbowicz, "Telegraph, Censorship, and Politics," 105; Towery, "Censorship of South Carolina Newspapers," 153.

80. Mathis, "Freedom of the Press in the Confederacy," 639.

81. Brian Dirck, "Communities of Sentiment: Jefferson Davis's Constitutionalism," *Journal of Mississippi History* 58, no. 2 (1996): 135.

82. Ibid., 136.

83. Ibid.

84. Ibid., 153.

85. Walter F. Leak to Jefferson Davis, March 12, 1864, in *The Papers of Jefferson Davis*, ed. Haskell M. Monroe Jr. and James T. McIntosh, 14 vols. (Baton Rouge: Louisiana State University Press, 1991–2015), 10:278; interview with North Carolina Delegation, January 23, 1864, in ibid., 10:199; Edwin S. Reade to Zebulon B. Vance, February 10, 1864, , Zebulon B. Vance Papers, State Archives of North Carolina, P.C. 15.4; Neely, *Southern Rights.*

86. Jefferson Davis, "Second Inaugural Address," available from the Jefferson Davis Papers, https://jeffersondavis.rice.edu/Content.aspx?id=107, accessed September 9, 2015.
87. Reid, "William W. Holden and 'Disloyalty' in the Civil War," 24.
88. "Brownlow's Knoxville Whig," reprinted in the *Macon Telegraph*, August 17, 1861.
89. Ibid., 178; Dirck, "Communities of Sentiment," 160–62.
90. Reid, "William W. Holden and 'Disloyalty' in the Civil War," 37.
91. Escott, *After Secession*, 170, 177.
92. Rose O'Neal Greenhow, *My Imprisonment and the First Year of Abolition Rule at Washington* (London: Richard Bentley, 1863), 233, available from Documenting the American South, http://docsouth.unc.edu/fpn/greenhow/greenhow.html, accessed August 13, 2009; "A Heavy Broadside against Jefferson Davis," *Daily True Delta*, October 4, 1864; "Southern Freedom of the Press," *Savannah Republican*, September 8, 1864.
93. Jefferson Davis to William M. Brooks, March 15, 1862, in *Papers of Jefferson Davis*, 8:100.
94. Charles J. Mitchell to Jefferson Davis, June 7, 1862, in ibid., 8:231.
95. Jefferson Davis to John Heiss, October 13, 1859, in ibid., 6:263.
96. Jones, "Confederate Press and the Government," 10–11.
97. Ibid., 12–13.
98. Ibid., 4; Dickerson, *Course of Tolerance*, 190–91; *Proceedings of the Confederate Congress*, Southern Historical Society Papers 46 (1953): 87–88, 98–99, 187; Jones, "Confederate Press and the Government," 12–13.
99. *Proceedings of the Second Congress of the Confederate States of America, First Session and Second Session in Part*, ed. Frank E. Vandiver, Southern Historical Society Papers, n.s. 13, whole 51 (Richmond: Virginia Historical Society, 1958), 98–99.
100. Jones, "Confederate Press and the Government," 12; Mathis, "Freedom of the Press in the Confederacy," 636; Dickerson, *Course of Tolerance*, 191; see the failed debates in *Journal of the Confederate Congress* 3 (1904): 100, 154, 156–57.
101. Mathis, "Freedom of the Press in the Confederacy," 635.
102. Wilbur J. Cash, *The Mind of the South* (New York: Alfred A. Knopf), 1941; James C. Cobb, "Does Mind No Longer Matter? The South, the Nation, and the Mind of the South, 1941–1991," *Journal of Southern History* 57, no. 4 (1991): 683; Robert E. May, "Psychobiography and Secession: The Southern Radical as Maladjusted 'Outsider,'" *Civil War History* 34, no. 1 (1988): 46–47; Clement Eaton, *The Freedom-of-Thought Struggle in the Old South* (New York: Harper and Row, 1964), 384, 102–3, 89–90, 92–93; Steven A. Channing, *Crisis of Fear: Secession in South Carolina* (New York: Norton, 1974), 20–21, 55; Eaton, "Freedom of the Press in the Upper South," 480.
103. Joseph R. Stromberg, "Country Ideology, Republicanism, and Libertarianism: The Thought of John Taylor of Caroline," *Journal of Libertarian Studies* 6, no. 1 (1982): 38; Levy, *Emergence of a Free Press*, 309; Robert E. Shalhope, "Thomas Jefferson's Republicanism and Antebellum Southern Thought," *Journal of Southern History* 42,

no. 4 (1976): 533; Earl E. Thorpe, *Eros and Freedom in Southern Life and Thought* (Durham: Seeman Printing, 1967), 10.

104. Gordon S. Wood, *The Creation of the American Republic, 1776–1787* (Chapel Hill: University of North Carolina Press, 1969), 19; Shalhope, "Thomas Jefferson's Republicanism," 545.

105. William Henry Trescot, "Oration before the South Carolina Historical Society, 1859," *Russell's Magazine*, July 1859, 289–307, cited in Lacy K. Ford Jr., *Origins of Southern Radicalism: The South Carolina Upcountry, 1800–1860* (New York: Oxford University Press, 1988), 362; Richard Reid, "Civil Liberties in the Confederacy—North Carolina," *Canadian Journal of History* 14, no. 2 (1979): 173–97; Stromberg, "Country Ideology," 38.

106. Ford, *Origins of Southern Radicalism*, 50, 128, 352, 357; Stephanie McCurry, *Masters of Small Worlds: Yeoman Households, Gender Relations, and the Political Culture of the Antebellum South Carolina Low Country* (New York: Oxford University Press, 1995), 6.

107. Moses Mather, "America's Appeal to the Impartial World," in *Political Sermons of the American Founding Era*, ed. Ellis Sandoz, vol. 1 (1730–88), Online Library of Liberty (Indianapolis: Liberty Fund), http://oll.libertyfund.org/?option=com_staticxt&staticfile=show.php%3Ftitle=816&chapter=69260&layout=html&Itemid=27, accessed July 9, 2009.

108. Ford, *Origins of Southern Radicalism*, 138.

109. Kruman, *Parties and Politics in North Carolina*, 243.

110. Ford, *Origins of Southern Radicalism*, 348.

111. Alexis de Tocqueville, *Democracy in America*, trans. Henry Reeve (New York: Bantam Books, 2004), 436.

112. May, "Psychobiography and Secession," 46–47; Eaton, *Freedom-of-Thought Struggle*, 384, 102–3, 89–90, 92–93.

113. Channing, *Crisis of Fear*, 20–21, 55; Eaton, "Freedom of the Press in the Upper South," 480; James Henry Hammond, "On the Admission of Kansas, under the Lecompton Constitution ('Cotton Is King') Speech before the United States Senate, 4 March 1858," http://www.sewanee.edu/faculty/Willis/Civil_War/documens/HammondCotton.html, accessed July 8, 2009.

114. Eaton, "Freedom of the Press in the Upper South," 479; Channing, *Crisis of Fear*, 20–21, 55.

4. FIGHT, FOLD, FLIP, OR FLEE

THE CONFEDERATE PRESS AND ENEMY OCCUPATION, 1861–65

DEBRA REDDIN VAN TUYLL,
NANCY MCKENZIE DUPONT,
AND JOSEPH HAYDEN

The experiences of newspapers in occupied areas of the Civil War South were varied, just like the experiences of the ordinary people who endured occupation. And, as ordinary people responded differently to their grim circumstances, so, too, did newspapers. Some stood their ground and decided "to live and die for Dixie." These journalists supported the Confederacy and were not about to back down—though that meant occasional suppression of their newspapers and sometimes personal danger for the newsmen themselves. Many publications simply folded, though that decision was often just as much a product of the war experience generally as of occupation. Others flipped to the Union side, capitulating at least to the point of publishing nothing that would offend occupiers. Still others decided that life under occupation was not something they wished to experience, and so they fled to Confederate territory.

None of these was a perfect choice. Publishing, even under the best of circumstances, was arduous during the war, as was just living day to day. Editors had to deal with shortages of men and materials, with haphazard means of acquiring news and subscribers who would not always pay their bills.[1] These hardships were only the starting point. Staying in business was tricky, even for newspapers run by known Union sympathizers. And those who refused to back away from their pro-Confederate stance risked, at best, harassment, destruction (often through arson), and suppression.

Prior to this study, the exact nature of what newspapers faced in areas occupied by enemy troops has remained a subject of conjecture and deductive reasoning for those who have given it any thought at all. Virtually nothing has been written previously about the experiences of Southern newspapers in Union-occupied areas. The few studies of the occupied press that have been done focus on the coastal regions of the Carolinas, Georgia, and Virginia, where few newspapers existed and most of the ones published during the occupation were founded and run by Republican journalists from the North.[2]

However, as James W. Carey and others have established, a newspaper is a social institution, and what happens within a society influences the press just as it does all other social institutions. The assumption has always been that the press in enemy-occupied areas had an even more difficult time during the war than those journals that published in unoccupied territory. That assumption is bolstered by Carey's argument, for Confederate citizens in occupied areas who retained their Southern loyalties faced harassment, loss or destruction of personal property, banishment, and other forms of punishment. But Confederate citizens in unoccupied areas did not always have an easy time of it—and even friendly troops can devastate an area when settled in for the duration. Still, at least loyal Confederates did not have to worry too much about being punished for saying good things about Jefferson Davis and his government.[3] This study, however, moves beyond the topic of Confederate journalism in Confederate-held areas to examine the experience of that other Southern press—the one that continued to publish despite the menacing presence of Union troops who were just itching, in many cases, for some reason to silence what they would have called "secesh" voices.

This chapter examines the experiences of newspapers in four Confederate cities. Taken together, these four examples demonstrate the range of experiences Confederate journalists had when they continued publishing within Union lines. The cities studied include Alexandria, Virginia, which contained the longest occupied newspaper of the war; New Orleans, Louisiana, the South's largest media market; Chattanooga, Tennessee, whose newspapers endured an almost constant ping-ponging between Union and Confederate troops until 1863; and Vicksburg, Mississippi, whose post-occupation newspaper was owned by a former Confederate and edited by a former Union soldier. Each of these cities had newspapers that decided to fold due to war exigencies as well as those that continued publishing in spite of the harrowing circumstances.

The newspapers chosen for the study were dailies and were located in places where Union troops settled for long occupations. Small villages did not have the resources to support occupying troops, nor were they typically important enough for long-term occupation. Larger towns and cities, on the other hand, had railroads passing through that could be used to transport troops and matériel—or to halt deliveries to Confederate armies. They also contained homes and businesses that could be confiscated for use as barracks and hospitals and commonly had telegraph offices that would simplify communications between the occupying forces and higher military commands.[4]

What this study finds is that Confederate journalists living and working in federally occupied territories faced the same day-to-day challenges as their comrades in unoccupied areas—and then some. Southern journalists, as well as citizens, in occupied areas were "literally a people without a country, a fact of which they were constantly reminded by the presence of masses of hostile enemy soldiers."[5]

Of the periodicals in the four cities chosen for this study, the Alexandria newspaper represents the group that stayed and fought. Its prewar rival, the *Virginia Sentinel*, fled and then folded. The New Orleans press had publications that exemplified each of the four categories, plus one other: founding. With Union occupation, it became possible for an African American press to emerge in New Orleans, and the result was the launch of *L'Union*. Chattanooga's prewar papers folded, though that city would give birth to one of the most virulent, effective, and best-written newspapers of the wartime South, the *Rebel*. That publication would be forced to flee once Union occupation began but would be replaced when a pro-Union editor returned to reopen his paper. And the one newspaper editor whose plant survived the siege of Vicksburg joined forces with a former federal soldier to flip his journal to a pro-Union, virulently anti-Copperhead publication.

ALEXANDRIA: FOUGHT

The *Alexandria Gazette* is an excellent example of a paper that stayed and fought, not only because it was the longest occupied newspaper of the war but also because its owners and editors—Edgar Snowden Sr. and Edgar Snowden Jr.—never backed down. Nothing could convince the once staunchly Unionist Snowden family to budge from their pro-Confederate stance—not multiple suspensions, multiple arrests, the threat of banishment, or even being used as a human shield to protect trains transporting troops to the front. The Snowdens and their publication would pay dearly for their loyalty.

Loyalties forged in the crucible of occupation were sometimes fluid and created by practicality. Formerly solid Unionists sometimes became rabid Confederates as the result of indignities and insults suffered at the hands of their occupiers—which, admittedly, were sometimes made worse because many Southerners, particularly women, were not reluctant either to initiate or to return said insults. Nor was clandestine violence against occupiers unknown. Guerrillas might attack sentries or lone soldiers, and women might just "accidentally" happen to dump the contents of chamber pots out their bedroom windows as Union soldiers passed on the street below. Such skirmishes encouraged retribution by Federal soldiers, which, in turn, typically only helped to solidify Confederate sentiments.[6] This was certainly true of the Snowdens of Alexandria. Although their publication was avowedly Unionist prior to, and even after, Lincoln's election, by the time Virginia seceded in May 1864, the editors' stance was definitely pro-secession. The Snowdens were so loyal to the Confederacy that it took less than a day for them to run afoul of Alexandria's first Union occupiers.

Colonel Orlando B. Willcox of the First Michigan, an attorney with a West Point education, was in charge of organizing the occupation of Alexandria. Willcox was perhaps the best possible person to oversee the Union takeover. He and the mayor, Lewis Mackenzie, were old friends, having met a decade earlier when Willcox was stationed at the nearby Fort Washington. Willcox had other friends in the city as well. In spite of, or perhaps because of, his connections to the town, it fell to Willcox to issue the call for martial law in Alexandria, and he sent the order to the *Gazette* to be included in the next edition. But the Snowdens refused to use their presses to print.[7]

According to the *Fayetteville Observer*, when the Snowdens received Willcox's order, they responded that they would not use "the type and presses of the Gazette . . . for any such purpose." Instead, they closed the office and suspended the paper. In retaliation, two Michigan soldiers by the names of Galloway and O'Donell made their way into the *Gazette* plant the next day and printed the order themselves. They then sacked the office and destroyed property and looted bonds and certificates. The newspaper would remain suspended for five months.[8]

Not long after they restarted their newspaper, the Snowdens once again overstepped the boundaries permitted by Union authorities. Snowden Jr., the sole editor at this point, was arrested and nearly banished from his home city during the autumn of 1861, the newspaper's plant was set ablaze in early 1862 in retaliation for his criticisms of Union officers who had arrested an Episcopalian priest in the midst of Sunday services, and later during the war he was used as a human shield to protect troop trains delivering soldiers to the front.[9] The paper was suspended no less than three times and threatened on another occasion for referring to the Virginia Senate as the "Virginia Legislature." The military governor objected to this term, for he said it gave credence to the assembly as a legitimate political body. The publication would continue covering the legislature, but the Snowdens would find ways to write around the name of the body.[10]

Such legal and extralegal actions were common occurrences across the occupied South. Unless or until they signed loyalty oaths, and sometimes even after they did so, Southerners in occupied areas might see their businesses closed or confiscated, as the Snowdens did; their homes looted, burned, or turned into military headquarters or hospitals; their mail intercepted and read; and perhaps passports and curfews imposed. If Confederates in occupied territories were too overt in their Southern sympathies, they risked arrest and banishment.

Edgar Jr. was threatened with banishment in January 1863 when he reported on a dead mule left on a city street. Similar stories had run in other editions of the paper, but for some reason this one caught the attention of the military authorities. None of the sources that report this incident indicate why the story was a problem. Presumably the Union military leaders believed the article to be a veiled criticism of their administration. Later that year, in July, Edgar Jr. again ran into trouble with the Union occupiers because of his relief work on behalf of families of Confederate soldiers. He was ordered to prove his loyalty to the United States or to leave Alexandria within forty-eight hours. Snowden refused to sign the loyalty oath, though ninety-eight other citizens did, and another fifty-nine signed paroles of honor. Fortunately for the Snowdens, victories at Gettysburg and Vicksburg captured Union attention, and the exile orders were dropped.[11]

Non-journalists also had to deal with constraints on their speech. E. A. Harnish of Vicksburg was arrested for publicly saying he wished "[Nathan Bedford] For[r]est would come and kill ever Yank in Vicks(burg)," as was his fellow citizen Nathan Renwick when he cheered for Jefferson Davis. Five women of that city were banished for walking out of a church service where a prayer was offered for President Lincoln.[12] Freedoms these people had taken for granted before the war were trampled under the boots of their occupiers even during the early years of the conflict, when the Union army employed a more conciliatory approach to dealing with citizens in federally held areas.

NEW ORLEANS: FLIPPED AND FOUNDED

Other newspapers, like those in New Orleans, the South's largest media market and home to one of the region's few penny newspapers, the *Picayune*, might have been able to continue publishing, but they really became only shells of their former selves. Early on, some New Orleans papers tried to maintain their Southern loyalties, but the harsh martial law imposed by General Benjamin Butler put a period to that sort of publication fairly quickly. The *Picayune,* which had been among the premier newspapers in the South before the war, was just a sad rag once New Orleans fell. Yet a positive effect of Union occupation was that it allowed for the genesis of an African American press in the South.

The *Picayune* had maintained a neutral stance during the secession debate, and its editors did manage to hang on and continue publishing through the war, but the once-robust newspaper circulated little more than local news that focused on crime and other non-war-related events. It avoided nearly all editorial discussion of war-related issues, and when it did make reference to the conflict, the product was little more than pabulum. One reader complained about how boring the paper had become, writing, "There is no news in the paper. The Old Yankee Picayune is as dull as ever."[13]

The *Daily True Delta,* one of the city's Unionist newspapers, also was targeted by military governor Butler, who would become known throughout New Orleans as "Beast Butler." When the *True Delta* declined to publish a proclamation from Butler, the military governor promptly closed the newspaper—which published the order the following day. Secessionist or pro-Confederate papers in the city did not stand a chance; Butler had them all closed in short order. Even

Artist John McLenan shows the impact of Major General Benjamin Butler's infamous "woman order" issued May 15, 1862, which instructed his soldiers to treat any women who insulted Union troops as prostitutes. The order shocked Union and Confederate citizens and led to Butler's vilification in America and England. *Harper's Weekly,* July 12, 1862; Library of Congress Prints and Photographs Division, Washington, D.C.

religious newspapers were not safe from suppression. Butler also shut down *La Propagateur Catholique* for its proslavery stance and accused the paper's editor, Napoléon-Joseph Perché, a future archbishop, of treason, placing the priest under house arrest.[14]

Interestingly, Butler did not act immediately against his worst critic, the *Daily Delta* (a different publication from the *Daily True Delta*). As the fall of the city became more and more a foregone conclusion, that newspaper boldly reminded New Orleans citizens that there was no disgrace in being conquered, only in surrendering freedom of conscience to the conquerors. The newspaper's editors considered suspending publication once Butler's troops occupied the city but concluded finally that their obligations to their readers and employees were more important than their physical safety. The publication did moderate its tone a bit, but that move brought new pressure from an unexpected source: the citizens of New Orleans, who wanted a much more defiant editorial stance in the paper, one that the editors just could not accommodate, given the restrictive orders they faced. As it was, they were skirting the edge of what was allowed. The editors reminded its readers that they were "virtually prisoners of war."[15]

Other newspapers were created during this time, such as the *Times*, of Unionist sentiment, and the *Era*, which was founded by General Nathaniel P. Banks himself, who replaced Butler at the end of 1862. For those whose interests coincided with occupation forces, who supported the military command without reservation, and who could be counted on to print announcements, ads, and even various articles, there were substantial rewards. General Banks favored at least three papers with several hundred dollars of patronage per month, no small compensation in a time of shortages and overextended credit. In these times of hardship and deprivation, journalists accepted income from wherever they could get it.[16]

The most significant new players in New Orleans journalism, however, were the proprietors of two African American newspapers that appeared in the South's largest media market following its occupation by Union forces, Louis-Charles Roudenez and Paul Trévigne. These men published *L'Union*, which appeared shortly after the occupation, and the *New Orleans Tribune*, which made its debut in 1864.[17]

L'Union was the first African American newspaper to be published in the South. It began soon after the occupation of New Orleans. Trévigne served as editor of *L'Union*, and Roudenez was the paper's chief financial backer. The *Tribune*, published by Roudenez, would follow two years later as a strong supporter of the Union occupiers. Both men were civil rights leaders in Louisiana, and they used the pages of their newspapers uncompromisingly to support the cause of emancipation and equality. Without Union occupation, these papers likely never would have been able to start up. The bilingual *L'Union*, which lasted until July 1864, published two editions, a biweekly and a triweekly. Here, too, journalistic opportunities followed changes in political authority, which in time of war depended on artillery and manpower.[18] Those changes in circumstance forced journalists to walk a very dangerous line. As the *Daily Delta* noted in May 1862, a newspaper had to do what it could in order to survive. And certainly staying in an occupied city meant reckoning with raw power:

> Under these circumstances, we have concluded on a course which we trust will meet with the approval of our friends. Whilst we shall abstain from the publications which are forbidden by the U.S. officer having military occupation of the city, we shall avoid the surrender of that inalienable privilege of all free and manly journalism, which revolts at the control of a censorship.[19]

CHATTANOOGA: FOLDED, FLIPPED, FOUNDED, AND FLED

Newspapers in Chattanooga, Tennessee, had an altogether different sort of experience, for between 1861 and 1863, that city regularly see-sawed between the Union and the Confederacy. The natural pass through the Appalachian Mountains at Chattanooga rendered that city essentially the military gateway to the western theater, meaning that publishing there would have been a challenge under any circumstances. Chattanooga papers would have been well positioned to acquire news from the different units passing through or possessing the city, but their problem was getting the news in print and distributed once it had been obtained.

This was particularly difficult when the city was in enemy hands—so much so that, for much of the war, Chattanooga's news industry simply collapsed. Newspapers had to be imported from other cities. The *Daily Rebel*, for a time run by Henry Watterson, lasted only a year. Even the city's prewar Unionist editor, who returned to publish the *Chattanooga Daily Gazette* once the Union took the city for good in November 1863, had some issues with the Federal military authorities.

James Hood, a twenty-three-year-old North Carolina native and pro-Union journalist, had been in Chattanooga before. His old version of the *Gazette* was published until 1861, when Confederate sentiment forced him to leave. A changing of the guard brought him back in 1864; he returned with a sense of righteous indignation at having to leave town in the first place. But he owed his second tenure, and what amounted to a printing monopoly, to those fortunes of war, the same military events that drove the pro-Confederate *Daily Rebel* to flee and seek refuge in cities farther south. He filled a void that was equal parts commercial, political, and journalistic.[20]

Once he was back, however, it was not long before he discovered a whispering campaign against him. As a result of one of his editorials that complained about differing policies concerning what to do with Confederate sympathizers, General Samuel P. Carter made it known he wanted to have the editor "muzzled," while General William T. Sherman warned him that "if he dont mind his own business we must take a short & summary way to make him. These little sheets are at best a nuisance and make more trouble than they are worth." Hood's friends in Nashville, particularly the governor, helped him survive the scare, but his fears never went away.

Hood's political convictions remained steadfast. He vigorously defended Lincoln and the cause of the Union in his newspaper, served on various associations, and campaigned for a state convention of Unionists as well as for the inclusion of Tennessee in the national convention. In an editorial titled "The President Our Friend," he expressed his commitment to the president: "We hope that no loyal East Tennessean will forget, in this hour of apprehension, that Abraham is the friend of the loyal people of East Tennessee."[21]

For much of the year, the *Gazette* dutifully carried a banner of the Lincoln/Johnson ticket in the first column of its second page—a reminder, if anyone required it, that this newspaper endorsed these men and Unionism without hesitation. Additionally, Hood helped to organize an "Abe and Andy" ratification meeting in July 1864.[22] He was also quick to defend Lincoln against attacks from various quarters. For instance, he excerpted a *New York Daily News* broadside that called the president a "despotic ruler," then lambasted the writer for what he deemed willful blindness. How was he able to write such things with impunity if Lincoln were the tyrant he made him out to be?[23] Hood could wax Jeffersonian in his impassioned defenses of freedom of the press while carefully circumscribing the people who deserved that freedom. His principles did not extend to editors with Confederate sympathies, and his journalism perfectly illustrated the power politics he played: might made right.[24]

Aside from his politics, the other characteristic of Hood's newspaper that stood out was his unceasing entrepreneurialism. He was ready to exploit any business opportunity. For Hood, commerce and political payback coincided merrily. He served as the city's postmaster, a position he aggressively capitalized on as editor of the only newspaper in town. The *Gazette* featured frequent stories about mail delivery, advertised postal services, and told readers of letters awaiting them at his office and of the one-cent fee Hood would charge them to pick up the items. Publishing was a dicey proposition during the war, and editors like Hood had to make money where they could. Hood also used his position as postmaster to serve his readers. In one editorial, Hood described the painstaking efforts he took to disseminate the latest news:

> About nine o'clock last night, Mr. Wm. L. Kelly with a week[']s Northern mail arrived from Nashville on the train. Every soldier in the army should thank Mr. Kelly for the energy he has displayed in this matter. The mail was brought in wagons to Murfreesboro, and is thus ahead of our express companies, and everything else. Mr. Kelly informs us that in Nashville they are as much in the dark about the condition of the road as we have been here.
>
> The Post Master at this place, worked his entire force nearly all night last night, and will thus be able to deliver the immense accumulation of mail matter at a reasonable hour this morning. The clerks had a huge job before them last night; but it is due to them to state that they went at it with a hearty good will.
>
> Mr. Kelly leaves for the front this morning and in less than twenty-four hours, our brave boys will be reading letters from the dear ones at home.[25]

Hood did not always use what he found in newspapers, however. In a brief notice from early 1865, for example, he wrote, "The Richmond papers of the 7th were received, and are entirely destitute of news."[26]

The vulnerability of Hood's position was never clearer than when military officers like Carter and Sherman questioned Hood's loyalty. That may explain why he also took every opportunity to demonstrate his patriotism and his "duty." Almost every week he printed an "honor roll" of the names of those recently killed or wounded, and he often commented on the sacred significance of this service in notes or editorials. Hood responded to criticism of the space he devoted to this column by writing,

> We understand that a few copperheads are complaining at the great amount of space taken up in our columns by the publication of the names of wounded. They say that there should be more general reading. We differ with you, rebs. The Gazette is a soldiers['] paper. The army and the loyal portion of the country will be interested to know the names of the sufferers for the good cause, and the Gazette will publish them to the exclusion of everything else.[27]

Despite Hood's claim of independence, at times the *Gazette* assumed the appearance of a quasi-governmental organ with regular news about the local quartermaster and the army-run news depot, stories about military minutiae, and ubiquitous legal notices. Hood was always quick to tip his hat to the local quartermaster and the army-run news depot and their proprietors, perhaps out of camaraderie, perhaps to emphasize for readers his own, vaguely soldierly contributions: "We are again indebted to the Army News Depot, for favors, on several late occasions, ahead of the mail."[28]

This quest for commercial success and maybe a certain official indispensability might have provided extra insurance in case Hood's political beliefs were insufficient. Hood was back to "rule the roost,"[29] as he put it, and he recognized that during time of war nothing was guaranteed and very little other than death was permanent. This editor, who ardently supported the Union and never found fault in public with anything Abraham Lincoln did, took no chances with the local commanders.

VICKSBURG: FLIPPED

The press in Vicksburg, Mississippi, experienced a situation both similar and dissimilar to the press in Chattanooga. While Vicksburg did not experience the see-sawing the Tennessee city did, its one newspaper, like the *Chattanooga Daily Gazette*, was published by a Yankee journalist once the city fell into Union hands.

Unionist newspapers in federally held territories were less likely to experience harsh treatment by Union occupiers. After Vicksburg fell on July 4, 1863, Ira Batterton, a former Union soldier, and James Swords, a Vicksburg printer, teamed up to begin publishing the *Daily Herald*. The paper focused on advertising, business news, and whatever Batterton could see from his second floor window. He even occasionally printed news from the Confederacy, although the paper was avowedly Unionist. Of the seven goals Batterton published on page 2 of his first edition, three dealt with the war and its aims. Batterton declared his support for the Union, for the Union war effort, and for forcing the states in rebellion back into the Union.[30]

Batterton had to be judicious in what he wrote, but he enjoyed more freedom to publish than many other editors in occupied cities. For one thing, he appears to have possessed a publishing monopoly and had the town to himself. For another, the generals who governed Vicksburg may have believed the threat of trouble gone when the *Whig* and the *Sun* closed. Then, too, Vicksburg was never regarded as a hotbed of secession in the first place, which may have eased military concerns about its vulnerability.

The former Union soldier sometimes evoked freedom of the press, but his devotion to the principle of civil liberty hinged on the particular politics of certain individuals and certain newspapers. He afforded no tolerance of Confederate sympathizers and reserved his greatest condemnation for the Copperhead press in places like Chicago and Cincinnati. "Destroy the rebel press North," Batterton inveighed, "and that in the south would lose its inspiration." In his mind, these editors were guilty of treason and deserved no forbearance from censors.[31]

Batterton had the freedom to criticize Vicksburg's occupiers, and he used it to urge military officials to do more to curb crime in the city, particularly crimes that targeted individuals. By all accounts, Batterton's paper was a success, even though it was out of step with public sentiment in Vicksburg. Within a year of establishing his paper, he was advertising for more newsboys, and he could afford a vacation to New Orleans.

All in all, Batterton's fierce anti-Confederate, anti-Copperhead sentiments won him far greater freedom to publish than newspapers that leaned more toward the Confederate perspective. He could get by with a bit more criticism of Federal authorities because there were no questions regarding his loyalties. However, even he had to watch to ensure that he did not step too far outside of approved boundaries of what could or could not be published.[32]

Batterton's journalistic career was short-lived, though by June 1865 he was well known and successful enough to have become a correspondent for the *Chicago Tribune*. However, before July was out, he would be dead, killed when a friend's pistol accidentally went off. Swords continued publishing the *Herald* without his partner.[33]

OCCUPATION AND ITS EFFECT ON THE CONFEDERATE PRESS

Occupation assumed different forms depending on the city where it took place. Its consequences were diverse and unpredictable but always had an impact. Occupation was not just temporary caretaking; it engendered conflict and so was transformative. The variety of experiences of editors in just four cities shows a complexity as wide-ranging as the military commanders in those regions themselves. No one explicitly prohibited local newspapers, as Japanese troops did in Korea in 1907. But editors might be forced to print certain announcements, as French journalists were by the Vichy government in 1940. It was not possible then to simply steer an utterly neutral, independent course. Neutrality was not an easily tenable position in this civil war, a "total war," in which everyone was expected to contribute—or to leave.

Given the touchiness of Union military commanders on matters of speech, newspapers in many occupied places, such as New Orleans, had to moderate or expunge any rebel sentiments from their pages. Federal authorities feared the power of these journals to stir up secessionist sentiment and thus complicate the task of occupation. This was often true even when Northern journalists edited the papers. In Brownsville, Texas, the *Loyal National Union Journal* published for about three months in the spring of 1864. It offered general news and articles that supported the reelection of Lincoln but virtually nothing that would give encouragement to Southern sympathizers in Brownsville. Similarly, when Sherman captured Savannah in December 1864, he allowed two newspapers to be published by Northern correspondents who were traveling with his army, but he warned the editors of both that they would be held strictly accountable for their content.[34]

The federal Articles of War did condone suppression of newspapers that military authorities had "deemed . . . to be injurious to the public's interests" or that might "excite opposition to the dominant authority or [encourage] the support of the enemy's cause." The Articles of War acknowledged that an enemy newspaper could be just as powerful a weapon "of war . . . as a fort or battery of the enemy in the field."[35]

Savannah's citizens flee in advance of a federal raid on the city in December 1861. *Frank Leslie's Illustrated Newspaper*, December 21, 1861.

Given the authority to control newspapers in occupied territories, Federal military officials in some places not only suppressed or harassed the Confederate press but also engaged in vindictive and punitive acts. When the *Rebel*, perhaps Tennessee's most vehemently anti-Union newspaper, fled Chattanooga, the Union commander ordered all the paper's materials and machinery to be piled up in the street and burned. Whatever could not be burned was to be broken up into tiny pieces with sledgehammers. At least three complete runs of the *Rebel*'s editions were destroyed in the conflagration. To avoid such interference from military authorities, many, including the *Rebel*, the storied "Moving *Appeal*" of Memphis, and all of Atlanta's newspapers, simply fled rather than submitted to Union occupiers, though at least one, the *Intelligencer*, returned home and resumed publication within only a few weeks after Union troops decamped. Newspapers that remained in occupied places like Memphis published under strict military supervision.[36]

In places that did not directly experience the war, such as Augusta, Georgia, where the anti–Jefferson Davis, pro-peace *Chronicle and Sentinel* and its pro-Davis, pro-war rival, the *Constitutionalist*, published with virtually no interference. Despite its harsh indictments of Davis and consistent calls for peace, the only retribution the *Chronicle and Sentinel* faced was the loss of Confederate advertising late in the war. There is some evidence that Confederate authorities visited the paper's editor, Nathan S. Morse, to warn him of dire consequences for his disloyalty, but his paper was never suppressed by Confederate authorities. The two Augusta papers continued to publish unfazed. After the fall of Atlanta, papers there were briefly suspended, but at least one was back in business only a few weeks after Sherman's troops moved out. In Atlanta, Macon (Sherman's troops feinted in that direction to destroy a pistol factory outside of town), and Milledgeville, publication of newspapers was only briefly interrupted when editors and printers were called into action as part of each city's defenders. The situation worked out differently in Savannah, for the editors of the two publications in that city abandoned their shops and fled as Sherman and his men marched in.[37]

Newspapers in areas that were occupied for long periods clearly had a more harrowing experience. Suspension, banishment, and arrest were common tactics Union military governors used to deal with pro-Confederate editors. Regular soldiers, given the opportunity to take matters into their own hands, sometimes went to extreme measures to silence what they considered to be abhorrent voices. John Vautier, a private serving in the Eighty-Eighth Pennsylvania Volunteers, affirmed this philosophy when he referred to the *Alexandria Gazette* as "a violent Rebel journal . . . [that] spits out its treason whenever it can." Some of his comrades went further than merely accusing the paper of treason; they decided to silence it in February 1862 by setting fire to its plant.[38]

Often, rather than allow a news vacuum to develop when Confederate editors were removed, Federal military governors would replace them with Union sympathizers. On February 11, 1864, the following paragraph appeared in the *Memphis Daily Appeal*:

> The Reconstruction Movement in Arkansas—The editor of the Little Rock Democrat has been arrested by the (Union) military authorities for publishing disloyal sentiments, and his paper suppressed. A new paper will soon be started by men of undoubted loyalty who will use their influence in favor of the reorganization movement.

The Memphis paper had some reason for sympathy. Its editors had chosen to flee occupation, and at the time of that editorial, the *Appeal* was being published from Atlanta, a haven for other journalistic fugitives from the Union army.

The findings of this work demonstrate that as military territory, and with it political authority, changed hands, the enterprise of journalism shifted as well. New players—sometimes homegrown, other times not—new partners, and new power struggles emerged. The situation remained fluid and often volatile. For whether these journalists were "men of undoubted loyalty" or "permanent members of the rebellion," editors in occupied Southern cities faced political uncertainty so often and economic pressure so keen that it is a wonder more newspapers did not disappear. The attrition rate among Southern newspapers was severe enough as it was. In several states, only about a tenth of the newspapers survived. Overall, the survival rate for Southern newspapers was about 52 percent for dailies and 31 percent for weeklies.[39] American journalism was tested by the war, then, and that predicament was as much met with resolve and courage as with surrender, opportunism, or vengeance.

The Civil War cemented the importance of journalism in the United States, a legacy made even clearer by occupation. Newspapers mattered for their communities. Fleeing editors or sabotaged printing presses left a vacuum in a city that could not be filled by sutlers, field commanders, or postal services. In time of war, information was a commodity or currency that profoundly affected morale. Towns like Alexandria, New Orleans, Chattanooga, and Vicksburg depended on journalism to contribute commercial as well as cultural cohesion. And when publications closed, anxiety rose because the absence of information stoked fear and uncertainty.

Occupation punished those journalists who continued to fight for the cause they believed in. They risked losing their livelihoods and lives. Journalism and citizens alike suffered, for in each instance examined here, occupation meant not just dealing with the everyday trials of having enemy troops in the environs but also limits on speech, assembly, and even religion. Preachers were arrested for failing to pray for the proper president. Journalists were threatened with banishment for noting the simplest of events that everyone in town probably already knew about before the newspaper appeared—a long-dead horse, after all, not only was a physical impediment to movement at the crossroads where it lay but was a stinky obstacle. When newspapers folded, fled, or flipped, citizens were left without any sort of information vehicle about the war, short of what they could learn from letters, word of mouth, or newspapers published from the enemy perspective. Most important, though, the presence of occupying troops prohibited journalists and citizens from discussing and critiquing actions of the government—the one thing Americans could all agree on was, without doubt, guaranteed by the First Amendment—even if there had been limits on speech about government throughout American history to that point. Even where occupation did not shutter newspapers, its constant interference discouraged both news coverage and editorial commentary. For while Unionist editors, for example, stood to gain from the suddenly reorganized field of competition, they were hardly spared military meddling. Generals were quick to rebuke or restrict editors no matter what their political beliefs. That fact was less a matter of politics than it was the age-old conflict between armies and civilians. Occupation did permit the cultivation of an African American press in New Orleans—one instance of journalists benefiting from new circumstances. Otherwise, martial law meant a net loss for the Southern press during the Civil War.

That casualty reflects the general diminution of freedom of the press one sees in other conflicts, particularly total wars such as World War I. Dissent in these eras was seldom tolerated and normally punished swiftly; "patriotism" and obedience were scrupulously demanded. Journalists James Hood and Ira Batterton, for example, believed in liberty for editors who thought as they did. They did not accord freedom to "traitors" and "rebels." And so often when they uttered words like "independence," they did not mean what we might think of today—an intellectually neutral third course. Their brand of independence was an exceptionally narrow one, applying only to beliefs held by the political victors, not to the viewpoints ousted by force of Springfield rifles or cavalry sabers.

Occupation brought the application of force to politics and journalism, then. But force is seldom final and often prompts resistance. While the presence of Union troops transformed the cities they overran, occupation hardly guaranteed a future for the newspapers it fostered. Some disappeared soon after the war ended, along with their editors. And in the same way that other repressive periods of American history—resulting in the Alien and Sedition Acts of 1798 or the Espionage and Sedition Acts of 1918, for instance—triggered a backlash among Americans weary of censorship, the Civil War's excesses likewise created skepticism, even fear, of centralized power. They also gradually underscored the significance of the nation's "public journals" and their role in American civic life and constitutional law.[40] Journalism survived the Civil War and would thrive in the last decades of the nineteenth century, growing in prestige, economic strength, and eventually editorial independence. The occupied press evoked a specter nobody wanted to see again.

Occupations like those experienced in the four cities studied for this chapter were not the only encounters Southern newspapers had with the Union army. However, enemy invasions or raids, such as those suffered by Georgia's newspapers in November 1864, were less of a problem for journalists than was occupation. Occupation left newspaper editors with three choices: capitulate, defy, or flee. As to which choice posed the most harrowing experience, there can be little debate. Certainly those editors who defied the local authorities faced harrowing times. Those who capitulated, though, became a sort of occupier themselves, for by their support of the Union perspective, they aided in the quest to suppress secessionist and war sentiment. They would set up an environment that gave Unionists their voices back while silencing Confederate opinion.

Among the choices an editor could make regarding how to respond to occupation, perhaps the most astounding one of all was the choice to continue publishing amid the chaos and chronic vexations of too few supplies and men to publish, too few subscribers willing to pay for their papers, and too little money to cover costs, much less to make a profit. It is easy to make heroes of such individuals and their publications, but such a perspective serves only to turn these real-life journalists into caricatures. As these case studies show, Confederate journalists were doing the best they could under trying—sometimes oppressively trying—conditions. Their stories constitute a mostly unknown chapter of American journalism history, a chapter that deserves attention for what it teaches about the impact of war on one of its most important social institutions—the press.

Notes

1. Mary Elizabeth Massey, *Ersatz in the Confederacy: Shortages and Substitutes on the Southern Home Front* (repr., Columbia: University of South Carolina Press, 1993); Charles W. Ramsdell and Wendell Holmes Stephenson, *Behind the Lines in the Southern Confederacy* (Baton Rouge: Louisiana State University, 1944); Andrew F. Smith, *Starving the South: How the North Won the Civil War* (New York: St. Martin's Press, 2011).

2. Stephen V. Ash, *When the Yankees Came: Conflict and Chaos in the Occupied South, 1861–1865* (Chapel Hill: University of North Carolina Press, 1995), 18, 169; Judkin Browning, *Shifting Loyalties: The Union Occupation of Eastern North Carolina* (Chapel Hill: University of North Carolina Press, 2011); George Hendricks, "Union Army Occupation of the Southern Seaboard, 1861–1865" (PhD diss., Columbia University, New York City, 1954); Jeanette M. Bergeron, "Occupation Newspapers of South Carolina, 1862–1865," in *South Carolina Journals and Journalists*, ed. James B. Meriwether (Spartanburg, S.C.: Reprint Co. Publishers, 1975), 135–45.

3. James W. Carey, *Communication as Culture: Essays on Media and Society* (Winchester, Mass.: Unwin Hyman, 1989), 20–23; Debra Reddin van Tuyll, *The Confederate Press in the Crucible of the American Civil War* (New York: Peter Lang, 2012), 262–66; Patricia G. McNeely, Debra Reddin van Tuyll, and Henry H. Schulte, *Knights of the Quill: Confederate Correspondents and Their Civil War Reporting* (West Lafayette, Ind.: Purdue University Press, 2010), 12–13.

4. Steven V. Ash, *Middle Tennessee Society Transformed, 1860-1870: War and Peace in the Upper South* (Baton Rouge: Louisiana State University Press, 1988), 88.

5. Gordon A. Cotton and Ralph E. Mason, *With Malice toward Some: The Military Occupation of Vicksburg, 1864–1865* (Vicksburg: Vicksburg and Warren County Historical Society, 1991).

6. General Benjamin Butler, General Order No. 28, *War of the Rebellion: A Compilation of the Official Records of the Union and Confederate Armies* (hereafter *Official Records*) (Washington, D.C.: Government Printing Office, 1880–1901), series 1, vol. 15, 21; Ash, *When the Yankees Came*, 44; Ash, *Middle Tennessee*, 87–88, 144–45; Browning, *Shifting Loyalties*, 4, 135–37, 180.

7. Marc Leepson, "The First Union Martyr: Elmer Ellsworth, Alexandria, and the American Flag," *Alexandria Chronicle*, Fall 2011, 11; Orlando B. Willcox, *Forgotten Valor: The Memoirs, Journals, and Civil War Letters of Orlando B. Willcox* (Kent: Kent State University Press, 1999), 267.

8. "Later from Alexandria," *Fayetteville (N.C.) Observer*, June 3, 1861; Lester J. Cappon, "The Yankee Press in Virginia, 1861–1865," *William and Mary College Quarterly Historical Magazine* 15, no. 1 (January 1935): 81; Willcox, *Forgotten Valor*, 273.

9. "The Alexandria Gazette," *Alexandria Gazette*, September 16, 1893. The incident involving Snowden being used as a human shield occurred on October 17, 1864.

10. "The Despot's Heel Is on Thy Neck!," *Raleigh Register*, March 15, 1862; untitled editorial, *Local News* (Alexandria, Va.), February 10, 1862; Cappon, "Yankee Press," 81; Carrol H. Quenzel, "Samuel Snowden, a Founding Father of Printing in Alexandria," unpublished manuscript, Local History Special Collections, Alexandria Public Library, Alexandria, Va., p. 42; Henry B. Whittington Diary, February 11, 1862, Alexandria Public Library; John D. Vautier, *History of the 88th Pennsylvania Volunteers in the War for the Union, 1861–1865* (Philadelphia: J. B. Lippincott, 1894), 22; "To the Patrons of the Alexandria Gazette," *Alexandria Gazette*, October 31, 1864; James G. Barber, *Alexandria in the Civil War* (Lynchburg: H. E. Howard, 1988); "To the Subscribers of the Gazette," *Alexandria Gazette*, July 8, 1863; Carroll H. Quenzel, *Edgar Snowden, Sr.: Virginia Journalist and Civic Leader* (Charlottesville: Bibliographical Society of the University of Virginia, 1954), 44–45; Diane Riker, "'This Long Agony': A Test of Civilian Loyalties in an Occupied City," *Alexandria Chronicle* (Spring 2011), http://www.alexandriahistorical.org/images/stories/Chronicle/2011_Sp2_Chronicle.pdf (accessed November 28, 2012), 3, 4, 7, 8; untitled story, *Alexandria Gazette*, September 12, 1863; "From the South," *Alexandria Gazette*, September 9, 1863.

11. Quenzel, *Edgar Snowden, Sr.*, 44–45; Browning, *Shifting Loyalties*, 153; Rebecca Downes, "The Occupation of Alexandria, Va. during the Civil War," *Carlyle House Docent Dispatch*, May 2011, http://www.nvrpa.org/uploads/Files/published_articles/5-May%202011-%20The%20Occupation%20of%20Alexandria.pdf, accessed July 27, 2013; "To the Subscribers of the Gazette."

12. *Official Records*, series 1, vol. 24, part 2, 62–66.

13. Elliott Ashkenazi, ed., *The Diary of Clara Solomon: Growing Up in New Orleans, 1861–1862* (Baton Rouge: Louisiana State University Press, 1995), 423.

14. Gerald M. Capers, *Occupied City: New Orleans under the Federals, 1862–1865* (Lexington: University of Kentucky Press, 1965), 177; Benjamin F. Butler, *Autobiography and Personal Reminiscences of Major-General Benjamin F. Butler* (Boston: A. M. Thayer, 1892), 377; *New Orleans Daily True Delta*, May 3, 1862; Chester G. Hearn, *When the Devil Came Down to Dixie: Ben Butler in New Orleans* (Baton Rouge: Louisiana State University Press, 1997), 100; Napoléon-Joseph Perché, quoted in William Lemuel Greene, *Spicing Ecclesiastical Gumbo: The Life of Napoléon-Joseph Perché, Third Archbishop of New Orleans, 1805–1883* (Baton Rouge: Claitor's, 2012), 77, 79.

15. *New Orleans Daily Delta*, May 4 and May 14, 1862.

16. Richard H. Abbott, *For Free Press and Equal Rights: Republican Newspapers in the Reconstruction South*, ed. John W. Quist (Athens: University of Georgia Press, 2004), 14.

17. Will Coviello, "Panel Marks 150th Anniversary of First Black-Owned Daily U.S. Paper," *Gambit: Best of New Orleans*, http://www.bestofneworleans.com/blogofneworleans/archives/2014/07/18/panel-marks-150th-anniversary-of-first-black-owned-daily-us-newspaper, accessed January 21, 2015.

18. Anna T. Micklin, "Trévigne, Paul," Black Past.org, http://www.blackpast.org/aah/trevigne-paul-1825–1908, accessed January 21, 2015; "*L'Union*," African American Registry, http://www.aaregistry.org/historic_events/view/lunion-first-black-daily-newspaper, accessed January 21, 2015.

19. *New Orleans Daily Delta*, May 4, 1862; Debra Reddin van Tuyll, Nancy McKenzie Dupont, and Joseph R. Hayden, *Journalism in the Fallen Confederacy* (New York: Palgrave, 2015), 79–81.

20. Hood to Johnson, October 16, 1863, in *The Papers of Andrew Johnson*, ed. Leroy P. Graf and Ralph W. Haskins (Knoxville: University of Tennessee Press, 1983), vol. 8, 420.

21. *Chattanooga Daily Gazette*, April 23, 1864, 2.

22. Ibid., June 26, 1864. See also "The National Union Ticket," ibid., June 10, 1864.

23. Ibid., April 27, 1864.

24. Hood to Andrew Johnson, March 17 and March 31, 1861, in *Papers of Andrew Johnson*, vol. 8, 455, 402.

25. "The Mail Ahead," *Chattanooga Daily Gazette*, September 10, 1864, 2; "Post Office Notice to Military Commanders," ibid., September 13, 1864, 3.

26. "All Quiet," *Chattanooga News*, March 10, 1865, 2.

27. *Chattanooga Daily Gazette*, June 2, 1864. For an example of the "honor roll," see the June 5, 1864, issue.

28. Ibid., April 14, 1864.

29. James R. Hood, "To the Patrons of the Chattanooga Daily Gazette," ibid., September 13, 1864.

30. Van Tuyll, Dupont, and Hayden, *Journalism in the Fallen Confederacy*, 99–105; William Gardner, unpublished memoirs, quoted in letter from Ruth MacGregory (Gardner's great-niece) to Edwin C. Bearss, Old Courthouse Museum, Vicksburg, Miss., July 2, 1965; "W. T. Gardner Dies; Veteran of Civil War," *New York Herald Tribune*, July 9, 1934; *Vicksburg Daily Citizen*, July 2, 1863.

31. *Vicksburg Daily Herald*, July 14, 1864.

32. Cotton and Mason, *With Malice toward Some*, 13; Ira A. Batterton, letter to his father dated January 17, 1864; Batterton letter, March 23, 1864; Batterton letter, October 11, 1863. Batterton's letters are privately held by Mrs. John Leonard Probasco of Rockford, Ill. They have been quoted and in some cases summarized by M. F. Batterton of Naperville, Ill. The abstract is held in a file at the Old Courthouse Museum in Vicksburg. *Vicksburg Daily Herald*, October 8, 1864, quoted in *Vicksburg Sunday Post*, October 26, 1987.

33. Van Tuyll, Dupont, and Hayden, *Journalism in the Fallen Confederacy*, 95–105.

34. Ash, *When the Yankees Came*, 58; James Martin, "For the Army, the People, and Abraham Lincoln: A Yankee Newspaper in Occupied Texas," *Civil War History* 32, no. 2 (1993): 126–47.

35. *A Digest of Opinions of the Judge Advocate General of the Army* (Washington: Government Printing Office, 1917), 1058.

36. "Our Paper," *Memphis Daily Appeal*, April 29, 1862; "Newspapers Received," *Columbus (Ga.) Daily Enquirer*, December 17, 1864; Barbara G. Ellis, *The Moving Appeal: Mr. McClanahan, Mrs. Dill, and the Civil War's Great Newspaper Run* (Macon: Mercer University Press, 2003); Robert Bailey, "The 'Bogus' Memphis Union Appeal: A Union Newspaper in Occupied Confederate Territory," *West Tennessee Historical Society Papers* 32 (1978): 32–47; van Tuyll, *Confederate Press*, 65; *Chattanooga Times*, January 9, 1949; *Chattanooga Daily Rebel*, August 30, 1863; William S. Speer, *Sketches of Prominent Tennesseans* (Nashville: Albert T. Tavel, 1888), 481.

37. "The Battle of Griswoldville," *Augusta Chronicle and Sentinel* (reprinted from the *Macon Telegraph* of November 24, 1864), November 30, 1864; van Tuyll, *Confederate Press*, 306–9.

38. Michael Ayoub, "Hessians in Our Midst: Provost Duty in Alexandria, 1861–1862: The 88th Pennsylvania Volunteers," *Alexandria Chronicle*, Fall 2008, 10, http://www.alexandriahistorical.org/images/stories/Chronicle/2008_Fall_Chronicle.pdf, accessed December 5, 2012.

39. J. Cutler Andrews, *The South Reports the Civil War* (Princeton: Princeton University Press, 1970), 45; van Tuyll, *Confederate Press*, 16–21.

40. Timothy W. Gleason, *The Watchdog Concept: The Press and the Courts in Nineteenth-Century America* (Ames: Iowa State University Press, 1990), 54.

5. DISTURBING THE PUBLIC PEACE

RADICAL AND CONSERVATIVE EDITORS IN THE RECONSTRUCTION SOUTH

ERIKA J. PRIBANIC-SMITH

Although the Civil War officially ended in 1865, the underlying ideological and political conflict lingered on through the era of Reconstruction. Officially beginning with the passage of the Emancipation Proclamation in 1863 and ending with the Compromise of 1877, Reconstruction pitted Southerners who aimed to rejoin the nation while continuing their white supremacy against newly freed African Americans and Northern Republicans who insisted that African Americans be granted equal rights. The era can be divided into two phases. During the first, very short phase, Presidents Abraham Lincoln and Andrew Johnson took a moderate approach that intended to return the South to normal as quickly as possible, requiring only that Southern states repeal their secession ordinances, officially declare their slaves free, and repudiate their war debts so that the United States would not be forced to absorb the cost of Confederate rebellion. Other than high-ranking civil and military officials, any former Confederate who swore an amnesty oath pledging loyalty to the United States would be pardoned and re-enfranchised. But despite Johnson's acceptance of the former Confederate states, Congress refused to seat their representatives. Contention between Johnson and Congress increased as the president vetoed several measures, including bills that would award rights and aid to freedmen.[1]

The second phase began as Radical Republicans gained control of Congress. They ensured the passage of the Civil Rights and Freedmen's Bureau Acts as well as of constitutional amendments making African Americans citizens (Fourteenth

Amendment) and granting them the right to vote (Fifteenth Amendment). Furthermore, the Radical Republicans enacted military rule in the ten Confederate states that had not granted adequate rights to freedmen—dividing those states into five military districts—and temporarily stripped former Confederate officials and military officers of the rights to vote and hold political office.[2] Congress organized the military districts as part of the Reconstruction Acts that became law in March 1867. The acts featured provisions for readmitting states and ending military authority, including framing new state constitutions and ratifying the Fourteenth Amendment.[3] Arkansas, Georgia, Louisiana, Florida, Alabama, and the Carolinas were readmitted in June 1868, though Georgia returned to military control from December 1869 to 1871.[4] By early 1870, Mississippi, Virginia, and Texas completed the necessary steps for readmission, which by then also included ratification of the Fifteenth Amendment.[5] Though the military no longer held control over civil affairs, it maintained a strong presence in the Southern states.

Readmission did not mean peace, however. As African Americans, sympathetic Southerners (termed "scalawags"), and Northern visitors ("carpetbaggers") installed biracial, Republican governments in the Southern states, Southerners resistant to change—known as Conservatives—reacted violently. Despite attempts by President Ulysses S. Grant to enforce the Civil Rights Act and subsequent constitutional amendments, the Ku Klux Klan and paramilitary organizations such as the White League and Red Shirts terrorized African Americans and white sympathizers. In part because of these violent organizations, Conservative Democrats known as "Redeemers" gradually gained control of Southern governments.[6] Reconstruction came to an official end in 1877, when Rutherford B. Hayes withdrew military troops from the former Confederate states as part of the alleged compromise that installed him as president.[7]

Operating in such an intense political environment, Southern newspapers of the Reconstruction era reverted to the partisan function that had been established for the press earlier in the nineteenth century. Republican editors defended Reconstruction policy, protected freedmen, and admonished the violent tactics of some Conservatives, whereas Democratic editors upheld Southern values and attacked the Reconstruction government and its military installments.[8] Although some military leaders and Conservative organizations aimed to quiet any newspaper that criticized them, only the most obnoxious partisan sheets suffered serious consequences. Loyal Southerners counted verbal abuse of Confederate veterans as treason, and they deemed language that could incite freedmen and other Radicals to violence as dangerous. Similarly, Republican leaders found

Conservative attempts to rouse insurrection intolerable, as was any language they considered a serious obstacle to Reconstruction policy.[9]

Suppressors labeled these extreme cases as abuses of the right to a free press. As long as the speech was not seen as harmful, though, the right to free expression generally was protected. Donna Dickerson argues that the First Amendment was "in the vortex" of social and political changes that occurred during the antebellum and Civil War eras. By the time of Reconstruction, the public and press were free to discuss issues "without the mailed glove of government censorship."[10] Thus, most Southern partisan newspapers enjoyed a great deal of liberty to circulate their views as passionate mouthpieces for their respective parties and vigorous attackers of their opponents.

Hodding Carter describes the newspapers of the Conservative Democrats as "bombastic organs" that "fulminated against the carpet-bagger, the Negro and the Yankee soldier of military reconstruction" with little regard for accuracy, and other historians have supported that.[11] Ted Tunnell argues that the Democratic press played an important role as "the only institution in the South fully under the control of native whites and in a position to oppose northern policy."[12] Conservative editors railed against Radical politicians and ideals with a vigor characteristic of the partisan press.[13] In particular, several scholars have emphasized that some Democratic newspapers undermined Republicans' efforts to achieve civil rights for freedmen by influencing the public to believe that African Americans were inferior and incapable of participating in the political sphere.[14] Although primarily occupied with disparaging their opponents, Democratic newspapers also did their part to support Conservative and Redemption candidates and measures.[15]

Carter labels their counterparts in the Radical Republican press as "vicious, wholly self-seeking journals" that earned reputations as dishonest and corrupt, pilfering thousands of dollars from the Republican regime in printing contracts and advertising.[16] Some historians assert that Radical politicians and military governments controlled the flow of information by favoring the Republican press with official advertisements and announcements and by economically strangling opposition papers, forcing them to suspend publication.[17] This was particularly true in the Third Military District, consisting of Florida, Georgia, and Alabama. General John Pope—whom James Sefton labels a "thorough-going Radical"—issued an order denying newspapers in his district that opposed congressional Reconstruction the patronage of their state or local governments. Pope explained in a report to Washington that his actions were intended to curb editorial abuse of military appointees and the intimidation of loyal papers by disloyal ones. Editors of all political stripes who were accustomed to penning partisan vitriol without consequence balked at the measure as a threat to free speech and criticized the action as an attempt to dictate the political tone of the press.[18]

Generally, though, historians deny that the Republican press held any advantages over the Democratic newspapers. Patronage was scarce, awarded to a precious few newspapers and quickly withdrawn if a paper displayed any shred of the wrong politics. Furthermore, Republican newspapers failed to achieve the

General John Pope issued two conflicting orders regarding the press as commander of the Third Military District. One order prohibited blatant infringements on press freedom by military personnel, but another attempted to control the press by refusing government patronage to newspapers that opposed congressional Reconstruction. Library of Congress Prints and Photographs Division, Washington, D.C.

same circulation and commercial advertising figures as their Democratic counterparts. Although some Republican editors were indeed corrupt and greedy, many operated their newspapers at a loss, and some endured terrorism by Conservative groups to support and sustain a party whose equal rights principles they truly believed in.[19] For example, Jason Clarke Swayze made enemies for his allegations against loyal Southerners and his invitations for Radicals to retaliate violently.

JASON CLARKE SWAYZE VERSUS GEORGIA CONSERVATIVES

The New Jersey–born Swayze began facing suppressive tactics almost immediately after he arrived in Griffin, Georgia, on the eve of the Civil War. Under Confederate law, Swayze was able to avoid military service as a printer, but his devout Unionism brought him endless harassment by local "rebels" and Confederate soldiers. In 1863, a mob seized Swayze at his office and rode him through town on a rail "with severe threats of tar and feathers, and hanging," for a "smutty article" he had published in his *Bugle Horn of Liberty.* Once Swayze escaped, the mob shouted after him that he had better blow his bugle horn somewhere else.[20]

Soon after, the Confederates arrested Swayze for his Union sentiments. While imprisoned, Swayze refused to pledge his loyalty to the Confederacy. As punishment, he was "balled and chained at Macon, and forced to 'mark time' on the head of a barrel, face to the street, with a placard hung upon his breast on which was written 'Traitor.'"[21] Near the end of the war, he was taken to the front of the Confederate lines but escaped to the Federal army; he became a scout and spy under General William Tecumseh Sherman.[22]

After the war, Swayze returned to his family in Griffin and became an agent of the Freedmen's Bureau, a government agency tasked with aiding freed slaves. Swayze resigned "for the sake of peace and harmony" after his actions generated too much controversy, and he occupied his time distributing propaganda to freedmen and writing letters about the state of affairs in Georgia to whatever newspapers would publish them, north and south.[23] Swayze continued to receive threats from loyal rebels who "did not like Captain Swayze's style of giving the Negro as much justice as the white."[24] On two occasions, Confederate veteran Littlejohn J. Bloodworth accosted Swayze, calling him a "damned Yankee son of a bitch" and accusing him of sexual relations with African Americans. During the second verbal assault, Bloodworth brandished a pistol. Swayze attempted justice through city and county tribunals, but neither jury found any evidence of wrongdoing.[25]

In a final attempt to silence Swayze, Bloodworth and five other men conspired to drive the Unionist printer out of town or kill him if he refused to leave. On December 1, 1866, the men met at a local restaurant, where a Swayze sympathizer overheard them plotting and alerted a mutual friend who ran to warn Swayze. The ally found Bloodworth's group already surrounding Swayze in his office. Swayze told the men he would go when he pleased, not at their suggestion. When the mob threatened to kill Swayze, his comrade stepped in and encouraged them to give Swayze time to reconsider. They told Swayze that he had forty-eight hours to vacate or they would return and hang him. The men left the office shouting, "Hurrah for Jeff Davis, and damn the man that won't say hurrah for him!"[26]

Swayze lamented, "I am satisfied that I cannot[,] neither can any acknowledged Union man[,] obtain justice in the local courts in that part of the state where I am acquainted."[27] Therefore, he appealed to his friends at the Freedmen's Bureau district office in Savannah, and General Davis Tillson insisted that Bloodworth's group be arrested as a test case for the Civil Rights Act.[28] In retaliation for the arrests, local newspapers emphasized the respectability of native Georgians while accusing the "treasonous" Swayze of all manner of wretchedness for harassing them. Rebel editors called Swayze an "incendiary abolitionist," a liar, and "a notorious scoundrel"; complained that his writings had vilified and misrepresented the noble Southern people; and averred that he would get what he deserved if his slanders continued.[29] Further, the citizens of Spalding County blamed Swayze for "all the difficulties between the freedmen and their former owners, in this community," and insisted his "improper conduct" could not be tolerated.[30] The newspapers argued that Swayze should be jailed, and they would rejoice when he was.

Meanwhile, Swayze continued lashing out at rebels for their treatment of nationalists and African Americans. He also chastised the government for its leniency toward former Confederates—whom he labeled traitors—and failure to protect loyal Unionists. Swayze asserted that "the rebellion is not crushed yet." He declared that the rebel press had boasted the Civil Rights Act could not be executed in Georgia and that if a Unionist or freedman depended on the state courts, "rebels, with impunity, laugh at any effort he may make." Swayze called for the state government to be overthrown and a new one installed that would protect true patriots.[31]

Swayze purchased the steadfastly Republican *American Union* in August 1867, and having his own outlet for tirades against Conservatives increased backlash from local citizens who wanted him silenced. Given his circulation woes, Swayze relied in part on patronage to stay afloat during military rule in Georgia. Richard Abbott notes that the *Union* particularly benefited from General Pope's order requiring that all federal, state, and local official advertisements and announcements be published in newspapers that supported congressional Reconstruction.[32]

Patronage offered little comfort, though, as Swayze continued to face hostility from neighbors who aimed to suppress his vitriolic articles against Conservatism. Swayze entered the *Union* office one day to find a note under the door advising him to close up shop and leave Griffin due to the number of political and personal enemies he had. The note called Swayze a "damned Radical" and warned, "If you should get tangled, blame no person but yourself."[33] Swayze consented to leave Griffin only after a mob destroyed the *Union* presses and burned down the building.[34]

Swayze relocated to Macon, where he reestablished the *American Union* with the assistance of his former employer Horace Greeley of the *New York Tribune*. But the locals of Macon were no more accepting of Swayze's Radical Republican rhetoric. His son Oscar, who apprenticed at the newspaper as a child, later recalled that being "shot at on the streets and threatened with hanging was part of the life of the *Union* editor."[35] Violent mobs threatened Swayze's life twice within his first three months in Macon, prompting him to write to Governor Rufus Bullock, "If I can't be protected for expressing Republican sentiments through my paper, then publication of it will be useless."[36]

Swayze's entire family required protection. Son Oscar recalled having to "dodge the dornicks" thrown at him when he ran errands for the paper.[37] Swayze lamented that none of his three children were able to attend school because they were constantly taunted and shunned by "young rebels."[38] Because the police were "too much engaged in politics, or too partizan [*sic*] to protect a child of mine," Swayze warned in his paper that he himself would teach the "pupils of treason" not to impose upon his family, so long as he was "alive and outside rebel jails."[39]

Swayze found himself inside a "rebel jail" soon enough. As other Georgia newspapers attempted to lure immigrants to aid the state's struggling postbellum economy, Swayze used every issue of the *Union* to proclaim them liars, supporting Governor Bullock's claims to Congress that the state had not been reconstructed and insisting that African Americans and Republicans lived in constant fear. By this time, the Ku Klux Klan had developed a stronghold in some sections of the state. Mildred Thompson has argued that the Reconstruction Acts made the African American a menace to the white citizens of Georgia.[40] The KKK threatened, beat, and murdered African Americans to control them and keep them down, reminding them of their inferior social status in spite of laws that purported them to be equal. In sections of the state where African Americans outnumbered the white population and their votes stood to affect elections, KKK "outrages" were politically motivated. The Georgia "chivalry" also targeted white leaders who were perceived as inciting African Americans against white citizens. Few of the perpetrators were arrested and even fewer convicted.[41]

In response to the violence, Swayze continued harping on the impotence of the federal government, lamenting that Congress had done nothing to protect the lives of innocent Georgians. He claimed in April 1869 that hundreds had been murdered in the prior year, and "hundreds more must spill their blood before the tardy hand of the government can be moved to protect its friends in a section of its

Thomas Nast, the famous illustrator for *Harper's Weekly*, produced this image titled "The Union as it was. The lost cause, worse than slavery" for the October 24, 1878, issue of the magazine to show that although the war was over and slavery as an institution had been ended, racist groups, including the Ku Klux Klan, used violence, murder, arson, and intimidation to curtail the rights granted African Americans during the Reconstruction era. Library of Congress Prints and Photographs Division, Washington, D.C.

domain which is filled with its enemies." Being that those who loyally supported the government before, during, and after the war had been "abandoned to their fate," Swayze encouraged Unionists to cement their ranks and pick up arms:

> Let them present an unbroken front and demand a tooth for a tooth, an eye for an eye! Let them show rebels that they have the nerve to defend themselves against lawlessness. Let the whole State organize into societies—secret societies; and when rebels commit their diabolical horrors upon them, because of their opinions, retaliate at a ten-fold ratio. For every life that is taken, lay every house in ashes within five miles of the spot where such blood is spilled—shoot down every rebel who opposes you, and turn the horrors back upon those who are daily repeating them upon loyal people. DO IT! And God will be your shield.[42]

The incessant violence against Republicans caused a delegation of state legislators to visit Congress and President Grant in the spring of 1869 to plead for protection. Yet as they returned home to Georgia, two of the delegates were murdered in separate incidents. Swayze of course railed against the government for its failure to protect loyal citizens and emphasized that Republicans must be prepared to protect themselves. The primary targets for his editorial rants, however, were the Ku Klux Klan and the *Atlanta New Era*. Swayze labeled the delegates' murders KKK assassinations and fingered *Era* editor Sam Bard as instigator because of an item he had published criticizing the legislative delegation for spreading lies in Washington about the state of affairs in Georgia, endangering the "the future prosperity and happiness of our people in order to promote their own wicked, selfish and diabolical ends." Bard called them "incarnate devils in human shape" and expressed hope that they would "perish by the wayside, and that the State may never again be cursed by their presence." Swayze took Bard's words as a call to action for KKK assassins.[43]

After the first murder, Swayze claimed he had been threatened by the KKK for trying to mourn his assassinated friend:

> So violent had this spirit become in several quarters before night, and so positive were the threats against the *Union* office, that our friends thought it prudent to guard it. So, here in a community that contains newspapers that insist that all men have all the rights and privileges that are enjoyed in any other State in the Union, loyal men have to band themselves together to protect the only Republican paper in the State that has not been made to yield to their demands, from being destroyed by a mob, because we dared to publicly mourn the untimely death of one of their victims.[44]

No *Union* appeared the following week. Swayze revealed that he had been arrested for his tirades, and for at least a few weeks he published his paper from jail. He had been charged with a high misdemeanor for violating a part of the Georgia penal code forbidding the circulation of "any paper, pamphlet, circular, or writing for the purpose of exciting insurrection."[45] The charge could not silence him, though. He avowed, "Though we are thrust into a rebel jail, and there rot, the paper will still go on." Even if an assassin were to take him down, Swayze promised his paper would continue under the editorship of his wife, "who is ten times more earnest and uncompromising" and "with a glorious cause to inspire her, will do her best to make treason odious."[46]

Though he eventually was released and never convicted of a crime, the ordeal inspired numerous editorials on the lack of press freedom in Georgia. Swayze declared that he had defended himself against innumerable prosecutions, and the "game will be repeated upon every man who dares to express himself as a Republican so long as rebels are allowed to fill the offices." He insisted that no freedom of speech or press existed in Georgia unless the speaker was of the appropriate politics or hue of skin.[47] In an editorial titled "Censors," he lambasted the local postmasters for withholding his paper from subscribers and for marking out or tearing out any item that was objectionable to rebels.[48] He offered as further proof of attempted censorship that the *Macon Telegraph* had called for the grand jury to take charge of the *American Union* and silence it.[49] A quote from Bard's *New Era* is telling of why the locals aimed to quiet Swayze: "This child of the devil is doing all he can to stir up riot and bloodshed in Georgia."[50]

When another Conservative newspaper reported that Swayze likely would be arrested again and incarcerated for many years, Swayze replied that locking him away was the next logical step, given that "money, threats and oppression already had been offered without avail." Swayze declared that all of the other Republican papers in the state had been "cowhided or bought into rebel service," leaving him alone to speak the truth and "give publicity to the hellish doings of treacherous rebels." He complained that the Confederate men who had been defeated on the battlefield nonetheless were winning the war of ideas in Georgia. Though they "commit treason and wicked, vile rebellion, the rebels are treated as gallant soldiers, and allowed to go scot free, and boast of their achievements on the domain of their conquerors." He begged to know why the rebel papers were allowed to "curse the air of nearly one half of our beloved country, and abuse not only every officer of the government, but the government itself," while he and others who had pledged to defend the government were left vulnerable.[51]

Yet despite Swayze's promise to carry on undeterred, he packed up his print shop in 1873 and moved to Kansas, where he established the *Topeka Blade*. Swayze told *Blade* readers that he had used in the *Union* "some sarcasm and a good deal of plain truth, which was 'mighty disagreeable' to traitors." He claimed that despite assorted schemes to break down the *Union*, it had gained a worldwide reputation and prospered financially. Nonetheless, once the Ku Klux Klan drove away or killed many of his supporters, he determined he had to "leave or starve." Furthermore, he had grown tired of the constant threats. He asserted that his "nerves were always strung up to their utmost tension, looking out for some treacherous assault."[52] However, Kansas proved no friendlier; within four years of relocating there, Swayze was silenced for good when a rival newspaperman gunned him down in front of the *Blade* office.[53]

SUPPRESSION BY THE MILITARY

While the greatest threat to Radical Republican editors like Swayze was the wrath of Conservatives, some disloyal newspapers faced suppression by military officials, particularly during the period of presidential Reconstruction. Donna Dickerson notes that the military governments installed in the Southern states continued wartime censorship practices, arresting enough newspaper editors for criticizing the government that other editors censored themselves to avoid the same fate.[54] Sefton avers that commanding generals regularly scanned the Southern press for evidence of disloyalty and stopped publication when necessary.[55] The first wave of suppression occurred as editors balked at the amnesty oath. Among the handful of newspapers punished for advising against taking the oath was the Democratic *Richmond Whig*, which called President Johnson's amnesty proclamation "heathenish." A local commander ordered the *Whig* office to be closed, although he allowed it to reopen ten days later because the editor generally had been loyal and friendly.[56] Military officials suspended for much longer other newspapers that criticized the oath, and one editor even was arrested. Following these acts of suppression, one Georgia editor announced that he would say no more about the civil or military governments in the state "until a mere editorial is not labeled as treason."[57]

A number of papers were silenced for criticism of the military itself.[58] Most trouble stemmed from editors bristling at the restrictions military units imposed, but a military commander stationed in Arkansas took exception to an assault on the troops' character in the *Camden Constitutional Eagle*. The *Eagle*'s editors accused the soldiers stationed there of

> coming up to town quite frequently and getting so inebriated as to be totally indifferent to decency, propriety, or anything else, and as they swagger and stagger toward camps use such profane and obscene language . . . as would make the most obdurate negro blush, if such a thing was possible, to say nothing of respectable ladies and children.[59]

The Little Rock *Arkansas Gazette* reported that the *Eagle* had been making unflattering comments about the military for some time, and the troops had grown tired of the abuse.[60] Although commanding officer Colonel Charles Champion Gilbert refused to censor the newspaper, second-in-command Major George S. Peirce led a group of thirty soldiers to destroy the *Eagle*'s press and dump its type into the nearby Ouachita River.[61]

Historians emphasize that in most cases, military suppression was imposed by locally stationed military personnel, not by the commanders of the Reconstruction military districts. District commanders generally were intolerant of such impositions on press freedom. Before the organization of the military districts under congressional Reconstruction, General Ulysses S. Grant issued an order that he alone had the authority to suspend newspapers as commanding general of the U.S. Army, and he declared that only the most hostile presses would be suppressed. He silenced only one in a year's time.[62] Even the openly Radical General Pope resented blatant and aggressive impositions on press freedom in his military district. Pope reprimanded an Alabama unit commander for intimidating a Mobile newspaper, which had published a letter to the editor encouraging African Americans to shoot their enemies rather than waste shots firing pistols into the air. Subsequently, Pope issued an order for the military to secure the greatest freedom of speech and press and do nothing to restrict it without authorization from Pope, even in cases deemed treasonous.[63]

The *Constitutional Eagle* incident prompted Fourth District commander General Edward O. C. Ord to issue a similar edict. Colonel Gilbert provided evidence that the *Eagle* had abused Ord himself, calling him "King Ord" and lamenting his ability to make laws and appointments in the name of the state of Arkansas, including appointing Radicals to key positions. Nonetheless, Ord had Major Peirce court-martialed and demoted and required him to forfeit his pay for a year. Ord insisted that military forces were to ensure the equal execution of laws upon all citizens, not to violate them "to gratify private revenge" and disturb the public peace.[64] Ord ignored his own advice in 1869, though, in perhaps the most famous case of military suppression during Reconstruction.

EX PARTE MCCARDLE AND THE SUPREME COURT

The significance of the case of *Vicksburg Times* editor William McCardle lay in its effect on the Supreme Court. Because Congress feared the case provided an opportunity for the high court to declare the Reconstruction Acts unconstitutional, legislators passed an act restricting the Supreme Court's appellate jurisdiction, forcing the McCardle case to be dismissed.[65]

William Harris has described McCardle as one of "a small corps of former Whig journalists who showered Mississippi during Reconstruction with sharp editorial darts aimed at those who carried out or acquiesced in the congressional settlement for the South." McCardle's Conservative *Vicksburg Times* became embroiled in an editorial battle with the Radical *Vicksburg Republican*. Embedded in McCardle's tirades were barbs against Ord and other military officials, attacks on a Freedmen's Bureau agent, opposition to the Fourteenth Amendment, calls for resistance to the military, and insistence that voters should refrain from voting in an election to submit to a convention for Mississippi's readmission to the Union.[66] On the latter issue, McCardle aimed to lead a boycott by white voters in order to prevent a majority of registered voters from approving the call for a convention. Any vote cast in the election, whether for or against a convention, was "indirectly countenancing, 'giving aid and comfort' to the infamous attempt to Africanize the State!"[67] Although the constitutional convention was approved, only eight white men out of more than twenty thousand voted in Vicksburg, which prompted McCardle to crow that "in the 'heroic city' of Vicksburg, the gallant Saragossa of the South, there were only eight cowards, dogs, and scoundrels."[68]

Fear of placing Mississippi under African American control inspired one of McCardle's tirades against Ord as well. Complaining that Ord was aiding the Loyal League—an African American Radical Republican organization—in taking possession of the state, McCardle claimed that Ord deserved to be hung, and when he was, "we shall endeavor to be on hand."[69] A few days later, on November 6, a *Times* editorial referred to all the district commanders of the South as "infamous, cowardly, and abandoned villains, who, instead of wearing shoulder straps and ruling millions of people, should have their heads shaved, their ears cropped, their foreheads branded, and their precious persons lodged in a penitentiary."[70]

On November 8, military officers arrested McCardle, and a military commission charged him with impeding Reconstruction, libeling individuals, and disturbing the public peace by inciting people to riot and insurrection.[71] Conservative newspapers across the South erupted in criticism of Ord's actions, inspiring him to present an illusion of impartiality by having the *Republican*'s editors arrested as well for their libelous assaults on McCardle.[72] Among the censures was an item in the *Charleston Daily News*, which averred that voting against a convention or advising others to do so did not violate any laws. "Intemperance of language, whether spoken or written, is not a crime justifying arrest and imprisonment," the Charleston paper argued.[73] The *Memphis Public Ledger* also stepped to McCardle's defense, accusing Ord of abusing and prostituting the power invested in him by the federal government to exact petty revenge for his own personal satisfaction.[74]

Meanwhile, McCardle's newspaper described the deplorable conditions of the confines his captors had thrust him into and promised to continue the fearless editor's fight against Reconstruction. The paper would be edited by its manager, S. Vernon, and its readers were told to expect no changes in sentiment or boldness: "Gen. Ord, backed by his hireling bayonets, may imprison the body of Major McCardle, but the free spirit and free pen cannot be shackled by his tyrannical ukase. If need be, an army of martyrs will step forward to take the place of the fallen hero."[75]

McCardle's attorneys—including former provisional governor William Lewis Sharkey and former U.S. senator Walker Brooke—petitioned the U.S. circuit court on November 12 for a writ of habeas corpus, citing *Ex parte Milligan* as precedent for the argument that McCardle had been charged and held illegally.[76] The *Milligan* case had addressed the question of whether the president and Congress could subject civilians to military trials when civilian courts were open and functioning. During the Civil War, Lambdin Milligan, an Indiana Copperhead Democrat, declared secession legal and argued that Lincoln and the Union had overstepped constitutional authority by pursuing war with the Confederacy. As "major general" of a society known as the Sons of Liberty, Milligan conspired to rebellion. He and his coconspirators were arrested and tried in a military tribunal, which found them guilty and sentenced them to death. Milligan filed for a writ of habeas corpus in an Indianapolis federal circuit court, which sent the case to the Supreme Court.[77] In a December 1866 decision, the high court indicated that military commissions had no jurisdiction over a citizen who was not a prisoner of war or a member of the armed forces, and neither the president nor Congress could impose martial law that overrode the constitutional protections of a criminal trial unless the courts and civil authorities had been overthrown by an invading nation.[78]

McCardle got a hearing before federal judge Robert A. Hill, whom Harris calls a "mild-mannered and respected Unionist" who strongly approved of congressional Reconstruction.[79] Hill denied the petition for a writ of habeas corpus, declaring the military's actions constitutional and Ord within his authority to arrest McCardle and hold him for trial by military commission. Placing states under military rule allowed military commanders to use commissions for citizen trials when civilian courts were thought inadequate.[80] McCardle quickly appealed to the Supreme Court under authority of the Habeas Corpus Act of February 5, 1867, which provided that all federal courts and judges could grant a writ of habeas corpus to any person restrained of liberty in violation of the Constitution or laws of the United States; the act had been designed to allow freedmen to seek the protection of federal courts.[81]

The Supreme Court began hearing the case in January 1868, and reports suggested that the court was sympathetic to McCardle's argument that the Reconstruction Acts violated the precedent set by *Milligan*.[82] House Republicans panicked in the wake of contentions by the Democratic press that the Court would use the McCardle case to strike down the Reconstruction Acts. After the Senate passed an unrelated amendment to the Judiciary Act of 1789, the House quietly tacked on a repeal of the Habeas Corpus Act of 1867, and the Senate accepted. Congress ultimately entered the act into law over a veto by President Johnson.[83] The Supreme Court had laid McCardle's case over to the next term as Congress and Johnson jockeyed over the Habeas Corpus Act. In the wake of the congressional decision to repeal the act, the high court announced in April 1869 that it lacked jurisdiction in the McCardle case, returning the editor to military authorities.[84] General Alvan Gillem dropped the charges against McCardle to avoid further contributing to his move toward martyrdom.[85]

As the Southern states recovered from their economic, political, and social Civil War wounds and attempted to reintegrate into the country they had seceded from, citizens of the South occupied one of two positions. Some sided with the federal government as it attempted to enforce new laws requiring the fair and equal treatment of newly freed slaves, whereas others chafed under what they perceived as oppressive oversight by a military and government that aimed to impose a drastic shift in Southern culture. Just as newspapers of prior eras evinced strong partisan views in accordance with their respective political affiliations, the Radical and Conservative editors of the postbellum era aggressively professed their beliefs either for or against Reconstruction policies while verbally assaulting their opponents.

Because of the conditions under which American newspapers developed, Hazel Dicken-Garcia has argued that partisanship was a firmly entrenched and accepted characteristic of the press through the end of the nineteenth century.[86] Therefore, although partisan editors and readers bristled at the expression of opposing views, they generally left each other alone, free to air their beliefs. Exceptions proved rare. A majority of the recorded attempts at suppression occurred during presidential Reconstruction and early in the congressional Reconstruction period, as residual from a more oppressive wartime military regime when seditious language was considered more dangerous.[87] Once high-ranking military officials withdrew from local commanders the authority to suspend publication of offending publications and impressed upon them the importance of a free press, few editors were subject to military sanction for views expressed in their publications. For most of the Reconstruction era, the only real threat the military posed to the press was the ability to withhold patronage from newspapers that espoused a disloyal position. During that time, most attempts at suppression came from angry Conservatives who threatened Radical editors and their families with physical violence.

Generally, the editors who faced suppression were the most obnoxious of their respective political stripes. Editors of the two Conservative newspapers mentioned in this chapter, the *Constitutional Eagle* and the *Vicksburg Times*, both found themselves in trouble after publishing a string of incendiary items over time and wearing down their targets. Other editors expressed similar views; Harris mentions four more anti-Reconstruction editors in Mississippi, but McCardle was the most vicious of them all.[88] Furthermore, McCardle's words not only were insulting but also clearly had influence over white readers in Mississippi and stood to hamper Reconstruction efforts there. Military officials worried that his rebellious spirit might even incite readers to insurrection.

Conversely, Swayze of the *American Union* sought to aid Reconstruction in Georgia, thereby making himself a nuisance to Conservatives in the state who perceived him as a threat to their way of life. Not only did he encourage African Americans to consider themselves equal and to partake in their newfound rights, but he also insulted the Southern gentlemen that Georgians considered noble and respectable; encouraged defiant, even violent behavior among his Radical readers; and sought protection from the U.S. government that would hamper the state's freedom and prosperity. Swayze was not the lone radical in Georgia; Elizabeth Nathans notes that about a half-dozen papers in Georgia were loyal to the Reconstruction cause.[89] None, though, were as incessantly vitriolic as Swayze.

Nonetheless, no type of suppressive tactics—legal or otherwise—proved particularly effective. Nathans argues that General Pope's attempts to control the tenor of the press in his military district failed, as his patronage policy did nothing to stem the tide of abuse that Democratic papers unleashed on Pope and his peers.[90] Nor did Major Peirce's raid on the *Eagle* office silence its editors for long. They quickly rebuilt and began publishing again, under the explicit protection of General Ord.[91] The ordeals of McCardle and Swayze similarly had the opposite effect of what their suppressors intended. McCardle's paper continued publishing with its characteristic vigor in his absence, and McCardle resumed his own torrent of abuse once his captors released him. Furthermore, McCardle's paper and others used his plight to elicit sympathy and support on behalf of the Conservative cause.[92] Swayze continued publication of his newspaper while in prison, complete with vitriolic rants against the Conservatives of his state. He swore that only death would silence him, and in that case, his paper would carry on under an editor as dedicated to the cause as he was. Although the Conservatives eventually ran him out of Georgia, Swayze continued speaking out against his foes there from afar, until a violent death did silence him.[93]

The partisan editors of the Reconstruction era were too impassioned and dedicated to their respective ideals to succumb to any entity that might threaten their freedom of speech or the press.

Notes

1. E. Merton Coulter, *The South during Reconstruction, 1865–1877* (Baton Rouge: Louisiana State University Press, 1947), 30–42; Eric Foner, *Reconstruction: America's Unfinished Revolution, 1863–1877* (New York: Harper and Row, 1988), 176–251.

2. Virginia had its own military district. The Second Military District encompassed the Carolinas. Georgia, Alabama, and Florida combined to form the Third Military District, while Arkansas and Mississippi made up the Fourth Military District. The Fifth Military District consisted of Texas and Louisiana. Tennessee had been readmitted to the Union in 1866 and was not placed under military rule. Coulter, *South during Reconstruction*, 43, 119; Foner, *Reconstruction*, 271–77; James E. Sefton, *The United States Army and Reconstruction, 1865–1877* (Baton Rouge: Louisiana State University Press, 1967), 113–14.

3. Coulter, *South during Reconstruction*, 119–20; Sefton, *United States Army and Reconstruction*, 110–11.

4. Georgia governor Rufus Bullock asked Congress to put the state back under military rule and force legislators to take an oath of loyalty to the Union. Foner, *Reconstruction*, 338; Elizabeth Studley Nathans, *Losing the Peace: Georgia Republicans and Reconstruction, 1865–1871* (Baton Rouge: Louisiana State University Press, 1968), 102, 150–66; Sefton, *United States Army and Reconstruction*, 186, 202–7; C. Mildred Thompson, *Reconstruction in Georgia: Economic, Social, Political, 1865–1872* (Gloucester, Mass.: Peter Smith, 1964), 255, 261–62.

5. Foner, *Reconstruction*, 452; Sefton, *United States Army and Reconstruction*, 198.

6. Coulter, *South during Reconstruction*, 340–65; Edmund L. Drago, *Hurrah for Hampton! Black Red Shirts in South Carolina during Reconstruction* (Fayetteville: University of Arkansas Press, 1998); Foner, *Reconstruction*, 425–44; J. Michael Martinez, *Carpetbaggers, Cavalry, and the Ku Klux Klan: Exposing the Invisible Empire during Reconstruction* (Lanham, Md.: Rowman and Littlefield, 2007); William Warren Rogers, "The Boyd Incident: Black Belt Violence during Reconstruction," *Civil War History* 21, no. 4 (1975): 309–29; Sefton, *United States Army and Reconstruction*, 220–29; James Smallwood, "When the Klan Rode: White Terror in Reconstruction Texas," *Journal of the West* 25, no. 4 (1986): 4–13; Frank J. Wetta, "'Bulldozing the Scalawags': Some Examples of the Persecution of Southern White Republicans in Louisiana during Reconstruction," *Louisiana History* 21, no. 1 (1980): 43–58; Lewis Nicholas Wynne and Milly St. Julien Vappie, "The Camilla Race Riot and the Failure of Reconstruction in Georgia," *Journal of South Georgia History* 16 (2004): 31–50.

7. Keith Ian Polakoff, *The Politics of Inertia: The Election of 1876 and the End of Reconstruction* (Baton Rouge: Louisiana State University Press, 1973); C. Vann Woodward, *Reunion and Reaction: The Compromise of 1877 and the End of Reconstruction* (Boston: Little, Brown, 1951).

8. Richard H. Abbott, *For Free Press and Equal Rights: Republican Newspapers in the Reconstruction South* (Athens: University of Georgia Press, 2004), 1–5; Hodding Carter, *Their Words Were Bullets: The Southern Press in War, Reconstruction, and Peace* (Athens: University of Georgia Press, 1969), 45–46; Donna L. Dickerson, "From Suspension to Subvention: The Southern Press during Reconstruction, 1863–1870," *American Journalism* 8, no. 4 (1991): 244–45; Donna L. Dickerson, "George T. Ruby: Reconstruction Politician/Journalist," *American Journalism* 15, no. 1 (1998): 53; Donna L. Dickerson, "Patronage and the Press: Gen. John Pope and Newspapers in Reconstruction Georgia," *Atlanta History* 36, no. 2 (1992): 39; Carl R. Osthaus, "From the Old South to the New South: The Editorial Career of William Tappan Thompson of the *Savannah Morning News*," *Southern Quarterly* 14 (April 1976): 248; Mark Wahlgren Summers, *The Press Gang: Newspapers and Politics, 1865–1878* (Chapel Hill: University of North Carolina Press, 1994), 208; Sarah Van V. Woolfolk, "The Political Cartoons of the Tuskaloosa *Independent Monitor* and Tuskaloosa *Blade*, 1867–1873," *Alabama Historical Quarterly* 27, no. 3–4 (1965): 140.

9. Coulter, *South during Reconstruction*, 287–88; Wendy Swanberg, "*Ex Parte McCardle* and the First Amendment during Reconstruction," in *A Press Divided: Newspaper Coverage of the Civil War*, ed. David B. Sachsman (New Brunswick, N.J.: Transaction, 2014), 335, 340; Thompson, *Reconstruction in Georgia*, 348.

10. Donna Lee Dickerson, *The Course of Tolerance: Freedom of the Press in Nineteenth-Century America* (New York: Greenwood Press, 1990), xii.

11. Carter, *Their Words Were Bullets*, 45.

12. Ted Tunnell, "Creating 'the Propaganda of History': Southern Editors and the Origins of *Carpetbagger* and *Scalawag*," *Journal of Southern History* 72, no. 4 (2006): 790.

13. John Kent Folmar, "Reaction to Reconstruction: John Forsyth and the Mobile *Advertiser and Register*, 1865–1867," *Alabama Historical Quarterly* 37, nos. 3–4 (1975): 245–64; Wilbur M. Hill, "Reconstruction in Richland Parish as Seen by the *Richland Beacon News*," *North Louisiana Historical Association Journal* 10, no. 1 (1979): 13–21; Osthaus, "From the Old South to the New South," 248; Woolfolk, "Political Cartoons," 140–65.

14. Edward J. Cashin Jr., "*The Banner of the South*, a Journal of the Reconstruction Era," *Richmond County History* 6, no. 1 (1974): 17; Mike Daniel, "The Arrest and Trial of Ryland Randolph, April–May 1868," *Alabama Historical Quarterly* 40, nos. 3–4 (1978): 127, 143; Dickerson, "Patronage and the Press," 32; Folmar, "Reaction to Reconstruction," 251; Stephanie C. Hardin, "Violence, Intimidation and Media Manipulation in Reconstruction Mobile, 1865–1876," *Gulf Coast Historical Review* 2 (1986): 39–52; Hill, "Reconstruction in Richland Parish," 17; Victor B. Howard, "The Kentucky Press and the Black Suffrage Controversy, 1865–1872," *Filson Club History Quarterly* 47 (1973): 215–37; Osthaus, "From the Old South to the New South," 247–50; Woolfolk, "Political Cartoons," 140, 151.

15. Folmar, "Reaction to Reconstruction"; Hill, "Reconstruction in Richland Parish."

16. Carter, *Their Words Were Bullets*, 45.

17. Ibid., 42–43; Frank Luther Mott, *American Journalism, a History: 1690–1960*, 3rd ed. (New York: Macmillan, 1962), 368; Margaret Ross, "Retaliation against Arkansas Newspaper Editors during Reconstruction," *Arkansas Historical Quarterly* 31, no. 2 (1972): 150.

18. James E. Bond, *No Easy Walk to Freedom: Reconstruction and the Ratification of the Fourteenth Amendment* (Westport, Conn.: Praeger, 1997), 240; Sefton, *United States Army and Reconstruction*, 149; Thompson, *Reconstruction in Georgia*, 177.

19. Abbott, *For Free Press and Equal Rights*, 6; Richard H. Abbott, "Jason Clarke Swayze, Republican Editor in Reconstruction Georgia," *Georgia Historical Quarterly* 79 (Summer 1995): 337–66; Richard H. Abbott, "The Republican Party Press in Reconstruction Georgia, 1867–1874," *Journal of Southern History* 61, no. 4 (1995): 725–60; Dickerson, "From Suspension to Subvention," 243–44; Dickerson, "George T. Ruby," 53; Dickerson, "Patronage and the Press," 31–33.

20. Observer, "Rode on a Rail," *Atlanta Intelligencer*, October 15, 1863; Justice, "J. Clarke Swayze: How Union Men Are Treated in the South," *Harper's Weekly*, January 5, 1867.

21. Justice, "J. Clarke Swayze."

22. Oscar K. Swayze, "Address to Craftsmen," box 3, folder 16, coll. 83, Oscar K. Swayze Papers, Kansas State Historical Society, Topeka; Justice, "J. Clarke Swayze"; "Prospectus of the *Topeka Blade*," *Topeka Blade*, August 13, 1873.

23. Justice, "J. Clarke Swayze"; *Topeka Blade*, June 7, 1875. See Special Orders, No. 19, Bureau of Refugees, Freedmen and Abandoned Lands, Office of the Assistant Commissioner for the State of Georgia, January 23, 1866, and Special Orders, No. 140, Bureau of Refugees, Freedmen and Abandoned Lands, Office of the Assistant

Commissioner for the State of Georgia, September 29, 1866, box 3, folder 18, coll. 83, Oscar K. Swayze Papers.

24. Justice, "J. Clarke Swayze."

25. J. Clarke Swayze, sworn affidavit submitted to H. C. Holcomb, clerk of the U.S. District Court for the Southern District of Georgia, December 5, 1866, box 3, folder 18, coll. 83, Oscar K. Swayze Papers.

26. "Arrested," *American Union* (Griffin, Ga.), December 14, 1866; Justice, "J. Clarke Swayze"; Swayze, sworn affidavit to Holcomb.

27. Swayze, sworn affidavit to Holcomb.

28. "Arrested"; Justice, "J. Clarke Swayze."

29. Clippings in box 3, folder 19, coll. 83, Oscar K. Swayze Papers: "Henry County Troubles," *Griffin (Ga.) Tri-Weekly Star*, October 23, 1866; "Our Boys—Pulaski," *Tri-Weekly Star*, December 11, 1866; "Military Arrests," *Macon (Ga.) Daily Telegraph*, December 12, 1866; "The Difficulty at Griffin and Its Results," *Americus (Ga.) Tri-Weekly Republican*, December 15, 1866; "Good," *Macon (Ga.) Journal and Messenger*, December 14, 1866; "Arrests in Griffin," *Journal and Messenger*, December 18, 1866; "Mr. J. C. Swayze," *Journal and Messenger*, January 12, 1867.

30. "Difference of Opinion," *Tri-Weekly Star*, February 14, 1867, and "The Martyr Swayze," *Journal and Messenger*, February 15, 1867, both in box 3, folder 19, coll. 83, Oscar K. Swayze Papers.

31. Justice, "J. Clarke Swayze." See also J. Clarke Swayze, "Southern Correspondence," *Bushnell (Ill.) Union Press*, March 28, 1867; "The Loyal Georgians' Greeting to Loyal Tennesseeans," *Nashville Daily Press and Times*, March 4, 1867; and J. Clarke Swayze, "Georgia Correspondence: How Union Men Are Treated," *Transcript* (unknown location), January 24, 1867, all in box 3, folder 19, coll. 83, Oscar K. Swayze Papers.

32. Abbott, "Jason Clarke Swayze," 344.

33. Per handwritten annotation by Swayze, the note came in an envelope with the return address G. A. & H. C. Cunningham, Griffin, Ga.; box 3, folder 18, coll. 83, Oscar K. Swayze Papers.

34. "Address to Craftsmen."

35. Ibid.

36. Swayze to Gov. Rufus Bullock, August 9, 1868, quoted in Abbott, "Jason Clarke Swayze," 349.

37. "Address to Craftsmen."

38. "Prospectus of the *Topeka Blade*."

39. J. Clarke Swayze, "Fair Notice," *American Union* (Macon, Ga.), May 7, 1869.

40. Thompson, *Reconstruction in Georgia*, 361.

41. Ibid., 361–94. See also Nathans, *Losing the Peace*, 131–35.

42. "The Situation," *American Union*, April 16, 1869. This issue contains a number of items listing "rebel outrages," including multiple items reporting the murder of a young churchgoing black mother by a teen of the Ku Klux Klan.

43. See multiple items in the *American Union* of April 23, May 7, May 14, and May 21, 1869. Bard's editorial is quoted in "Bard the Instigator of Assassination," *American Union*, April 23, 1869.

44. "Murder! Another Republican Killed!," ibid., April 23, 1869. See also "Hidden Fangs," ibid., May 7, 1869.

45. "The Blood-Hounds on a Fresh Scent," ibid., May 28, 1869.

46. "Censors," ibid., May 21, 1869.

47. "Hidden Fangs"; "Loyalty Exemplified," *American Union*, May 14, 1869.

48. "Censors."

49. *American Union*, May 7, 1869.

50. "Prospectus of the *Topeka Blade*."

51. "The Blood-Hounds on a Fresh Scent," and "Georgia, the Situation," *American Union*, May 28, 1869.

52. *Topeka Blade*, August 13, 1873; June 7, 1875; June 22, 1875.

53. *The Assassination of J. Clarke Swayze and Trial of John W. Wilson* (Topeka: Blade Printing Office, 1877).

54. Dickerson, "From Suspension to Subvention," 231.

55. Sefton, *United States Army and Reconstruction*, 55.

56. Dickerson, "From Suspension to Subvention," 233; Sefton, *United States Army and Reconstruction*, 55.

57. Quoted in Dickerson, "From Suspension to Subvention," 232–33.

58. Ibid., 233–34.

59. "Decided Nuisance," *Camden (Ark.) Constitutional Eagle*, quoted in *Arkansas Gazette* (Little Rock), August 13, 1867.

60. *Arkansas Gazette*, August 27, 1867.

61. Ross, "Retaliation against Arkansas Newspaper Editors," 150–52; Sefton, *United States Army and Reconstruction*, 151.

62. Dickerson, *Course of Tolerance*, 205–6; Dickerson, "From Suspension to Subvention," 234.

63. Dickerson, *Course of Tolerance*, 207; Dickerson, "From Suspension to Subvention," 236–37; Sefton, *United States Army and Reconstruction*, 149–50.

64. Dickerson, "From Suspension to Subvention," 237; Ross, "Retaliation against Arkansas Newspaper Editors," 153–54; Sefton, *United States Army and Reconstruction*, 151–52.

65. Dickerson, "From Suspension to Subvention," 237; James Wilford Garner, *Reconstruction in Mississippi* (Gloucester, Mass.: Peter Smith, 1964), 159, 168; William C. Harris, *The Day of the Carpetbagger: Republican Reconstruction in Mississippi* (Baton Rouge: Louisiana State University Press, 1979), 18; Sefton, *United States Army and Reconstruction*, 152.

66. Garner, *Reconstruction in Mississippi*, 168; Harris, *Day of the Carpetbagger*, 16; John Yoo, "*Merryman* and *Milligan* (and *McCardle*)," *Journal of Supreme Court History* 34, no. 3 (2009): 257.

67. *Vicksburg Times*, October 23, 1867.
68. *Vicksburg Times*, quoted in *Natchez (Miss.) Tri-Weekly Democrat*, November 12, 1867.
69. *Vicksburg Times*, November 2, 1867, quoted in *Shreveport (La.) South-western*, November 27, 1867.
70. "The Scoundrelism of Straps," *Vicksburg Times*, November 6, 1867, quoted in Harris, *Day of the Carpetbagger*, 16.
71. Harris, *Day of the Carpetbagger*, 16; Yoo, "*Merryman* and *Milligan*," 257.
72. Harris, *Day of the Carpetbagger*, 17.
73. "The Case of the Vicksburg Editor," *Charleston Daily News*, November 25, 1867.
74. *Memphis Public Ledger*, November 9, 1867.
75. *Vicksburg Times*, quoted in *Louisiana Democrat* (Alexandria), November 20, 1867, and *Winchester (Tenn.) Home Journal*, December 5, 1867.
76. Garner, *Reconstruction in Mississippi*, 168; Harris, *Day of the Carpetbagger*, 17; Stanley I. Kutler, "*Ex parte McCardle*: Judicial Impotency? The Supreme Court and Reconstruction Reconsidered," *American Historical Review* 72, no. 3 (April 1967): 839; Yoo, "*Merryman* and *Milligan*," 257.
77. Yoo, "*Merryman* and *Milligan*," 251–54.
78. Ibid., 254–55; Kutler, "*Ex parte McCardle*," 836.
79. Harris, *Day of the Carpetbagger*, 17.
80. Garner, *Reconstruction in Mississippi*, 168; Harris, *Day of the Carpetbagger*, 17; Kutler, "*Ex parte McCardle*," 839; Yoo, "*Merryman* and *Milligan*," 256–57.
81. Kutler, "*Ex parte McCardle*," 839; Yoo, "*Merryman* and *Milligan*," 256–57.
82. Yoo, "*Merryman* and *Milligan*," 257.
83. Kutler, "*Ex parte McCardle*," 840–42.
84. Ibid., 844.
85. Harris, *Day of the Carpetbagger*, 18.
86. Hazel Dicken-Garcia, *Journalistic Standards in Nineteenth-Century America* (Madison: University of Wisconsin Press, 1989), 97.
87. See Dickerson, *Course of Tolerance*, 147–81, 189–200.
88. Harris, *Day of the Carpetbagger*, 16.
89. Nathans, *Losing the Peace*, 52.
90. Ibid., 52–53.
91. Ross, "Retaliation against Arkansas Newspaper Editors," 153.
92. Harris, *Day of the Carpetbagger*, 17–18; Swanberg, "*Ex Parte McCardle*," 333–57.
93. *Topeka Blade*, June 7, 1875, and June 22, 1875.

PART 2

THE FIGHT FOR FREEDOM OF EXPRESSION

6. THE ROCKY ROAD TO TRUTH AS A DEFENSE

LIBEL CONSTRUCTION IN THE NINETEENTH CENTURY

SANDRA DAVIDSON

Truth, the illustrious goal for journalists, has a tarnished history as a libel defense. This chapter explores how truth as a defense took hold in the United States in the nineteenth century.

Nineteenth-century law on free expression is surprisingly little explored. In 1986, Michael T. Gibson observed, "Except for a few studies of isolated incidents concerning the first amendment, scholars jump from the Sedition Act of 1798 to the Espionage Act of 1917 and Justice Holmes's 'clear and present danger' opinions of 1919, paying little, if any, attention to the intervening period."[1] Gibson's observation seems generally true nearly thirty years later.[2] He lists sixteen "early state constitutions that made truth a defense in libel actions"[3] but does not dwell on libel cases. By the end of the nineteenth century, at least twenty-eight states had constitutions making truth a defense.[4] The U.S. Supreme Court in 1964 enumerated many constitutional provisions.[5] Looking at the development of truth as a defense in the nineteenth century first requires a brief look back for context.

THE BACKDROP

Certainly, some British authors paid tribute to truth. John Milton in his *Areopagitica* (1645) wrote of truth, "Let her and Fals[e]hood grapple; who ever knew Truth put to the wors[e], in a free and open encounter."[6] But British courts clobbered truth in libel cases. Truth was no defense, and that doctrine came ashore with British settlers in America, as did the doctrine of seditious libel—the crime of criticizing government. These two doctrinal imports posed a danger for journalists.

Truth as a defense had to progress from a deep hole before gaining ascendency. Early on, truth was considered an "aggravating circumstance": "The greater the truth the greater the libel."[7] Here is the logic: libel law's purpose was to keep the peace, which meant, in large part, averting duels. Add the assumption that if a criticism were true, then it would be more likely to inflame than if it were false. Thus, true criticism would be more likely to provoke revenge and disrupt peace.[8]

But an early seditious libel precedent, the prosecution of colonial printer John Peter Zenger in 1735, showed promise for truth as a defense. In his *New York Weekly Journal*, Zenger published an anonymous piece criticizing the Crown's New York governor, calling him a tyrant and oppressor. When Zenger refused to name the anonymous critic, prosecutors pursued Zenger. At trial, Zenger's lawyer, Andrew Hamilton, conceded that Zenger published the newspaper, as charged.[9] But Hamilton asked jurors to consider the publication's truth, despite the prosecution saying not to do so. Hamilton said,

> I hope it is not our bare printing and publishing a paper that will make it a libel. . . . [W]e are charged with . . . publishing "a certain false, malicious, seditious and scandalous libel." This word *false* must have some meaning, or else how came it there?[10]

He closed with these words: "The question before the Court and you, Gentlemen of the jury, is not . . . the cause of one poor printer. . . . It is the cause of liberty." The Crown judge, however, then instructed the jurors that the only question they could decide was whether Zenger published the words.[11] The more important question of whether the words constituted seditious libel would be left up to the judge.[12] Nonetheless, the jury disregarded the judge's instructions, acquitting Zenger within minutes.[13]

U.S. Supreme Court justice Clarence Thomas called Zenger's case "the earliest and most famous American experience with freedom of the press." Zenger's acquittal, he said, "set the colonies afire for its example of a jury refusing to convict a defendant of seditious libel against Crown authorities."[14] But while Zenger's acquittal quelled some prosecutors' ardor for prosecuting journalists, it did not establish truth as a defense, and neither casting off the colonial yoke in 1776 nor ratifying the First Amendment of the U.S. Constitution in 1791 stopped seditious libel prosecutions.

The First Amendment declared that "Congress shall make no law . . . abridging the freedom of speech, or of the press . . ." But that declaration did not stop the second president of the United States, John Adams, and his followers from passing the Alien and Sedition Acts of 1798. Adams's targets for suppression included Thomas Jefferson and his followers.[15] The acts' provision most alarming for journalists criminalized publishing "any false, scandalous or malicious . . . writings" against the U.S. government, president, or Congress to bring them into "contempt or disrepute."[16] In sweet revenge, Jefferson defeated Adams for the presidency in 1800. By 1802, all of the Alien and Sedition Acts' provisions either expired or were repealed.[17] The U.S. Supreme Court would later say, "Although the Sedition Act was never tested in this Court, the attack upon its validity has carried the day in the court of history."[18]

CROSWELL, HAMILTON, AND DENNIE

Early in the nineteenth century, in *People v. Croswell* (1804),[19] seditious libel stung journalist Harry Croswell. The *Wasp*, his newspaper, accused third U.S. president Thomas Jefferson of paying a man to call first president George Washington "a traitor, a robber, and a perjurer" and to call second president John Adams a "hoary-headed incendiary." The indictment characterized Croswell as "a malicious and seditious man, of a depraved mind and wicked and diabolical disposition," who "deceitfully, wickedly, and maliciously" intended to "scandalize" and "villify" Jefferson and to "wickedly and seditiously" disturb the peace (337–38). Convicted, Croswell appealed to New York's highest court.

Croswell's attorney, Alexander Hamilton (not to be confused with Peter Zenger's attorney, Andrew Hamilton), argued for truth as a defense. He said truth had been a defense in "ancient times." It was part of "common law," or judge-made law, which set "ancient precedents." But what had happened to truth as a defense? Hamilton said, "The opposite doctrine, which mentions that a writing is equally libelous, whether true or false, originated in a polluted source, the despotic tribunal of the Star Chamber" (343–44).

The infamous, juryless Star Chamber's name derived from stars painted on its ceiling.[20] The U.S. Supreme Court would later say of the Star Chamber, "That curious institution, which flourished in the late sixteenth and early seventeenth centuries, was of mixed executive and judicial character, and characteristically departed from common-law traditions. For those reasons, and because it specialized in trying 'political' offenses, the Star Chamber has for centuries

President Thomas Jefferson felt the sting of criticism in the *Wasp*, published by Harry Croswell. Jefferson retaliated, and Croswell felt the sting of prosecution for seditious libel. But Croswell avoided jail. The brilliance of Andrew Hamilton's advocacy for the concept of truth as a defense ultimately prevailed, although Hamilton did not live to see that day. Mead Art Museum, Amherst College, Amherst, Massachusetts.

symbolized disregard of basic individual rights."[21] People who suffered its brutal justice perhaps "saw stars" from being tortured. Several American courts have quoted this language: "The court of star chamber in England, once exercised the power of cutting off the ears, branding the foreheads, and slitting the noses of the libellers of important personages."[22] Supreme Court justice Hugo Black said this "ill-famed" court's "arbitrary procedures and gross excesses brought forth many of the safeguards included in our Constitution." Parliament abolished the Star Chamber in 1641.[23] Still, that court's grim legacy haunted the early nineteenth century.

Hamilton, in *People v. Croswell*, denounced both the Star Chamber and the judge in Zenger's case for trying to abolish truth as a defense. "The Star Chamber had no authority to alter the common law," he said. "Our ancestors, when they emigrated to this country, brought with them the common law, as their inheritance and birthright." And the judge's decision in *Zenger* "was of no great authority" because it displayed "no great research or temper . . . , and the decision was reprobated by the public" (344). The prosecution took an opposite view, contending that "the law is well settled, that, on an indictment for a libel, the truth cannot be given in evidence; and this rule of law rests upon the most solid grounds, notwithstanding the popular and captivating impression of the contrary doctrine" (348–49).

Hamilton replied, arguing for protection of truthful publications. The "brief summary" of his oration in the reported case includes this:

> The liberty of the press consisted in publishing with impunity, truth with good motives, and for justifiable ends. . . . If this right was not permitted to exist in vigor and in exercise, good men would become silent; corruption and tyranny would go on, step by step, in usurpation, until, at last, nothing that was worth speaking, or writing, or acting for, would be left in our country. (352–53)

Hamilton advocated jury power to truly decide libel cases, not just to decide if words were published. He contended that "to confine the jury to the mere question of publication . . . is calculated to render nugatory the function of the jury; enabling the court to make a libel of any writing whatsoever, the most innocent or commendable" (360). He wanted a new trial for Croswell because the jury was permitted only to determine if words had been published and because the defendant was not permitted to present evidence of truth (363–64).

Despite powerful oratory, Hamilton persuaded only half of the four judges, a stalemate. Jurors could consider evidence of truth or falsity only to determine whether the defendant had a malicious intent to damage a reputation (377). In short, truth did not prohibit a libel conviction if the defendant acted with malicious intent to damage reputation. To be not guilty, the defendant must have published with good motives, or good intent, even if the words were true. This viewpoint included elements of invasion of privacy as well as libel:

> And what can be a more important circumstance than the truth of the charge, to determine the goodness of the motive in making it, if it be a charge against the competency or purity . . . of a candidate for public favor, or a charge of actions in which the community have an interest, and are deeply concerned?

> . . . At the same time, this doctrine will not go to tolerate libels upon private character, . . . or to justify exposing to the public eye one's personal defects or misfortunes. (377–78)

Like Hamilton, these judges blamed the Star Chamber for the doctrine that truth was no defense (380, 390).[24] They also made clear that the English people disliked this doctrine, saying, "It was no doubt considered at the time as an oppressive innovation; but opposition must have been feeble to a court whose action and whose terrors were then at the greatest height" (385).

In other words, these judges said, in effect, "might meant right" in jolly old England: the Star Chamber had physical power to assert that truth was no defense, and nobody had the wherewithal to resist. With the Star Chamber's demise, however, British courts could turn back to common law, where truth *was* a defense. But the results were spotty, with truth sometimes a defense, sometimes not (386–90).

A bright note in the case analysis of Judge Kent, one of the four judges deciding *Croswell*, is this: "I have . . . shown that the rule denying permission to give the truth in evidence was not an original rule of the common law. The ancient statutes and precedents, which are the only memorials to which we can resort, all place the crime on its falsity" (390). Judges Kent and Thompson concluded that Croswell should receive a new trial and be "entitled to give in evidence . . . the truth of the libel" (394).

But two judges (Lewis writing the opinion, Livingston concurring) disagreed (411). Judge Lewis slammed Croswell and Hamilton, saying, "A petitioner, charged with a libelous and malicious publication, has called forth, in his defense, the gratuitous exertion of the choicest talents that grace this bar" (394). He then countered the conclusions of Judge Kent: "I now pronounce, with confidence, that it ever has been invariably, and still is, the law of England that the truth cannot be given in evidence, as a justification in a criminal prosecution for a libel, at common law" (395). After writing his analysis of case law, he declared, "I believe I have noticed all the leading authorities on the subject" (395–402). Then, after acknowledging that "popular sentiment" was against his view that truth could not be given in evidence, he continued:

> I am free to confess that, before I had fully considered the subject, the inclination of my own mind was strong that way. But on reflection I have discarded the opinion, satisfied that truth may be as dangerous to society as falsehood, when exhibited in a way calculated to disturb the public tranquility, or to excite to a breach of the peace. (402–3)

With New York's highest court evenly splitting in February 1804, truth as a defense remained in limbo in New York—but not for long. *People v. Croswell* notes, at the end of the published case, what happened next. In April 1804, on the last day of the New York legislature's session, a bill titled "An Act Relative to Libels" was introduced. It failed to pass, but a new bill, introduced during the following session, passed unanimously and became law in April 1805.[25]

This law, quoted at the end of *People v. Croswell*, overturned the doctrine that juries could determine only whether a defendant had published allegedly libelous material: "[T]he jury . . . shall not be directed . . . by the court . . . to find the defendant guilty, merely on the proof of the publication by the defendant, of the matter charged to be libelous" (412). Even more important, *the new law established truth as a defense*: "[I]n every prosecution for . . . any libel, it shall be lawful for the defendant . . . to give in evidence, in his defense, the truth of the matter contained in the publication charged as libelous." However, the law also said that evidence of truth "shall not be a justification, unless, on the trial, it shall be further made satisfactorily to appear that the matter charged as libelous was published with good motives and for justifiable ends." The law also limited imprisonment to eighteen months (412).

Truth as a defense had scored a victory in the New York legislature in April 1805. Then in August, "in consequence of this declaratory statute," Croswell's court unanimously awarded him a new trial. But he was never retried.[26] Sadly, Croswell's attorney did not live to see the legislative or judicial victories. On July 11, 1804, Hamilton and Aaron Burr, both from New York, dueled with pistols in Weehawken, New Jersey. Burr killed Hamilton.[27]

Hamilton and Burr were political giants. Hamilton was an author of *The Federalist Papers*, and his essays profoundly influenced the U.S. Supreme Court.[28] He was also President George Washington's secretary of the treasury while Thomas Jefferson was secretary of state.[29] Then, the presidential election of 1800 saw a protracted battle between Jefferson and Burr. Jefferson won and Burr became vice president. Hamilton's influence contributed significantly to Burr's loss.[30] Bad blood brewed. Historian Alison L. LaCroix calls the ensuing "affair of honor" the "most famous duel in the history of the United States":

> [I]t was the culmination of decades of political and personal animosity between the two leaders. It was also a particularly nineteenth-century moment that contained elements of public and private, honor and virtue, and legality and illegality, all of which existed in uneasy tension at a transitional moment in the history of American law.[31]

Political giant Alexander Hamilton, whose accomplishments include writing much of *The Federalist Papers* and serving as George Washington's secretary of the treasury, arguably did more to advance the cause of truth as a defense in seditious libel cases than anybody else. Tragically, Aaron Burr, who at the time was the U.S. vice president, fatally shot Hamilton in a duel. Library of Congress Prints and Photographs Division, Washington, D.C.

Vice President Burr was indicted for murder in New York and New Jersey[32] but ultimately stood trial for treason, in 1807 after leaving office, for allegedly trying to get some new western territories to separate from the United States. He was acquitted.[33] Hamilton's legacy includes movement toward truth as a libel defense—and citation in more than nineteen hundred U.S. cases.[34]

In 1805, *Croswell* and the defense of truth played a part in a Pennsylvania case, *Respublica v. Dennie.*[35] The libel prosecution of Joseph Dennie resulted from his attacks on democracy as a form of government. The indictment, in florid language, perhaps sounded more like a charge of incitement than libel:

> The defendant stands indicted, as a factious and seditious person, of a wicked mind, and unquiet and turbulent disposition and conversation, seditiously, maliciously and wilfully intending . . . to bring into contempt and hatred, the independence of the United States, . . . to excite popular discontent and dissatisfaction . . . , to molest, disturb and destroy the peace and public tranquility of the said *United States*, . . . to condemn the principles of the revolution, and revile, depreciate and scandalize the characters of the revolutionary patriots and statesmen, to endanger, subvert and totally destroy the republican constitutions and free governments of the said *United States* . . . (268)[36]

What language could be so vile? According to the indictment, Dennie's weekly Philadelphia newspaper, *Port Folio*, which has been called a "leading periodical" of its time,[37] "falsely, maliciously, factiously and seditiously" printed language such as, "A *democracy* is scarcely tolerable . . . and its powers are *unpropitious*." He spoke of the "futility" of democracy, saying it was "*wicked* at *Athens*, . . . *bad* in *Sparta*, and *worse* in *Rome*." Democracy in France "terminated in *despotism*"; in England, it was "rejected with the utmost *loathing and abhorrence*"; and in the United States, it was on trial and would result in "*civil war, desolation and anarchy*." He said "no good man but shudders at its *miseries*" and called democracy "*radically contemptible and vicious*" and an "example of what the villainy of some men can devise" (268). Clearly, Dennie was engaging in political speech, and, just as clearly, the prosecutor did not want to hear him.

In deciding this case, the Pennsylvania Supreme Court was bound by its state constitution, which declared that "printing presses shall be *free* to every person" examining the proceedings of any governmental branch and that no law could restrain that right. Furthermore, the constitution called free expression of opinions an "invaluable" right. But while all citizens could "*freely* speak, write or print on any subject," they were "*responsible for the abuse of that liberty*" (269).

This language advocating free speech in Pennsylvania's constitution dated back to 1790.[38] And what about truth as a defense? The constitution embodied that concept, decreeing that in libel indictments involving publications "investigating the official conduct" of public officials "or where the matter published is *proper for public information*," the truth could be "given in evidence." Furthermore, the constitution stated that the jury had the "right to determine the law and the facts," thus rejecting the doctrine that the jury could determine only if words had been published.[39]

The *Dennie* case said:

> Thus it is evident, that . . . every citizen may freely speak, write or print *on any subject*, but is accountable for the *abuse* of that privilege. . . . But "if one uses the weapon of truth" *wantonly*, for disturbing the peace of families, he is "guilty of a libel." (269–70)

For this principle, *Dennie* cited Hamilton in *Croswell*.[40]

And who should decide if an abuse of liberty occurred? The jury (270–71).

Dennie made clear that "[i]t is no infraction of the law to publish temperate investigation of the nature and forms of government." On the other hand, publications "plainly accompanied with a *criminal intent* . . . totally to unhinge the minds of the citizens, and to produce popular discontent," are "subversive of all government and good order." And here *Dennie* cited Hamilton in *Croswell* for the principle that "liberty of the press consists in publishing the truth, from *good motives* and for *justifiable ends*" (270).[41]

The bottom line for the jury was this:

> [I]f the consciences of the jury shall be clearly satisfied that the publication was *seditiously*, *maliciously*, and *wilfully* aimed at the independence of the *United States*, the constitution thereof, or of this state, they should convict the defendant. If on the other hand, the production was *honestly* meant to inform the public mind, and warn them against supposed dangers in society, though the subject may have been treated *erroneously*, . . . they should acquit the defendant. (271)

The verdict in *Dennie*: "not guilty" (271).

Thomas Jefferson's faithful political allies in Pennsylvania were behind the arrest of Federalist Joseph Dennie, just as Jefferson's allies in New York had been behind the arrest of Federalist Harry Croswell.[42] Jefferson supported suppression of his enemies. As one commentator noted,

> According to Jefferson's myth . . . Jefferson opposed the Alien and Sedition Acts because they restrained free speech. This perception of Jefferson's position does not comport with reality, but the propaganda surrounding the 1800 campaign assured that Jefferson and his . . . allies would be remembered for advocating extreme libertarian protections for expression.[43]

The political game in the late eighteenth and early nineteenth centuries was rough-and-tumble, to say the least.

CONSTITUTIONAL PROVISIONS AND A COUPLE OF CASE FUMBLES

Pennsylvania's legislators were the first to suppress suppression by enacting a constitutional provision embodying truth as a defense.[44] The year was 1790, the year before ratification of the First Amendment. In 1792, two more states enacted constitutional provisions: Delaware and Kentucky picked up Pennsylvania's language establishing truth as a defense when publications were investigating "official conduct" of public officials or "matters . . . proper for public information."[45] In 1796, Tennessee adopted truth as a defense for investigations into "official conduct" only.[46]

Twenty years passed before more states embodied truth as a defense in their constitutions. Indiana in 1816 picked up the language restricting truth as a defense to cases involving the "watchdog" function of the press.[47] In 1817, Mississippi became the first state to broaden the protection of truth, saying, "In *all* prosecutions or indictments for libels, the truth may be given in evidence."[48] The following year, 1818, Connecticut enacted that same broad language,[49] but Illinois enacted the more restrictive language used by Pennsylvania, Delaware, and Kentucky.[50] In 1820, Maine also enacted restrictive language: "the truth . . . may be given in evidence" but only "in prosecutions for any publications respecting official conduct" or candidates' qualifications or "matter . . . proper for public information."[51] But that year Missouri enacted broad protection: "In all *suits and prosecutions* for libel, the truth thereof may be given in evidence."[52] Thus, Missouri clearly mandated truth for both civil suits and criminal prosecutions.

Nine of the ten states included language that said "the jury may determine the law and the facts, under the direction of the court," with Maine using a variation on that same theme.[53] The sentiment was good, but in *State v. Jeandell & Vincent* (1854),[54] involving the *Blue Hen's Chicken* newspaper, Delaware's Supreme Court pointed out how problematic that putative right of the jury to declare the law was in practice:

> But to say that the jury are judges of the law in the same sense as they are judges of the facts, would be an exceedingly dangerous principle. The law of one jury might not be the law of another jury; and if they erred through ignorance or otherwise, there would be no correction. If the judge err in misstating a legal principle, the remedy is easy; by motion for a new trial or other proceeding to review his principles. (484)

The court made clear that juries as "judges of the law" were particularly dangerous in criminal cases—and then totally rejected that principle:

> There is no such principle, and never has been, in Delaware. The question . . . is not new in our courts; it is as old as the courts are; but as a legal principle it has been repudiated and turned out of court, as often as it has been presented; and often with much less courtesy than we have thought proper to treat it. (484)

In both criminal and civil cases of libel, truth as a defense had failures early on. For example, truth took a bludgeoning in 1825 in *Commonwealth v. Blanding*,[55] in which the Massachusetts Supreme Court ruled that truth was no defense in a criminal libel case. The *Providence (R.I.) Gazette* had published derogatory statements about an innkeeper. The newspaper's attorney argued vociferously for truth as a defense. He criticized British law (307). He invoked Hamilton's viewpoint in *People v. Croswell* (308). He called the view that "a libel, though true, is criminal, because it tends to a breach of the peace" a "gross fiction" (309). All to no avail.

The Massachusetts Supreme Court said "the gist" of libel is "it tends to provoke a breach of the peace." The court also said, "There are certain cases in which the defendant in a prosecution for a libel may acquit himself by showing an honest purpose and *proving the truth* of his allegations" (311–12).[56] But the "general principle" of Massachusetts's law was that "it is immaterial to the character of a libel as a public offence, whether the matter of it be true or false" (312).

The court was unapologetic in announcing that truth was no defense in libel prosecutions. Quite the contrary, the court presented a passionate defense for this position:

> No state of society would be more deplorable than that which would admit an indiscriminate right in every citizen to arraign the conduct of every other, before the public, in newspapers, handbills or other modes of publication, not only for crimes, but for faults, foibles, deformities of mind or person, even admitting all such allegations to be true. (312–13)

However, even this court recognized that "there may be cases where (there being no other mode by which great mischief can be warded off from the public) a newspaper communication, made with the sole view of preserving the citizens from injury to their life or health, would be justifiable" (312). The court gave this example: "an apothecary selling and distributing poison in the form of medicine." But the court called this "an extreme case" (320). So, generally, truth was no defense.

In 1827, in *Root v. King & Verplanck*,[57] truth as a defense was *available* but did not work in a civil libel case brought by New York lieutenant governor Erastus Root. An Albany newspaper, the *New York American*, said, "The facts are these: we speak only what we saw." Then it described Root's condition as he presided over the New York Senate:

> Lieutenant-Governor Root, holding on to each arm of his chair, looked round with inflamed face, with blood-shot eyes, and half open mouth, and with an expression altogether so stolid and drunken, as in any other situation . . . could not have failed to excite the derision of all present.
>
> . . . [B]y the all-important aid of the arms of his chair and his desk in front, he did rise, and stood for a moment, as if in preparation, silent before several hundreds of his fellow-citizens, an object, from his appearance and manner, we will venture to say, of loathing and disgust to every unprejudiced man among them; unwashed, unshaven, haggard, the tobacco juice trickling from the corners of his mouth to be wiped away with his coat sleeve; with unsteady footing, this second officer of the great State of New York, commenced his address to the Senate. (614–15)

Root filed a civil suit for libel.

Did a description of how a *public officer* performed his *public duties* receive protection? No. What was the root cause of the *Root* decision? The fault lay with the jury, perhaps, and not with the law. Or perhaps the judge's instructions confused the jury? The New York appellate court said,

> The judge addressed the jury at considerable length, and with much ability. He informed them, that if the publication admitted to have been made by the defendants held the plaintiff up to reproach or disgrace, either in his public or private character, it was a libel. . . . He stated that *the publication was libelous*, and the contrary had not been contended for on the part of the defendants. That they asserted its truth. *He instructed the jury, that, if true, this amounted to a perfect answer and bar to the plaintiff's suit*, though the defendants' motives might have been ever so malicious and vindictive. (618)[58]

Also, the judge commented on the evidence:

> The judge . . . stated that there was much contradictory testimony; that the witnesses were all credible and respectable. He commented on the testimony, and then called the attention of the jury to the question of intoxication—concluding, that if the plaintiff was intoxicated, the defendants must be acquitted; if not, the plaintiff was entitled to a verdict. (619)

The jury ruled for Root (620). After lengthy analysis of libel law, the appellate court refused to grant the newspaper a new trial (637). "Was the verdict against evidence?" the appellate court asked and then continued, "Whether the libel was true or not, was the question before the jury. The evidence was contradictory. It was the province of the jury to weigh it; and the court ought not to set aside the verdict unless in a clear case" (636). So perhaps the law on truth as a defense in New York was strong, but so was the plaintiff's attorney.

Although the watchdog press arguably got muzzled in *Root,* truth as a defense was gaining a real foothold. As mentioned earlier, by 1820, ten states had passed constitutional provisions recognizing truth as a defense.[59] More than a decade passed before another state enacted a constitutional provision. Michigan in 1835 permitted truth as a defense in "all" libel prosecutions, with this limitation: "The matter . . . was published with good motives and for justifiable ends."[60] The following year, 1836, Arkansas passed a provision harkening back to older, more restrictive language establishing truth as a defense when publications investigate "official conduct" of public officials or "matters . . . proper for public information."[61] In 1838, Florida enacted a constitutional provision similar to Michigan's, with truth a defense in "all" libel prosecutions if "published with good motives and for justifiable ends."[62]

Rhode Island in 1843 provided truth as a defense "in all trials for libel, both civil and criminal, . . . unless published from malicious motives."[63] Thus Rhode Island broadened its truth-as-a-defense horizon to include not just criminal prosecutions but "*all trials,*" explicitly adding "civil" trials.

New Jersey in 1844 passed a longer constitutional provision, extolling every person's right to "freely speak, write, and publish" and forbidding laws restricting free speech or press; truth was a defense in all libel prosecutions if "the matter . . . was published with good motives and for justifiable ends."[64] Iowa in 1846 enacted language almost identical to that in New Jersey's constitution, except Iowa dropped "the jury shall have the right to determine the law and the fact."[65] In 1848, Wisconsin passed a constitution almost identical to New Jersey's,[66] as did California in 1849.[67] So did Ohio in 1851, but, like Iowa, the state dropped "the jury shall have the right to determine the law and the fact."[68]

In 1859, Kansas said that press liberty is "inviolate" and that all may "freely" express themselves, "being responsible for the abuse." Of note, Kansas said that in "all *civil or criminal*" libel actions, "truth may be given in evidence": this, like Rhode Island's law, made clear that truth was a defense in civil suits, not just in criminal prosecutions. Kansas did require "justifiable ends" but did not mention "good motives."[69] In 1864, Nevada also said truth was a defense in "all civil or criminal" libel actions but required both "justifiable ends" and "good motives."[70]

In 1876, Colorado, similarly to Kansas and Nevada, provided that "in all suits and prosecutions for libel the truth thereof may be given in evidence"; "suits" clearly added truth as a defense in civil cases.[71] That same year, 1876, Texas used language similar to Colorado's on the jury determining law and facts "under the direction of the court" but limited truth as a defense to "prosecutions" for papers investigating public officials' conduct or matters "proper for public information."[72]

Over a decade later, in 1889, Montana picked up the broader language of truth as a defense "in all suits and prosecutions of libel."[73] That same year, North Dakota also used broad language of truth as a defense in "all civil and criminal" libel trials but throttled back somewhat by saying truth could only be "a sufficient defense when the matter is published with good motives and for justifiable ends."[74] The next year, 1890, Wyoming picked up North Dakota's framework for truth as a defense but differed in saying "good intent" instead of "good motives."[75] Montana, North Dakota, and Wyoming all mandated that the jury determine the law and facts "under the direction of the court."

South Carolina, in 1895, limited truth as a defense to "prosecutions" for libel and knocked out the phrase "under the direction of the court," simply saying, "[T]he jury shall be the judge of the law and the facts."[76] Two years later, in 1897, New York added back "under the direction of the court" language when stating that the jury "shall determine the law and the fact."[77] More important, New York, like South Carolina, did not mention truth as a defense in civil libel cases. Instead, New York allowed evidence of truth only in "all criminal prosecutions" and then only if "published with good motives and justifiable ends."[78]

In short, these twenty-eight states addressing truth as a defense in their constitutions did so with varying degrees of grace—but at least they made the effort. This left courts to fill in the gaps. And the courts, by and large, did their job.

THE LAST HALF OF THE CENTURY: MOSTLY GOOD NEWS FOR TRUTH

Even when plaintiffs prevailed, the principle of truth as a defense could remain intact. For example, in California in *Thrall v. Smiley* (1858),[79] two newspapers published a "card" submitted by George Smiley, a former patient not enthralled by Dr. Thrall, a dentist. Smiley's smile was destroyed, he claimed, when the dentist broke Smiley's front teeth while extracting a molar. The card said, "The public are hereby cautioned against employing the professional services of the above-named individual, whom I hereby denounce as a miserable bungler, and a disgrace on the profession he presumes to follow" (530). The dentist sued Smiley and won. Unfortunately, Smiley did not "aver the truth" of the matter (531). Form matters. The California Supreme Court said,

> The answer of the defendant, George Smiley, does not contain a justification of the publication. To constitute a justification, the answer should have averred the truth of the defamatory matter charged. It was not sufficient to set up facts which only tended to establish the truth of such matter. . . . The injury . . . may have been occasioned by the unskillfulness of the plaintiff; still, under the answer, it could not justify the sweeping denunciation that he was "a miserable bungler, and a disgrace" to his profession. (536)

Nearly a decade before this case, California had enacted its constitutional provision establishing truth as a defense.[80]

In 1860, Ohio's Supreme Court upheld a defendant's loss while also embracing truth as a defense. *Gazette Co. v. Timberlake*[81] started when the *Cincinnati Gazette* published this:

> SWINDLING—Amongst the arrests at the Ninth Street station-house yesterday, appeared the name of C. L. Timberlake, who is charged with petty larceny; he having, according to the statement made, bought a land warrant of a lady for ninety-five dollars, and when the lady had signed the documents making the warrant over to him, he gave her seventy-six dollars, and would give her no more. (549)

Timberlake indeed had been arrested. The next day the newspaper published the story, and later that same day the police court acquitted Timberlake. He then sued for libel and won (550–51). The Ohio Supreme Court opined that "a full, fair and impartial report of a judicial trial, had in open court, . . . may be published with impunity." But the question was whether this privilege extended to "the publication of mere preliminary proceedings, such as an ex parte affidavit, made before a proper officer, with a view to the arrest of the party, thereby falsely charged with crime" (552). The court said no, but the court also paid homage to the press and truth, saying, "We are by no means disposed to underestimate the importance of a free press. . . . But, in this case, there is no claim that the charge against the plaintiff below, was, in fact, *true*. The defense rests wholly on the claim of privilege" (555).[82] The court made clear that "such publication can only be justified by showing the truth of the charge" (556).

In 1877, interpretation of Kansas law on truth as a defense fell to the Kansas Supreme Court in *Castle v. Houston*.[83] The *Leavenworth Daily Commercial* printed that the Kansas legislature would be investigating the state's insurance department and that a "cadaverous-looking" and "completely played-out insurance agent" (Castle) had instigated the investigation by crying "fraud"—in hopes of unseating the current superintendent of insurance and becoming a clerk (418–19). In the ensuing libel trial, the judge instructed the jury that "the fact of the language being true, is not alone an answer to the charge, but can only be shown in mitigation of damages" and that "it is not a defense simply to show the truth of the matter published, but the party must go further, and show . . . that he acted with good motives and for a justifiable end" (420).

The Kansas Supreme Court explained, "It was at one time the rule of the common law, that the truth of the charge . . . could not be given in evidence in a criminal prosecution" (420).[84] But the "wise framers" of the Kansas Constitution "modified the tyrannical and harsh rule of the common law as stated in the star-chamber of England" (422).[85] And the Kansas legislature then followed with a statute providing that "in all prosecutions or indictments for libel, the truth thereof may be given in evidence to the jury, and if it appears to them that the matter as charged as libelous was true, and was published with good motives and for justifiable ends, the defendant shall be acquitted" (422–23).[86]

Here the Kansas court drew an important distinction between *criminal* and *civil* libel cases. For criminal cases, the court said, "There are many good and sufficient reasons why a publisher of a statement, true in fact, yet given to the public with a malicious design to create mischief, should be amenable to the criminal laws, and yet not be liable in a civil action" (424). So truth might not be a complete defense in criminal cases. And the court looked at the Kansas civil code and concluded that "under the code, the truth is a full justification in a civil action." Furthermore, the view that the constitution requires "justifiable ends" in civil cases "is not in accordance with the spirit or the letter of that instrument" (426). The Kansas Constitution says, "[I]n all civil or criminal actions for libel, truth may be given in evidence to the jury, and if it should appear that the alleged libelous matter was published for justifiable ends, the accused party shall be acquitted."[87] (The constitution does not mention "good motives.") The court focused on the language that said "the *accused* party shall be *acquitted*," pointing out that this language applies to criminal prosecutions (427).

Fortunately for the defendant, this was a civil suit, and truth alone was a "full justification." The trial judge "misdirected the jury in a very material point," the Kansas Supreme Court said. The defendant received a new trial (428–29).

In 1881 in *Sullings v. Shakespeare*,[88] the Michigan Supreme Court echoed the Kansas Supreme Court's language, saying,

> A considerable number of objections assume that if an article is maliciously libelous, its truth alone will not be a defence. In this there is a confusion of civil and criminal remedies. In a criminal prosecution the truth alone, if not published with good motives and for justifiable ends, is not always a complete defence. But in civil cases it is well settled that no damages can be given for a libel that contains no falsehood. (411)

This case involved a doctor with stereotypically poor penmanship. Considering himself sullied, Dr. Sullings sued Shakespeare, publisher of the *Kalamazoo (Mich.) Gazette*, for publishing alleged libels, including that the doctor removed a "patty tuber" from a patient's "hypogastrium" (410). But the defendant's uncontested testimony showed that the doctor himself wrote the article and gave it to the newspaper to publish. Calling the doctor's article "a gratuitous puff of himself," the Michigan court said evidence also showed that the article was "very illegibly written." The errors were but a "printer's blunder," the court concluded, adding, "[W]e do not see how a mistake of the printers without wrongful intent could be held a malicious libel" (412).[89]

That same year, 1881, the Massachusetts Supreme Court, which did not allow truth as a defense in a criminal libel case in 1825,[90] also denied truth as an absolute defense in a civil case. *Lothrop v. Adams*[91] involved a newspaper story in the *Springfield Republican* that called a minister cruel for kicking one daughter and whipping another with a riding whip (477–78). The story concerned the minister's trial in front of a Congregational church (482).

The court quoted a Massachusetts statute that said,

> *In every prosecution and in every civil action* for writing or for publishing a libel, *the defendant may upon the trial give in evidence the truth of the matter* contained in the publication charged as libellous; *and such evidence shall be deemed a sufficient justification, unless malicious intention shall be proved.* (478)[92]

The court then explained that under the statutory language, truth was not an "absolute defence." Thus, "the plaintiff may, notwithstanding the words are true, maintain his action if he can show that they were published with malicious intention" (478).

The minister won his libel case, and the Massachusetts Supreme Court upheld his win, even saying that it did not appear that the newspaper story was "a fair and accurate report of the proceedings before the church, made bona fide and without malice" (482).

In 1882 in *Wallis v. Bazet*,[93] the Louisiana Supreme Court heard a libel case springing from a newspaper's coverage of an open meeting of the Houma city council. The mayor awarded an oral contract for bridge cleaning without the customary bidding process. The council did not approve, and the newspaper quoted one of the aldermen:

> Mr. J. W. Board states publicly, that it was a put up job by the Mayor, and the reason why the contract was not written was because the Mayor's son was interested in the contract. He further states that the work they want one hundred dollars for is worth about thirty dollars. "There is something rotten in Denmark." "More whitewash needed." (132)

The mayor sued the newspaper (131). The newspaper responded that its publication was "privileged" and "a just, fair and true comment on the conduct of a public official" (132). The mayor lost, and the foreman of the jury, in open court, read this statement, which said, essentially, a pox on both your houses:

> The loose and unbusiness-like manner of proceeding with the disbursement of the public funds of the town of Houma, by the Council and the Mayor of said town, gave rise to the allegations against Mayor Wallis, in the article of the Houma Courier, of 8th October, 1881. Said article, though not libellous, is ungentlemanly in tone, and beneath the dignity of correct and honorable journalism[.] (133)

The Louisiana Supreme Court agreed on both counts—"not malicious or libelous" but "not indicating the highest cultivation of taste and refined journalism" in using the "rotten in Denmark" and "whitewash" quotes (134).

Courts continued to extol truth in the late nineteenth century. The Kentucky Supreme Court in 1889 *demanded* truth if a newspaper printed content provided by another:

> [I]t is said that it would be a harsh rule to require conductors of newspapers to be responsible for the truth of the information that they furnish the public. The answer is, that the press must not be the vehicle of attacks upon the character and reputation of a person unless the attack is known to be true; if it is not known to be true, do not publish it.[94]

In 1890, the Texas Supreme Court, in a case involving a newspaper report about a man's involuntary commitment for insanity, explained why truth is a complete defense:

> If the truth of the charge is established by proof[,] the plaintiff would not be entitled to recover, because he can not be said to be damaged by the loss of or injury to a character he did not possess. Such is the principal reason given why it is a defense complete in itself.[95]

Three years later, however, *Johnson v. State*[96] showed that sometimes truth was not a complete defense in Texas. A Dallas trial court denied truth as a defense in a criminal libel case. In one of a series of cases against the *Kansas City Sunday Sun*, distributed in Dallas, the court fined the newspaper $100 for publishing that Owen Parry, of Dallas, lived with a prostitute for a year (criminal intimacy), caught her in flagrante delicto with another man, broke a lot of her furniture, and then came back several times later, drunk and disorderly (464–66).

The trial court relied on a Texas statute that said,

> [W]hen a libel charges a penal offense, and states the time, place, and nature of the offense, the truth of the libel may be offered in evidence. If the penal offense is charged generally, without the specifications required, the truth can not be proved, though in fact the libel may be true. (464)[97]

The Texas Court of Criminal Appeals did not take issue with that statute but instead appeared to support it. The court said, "It is the policy of the law to suppress the publication of all scandalous matter which simply tends to bring disgrace and trouble upon the citizen, but it is not its policy to suppress the discovery of crime" (465). Here the court pointed to Article 1, § 8 of the Texas Constitution of 1876, which says, "In prosecutions for the publication of papers, . . . when the matter published is proper for public information, the truth thereof may be given in evidence." The court said that discovery of crime is "*proper for public information*" because "it always concerns the public interest that crimes be revealed and punished." The court continued, however, with some troubling language:

> But the law will permit no criminal charge to be publicly made by any person without such specific statement as to time, place, and the nature of the offense. . . . *If he makes the publication without the specifications, he will be guilty of libel, though the facts be true.* (465)[98]

So sometimes truth was not enough. *Johnson* showed that a weakness still existed in Texas in the legal armor of truth as a defense. But in this case, the appellate court ruled, "The charges here made were sufficiently specific as to the penal offenses charged" (465). The court reversed and remanded the case (466).

Similarly, in another case in this *Kansas City Sunday Sun* series, the Texas appellate court overturned a $200 fine and remanded the case to permit truth as a defense of the "innuendo" that county attorneys bribed or intimidated witnesses, such as the prostitute, to keep them away from the courthouse so truth could not be shown in the criminal libel prosecution involving Owen Parry.[99]

The next year, 1894, the Indiana Supreme Court embraced truth as a defense in *Palmer v. Adams*.[100] A newspaper published a story under these headlines "in large capital letters": "Kidnapped the Girl. A thirty-five year old masher spirits away a fifteen year old girl. Reward offered for the capture. A school girl stolen." The article then told about the elopement of the girl, Pearlie Wolfe, with a thirty-five-year-old man, Palmer. He sued for libel, lost, and appealed (72). Indiana's supreme court ruled against the "masher," saying, "The constitution of the State, article 1, section 10, provides that: 'In all prosecutions for libel, the truth of the matters alleged to be libelous may be given in justification.' It is never libelous to publish the truth." The court called truth a "complete defense" (73–74).

In 1895 in *McGuire v. Vaughan*,[101] the Michigan Supreme Court ruled for a newspaper in a pitched battle over a pitchforking. A newspaper said McGuire had landlord troubles and, "it is alleged," that the landlord's agent, McClintock, came to seize some of McGuire's cattle. Then

> an altercation ensued, in which McGuire, it is charged, finally seized a pitchfork, and ran it into the thigh of the man who wanted the cattle. It is claimed that he was in a great rage, and sent his daughter into his house after a revolver, threatening to kill somebody when he got it. (281)

McGuire, the newspaper said, was arrested for "assault with intent to do great bodily harm, less than murder" (281).

McGuire sued for libel. He lost, appealed, and lost again (287). The Michigan Supreme Court said that at trial, "the proof tended only to show, that the fork was run through the pants, and not into the thigh." Was this fatal to the defense of truth? No. "The other facts, however, as developed on the trial, showed that the jury believed that the plaintiff was guilty of the offense charged [assault with intent to do great bodily harm], though the fork did not penetrate McClintock's thigh." The article, in effect, was true enough: "[T]he statement in it that the fork was run into and through McClintock's pants, instead of his thigh, would not necessarily add to or lessen the degree of the crime which was imputed to him in the article" (286).

But truth as a defense did not save clearly inaccurate portrayals in two Pennsylvania cases in 1896. In *Shelly v. Dampman*, a newspaper reporter conversed with police and got confused, resulting in a story that, in big headlines, portrayed a respectable widow as running a "bawdyhouse."[102] Nor could truth as a defense do any magic in an erroneous *Pittsburgh Times* report that a woman was a witch who caused a boy's illness.[103]

In sum, although there were a few wobbles, the nineteenth century saw a swing in attitude, the pendulum moving decidedly in favor of truth as a defense. Arguably, the value of freedom of the press to tell the truth, and its protection in courts of law, gained ascendancy during this fascinating century.

Notes

1. Michael T. Gibson, "The Supreme Court and Freedom of Expression from 1791 to 1917," *Fordham Law Review* 55 (December 1986): 263–64 (footnotes omitted).

2. In 2008, Stewart Jay wrote a general exploration. See Stewart Jay, "The First Amendment: The Creation of the First Amendment Right to Free Expression from the Eighteenth Century to the Mid-Twentieth Century," *William Mitchell Law Review* 34 (2008): 773. He says, "Libel was a criminal offense in almost all the founding states, and seditious utterances were regarded as a form of libel." Ibid., 784 (citing David J. Jenkins, "The Sedition Act of 1798 and the Incorporation of Seditious Libel into First-Amendment Jurisprudence," *American Journal of Legal History* 45 [2001]: 154, 171). But Jay does not focus on nineteenth-century libel cases.

3. Following "*See, e.g.*," Gibson alphabetically lists these state constitutions making truth a defense during the nineteenth century: Arkansas, California, Colorado, Connecticut, Delaware, Florida, Illinois, Indiana, Iowa, Kentucky, Michigan, Mississippi, Missouri, New Jersey, New York, and Pennsylvania. See Gibson, "Supreme Court and Freedom of Expression," 287n149. (Note: He mistakenly says Florida's law declares "truth admissible in libel actions concerning public officials or public matters." For Florida's law, see note 62 and accompanying text.)

4. Kansas, Maine, Montana, Nevada, North Dakota, Ohio, Rhode Island, South Carolina, Tennessee, Texas, Wisconsin, and Wyoming also passed constitutions with truth as a defense. See nn. 44–52 and 59–78 and accompanying text for constitutional provisions on truth as a defense.

5. See Garrison v. Louisiana, 379 U.S. 64, 70 note 7 (1964).

6. John Milton, *Areopagitica*, 1645, third paragraph from the end, available at https://www.dartmouth.edu/~milton/reading_room/areopagitica/text.shtml, accessed August 2014.

7. State v. Haskins, 109 Iowa 656, 657, 80 N.W. 1063 (1899).

8. See, e.g., Garrison v. Louisiana, 379 U.S. 64, 67–68 (1964). See also People v. Croswell, 3 Johns. Cas. 337, 379 (1804):

> The English decisions on the subject of libels have not been consistent in principle. The reason assigned for the punishment of libels, whether true or false, is because they tend to a breach of the peace, by inciting the libelled party to revenge, or the people to sedition. It is not the matter, but the manner, say the books, which is punishable.

9. "Crown v. John Peter Zenger," *Legal History: 1674–1776*, http://www.nycourts.gov/history/legal-history-new-york/legal-history-eras-01/history-new-york-legal-erascrown-zenger.html, accessed August 2014.

10. "August 4, 1735: John Peter Zenger Acquitted," *ABA Journal* 68, no. 4 (August 2013), http://www.abajournal.com/magazine/article/august_4_1735_john_peter_zenger_acquitted/, accessed September 19, 2015.

11. "Crown v. John Peter Zenger."

12. See, e.g., Jones v. United States, 526 U.S. 227, 446 (1999).

13. See, e.g., "August 4, 1735: John Peter Zenger Acquitted" and "The Beginnings of Revolutionary Thinking: The Trial of John Peter Zenger," http://www.ushistory.org/us/7c.asp, accessed August 2014.

14. McIntyre v. Ohio Elections Comm'n, 514 U.S. 334, 361 (1995) (J. Thomas, concurring). Andrew Hamilton also carved a place for himself in linguistic history. The phrase "Philadelphia lawyer," meaning a "shrewd lawyer," refers to him. See, e.g., "Philadelphia lawyer," Wordsmith.org, http://wordsmith.org/words/philadelphia_lawyer.html, accessed August 2014.

15. See, e.g., Gregg Costa, "Note: John Marshall, the Sedition Act, and Free Speech in the Early Republic," *Texas Law Review* 77 (March 1999): 1011 and throughout (in part, covering the XYZ Affair and arguing that the Alien and Sedition Acts were more about federalism than free speech).

16. See, e.g., New York Times Co. v. Sullivan, 376 U.S. 254, 274–75 (1964). As an example of a conviction for seditious libel under the Alien and Sedition Acts for a publication's criticism of President Adams, see U.S. v. Cooper, 25 F. Cas. 631 (D. Pa. 1800). Falsity and malicious intent were necessary for conviction. The judge charged the jury, "If you believe that he has published . . . without malice, or an intent to defame the president of the United States, you must acquit him. If he has proved . . . truth of the facts asserted by him, you must find him not guilty" (643). The judge sentenced Cooper to six months' imprisonment and a $400 fine (644).

17. See, e.g., Jerry L. Mashaw, "Reluctant Nationalists: Federal Administration and Administrative Law in the Republican Era, 1801–1829," *Yale Law Journal* 116 (June 2007): 1636, 1641n14.

18. New York Times Co. v. Sullivan, 376 U.S. at 276.

19. People v. Croswell, 3 Johns Cas. 337 (N.Y. 1804). Parenthetical page numbers in this section are from this case.

20. See, e.g., Warren Moise, "Beyond the Bar: Halloween, and the Monster outside Your Courtroom Door," *South Carolina Lawyer* 23 (2011), 15 (focusing on the Star Chamber's relevance to current trials).

21. Faretta v. California, 422 U.S. 806, 821 (1975).

22. See, e.g., Kwass v. Kersey, 139 W. Va. 497, 508; 81 S.E.2d 237 (1954) (citing "Brandreth v. Lance, 8 New York Chancery Reports, 24 Paige Ch. 8, decided in 1839," which, in turn, cited "Hudson's Star Chamber, 2 Collect. Jurid. 224"). See also Balboa Island Village Inn, Inc., v. Lemen, 40 Cal. 4th 1141, 1149 note 3, 156 P.3d 339 (2007), and Murphy v. Daytona Beach Humane Society, Inc., 176 So. 2d 922, 924 (1965).

23. Green v. United States, 356 U.S. 165, 203 (1958) (J. Black, dissenting).

24. Justice William O. Douglas, in a 1964 concurring opinion in *Garrison v. Louisiana*, said, "Irving Brant has shown that seditious libel was 'entirely the creation of the Star Chamber.'" 379 U.S. at 83 (citing Brant Irving, "Seditious Libel: Myth and Reality," *New York University Law Review* 39 [1964]: 1, 11).

25. People v. Croswell at 411, 412. See "An Act Concerning Libels," ch. 90, 1805 *New York Session Laws* 450, cited in Thomas J. Finkelman, "Thomas Jefferson, Original Intent, and the Shaping of American Law: Learning Constitutional Law from the Writings of Jefferson," *New York University Annual Survey of American Law* 62 (2006): 45, 78n143 and accompanying text.

26. See, e.g., Finkelman, "Thomas Jefferson," 78.

27. See, e.g., "Alexander Hamilton and Aaron Burr Dueled to the Death: July 11, 1804," available at http://www.americaslibrary.gov/jb/nation/jb_nation_hamburr_1.html, accessed August 16, 2014.

28. For an extensive article on how the U.S. Supreme Court used Hamilton's *Federalist* essays, see David McGowan, "Ethos in Law and History: Alexander Hamilton, *The Federalist*, and the Supreme Court," *Minnesota Law Review* 85 (February 2000): 755.

29. David Sloss, "Judicial Foreign Policy: Lessons from the 1790s," *Saint Louis University Law Journal* 53 (Fall 2008): 145, 154.

30. Louise Weinberg, "Our Marbury," *Virginia Law Review* 89 (October 2003): 1235, 1245, 1279.

31. Alison L. LaCroix, "To Gain the Whole World and Lose His Own Soul: Nineteenth-Century American Dueling as Public Law and Private Code," *Hofstra Law Review* 33 (Winter 2004): 501. This article discusses in depth the history of dueling in the North and South.

32. Eric M. Freedman, "On Protecting Accountability," *Hofstra Law Review* 27 (Summer 1999): 677, 688–89.

33. Ibid., 714–15.

34. Lexis database search for "Alexander Hamilton," "cases" files, August 30, 2014: 1,939 hits.

35. Respublica v. Dennie, 4 Yeates 267 (Pa. 1805). Parenthetical page numbers in this section are from this case. The case includes this at the end: "Editor's Note: No Majority Opinion Appears at this Cite." Ibid., 271.

36. All italics in *Respublica* are from the original case.

37. David Abrahamson and Christina Bryza, "Magazine Publishers," *Encyclopedia of American Journalism*, Stephen L. Vaughn, ed. (Taylor & Francis, 2007), 281.

38. State v. Marshall, 859 S.W.2d 289, 292 (Tenn. 1993) (an obscenity case). This language appeared in Article 9, Section 7 in the 1790 constitution. "The same language is currently contained in Article I, Section 7 of Pennsylvania's current Constitution" (292).

39. Respublica v. Dennie at 269.

40. Citing *Croswell* at pa. 70.

41. Citing *Croswell* at pa. 63–64.

42. Finkelman, "Thomas Jefferson," 78.

43. See Michael P. Downey, "Note: The Jeffersonian Myth in Supreme Court Sedition Jurisprudence," *Washington University Law Quarterly* 76 (Summer 1998): 683, 693 (footnotes omitted). See also Costa, "John Marshall, the Sedition Act, and Free Speech," 1,038.

44. Pa. Const. of 1790, art. 9, § 7.
45. Del. Const. of 1792, art. 1, § 5; Ky. Const. of 1792, art. 12, § 8.
46. Tenn. Const. of 1796, art. 11, § 19.
47. Ind. Const. of 1816, art. 1, § 10.
48. Miss. Const. of 1817, art. 1, § 8 (emphasis added).
49. Conn. Const. of 1818, art. 1 § 7.
50. Ill. Const. of 1818, art. 8, § 23.
51. Maine Const. of 1820, art. 1, § 4.
52. Mo. Const. of 1820, art. 12, § 16 (emphasis added).
53. "The Jury, after having received the direction of the Court, shall have a right to determine, at their discretion, the law and the fact." Maine Const. of 1820, art. 1, § 4.
54. State v. Jeandell & Vincent, 5 Del 475 (1854). Parenthetical page numbers in this paragraph and the next are from this case.
55. Commonwealth v. Blanding, 20 Mass. 304 (Mass. 1925). Parenthetical page numbers in this section are from this case.
56. Emphasis added.
57. Root v. King & Verplanck, 7 Cow. 613 (N.Y. 1827). Parenthetical page numbers in this section are from this case.
58. Emphasis added.
59. See nn. 44–52 and accompanying text.
60. Mich. Const. of 1835, art. 1, § 7.
61. Ark. Const. of 1836, art. 2, § 8.
62. Fla. Const. of 1838, art. 1, § 15.
63. R.I. Const. of 1843, art. 1, § 20.
64. N.J. Const. of 1844, art. 1, § 5.
65. Iowa Const. of 1846, art 11, § 7.
66. Wis. Const. of 1848, art 1, § 3.
67. Calif. Const. of 1849, art. 1, § 9.
68. Ohio Const. of 1851, art. 1, § 11.
69. Kans. Const. of 1859, Bill of Rights, § 11.
70. Nev. Const. of 1864, art. 1, § 9.
71. Colo. Const. of 1876, art. 2, § 10. Colorado says that "the jury . . . shall determine the law and the fact."
72. Tex. Const. of 1876, art. 1, § 8.
73. Mont. Const. of 1889, art. 2, § 10.
74. N.D. Const. of 1889, art. 1, § 4.
75. Wyo. Const. of 1990, art. 1, § 20.
76. S.C. Const. of 1895, art. 1, § 21.
77. N.Y. Const. of 1897, art. 1, § 8. New York, like Colorado, used the singular "fact."
78. Ibid.

79. Thrall v. Smiley, 9 Cal. 529 (1858). (George's brother was also a defendant because he "aided and counseled" George. Ibid. at 530.) Parenthetical page numbers in this paragraph are from this case.

80. See note 67 and accompanying text.

81. Gazette Co. v. Timberlake, 10 Ohio St. 548 (1860). Parenthetical page numbers in this paragraph are from this case.

82. Emphasis in original.

83. Castle v. Houston, 19 Kan. 417 (1877). Parenthetical page numbers in this section are from this case.

84. The court continued, "Hence originated the familiar maxim, 'The greater the truth the greater the libel'" (420). The theory, the court said, was that a truthful libel was more likely to lead to a breach of the peace. Ibid., 420–21 (citing *People v. Croswell*). For *Croswell*, see nn. 19–26 and accompanying text.

85. For the Star Chamber, see nn. 20–24 and accompanying text.

86. Quoting Sec. 272, Gen. Stat. 376.

87. See Kans. Const. of 1859, Bill of Rights, § 11.

88. Sullings v. Shakespeare, 46 Mich. 408, 9 N.W. 451 (1881). Parenthetical page numbers in this paragraph are from this case.

89. Another article, "undoubtedly written in a manner open to criticism," combined "fact" and "comment." It concerned an "ostentatious style" ride by the doctor in a chariot and his suit against the Vulcanite Rubber Company (ibid., 413–14).

90. See *Commonwealth v. Blanding*, nn. 55–56 and accompanying text.

91. Lothrop v. Adams, 133 Mass. 471 (1881). Parenthetical page numbers in this section are from this case.

92. Quoting Gen. Sts. c. 129, § 77 (emphasis added).

93. Wallis v. Bazet, 34 La. Ann. 131 (1882). Parenthetical page numbers in this paragraph and the next are from this case.

94. Riley v. Lee, 88 Ky. 603, 614, 11 S.W. 713 (1889).

95. Patten v. Belo, 79 Tex. 41, 46 14 S.W. 1037 (1890).

96. Johnson v. State, 31 Tex. Crim. 464, 20 S.W. 980 (1893). Parenthetical page numbers in this section are from this case.

97. The statute is Tex. Penal Code, art. 642. See 31 Tex. Crim. 464, headnote 1.

98. Emphasis added.

99. Johnson v. State, 31 Tex. Crim. 569, 569–71, 21 S.W. 541 (1893).

100. Palmer v. Adams, 137 Ind. 72, 36 N.E. 695 (1894). Parenthetical page numbers in this paragraph come from this case.

101. McGuire v. Vaughan, 106 Mich. 280, 64 N.W. 44 (1895). Parenthetical page numbers in this paragraph and the next come from this case.

102. Shelly v. Dampman, 1 Pa. Super. 115, 120–21 (1895).

103. Oles v. Pittsburg Times, 2 Pa. Super. 130 (1896).

7. KEEPING THE LIGHT UNDER THE BUSHEL

LAWS, MORES, AND READING

PAULETTE D. KILMER

Tyrants fear the power of the spoken word and create a secular mythology of self to control public discourse. Therein, folklore has preserved this tension between maintaining order and allowing dissension. Civic institutions, like the church, school, and local government, often have defined dissent as the enemy of the common good. By the nineteenth century, Wendell Phillips, an abolitionist lawyer, pointed out, "Law is nothing unless close behind it stands a warm living public opinion."[1] Law evolves through consensus to determine acceptable behaviors essential for inspiring harmony under a social contract. Of course, the stories exchanged through the oral tradition, cave paintings, songs, and eventually newspapers, pamphlets, and books reinforced the shared moral code.

Nevertheless, clever critics of the status quo have always circulated their misgivings through narratives. Monarchs naturally considered these stories, which were often sung as ballads, treasonous threats to their authority. Even nursery rhymes, which still amuse children today, centuries ago informed commoners of current events that aristocrats did not want publicized. For example, via an allegorical code, "Hey, diddle, diddle / The cat and fiddle . . ." mocked King Richard III's rise to power in England.[2]

Social values shape laws. Late in the nineteenth century, Emile Durkheim, the founder of sociology in France, pointed out that legal changes occurred only because visionaries chose to commit the criminal act (in their day) of speaking freely. "Liberal philosophy has as its precursors the heretics of all kinds who were justly (*sic*) punished by secular authorities during the entire course of the Middle Ages and until the eve of Modern times."[3] Ironically, in trying to serve the greater good, citizens have enforced unjust statutes. For example, intending to promote decency and, thus, generate social tranquillity, politicians have passed laws restricting the right to read and think freely.

To examine the evolution of nineteenth-century obscenity laws, this chapter is divided into three parts. Since people write laws to enforce community values, the first section examines the cultural mindset of Victorian expectations that muffled unwelcome voices. The second part traces the English common-law roots of American jurisprudence. The final division explains how cultural and legal developments after the Civil War prompted Congress to pass the "Act of the Suppression of Trade in, and Circulation of, Obscene Literature and Articles of Immoral Use," which was called the Comstock Act.

WORSE THAN DANTE'S HELL: THE PUBLIC LIBRARY'S INFERNO

As early as 1806, the *Newport (R.I.) Mercury* warned that certain obscene, radical, and sensational "volumes, which usually crowd the shelves of a circulating library or are seen tumbling on the sophas of a fashionable drawing room," debased the English language.[4] These devil seeds, or so censors believed, could grow into destructive ideas that would stunt the moral growth of youth. More than forty years later, the *Hillsdale (Mich.) Whig Standard* offered speeches for twenty-five dollars each about topics essential to educating people of all ages; one of "the best practical [lectures]" outlined "the Evil Influence of Light Reading, pointing out a remedy in the diffusion of *useful* knowledge, the formation of Public Libraries." A follow-up talk urged citizens to embrace the "Suppression of Vicious Literature."[5]

Censors wish to protect youth and fear that ideas might undermine social order. Social institutions like the church, school, or government preserve community standards. The news and entertainment media (including songs, books, plays, and art) have instilled within citizens a sense of shared national identity, heroes, and goals. Shielding children and the weak-minded from harmful writing, speech, drama, and art has kept censors busy for eons. In 1787, King George III ordered his officials to "suppress all loose and licentious printing, books and publications, dispensing poison to the minds of the young and unwary, and to punish publishers and vendors thereof."[6] Nineteenth-century newspapers ran many articles about the perils of reading. Some condemned romances or story papers. Others warned that dime novels taught children shameful, criminal, and sometimes fatal habits. Women were assumed incapable of understanding the nuances of fine literature and susceptible to the mischief and wicked suggestions of the cheap paperbacks or story papers.

Many libraries locked up questionable books in a room called "The Inferno," inspired by Dante's classic study of Hades, and limited their access to certain gentlemen. In 1889, Congregational minister James M. Hubbard, who graduated from Yale College and a theological school and who edited the religious magazine the *Youth's Companion*, warned that libraries were "a grave evil" to communities because they allowed children to read fiction. Hubbard noted that past New Englanders had considered novel reading a sin, but over time people had changed their minds. "In some city libraries and possibly in some of the town libraries . . . a department technically known by some as 'The Inferno' [shelves] books of unquestioned and undisguised immorality . . . which are remarkable merely on account of their gross obscenity." Hubbard feared that these books, which he said mostly came from Europe, would cause "a moral pestilence."[7]

A letter writer disputed Hubbard's conclusion that most library patrons were children who checked out fiction exclusively. After listing statistics from Detroit, St. Louis, Indianapolis, Cleveland, Providence, and the Morse Institute in Natick, Massachusetts, the correspondent concluded, "Children do not make up more than one fifth of the readers in our public libraries." Moreover, these youths read histories, biographies, scientific works, and travel books tailored to fit their intellectual needs as well as storybooks. This critic disagreed with Hubbard's assessment of fiction as pernicious and cautioned him not to "cramp the mind and sensibility of a youth by excluding him or her from an intimacy with the beautiful, inspiring and elevating products of imaginative literature."[8]

Ironically, restricting books generated interest in them. The *Boston Daily Globe* lamented on August 7, 1897, the "sad commentary on human nature" reflected in the Boston Public Library's refusal to not give the newspaper a list of the "immoral books in the Inferno" because then "we should have a lot of people coming in and asking for them."[9]

Requesting books from the Inferno did not necessarily gain petitioners entry, and women were not allowed access at all. The Inferno at the Boston Athenaeum Library was located in "the back part of the large burglar and fireproof vault where the valuables of the institution were kept." While W. I. Fletcher worked as a delivery clerk there, only once in the five years of his employment did a craven soul, a middle-aged member of a reputable family who seemed like a respectable gentleman, succeed in acquiring "a book, which had been wisely sequestrated," in order "to gratify" his "prurient curiosity." However, upon returning early from lunch, the "chief" of the Inferno seized the miscreant's "prize" and "took the book from before his face and had it locked up again before the person could get halfway to the door in his ignominious flight."[10]

In addition to fiction deemed obscene, works judged politically explosive also filled the Inferno. Boston Library administrators explained that uneducated socialists and anarchists might misinterpret certain authors' intentions and do irreparable harm. In 1897 an assistant librarian to Herbert Putnam pointed out to a reporter that despite protests from skeptics, the general public agreed with Putnam and trusted his judgment. He described the Inferno in the Boston Library:

> Outside of the anarchistic and socialistic works . . . there are many other books, which are unsuitable for general circulation. These we have gathered together in a certain section of the building, . . . "the Inferno." Among the works here are Roccacio's [*sic*] *Decameron* unabridged, the *Heptameron* of Margaret of Navarre, and the unexpurgated editions of the earlier English and French dramatists, Beaumont and Fletcher, Webster, Racine, and so on. Of course, the Inferno is open to readers as well as any other part of the library, but we have to discriminate between them.

The assistant librarian noted that parents would not want their children to freely check out literature beyond their experience or maturity and that some adults also lacked the sophistication to read whatever they wished.[11]

The Inferno's restrictions on reading arose from community standards and library practices rather than from laws or ordinances. On March 25, 1882, the *Daily Republican* in Decatur, Illinois, reported on the Boston Library's survey to acquire information about limiting readers' choices. The librarian from the New York Mercantile Public Library explained that the American Library Association had circulated the questionnaire to learn how banning books had affected communities as well as to gather statistics about how many libraries imposed bans, which books were pulled from collections, and, empirically, the impact of the Inferno on library usage. Sadly, Infernos denied the intended audience of ordinary readers access to E. D. E. N. Southworth, Horatio Alger, and many other authors who wrote for story papers or whose stories (like those of Wilkie Collins) challenged prevailing social conventions and cherished ideals. The ALA survey asked librarians to place a check mark beside "the authors whose works were formerly in the library but have since been withdrawn on the grounds of sensational or immoral qualities."[12]

The librarian at the New York Mercantile Library reasoned that all libraries enforced rules on taste and decency, adding that his library had "drawn the line

Librarian Herbert Putnam supervises students in the Reading Room at the Library of Congress. Previously, during his tenure at the Boston Public Library, Putnam declined a request in August 1897 by an editor at the *Boston Globe* for a list of books in that library's "Inferno" because Putnam feared that publication of the immoral titles would increase patrons' demand to read these "tickets to hell." Library of Congress Prints and Photographs Division, Washington, D.C.

at translations of [Émile] Zola's works." On the other hand, he admitted, "it would be impossible to exclude Mrs. [Mary Jane] Holmes' books, for instance, because she was one of the most popular authors represented in the library."[13]

THE DANGERS OF READING

The laws for regulating obscenity and incendiary speech grew in a cultural milieu of suspicion that pornography as well as the proliferation of dime novels, romances, whodunits, horse operas, and cheap story papers helped fuel. Pears soap tucked paperbacks into boxes to increase sales. Vending machines in railroad stations offered passersby the latest potboilers for a few coins. As the interest in these urban fairy tales surged, newspapers also featured serial cliff-hangers, ghost tales, and love stories. The *Experiment* of Norwalk, in Huron County, Ohio, estimated that 75 percent of "the female sex" preferred sentimental novels, rather than worthwhile literature and edifying books on history or science. "Yes, so widespread and pernicious is this passion for fiction, that it vitiates the taste for lofty conceptions and blinds the eye to all that is splendid in substantial literature."[14]

Boys, too, lost their souls through reading, according to the *Cincinnati Christian Age* in 1850, which particularly pointed out European authors like Byron. The correspondent quoted a lad who lamented reading novels on the Sabbath: "I am ruined! Yes! Eternally ruined in soul and body. I see nothing before me . . . but the blackness of darkness forever!"[15]

The diffusion of dime novels across the nation and through the middle and even upper classes as well as among the less fortunate alarmed many reformers, librarians, teachers, parents, and newspaper contributors. In 1884, the *Daily News* of Frederick, Maryland, lumped dime novels with the *National Police Gazette* as examples of "pernicious literature" and called for legislation to end such "abuses of the liberty of the press." Reading thrilling plots excited boys, emboldening them to emulate the heroes' exploits. The attacks on property and some robberies in a northern state illustrated the power of the trashy stories over the juveniles who formed a gang of road bandits, resembling the penny-dreadful thugs. Certainly, youths read crime news, which emphasized the bitter harvest of breaking the law, often without learning from these cautionary accounts. On the other hand, "the novelist [kept] the punishment carefully in the background and, with the aid of a depraved imagination, [threw] a halo of romance over the crime itself."[16]

Newspapers published articles about the psychological as well as the moral harm in reading dime novels. In 1879, the spell of western thrillers so completely hypnotized J. L. Cameron, who was forty-seven, that he could not distinguish his nightmares from reality. "Under the crazy belief that Indians had attacked the house," he leaped through the window. After Cameron disappeared from Red Lake Ranche near Fort Thompson, Arizona, he roamed "the prairies five days without food and with nothing on but his shirt." Finally, rescuers took Cameron to Brule City, where he received medical treatment. He attributed "his hallucination to too much dime novel reading, followed by several blood curdling dreams."[17]

In the same column, the *Freeport (Ill.) Daily Bulletin* noted that Sitting Bull's hungry braves were returning from Canada to the Red Cloud agency. The commissioner had sent orders to feed them but to treat them as prisoners of war. Another item reported that "fifty-six lodges of the Minneconjon Sioux, under Chief Burnt Face, left Cheyenne agency and started out on the warpath."[18] They attacked a wagon train in the Black Hills but left empty-handed; soon, two companies of the Eleventh Infantry began searching for the Native Americans.

On the March 17, 1897, cover of *Puck*, artist Samuel D. Ehrhart satirized the Victorian elite's fear of popular literature. The respectable gentleman in the background holds a dime novel whodunit, *Old Sleuth, The Detective*, and the children are reading newspapers labeled *Morning Cyclone of Crime* and *Daily Scandal Monger*. The newsstands bear signs: "All the Sensation Papers," "Daily Rot," "Daily Scooper," "Morning Scavenger," and "Don't Fail to Buy the Sunday Slop Bucket." The headlines include "How to Poison a Whole City," "Murder," and "Crime." Library of Congress Prints and Photographs Division, Washington, D.C.

This series of brief news items used the same kind of language and reflected similar prejudices as those found in the dime novels. In fact, some critics as well as editors drew parallels between the daring, highly improbable westerns and sensationalized reports from the frontier. In one account, "Detective Looney" concluded, "The arrest of the youth upon suspicion of having committed so dastardly a crime has brought out a story that is as replete with dramatic situations as any dime novel."[19]

Newspapers warned readers that "mashers" preyed upon girls who read romances and that boys addicted to dime novels risked losing everything. Indeed, some ran away to join the circus or fight Indians while others languished in reform schools. One such book even killed a judge's son: Joseph Hennessey, a feeble-minded boy in Colorado Springs, perished from injuries he sustained acting out scenes from a yellow-covered thriller.[20]

THE COMMON-LAW ROOTS OF OBSCENITY ORDINANCES AND STATE LAWS

The Court of the King's Bench tried the first case involving printed obscenity in 1727. The defendant, Curll, a printer, had published *Venus in the Cloister; or, The Nun in Her Smock*. The judge decided that Jean Barrin's 1683 novel contained blasphemy and heresy as well as obscenity.[21] In the New World, along with John Cleland's *Fanny Hill* and numerous other books that most considered indecent, a naughty item from Benjamin Franklin, *Advice to a Young Man Choosing a Mistress*, circulated among the upper crust of society. Very few trials occurred, and no obscenity laws existed in the United States or Great Britain until the nineteenth century. For instance, in a 1708 case, the court ruled that "since *Fifteen Plagues of Maidenhead* did not insult the church, the government, or any individual . . . no harm has been done" and dropped the charges.[22]

Early in the nineteenth century, John Ruggles challenged common-law blasphemy strictures. He publicly declared, "Jesus was a bastard and his mother must be a whore" and then demanded the court protect his religious liberty under the New York state constitution of 1777, but the chief judge of the New York Supreme Court, James Kent, not only enforced the English law for blasphemy but also added obscene libel. Although this case in 1811 did not involve obscenity, Kent felt that attacking Christianity undermined the community's ethics and might jeopardize public order.[23] By 1821, under the common-law category of obscene libel, appellate court judges had established precedents for prosecuting those who offended community moral standards.[24]

During the nineteenth century, as popular story formats increased, Sunday schools as well as public libraries banned light reading. People wrote letters to newspaper editors denouncing dime novels, story papers, and newspaper serials as corrupters of children and other innocents. News items warned about the consequences of "pernicious literature." The *Hour* magazine estimated that "millions of young girls and thousands of boys were *novelized* into absolute idiocy."[25]

Cheap books swelled in popularity throughout the nineteenth century, despite the recession of 1880. The publishers' financial crisis inspired other business leaders to buy entire warehouses of books to give away with their products, and one entrepreneur registered a new brand, "book soap." These cheap paperbacks were packed in boxes of soap and cereal and were given to those who purchased patent medicines. Vending machines with simple crank handles, full of these books, appeared in parks, popular restaurants, and other places where people congregated. "Book soap" authors included such popular American writers as Edgar Allan Poe, Nathaniel Hawthorne, and Emily Dickinson as well as Europeans like Sir Walter Scott.[26]

The targets of library censorship, writing modern fairy tales full of action and of love lost but retrieved and developing formula characters, often adjusted to the demand for "clean" stories. In his memoir about writing potboilers, *The Fiction Factory*, William Wallace Cook explained that to succeed, writers must respect their readers: "Their awakened moral sense makes possible the muckraker; and when they weary of the day's evil and the day's toil, it is their habit to divert themselves with pleasant and exciting reading, and it must be CLEAN."[27]

Victorian concerns about public order and morality in the vortex of progress triggered suspicion of reading. Immigration, industrialization, and innovation transformed cities into metropolitan hubs of commerce and culture. However, relentless change raised concerns about maintaining social cohesion and preserving values. For example, rejecting the passive role assigned to women in the home, the suffragists rocked the nation to its core. The right to vote would empower women to participate politically in the public sphere, which opponents feared would destroy domestic tranquillity and shatter public order.

Throughout the nineteenth century, many religious, educational, political, and social leaders considered unnatural those books featuring happy, independent women fulfilling roles reserved for men. One of the longest-running banned books in U.S. history, John Cleland's *Memoirs of a Woman of Pleasure or Fanny Hill*, upset ministers and civic leaders partly because, despite the heroine's boudoir adventures with multiple partners, she married her true love and lived happily ever after. Strict modesty codes emphasized paternalistic assumptions concerning women's helplessness outside their homes and their need for protection from corrupting forces, like lewd references to "arms" or "legs" rather than "limbs."

Despite these cultural taboos, women read newspapers, which increased their knowledge of politics, science, and other topics considered too coarse for them. In 1892 the *New York World* added a section devoted entirely to female interests, and the *San Antonio Daily Light* as well as the *Atlanta Journal* lamented that the "newspaper reading habit is working its insidious way into the drawing rooms and the very inmost recesses of the home circle. Its growth is in harmony with and the natural consequence of the broadening of woman's field and the elevation of female education."[28]

When authors like Stephen Crane or Theodore Dreiser challenged the status quo of rigid social rules in their novels, they made many people uncomfortable. "By either supporting or not opposing majoritarian will," notes Mary M. Cronin, "much of the public was willing to exclude unpopular social expression when such discussion seemed threatening to the public order."[29]

THE URBAN ABUNDANCE OF VISIBLE SMUT

Readers had to open books to discover their contents. On the other hand, smut dealers displayed in shop windows various photos, books, and items like packs of cards illustrated with obscene images. Prostitutes walked the streets day and night. Starting in the 1830s, New York City's "sporting gentlemen" bought guidebooks to brothels, delineating what each madam offered.[30] A decade later, a new kind of journalism for the Big Apple emerged, the "flash press," which took its name from the slang term for thieves. The flash press catered to the "man-about-town readership" with articles rich in flamboyant details about naughty nightlife and containing gossip about real people identified with their initials or full names.[31] Editors satirized stories, often feigning horror and disbelief at the scandalous activity among the sleazy crowd. Of course, the mostly male readership soared.

Although flash papers were very popular in their day, they dropped out of historical, legal, and pop cultural consciousness for decades. Patricia Cline Cohen, Timothy J. Gilfoyle, and Helen Lefkowitz Horowitz note that "twentieth-century lawyers and judges arguing obscenity cases did not know to use them as legal precedent, and historians studying the history of sex, gender, and sport were ignorant of them."[32] During their short run roughly from the fall of 1841 to the spring of 1843, sleazy weeklies (or "prickly rags") like the *Whip*,

Rake, *Libertine*, and *Flash* targeted businessmen and civic leaders who filed libel suits.[33] In a twist of fate worthy of a cheap novel, a judge satirized in the flash press, Frederick A. Tallmadge, emphasized obscenity libel, directing the grand jury in October 1841 to censor the flash press to protect the public interest. The publishers of the *Flash*, *Rake*, and *Libertine* all were indicted in 1842 and 1843 under common-law statutes; the litigation shut down the sporting journals.

Ironically, one case against a flash paper publisher resulted in a precedent that echoed later free speech advocates. On January 14, 1842, George Wilkes, William Joseph Snelling, and George B. Wooldridge faced charges of criminal and obscene libel in the New York General Sessions Court. Wooldridge testified against his former colleagues, who both pled guilty to libel but not to obscenity. The obscenity charges were dropped. In April, they faced new charges of obscenity, and Wilkes, who pled guilty, received a suspended sentence. The jury found Snelling, who proclaimed he was innocent, guilty and ordered him to finish his sentence, slated to end in about thirty days.

In the fall of 1843, Wilkes was tried again on obscenity charges, and although he lost, his argument remains important. Wilkes challenged English judge William Blackstone's logic on obscenity, claiming the common-law standards were too vague, and raised questions about determining obscenity that continue to interest First Amendment proponents. Yet his arguments did not impress Judge Tallmadge, and the jury found Wilkes guilty. Cohen, Gilfoyle, and Horowitz observe that "Tallmadge's position and many of the practices of his court held sway over the law of obscenity until early in the twentieth century."[34]

Until municipalities, states, and eventually the nation passed laws in the nineteenth century, cases were tried under obscene libel or public nuisance provisions of the common law. Blackstone explained that libel "signified any writings, pictures, or the like, of an immoral or illegal tendency."[35] Acts in the privacy of one's home were not illegal, but those same deeds done in public set a bad example and were punishable. Blackstone listed these examples of "gross improprieties and general immoralities: lewdness, swearing and cursing, and blasphemy." He defined lewdness as "'some grossly scandalous and public indecency' and linked it with obscenity."[36]

The indignation over public indecency and obscenity inspired the Hicklin test in England, which originated at the Queen's Bench in 1868. The law defined obscenity in terms of harm to children and others susceptible to suggestion. "The Hicklin test entered American legal doctrine in the Court of Appeals case, *United States v. Bennett* (1879), and its place was consolidated by the Supreme Court in *Rosen v. United States* (1896)."[37]

RELENTLESS MONSTER OR CHRISTIAN HERO?

For forty years, Anthony Comstock, a former dry goods merchant, answered what he considered a divine call from God to rid the world of vice as a U.S. post office agent. His biographer, Charles Gallaudet Trumbull, offered as evidence of Comstock's success in his mission this list of items the zealot destroyed: more than fifty tons of "vile" books, more than twenty-eight thousand pounds of plates used to print those volumes, and almost 4 million obscene photos. Of the 3,646 people he arrested, 2,682 were convicted or entered guilty pleas, with 2,180 of the latter group sentenced. If someone had rented a train to transport the materials Comstock identified as indecent and the people he prosecuted, then that "Taboo Express" would have pulled sixteen freight and sixty-one passenger cars.[38]

To his opponents, Comstock's religious mania blinded him to individual rights under the First Amendment, rendering him a lethal freak. But to the many who shared his concern about the erosion of the Protestant ethic, he slayed the dragons of irresponsibility and decadence, thus preventing the devil from snaring victims.[39] A reviewer of Trumbull's book exclaimed, "If you like to read about Sherlock Holmes and his imaginary adventures in the world of crime, you will not fail to be absorbed in this narrative about a real man, a Christian hero fighting against the rule of the kingdom of darkness."[40]

The truth about Comstock's legacy probably falls somewhere between the extremes of freedom hobgoblin and God's emissary. Comstock never faltered in his belief that the Lord had chosen him. "The weeds of sin, thus planted in weak human nature, are forced to a rapid growth, choking virtue and truth, and stunting all the higher and holier instincts," Comstock warned in *Traps for the Young*.[41] He liked this gardening imagery and arrogantly invoked it to dismiss criticism of his tactics that had compelled Ida Craddock, who wrote a manual for newlyweds, to commit suicide rather than face sentencing for sending pornography through the mail.[42]

Every time he succeeded in uprooting vice, Comstock rejoiced, and he boasted that he had pushed fifteen reprobates so hard that they took their own lives.[43] This fiery pruner's views seem extreme today, but many disapproved of shocking accounts they read in newspapers and the sin they witnessed firsthand on visits to cities. According to Anna Louise Bates, another Comstock biographer, "That the Victorian bourgeoisie shared his values is no coincidence."[44] Like many children, Anthony, who grew up on a farm, learned Bible stories that he repeated years later at home as well as in the Congregational Church. His mother, Polly Lockwood Comstock, enforced Victorian era mores, drawing inspiration from

Calvinism and traditional views of motherhood,[45] and "although his mother died when he was ten, the religion she had taught Anthony—one of hellfire and damnation—he carried with him for the rest of his life," notes Marianne Mussett in her study of the crusader.[46]

Many mothers instilled Protestant values in their children, but working mothers in poor neighborhoods could not stay home all day, and children often helped support the family. "Child street sellers, or hucksters, while acceptable to the working class, looked like products of neglect to polite middle-class reformers," says Bates.[47]

Inevitably, the working class and advocates for women's rights challenged the male-dominated society of patriarchy, which Comstock and his financial backers regarded as the skeleton of civilization. Victorian gender roles specified that men played magnanimous rulers of their castles over their subservient wives, too weak in mind and body to thrive in the public sphere. Comstock despised newspaper items that contradicted his expectations. As one such example, in 1879, the *Fort Wayne (Ind.) Daily Sentinel* reported that Anna F. Kennedy, who lived near Monroeville, Indiana, defended herself from the advances of a traveling picture peddler. When the masher cooed indecently, Kennedy brandished a poker and thwarted his "attempt to conquer her with a chair." Then she reported the incident to the sheriff, who put out a warrant for the cad's arrest.[48] These stories about strong, capable women as well as accounts describing the new woman who earned a college degree, acquired a medical or legal license, or made a difference as a reformer offered the public an alternative view of society where men and women served their communities together. The anecdotes, like bricks striking a glass house, shattered the gender assumptions of patriarchy; of course, like glue, the status quo repaired most of the cracks.

By the late nineteenth century, women finishing high school and college sought advice about family planning. Comstock considered fertility information particularly lewd because it empowered wives to control reproduction, thus subverting husbands' authority. "Literature about women's rights violated everything he perceived to be natural and was, therefore, as obscene to Comstock as the most licentious pornography," says Bates.[49] The notes in his ledger reveal that on March 2, 1872, he seized flyers announcing a woman's rights convention from a man's house and persuaded the judge to fine the offender $500 as well as to send him to prison for one year to punish him for circulating obscene material. Comstock cherished his image as the savior of youth from depravity; thus, the suffrage sympathizer's tactic of making reform a family affair in which his two young sons helped hand out the "vile" literature outraged Comstock.[50]

Comstock's crusade against evil covered providing information about the human body, abortion, and sex. He opposed teaching adolescents anatomy because he feared knowledge of the reproductive system would prompt lewd thoughts and even "self-abuse" (masturbation), which many people then believed led to insanity or criminal behavior.[51] But despite the hundreds of arrests Comstock had made as an official agent of the U.S. Postal Service in the 1870s, products he considered shocking still appeared in newspaper ads, and some capitalized on the purist's war on filth.

For example, an advertisement on the front page of the *Jeffersonville (Ind.) National Democrat* on December 11, 1879, promised "MARRIED WOMEN" the "Comstock Syringe," describing it as "the most perfect article" for "purity," for preventing and curing diseases, and for "judicious and healthy regulation of the Female Functions, that is a blessing to Womankind." The "lady physician of this city" closed the ad with the address and price, "Five dollars plus express charges."[52]

A year before, the "lady physician," "Mrs." Dr. Sara Blakeslee Chase, had gone to the Tombs (New York City jail) for selling two of her syringes and had been fined $1,500 in May 1878. "The charges against her," says Linda Gordon in her history of birth control politics, "read in part, '. . . by the syringes, which she recommends and sells, she places it in the power of wives to prevent conception.'"[53] Chase countersued. In a lecture at Chickering Hall, in New York City, she vowed to take her case to the U.S. Supreme Court. "He [Comstock] needs a victim constantly," she said. "He doesn't know the difference between an immoral picture and a work of art. If we physicians are to obey the law as he interprets it, and if we do our duty there is reason for every one of us to be in fear to close our offices."[54] Chase had Comstock arrested for false imprisonment and defamation on June 25, 1878. Her list of losses indicated the ramifications even for people found innocent. She said many patients stopped requesting her services and her tenants had moved out.[55]

Other physicians also faced persecution for trying to educate the public about medical conditions. Dr. James S. Sherman mailed circulars offering a hernia cure complete with illustrations, and the warrant accused him of sending the pamphlet to women and young girls. Comstock had Sherman arrested in Boston and other cities, but he was not prosecuted. Then, in 1885, a grand jury indicted Sherman, ordering him to return to Philadelphia to face charges, and the doctor paid a $2,500 bail.[56]

Prior to the Comstock Act, newspapers used more direct language than the *Jefferson National Democrat* and pointed out the "Comstock syringe's" value in family planning. For instance, Ezra Heywood, a free love advocate, made the syringe an icon for reproductive freedom, taking every opportunity, including when he was on trial for violating the Comstock Act, to educate the public about his views. An advertisement for Dr. Chase's syringe that he published in his magazine, the *Word*, "had one sole . . . purpose . . . the assertion of Woman's Natural Right to ownership of and control over her own body-self—a right inseparable from Women's intelligent existence; a right unquestionable, precious, inalienable, real—beyond words to express."[57] He changed the name of the contraceptive to the "Vaginal Syringe" to remove the association with "the pious scamp who thinks Congress gives him legal right of way to and control over every American Woman's Womb."[58] Outlawing information about conception, birth, and sexual health complicated people's lives and jeopardized their happiness. But the First Amendment did not protect pornography, and Comstock decided what was obscene.

Midwives also got into trouble, especially those who supplemented their incomes with abortion potions or devices. A famous dealer in the powders she concocted as well as in abortions, New York City's Madame Restell (Ann Lohman) traveled in a stylish carriage, relying on the mail order business to reach customers. The press claimed the rich woman's mansion was built on baby skulls, near a special sewer designed to whisk away the corpses, in a wealthy neighborhood where only an "Office" sign on the basement gate revealed the house's true purposes.[59]

Lohman—who had previously served one sentence, had spent months incarcerated without bail, and had been arrested at least five times—swore she would never return to prison, despite Comstock's evidence against her.[60] According to the *Hagerstown (Md.) Herald and Torch Light*, "Mr. Shannon, the husband of Restell's granddaughter, stated to a reporter that Madame Restell seemed very much depressed all day Sunday walking from room to room, wringing her hands and asking why she should be so persecuted, as she had never done anybody any harm in her life."[61] *The Goshen (Ind.) Democrat* disagreed, decried her "vile limbs" hidden in furs and the diamonds dripping from her neck, and denounced the corruption in New York City that allowed her to horde millions from her "business at which Divinity shudders and even humanity revolts."[62]

The midwife worried that the court case was tarnishing her grandchildren's reputations and that a long prison term would punish them more than her. As she finished chatting with her granddaughter and Mr. Shannon, Lohman told them to get up early for court in the morning. Her last words were, "Good night. Oh, how I dread two o'clock."[63] Sometime early the next morning, Lohman slit her throat ear-to-ear with a huge carving knife. The water from the spigots in her bathtub where she had lain down had washed away the blood. When the maid found her naked body, both it and the water were cold.[64]

Papers across the country ran lurid details about Lohman's suicide. "'A bloody ending to a bloody life,' Comstock commented upon hearing of her death," noted Kate Manning. "The newspapers echoed his sentiments. 'The end of sin is death,' wrote the *New York Tribune*, and the *Times* editorialized that Lohman's death was 'a fit ending to an odious career.'"[65]

LEGISLATING MORALITY

The pornographers who lined their shop windows with graphic photos and merchandise as well as filled mailbags with illicit goods generated a public backlash against the flood of obscene newspapers, photos, cards, illustrations, and other wares that flowed across the nation by the end of the Civil War.[66] The purity crusader probably would not have convinced Congress to pass the Comstock Act in 1873 without the urban hubs of saloons, brothels, gambling parlors, and opium dens.[67] Any visitor to a big city's sin zone could purchase guidebooks to houses of prostitution in elegant hotels as well as flash papers full of sex and sports, sensational pulp fiction, and racy photographs.

In the countryside, the U.S. mail delivered ads and publications from pornographers as well as dime novels, cheap romances, and other light fiction. The newspapers frequently carried graphic descriptions of gruesome crimes, scandals, and detailed morality tales rivaling any thriller. Starting in 1844, the first popular men's magazine, the *Police Gazette*, featured spicy accounts of crimes. A radical trade organ of Lima, Ohio, declared in 1894, "In winter months, if you haven't room for a stove, hang up a few extra *Police Gazettes* and one copy of the *Standard*, not more than one of the latter."[68] But the Sunday school movement, Dwight L. Moody and Billy Sunday revivals, the U.S. Salvation Army (launched in Philadelphia in the 1880s), civic committees, libraries, and public schools supported Comstock's purity crusade.[69]

In the post–Civil War decades, anxiety over gambling, drinking, cursing, blasphemy, and sloth swept over the nation. The imperative to maintain the Protestant ethic and patriarchy added family planning, seeking women's rights, and reading to the taboos. As George Bernard Shaw said, referring to those who promoted "Comstockery," cultural changes that accompanied industrialization, immigration, and innovation during the late nineteenth century threatened the Bible-centered, white-male-dominated world.[70] Nevertheless, hypocrisy kept purity crusaders from prosecuting high-class violators who bought pornography, kept mistresses, picked up business cards from madams of elite brothels at luxury hotels, and frequented public library Infernos.[71]

In the early twentieth century, Comstock's agents worked with sympathizers in libraries, churches, schools, and civic organizations to make the U.S. publishing capitals, Boston and New York, centers of book banning. The Comstockery disciples targeted literary lions like Shaw, Dreiser, Sherwood Anderson, Upton Sinclair, Aldous Huxley, Ernest Hemingway, and Erich Maria Remarque.[72]

Two lessons emerge from this era in legal history. First, some values rooted deeply in Western thought reflect universal concerns. The Comstock Act arose from concern for children that began long before the purist was born. Circa 380 B.C. in *The Republic*, Plato recommended censoring fiction writers, thus raising a question still pondered today: "Shall we just carelessly allow children to hear any casual tales, which may be devised by casual persons and to receive into their minds ideas for the most part the very opposite of those which we should wish them to have when they are growing up?"[73] This desire to protect the young from exposure to adult themes has permeated culture for centuries.

Ironically, Victorian newspaper editors recognized the second lesson people learned from Comstock: his solution of publicly proclaiming books too evil to exist often backfired. After calling Comstock a "whippersnapper," the *Goshen (Ind.) Independent* described D. M. Bennett's *Cupid's Yokes* as "an insignificant, puerile, trashy piece of ten cent literature" containing "nothing more obscene in it than is every day in our papers."[74] Reputable dealers sold the pamphlet about the tyranny of marriage, the *Independent* explained, and "the incarceration of Bennett [under the Comstock Act was] the best possible advertisement." Banning books increased sales then as well as today.[75]

Notes

1. Wendell Phillips, *Speeches, Lectures, and Letters* (Cambridge, Mass.: University Press, 1864), 264.

2. Albert Jack, *Pop Goes the Weasel: The Secret Meanings of Nursery Rhymes*, illus. Lara Carlini (New York: Penguin [Perigree Book], 2009), no page given. See, from *Mother Goose Rhymes*,

> Hey diddle, diddle,
> The cat and the fiddle,
> The cow jumped over the moon;
> The little dog laughed
> To see such sport,
> And the dish ran away with the spoon

at www3.amherst.edu/~rjyanco94/literature/mothergoose/rhymes/heydiddlediddle, accessed February 21, 2015.

3. Emile Durkheim, *Rules of Sociological Method*, 1895, 71–72, extracts at http://studymore.org.uk/xDur.html.

4. *Newport (R.I.) Mercury*, September 20, 1806.

5. The quotations originated in the same advertisement, "To Teachers and Others," *Hillsdale (Mich.) Whig Standard*, August 22, 1848.

6. Quoted in Donna Dennis, *Licentious Gotham: Erotic Publishing and Its Prosecution in Nineteenth-Century New York* (Cambridge, Mass.: Harvard University Press, 2009), 29–30.

7. For biographical details, see "Obituary Record of Graduates of Yale University Deceased during the Year 1931–32," *Bulletin of Yale University* (New Haven: Yale University, 1932), 6–7; and his obituary in the *New York Times*, January 8, 1932. The rest of the information originated in James M. Hubbard, "Are Public Libraries Public Blessings?," *North American Review* 149 (September 1889): 339–446, reprinted in *Library Journal* 14, no. 10 (October 1889): 407–9. Also see Leonard Schulp with Stephen H. Paschen, *Librarianship in Gilded Age America: An Anthology of Writings, 1868–1901* (Jefferson, N.C.: McFarland, 2009), 107.

8. Max Cohen, "A Letter Responding to Hubbard," *Library Journal* 14, no. 10 (October 1889): 400.

9. "Editorial Points," *Boston Daily Globe*, August 7, 1897.

10. W. I. Fletcher, "The Inferno in Public Libraries" [letter to the editor], *Critic*, no. 309 (November 30, 1889): 275. The quotations in this paragraph originated in this source. Also see Mary M. Cronin, "The Liberty to Argue Freely: Nineteenth-Century Obscenity Prosecutions and the Emergence of Modern Libertarian Free Speech Discourse," *Journalism and Communication Monographs* 8, no. 3 (September 2006): 173.

11. "Boston's Forbidden Books. Index Expurgations of the Public Library Has on It Political Literature as Well as Obscene—Is the Librarian Infallible?," *Boston Sunday Globe*, August 1, 1897.

12. "A Library Black List: Books That Are Sometimes Excluded as Sensational or Immoral," *Decatur (Ill.) Daily Republican*, March 25, 1882. The list of authors resembled a who's who of dime novel and popular authors: Mrs. A. S. Stephens, Mrs. E. D. E. N. Southworth, Mrs. M. J. Holmes, Mrs. A. J. Evans, Mrs. C. L. Hentz, Mrs. M. F. Finley, Mrs. Henry Wood, Mrs. Forrester, Miss Rhoda Broughton, Miss Helen Mathers, Miss Jessie Fothergill, Miss M. E. Braddon, Miss Florence Marryat (Mrs. Leano), Ouida, Horatio Alger, Mayne Reid, W. H. G. Kingston, E. Kellogg, G. W. M. Reynolds, Oliver Optic, G. A. Lawrence, Edmund Yates, E. C. Greenville Murray, W. H. Ainsworth, Wilkie Collins, F. L. Bulwer (Lord Lytton), and Wm. H. Thomas.

13. "Library Black List."

14. *Norwalk (Ohio) Experiment*, December 8, 1841.

15. "Novel Reading," *Cincinnati Christian Age*, May 10, 1850.

16. "Dime Novel Literature," *Frederick (Md.) Daily News*, December 6, 1884, 2.

17. "Result of Reading Dime Novels," *Freeport (Ill.) Daily Bulletin*, October 25, 1879.

18. "The Indians. Dakota Sioux on the War Path—Return of a Few of Sitting Bull's Braves," *Freeport Daily Bulletin*, October 25, 1879. See "Strange, but True: A Case in Which Fact Beats the Wildest Dreams of Fiction," *Edwardsville (Ill.) Intelligencer*, March 9, 1892. The author compares the real incident to a dime novel plot.

19. "Suspected of Being Assassin: Arrest of Alexander Mitchell, a Youth Yesterday. Crime Laid [*sic*] at His Door. Officials Say He May Have Been the Tool of Alexander's Relatives. Prisoner Denies That He Is Guilty. He Talks in His Cell—His Sweatheart [*sic*] Calls to Him—She Is Alexander's Sister-in-Law. What the Theory of the Detective Is," *Atlanta Constitution*, August 26, 1899.

20. *Colorado Springs Weekly Gazette*, June 25, 1881. No headline appeared over the brief. For an example of a news story linking reading romances with falling for mashers, see "Runaway Matches," reprinted from the *New York Evangelist* in the *Alton (Ill.) Observer*, January 25, 1838. For a typical news account of lads running away, see "A Dime Novel Boy from Chicago," *Alton (Ill.) Telegraph*, May 5, 1888; and "Effect of Dime Novels," *Colorado Springs Daily Gazette*, August 12, 1870. For the homicide of the judge's son, see "Shoots Son of Judge Hughs," in "Around a Big State. Brief Compilation of Illinois News. Collapse of Pekin's Bridge—Dime Novel Reader Commits Murder—To Answer for Murder Committed Years Ago," *Wyoming (Ill.) Post Herald*, September 20, 1899.

21. Dennis, *Licentious Gotham*, 29.

22. Marjorie Heins, *Sex, Sin, and Blasphemy: A Guide to America's Censorship Wars* (New York: New Press, 1994), 19.

23. Dennis, *Licentious Gotham*, 297; and People v. Ruggles, 8 Johns (1811).

24. Dennis, *Licentious Gotham*, 54. Some representative cases include Commonwealth v. Sharpless, 1 S. & R (Pa.) 91 (1815), reprinted in Edward De Grazia, *Censorship Landmarks* (New York: Bowker, 1969), 35–40; and Commonwealth v. Holmes, 17 Mass. 335 (1821), reprinted in De Grazia, *Censorship Landmarks*, 40–41.

25. "A Lesson from the Revolution," *Publishers Weekly* 18, no. 7 (1875): 186–87, quoted in John Tebbel, *The History of Book Publishing in the United States: The Expansion of an Industry*, vol. 2 (New York: Bowker, 1975), 5–6.

26. Paulette D. Kilmer, "Book Soap," *The Fear of Sinking: The American Success Formula in the Gilded Age* (Knoxville: University of Tennessee Press, 1996), 31.

27. Ibid., 23. See William Wallace Cook, *The Fiction Factory* (Ridgewood, N.J.: Editor Company, 1912), 41.

28. "Women Newspaper Readers," *San Antonio Daily Light*, August 9, 1892.

29. Cronin, "Liberty to Argue Freely," 168. See Margaret A. Blanchard, *Revolutionary Sparks: Freedom of Expression in Modern America* (New York: Oxford University Press, 1992), 1–109; Mark Graber, *Transforming Free Speech: The Ambiguous Legacy of Civil Libertarianism* (Berkeley: University of California Press, 1991); and David M. Rabban, *Free Speech in Its Forgotten Years* (New York: Cambridge University Press, 1997).

30. Dennis, *Licentious Gotham*, 22.

31. Patricia Cline Cohen, Timothy J. Gilfoyle, and Helen Lefkowitz Horowitz, *The Flash Press: Sporting Male Weeklies in 1840s New York* (Chicago: University of Chicago Press, 2008), 6.

32. Ibid., 3.

33. Ibid., 1.

34. Ibid., 108.

35. Ibid., 83.

36. Ibid.

37. Sergey Tokarev, "Regina v. Hicklin, L.R. 2 Q.B. 360 (1868)," at http://uscivilliberties.org/cases/4353-regina-v-hicklin-lr-2-qb-360-1868.html.

38. Charles Gallaudet Trumbull, *Anthony Comstock, Fighter: Some Impressions of a Lifetime Adventure in Conflict with the Powers of Evil* (New York: Fleming H. Revell, 1913), 253.

39. Ibid., 240. After estimating that Comstock saved 42 million children from degradation, Trumbull invokes the devil imagery.

40. "Book Notices: *Anthony Comstock, Fighter*," *Biblical World* 43, no. 1 (January 1914): 63.

41. Anthony Comstock, *Traps for the Young*, ed. Robert Bremer (Cambridge, Mass.: Belknap Press of Harvard University Press, 1967), 138.

42. Anna Louise Bates, *Weeder in the Garden of the Lord: Anthony Comstock's Life and Career* (Lanham, Md.: University Press of America, 1995), 15.

43. Ibid., 13.

44. Ibid., 14.

45. Ibid.

46. Marianne Mussett, "Anthony Comstock and His Adversaries: The Mixed Legacy of This Battle for Free Speech," *Communication Law and Policy* 11, no. 317 (Summer 2006): 317.

47. Bates, *Weeder in the Garden of the Lord*, 7.

48. "Brevities," *Fort Wayne (Ind.) Daily Sentinel*, April 11, 1879.

49. Bates, *Weeder in the Garden of the Lord*, 61.

50. Ibid.

51. Ibid., 15.

52. "Anthony Comstock Has Been Arrested and Held to Bail to Answer the Suit of a Lady Physician of This City . . ." *Jefferson (Ind.) National Democrat*, December 11, 1879.

53. Linda Gordon, *The Moral Property of Women: A History of Birth Control Politics in America* (Champaign: University of Illinois Press, 2002), 34.

54. "Anthony Comstock Criticized. Mrs. Sara H. Chase Answers in Public Two Letters Concerning Him," *New York World*, November 23, 1878. The *Eau Claire (Wis.) Daily Free Press* mentioned Dr. Sara Chase's case and several others, including one in which Comstock and his men infiltrated a house of ill repute and then arrested the women for lewd conduct. "These atrocious cases entirely take from Comstock the credit which we were once disposed to allow him, of being a one-ideaed [*sic*] fanatic." See the July 3, 1878, issue.

55. "Anthony Comstock Arrested," *New York Times*, June 26, 1878.

56. "Anthony Comstock Complainant," ibid., May 22, 1885.

57. Gordon, *Moral Property of Women*, 34.

58. Ibid.

59. Kate Manning, "Abortion Wars, the First Time Around," *New York Times*, June 5, 2009; "MME. Restell's Arrest. Efforts to Procure Her Release. Judge Donohue Grants and Dismisses a Writ of Habeas Corpus—Justice Kilbreth Announces That He Will Accept Bail, but Declines to Conceal the Bondsmen's Names—No One Found Willing to Be Known as the Noted Woman's Surety," *New York Times*, February 14, 1878; "Madame Restelle [*sic*] Dead: Or Was Her Reported Suicide All a Sham and a Pauper's Body Buried for Hers?," *Boston Daily Globe*, April 5, 1878.

60. "End of a Notorious Criminal," *Fitchburg (Mass.) Daily Sentinel*, April 2, 1878.

61. "Suicide of the Notorious Madam," *Hagerstown (Md.) Herald and Torch Light*, April 17, 1878.

62. "The Luxury of Crime," *Goshen (Ind.) Democrat*, April 2, 1879. The writer said, "Money came easy; terror made her dupes disgorge almost fabulous sums. . . . She held her head high and swept on in luxury and infamy to the grave."

63. "Suicide of the Notorious Madam." This paper estimated her fortune at between a million and a million and half dollars.

64. The sign on the gate and details about her concern for her grandchildren are mentioned in "End of a Notorious Criminal."

65. Manning, "Abortion Wars."

66. Dennis, *Licentious Gotham*, 9.

67. Ibid., 12.

68. *Bookseller's Friend (A Radical Trade Organ)* 1, no. 1 (July 1894): 5.

69. Mussett, "Anthony Comstock and His Adversaries," 318.

70. Robert W. Haney, *Comstockery in America: Patterns of Censorship and Control* (Boston: Beacon Hill Press, 1960), 21. When in 1905 the New York Public Library put his play, *Man and Superman*, in its Inferno, Shaw assumed Comstock was responsible and coined the term "Comstockery." He said, "Comstockery is the world's standing joke at the expense of the United States. Europe likes to hear of such things. It confirms the deep-seated conviction of the Old World that America is a provincial place, a second-rate country-town civilization after all."

71. Cronin, "Liberty to Argue Freely," 169. The *Bookseller's Friend* charged repeatedly in the July 1894 issue that the big dealers circulated items that Comstock's agents punished small operators for offering.

72. Haney, *Comstockery in America*, 22. The books banned in Boston and/or New York included *The Genius* and *An American Tragedy* (Theodore Dreiser), *Dark Laughter* (Sherwood Anderson), *Oil!* (Upton Sinclair), *Antic Hay* (Aldous Huxley), *The Sun Also Rises* (Ernest Hemingway), and *All Quiet on the Western Front* (Erich Maria Remarque).

73. Quoted in Haney, *Comstockery in America*, 9.

74. "Cupid's Yokes vs. Anthony Comstock," *Goshen (Ind.) Independent*, August 2, 1879. The editor also referred to Comstock as "Stumcock" and said he and "his fanatical followers" persecuted D. M. Bennett to silence his atheistic newspaper, the *Truth Seeker*.

75. Dennis, *Licentious Gotham*, 9.

8. NO RIGHTS FOR THE WORKING MAN

LABORING BEFORE THE FIRST AMENDMENT HAD FORCE

JON BEKKEN

This chapter examines legal and extralegal restrictions on the labor movement in the nineteenth century. This early labor movement was multifaceted, encompassing both local (and later national) craft unions and labor reform societies that tackled a range of issues including abolition, economic and political reform, shorter hours, and universal education. Labor's struggles for equality encompassed both working conditions and workers' place in the broader society. But that role was sharply constrained. Throughout this period, courts held that activities such as boycotts and strikes constituted unlawful conspiracies, that authorities had unfettered license to restrict workers' public meetings and speeches, that their publications could be barred from the mails, and even that labor activists could be imprisoned or hanged for writing articles and giving speeches. Outside of the formal legal arena, workers and their organizations faced not only economic coercion but also in many instances armed attacks by private armies and state militias. Unionists more than once found themselves blacklisted or herded into concentration camps.

Although there is an extensive literature on American battles for free speech, traditionally this has focused on debates in the earliest years of the Republic and on the post–World War I era when free speech rights began to gain traction in the federal courts.[1] African Americans, abolitionists, and women's rights and labor activists frequently raised free speech arguments throughout the nineteenth century, but these claims were largely ignored by the courts and until recently received little attention from historians. As Jim Hawkins notes, "The early labor movement . . . remains an unexplored chapter in the history of free speech—it remains *truly* forgotten."[2]

The judiciary and much of the press simply could not conceive of workers' and other marginalized groups' advocacy for their interests as a legitimate exercise of freedom of speech. As David M. Rabban has observed,

> Judges who denied free speech claims before World War I, and even vigilantes who physically attacked the soapbox speakers of the Industrial Workers of the World (IWW) during their free speech fights . . . often emphasized their own deep commitment to what they deemed proper conceptions of free speech.[3]

Similarly, John Nerone notes that mob actions to silence radical speakers and minority voices were often championed in the establishment press, which bemoaned the "abusive" behavior of the victims in raising their voices despite the admonition of their betters.[4]

The federal government was quite open in its belief that only respectable citizens enjoyed free speech rights. The successful brief defending the deportation of English anarchist John Turner termed his First Amendment claims "incomprehensible. . . . Abridgement of the freedom of speech or of the press is no more brought about by the exclusion or expulsion of anarchists than by similar treatment of the followers of Confucius."[5]

The consequences of speaking and publishing could be severe, as the Haymarket Martyrs found when they were sentenced to death on the basis of speeches and newspaper articles calling upon workers to organize and to defend themselves against the armed attacks of guards and police. In *Spies v. Illinois* (1887), the Chicago anarchists unsuccessfully argued that the Fourteenth Amendment applied the First Amendment to the states. A similar argument had been accepted by a federal judge in 1871 but was not seriously considered by the U.S. Supreme Court until 1907 and not adopted for another two decades.[6]

Nonetheless, free expression remained a crucial part of labor's strategy throughout the 1800s despite the hostile legal arena, and union leaders explicitly grounded their right to expression in the First Amendment and in democratic theory. Labor activists used newspapers, advertisements, petitions, handbills, parades, and public demonstrations to promote their cause. During the great labor unrest of 1833, "processions and festivals enlivened the unionists' efforts, proclaiming to all their public identity and social ideals." In 1836, the attorney representing tailors in a conspiracy trial argued that it was unconstitutional to restrict workers' rights: "Shall all others, except only the industrious mechanic, be allowed to meet? . . . I ask again, is this repugnant to the rights of man? If it be, is it not repugnant to our constitution?"[7]

Labor was equally alert to suppression of its rights by extrajudicial means. A coordinating committee of German-speaking trade unions joined other unions in condemning the brutality and arrests police used to suppress the 1850 tailors' strike: "We did not expect to find in this free country a Russian Police, nor do we believe that the people will sustain these officials in their evident abuse of power."[8]

SOCIAL REFORMERS AND A FREE PRESS

The nineteenth century saw several waves of reform agitation, from the labor reform associations that pursued abolitionism and labor and women's rights to social reformers such as Wendell Phillips and Victoria Woodhull in the post–Civil War era. These reformers were an eclectic lot. Their sometimes-radical views arose in a context of social ferment that saw the *New York Tribune* hire Karl Marx as a correspondent and publish articles expounding the ideas of the French anarchist Pierre-Joseph Proudhon.[9] Among those reformers was Ezra Heywood, who pursued "negro emancipation, peace, women's enfranchisement, temperance, labor and love reform" but is perhaps best remembered for several obscenity prosecutions stemming from his pamphlet *Cupid's Yokes*, which criticized the marriage institution as an infringement of women's rights. While Heywood appealed his conviction on First Amendment grounds, the courts summarily rejected the argument that free expression applied to "matter deemed injurious to the public morals."[10]

Expression was central to labor activism from its very origins, although a labor press arose only in the 1820s.[11] Labor newspapers become more firmly established after the U.S. Civil War and more closely linked to particular immigrant groups, political tendencies, or unions. They largely escaped the waves of repression following the 1877 national railroad strike, the 1886 Haymarket affair (the *Arbeiter-Zeitung* continued daily publication even with most of its staff in prison),[12] and the labor strife of the 1890s. Labor papers, Nerone states, "were rarely the first target of anti-labor violence. First were usually picketers and demonstrators. They were closely followed by labor organizers and orators, and people distributing leaflets and other literature. Labor's newspapers were not usually its most public face."[13]

However, several criminal libel actions were brought against labor editors in the 1880s, and labor newspapers were often included in injunctions against strikes and boycotts.[14] J. P. McDonnell, editor of the Paterson, New Jersey, *Labor Standard*, was twice convicted of libel (in 1878 for referring to strikebreakers as "scabs" and in 1880 for publishing a letter describing working conditions at a brickyard), serving a two-month prison sentence for the second offense.[15] *Freiheit* editor Johann Most was convicted of endangering the peace following a speech (the day after the hanging of the Haymarket Martyrs) urging workers to prepare for the day of revolution, and later for publishing an article maintaining that all government is founded on murder.[16]

Labor supporters' exercise of their free speech rights remained on shaky legal ground throughout the nineteenth century. In 1894, the Massachusetts Supreme Court, in an opinion by Oliver Wendell Holmes, rejected a social gospel preacher's argument that there was a "constitutional right of citizens to the use of public grounds and places," ruling that the authorities had the unfettered right to determine who would be permitted to speak in public.[17]

THE RIGHT TO ASSEMBLE

Most early case law treated any combination of workers to advance their economic interests as an unlawful conspiracy against the public. Under this theory, union workers were barred from striking, refusing to work with nonunion workers, encouraging others to withdraw their labor, picketing, or asking union members or the general public to withhold patronage from particular employers with whom unions had disputes. Such activities could lead to prosecutions under common-law conspiracy theories, fines and imprisonment, and, later, to injunctions and imprisonment through contempt proceedings.[18] While the judiciary upheld the right of individual workers to withdraw their labor (at least where they had not contracted for some fixed period) or negotiate their wages, to do so in concert with other workers raised the specter of conspiracy. Even the 1842 decision commonly cited as bringing an end to this presumption coupled its ruling that workers had a theoretical right to organize and to seek to control the terms of their labor with severe strictures upon any effort to "coerce" employers into compliance.[19]

An extensive literature has developed on the judiciary's efforts to prevent labor organization as conspiracies.[20] While workers recognized these prosecutions as a clear infringement of their rights of freedom of association[21] and speech, and often could persuade juries of this, judges by and large found such claims incomprehensible. In 1805, for example, Philadelphia shoemakers published an appeal against their impending prosecution:

> In the constitution of this state, it is declared . . . "that the citizens have a right in a peaceable manner to assemble together for the common good." For fifteen years and upwards we have assembled together in a peaceable manner. . . . The master shoemakers, as they are called after the slavish style of Europe . . . [also] have their associations, their meetings, and they pass their resolutions; but as they are rich and we are poor—they seem to think that we are not protected by the constitution.[22]

There were at least twenty-three conspiracy prosecutions against labor organizations from 1806 to 1847, by which time courts were becoming more skeptical of the offense. In early cases the defendants were usually convicted, touching off intense controversy, until judges felt compelled to shift their rationale from combinations being unlawful per se to finding particular purposes or tactics unlawful. Thus, in 1806 the prosecutor condemned the cordwainers (shoemakers) as "men who can pack up their all in a knapsack" and their union as a "secret association, this private club" that undermined public order by its very existence. The judge instructed the jury to convict, stating,

> What is the case now before us? A combination of workmen to raise their wages may be considered in a two-fold point of view: one is to benefit themselves . . . the other is to injure those who do not join their society. The rule of law condemns both.[23]

Three years later, New York City cordwainers were similarly convicted of conspiring to raise wages, although the judge ruled that the offense was not forming their association but rather their concerted refusal to work for any employer who paid less than the agreed rate. In 1815, shoemakers were indicted in Pittsburgh, where the prosecution claimed that organizing to seek higher wages was a criminal conspiracy in itself.

In the 1820s, courts began requiring prosecutors to allege unlawful behavior, not mere association, resulting in a growing number of acquittals.[24] But in 1835, New York's appellate court overturned a trial court ruling that Geneva shoemakers had a legal right to collectively set their wages, concluding that their actions were indictable as they tended to raise the price of boots and so make local manufacturers uncompetitive.[25] A wave of similar prosecutions followed, but most did not result in convictions. In the face of these prosecutions, but also with a growing sense of their power, workers vigorously proclaimed their right to assemble, formed local and national labor federations, demonstrated, and continued to strike. Juries often were sympathetic to labor's appeals, proving reluctant to convict. As Hawkins has stated,

> In the five major trials against workers between 1833 and 1836, three declared the workers not guilty, the three in which juries were given free reign to apply the law to the facts on their own. In the other two trials, the judges essentially directed verdicts against the workers. . . . The unfavorable public response to the decisions against workers, generating protest crowds estimated at 30,000, gives reason to believe that the jury, representing the community, might have acted differently had they been truly autonomous. . . . The relative success of workers in front of juries gave way to profound failure in front of judges when judges later took over for juries and began issuing injunctions.[26]

The case law is replete with workers exercising their right to assembly. In 1836, twenty New York tailors were tried on criminal conspiracy charges—ostensibly for seeking to raise wages and intimidate nonunion workers, but actually over employers' repudiation of the existing wage scale and their declaration that they would no longer employ union members. Popular outrage was pronounced, and thousands joined a parade protesting the indictment. At trial, the employers conceded that there was no violence from the strikers (though they had been beaten by police), but this was of no consequence. Tailors had "paraded before the doors and windows [of shops] . . . insulting, vilifying, and applying the most opprobrious epithets to journeymen who continued in employ." To rid themselves of these "annoyances and interruptions to trade," the employers had the police arrest the tailors' leaders.[27] The judge's jury instructions demanded conviction, though jurors requested leniency. Judge Ogden Edwards imposed what he described as "a very mild punishment"—a fine of $1,150 (nearly three years' wages).

The court did not have even an inchoate notion that any law protected the right of free labor expression. In contrast, workers recognized that liberty, not just economics, was at stake. The "Coffin Handbill" anonymously distributed in response to the trial sarcastically demanded that workers "bend meekly, and receive the chains wherewith you are to be bound!" Workers denounced the "concerted plan of the aristocracy to take from them that Liberty which was bequeathed to them" and rejected the conspiracy law as "subversive of the rights and liberties of American citizens." Thirty thousand workers jammed City Hall Park to protest, burning the judge in effigy, and unions around the country protested with resolutions, effigies, and a ceremonial "burial of liberty."[28] Weeks later, a New York jury acquitted eight shoemakers facing similar charges, concluding that no coercion had taken place.[29]

Eight hundred women operatives joined the shoemakers' strike in Lynn, Massachusetts, which took place during a snowstorm on March 7, 1860. Despite the weather, the strikers carried banners and were preceded by the Lynn City Guards with music. Approximately four thousand workmen, firemen, and others joined the march. *Frank Leslie's Illustrated Newspaper*, March 17, 1860; Library of Congress Prints and Photographs Division, Washington, D.C.

By midcentury it was difficult to secure a conviction on the mere facts of having formed a labor association or sought higher wages; something more—such as an appeal to consumers not to patronize nonunion firms or other efforts at pressuring employers—was needed. Picketing against the employers' concerted action to cut wages might suffice, as in the 1842 case of eighteen Rockdale, Pennsylvania, workers indicted for conspiracy and riot, where the presiding judge declared that it was not the strike itself that was unlawful (presumably rejecting the prosecution's argument that "the prices of labor must be regulated by the manufacturers" rather than by "arbitrary rules" adopted by the workers) but rather the picketing and other means employed.[30] A similar distinction between combination and the means used was drawn in the Massachusetts case of *Commonwealth v. Hunt*, also decided in 1842.[31]

Just as criminal libel prosecutions did not silence the partisan press, so unions continued to organize (though sometimes as secret societies) and strike despite their legally precarious situation. There were hundreds of recorded strikes during the period when the courts considered labor unions criminal per se, with only a handful drawing judicial attention.[32] Judges seemingly preferred admonishing workers to crushing them. Much of the literature focuses on the relatively modest penalties imposed.[33] There is no known instance of a prison sentence in these cases, though many defendants were held for trial at exorbitant bail or held after sentencing until fines were paid.[34] In 1806, the cordwainers were fined eight dollars each (a bit more than a week's wages) plus court costs and ordered imprisoned until their fines were paid. In 1836, more than five thousand workers rallied in Philadelphia's Independence Square to protest prosecution (brought despite the refusal of the grand jury to indict) of several coal heavers and the court's imposition of $2,500 bail, resulting in the men's imprisonment awaiting trial. Philadelphia's mayor proclaimed that the prosecution was an attempt to "fell the tree [of the Philadelphia Trades' Union] that it might lay and rot"; the jury ultimately acquitted the men, and they were released from prison.[35]

Conspiracy prosecutions remained a common means of regulating union activities through the century. New York courts held, in 1867, that it was an indictable offense to demand that employers accept a union's wage scale; a New Jersey court held that union members could not refuse to work alongside nonunion men. When a single member of the Morrisania (New York) Bricklayers' Union quit work rather than teach a young man the craft outside of the union-controlled apprentice system, the union was convicted on conspiracy charges and seven of its officials fined.[36] In 1887, criminal conspiracy charges were brought against printers who waged a boycott campaign to try to compel the *Journal and Courier* of New Haven, Connecticut, to hire a union workforce.[37] But such prosecutions were increasingly difficult to sustain in the court of public opinion, and several legislatures passed laws expressly permitting unionization, to little effect. Felix Frankfurter and Nathan Greene noted in 1930, "On the whole, legislation has done little to restrict the courts in applying common law notions of conspiracy to labor disputes."[38]

As conspiracy convictions became more difficult to secure from juries, the level of violence deployed against unionists increased. Josiah Lambert finds only one instance of federal troops being deployed against strikers in the pre–Civil War era, during an 1835 strike by canal builders, and terms the show of force "purely symbolic." Similarly, the National Guard was called out in 1836 to intimidate striking dockworkers, but since they quickly returned to work he again does not see this as forceful suppression. Police more often were deployed against strikers, as in 1850 when New York police killed two strikers and seriously wounded dozens more. Though presented by Lambert as evidence of restraint (as the only known case of lethal force used against unionists by government in this era), there are many accounts of police beatings and forcible dispersal of demonstrations and picket lines.[39]

David Montgomery notes the repeated use of the army to break strikes, including the dispatch in 1864 of two companies of troops who imposed martial law and jailed strike leaders for seven weeks, until the strikers capitulated. (The pretext was the army's need for the guns they produced.) In St. Louis, the military outlawed union meetings, picketing, and strikes the same year. In 1865, hundreds of troops and a sheriff's posse raided company towns, evicting some four thousand striking coal miners and their families, arresting union leaders, and enabling operators to cut wages in half and employ only workers who pledged never to join a union.[40]

Police and military intervention increased in the post–Civil War years. Beginning with the 1877 railroad strikes, repression of strikes became more violent and more routine, with the National Guard deployed at least 118 times in a single decade; in addition, repression by local police and private security forces continued. This increasingly violent response to labor activities led, Lambert concludes, to most unions abandoning broader social goals and mobilizing strategies in favor of modest actions in pursuit of narrow goals less likely to draw the wrath of the state. "The emergence of pure-and-simple unionism and the transformation of the right to strike were a reaction to the state's use of force to suppress strikes," Lambert says. "Officials within the executive branch during this era had little difficulty finding compliant judges to sign formulaic strike injunction orders. If none were available, they could declare martial law and suspend the authority of the civil courts."[41]

These conflicts led to an increasingly militarized rhetoric in which all sides spoke of class warfare.[42] Deaths and injuries were increasingly common, with twenty Pittsburgh workers killed in a single incident when the militia opened fire on railroad strike sympathizers. The massacre touched off a riot that resulted in destruction of rail cars and property, but the resultant deployment of the U.S. Army quickly broke the strike.[43] While deployed in the name of "restoring order," Melvyn Dubofsky concludes the army's real role in these disputes was strikebreaking.[44]

Police routinely broke up peaceful labor demonstrations, as on January 13, 1874, when New York City police attacked thousands of unemployed workers rallying in Tompkins Square Park, even though they had secured a permit from city officials.[45] Arrests were common throughout this period, though most did not result in prosecution. By the end of the century, the police and courts were centrally involved in labor disputes, regularly arresting large numbers of workers during strikes and issuing sweeping injunctions against any efforts

Upper-class men and women hoot at coal miners in Mahanoy City, Pennsylvania, during a miners' strike. *Frank Leslie's Illustrated Newspaper*, March 25, 1871; Library of Congress Prints and Photographs Division, Washington, D.C.

to mobilize solidarity or otherwise promote labor's cause. In this increasingly repressive context, labor leaders began to develop a far more elaborated sense of their constitutional rights and devoted substantial energies to legislative and political action to rein in the courts and police.

In many instances, it can be difficult to disentangle allegations of violence from suppression of labor activities. Federal troops seized hundreds of Western Federation of Miners members in the Coeur d'Alene, Idaho, mining district after miners fired for union membership blew up the Bunker Hill mill. The striking miners were held for a year in concentration camps, with no effort to distinguish those responsible for the explosion. When the WFM passed a resolution denouncing the violation of "these fundamental principles of right, justice and humanity guaranteed to the people by the Constitution," prosecutors used it as a pretext to build a murder charge against union officials.[46]

In 1903, state troopers again rounded up striking miners and union sympathizers (including the entire staff of the *Victor Record*) in concentration camps, this time without the pretext of strike violence, and trained a Gatling gun on a courthouse where habeas corpus proceedings were underway. The next year, prosecutors indicted WFM secretary-treasurer William D. Haywood for a poster, "Is Colorado in America?," which detailed on each of the flag's thirteen stripes violations of workers' rights.[47]

This war against the miners' union had so little to do with actual union violence that Colorado authorities prosecuted a WFM official on murder charges even though they had met with the alleged victim shortly before the trial began. (Vincent St. John was acquitted because of insufficient evidence; the fabricated nature of the charges was discovered only recently.)[48]

THE LABOR INJUNCTION

Although conspiracy prosecutions continued throughout the century, particularly in cases where intimidation (moral or otherwise) could be alleged, by the 1880s injunctions had replaced criminal conspiracy prosecutions as the primary means of controlling labor.[49] According to Frankfurter and Greene, "During the remaining years of the century the cases grew in volume like a rolling snowball."[50] Injunctions prohibited workers on railroads from striking, barred picketing or attempts to persuade scabs to quit work, enjoined boycotts and peaceable appeals for community support, and banned strike meetings and demonstrations.[51] With injunctions, workers could be arrested, compelled to testify against themselves (as these were not technically criminal proceedings),[52] and sentenced to prison without the risk of a jury trial. As the dissent in *Hopkins et al. v. Oxley Stove Co.* concluded, the injunction

> is, indeed, the revival of despotism for laborers, and means their practical enslavement to great aggregations of capital, whose greed takes no note of human destitution and suffering. Their adversaries combine to act collectively, and it is not a conspiracy. . . . Let the constitutional mode of trial remain inviolate. The necessity for this is illustrated in this case. No American jury could be found who would say these defendants were guilty of a "conspiracy," or of making "threats" to injure any one.[53]

During the American Railway Union's 1894 strike against the Pullman Company, more than one hundred injunctions were served on union officials and supporters. The railroads responded in ways designed to maximize the disruption in order to obtain sweeping injunctions against the union, its members, and, in the words of the injunction against ARU president Eugene V. Debs, "all other persons whomsoever" inclined to support them.[54] A ruling sentencing ARU organizer F. W. Phelan to six months' imprisonment on contempt charges noted that "he has made as many as 20 speeches" in which "he has continued to explain the Pullman trouble." The fact that he asked workers to act not in their own behalf but in support of others was an aggravating factor. The judge in the case noted, "Something has been said about the right of assembly and free speech secured by the constitution of Ohio. It would be strange, indeed, if that right could be used to sustain the carrying out of such an unlawful and criminal conspiracy."[55] Yet while ARU president Eugene V. Debs blamed the injunctions for the strike's defeat, Lambert argues that "government by injunction . . . would have failed without the deployment of thousands of federal troops."[56] Dubofsky agrees; although the strike was essentially peaceful, "only the army could break the boycott."[57]

Although the U.S. Supreme Court ruled on the validity of a labor injunction for the first time in 1895 and the Massachusetts chief justice noted that issuance of such injunctions was "of very recent origin" the next year,[58] these merely continued the courts' long-standing hostility toward unions. The injunction upheld in *Vegelahn v. Guntner* shows the depth of this judicial animosity; the majority opinion charges that the union

> conspired to prevent [the employer] from getting workmen . . . unless and until he should adopt a certain schedule of prices [wages]. The means adopted were persuasion and social pressure . . . and a patrol of two men in front of the plaintiff's factory. . . . Intimidation is not limited to threats of violence or of physical injury to person or property. It has a broader signification, and there also may be a *moral intimidation* which is illegal.[59]

The chief justice dissented, questioning the wisdom of such injunctions and arguing that, contrary to the majority holding, it was lawful "to persuade one man not to enter into the employment of another, by telling the truth to him about such other person and his business," so long as no contract was interfered with.[60]

However, First Amendment issues could not be entirely ignored. In a Massachusetts case[61] the *Vegelahn* court relied upon for precedent, the court argued it was enjoining picketing not as defamation, which would be protected from prior restraint even by its crabbed notion of freedom of speech, but rather as a public nuisance. Similarly, an Ohio court refused to prohibit picketers from displaying placards and handing out leaflets, arguing that enjoining a libel violated the defendants' freedom of speech: "Abuse of the right may be punished criminally, or by civil suit for damages; but the constitution . . . has wisely provided, by implication at least, that the abuse of the right shall not be anticipated by the courts and enjoined."[62]

Overall, however, injunctions not only proliferated but became more sweeping—prohibiting picketing, strike rallies, private meetings, letters and telephone conversations, strike announcements, boycotts, and the like—extending their scope from union members and officials to entire communities and "all persons whomsoever." Failure to comply subjected union officials to contempt proceedings heard by the judge issuing the order, with no right to trial by jury as the courts held that these were not criminal proceedings.[63]

PUBLIC APPEALS UNLAWFUL

A common target of injunctions was boycott campaigns, where labor activists published lists of "unfair" employers and urged workers and sympathizers not to patronize them. The boycott, notes historian Norman Ware, was the most successful form of union activity in the Knights of Labor era (which peaked in the mid-1880s), in large part because unionists could count upon support from the wider community and, initially at least, boycotts were less likely to draw hostile action from the courts than strike action.[64] Class consciousness was relatively well entrenched, and workers were served by distinctive brands and products that were quite vulnerable to labor boycotts. But by 1886 courts were increasingly inclined to intervene against boycotts, on the theory that workers' peaceably distributing circulars and discussing their labor dispute with passersby constituted intimidation and/or extortion.[65]

In 1894, an injunction was issued against the Essex Trades Council in New Jersey against distribution of circulars placing the daily *Newark Times* on its unfair list and urging advertisers to cease doing business with the paper. The Essex unions appear to have been particularly vigorous in encouraging their members to use their purchasing power to support union organization, and the boycott resulted in much reduced circulation and advertising. While conceding the typographers' right to withdraw their labor (even collectively), they had no right to notify other unions that the *Times* was no longer a union shop, nor did other unions have the right to issue resolutions and circulars urging advertisers and subscribers to withdraw their patronage, as these constituted "moral intimidation." The court stated,

> What other result than injury could ensue to the business of the Newark Times . . . if organizations of individuals representing there a purchasing power of $400,000 a week . . . not only determined not to patronize the paper or to buy it, but, by resolutions passed in their various organizations, call upon the trading community to cease advertising in it. . . . Loss of business is the only natural result to be expected from such a condition of affairs, and, if continued, the failure of the enterprise would seem to be inevitable.

And so, because unionists' use of their purchasing power was an effective weapon, the court issued an injunction against it. "It is true there was no public disturbance, no physical injury, no direct threats of personal violence, or of actual attack on or destruction of tangible property," the court acknowledged. However, "every one is entitled to a chance for the patronage of the public, uninfluenced by malicious interference to excite prejudice."[66]

Similarly, in *Casey v. Cincinnati Typographical Union No. 3*, the union raised free speech arguments in defending its efforts to compel an employer to end his two-year lockout of union typographers. However, the court ruled,

> No case has been cited where, upon a proper showing of facts, an unsuccessful appeal has been made to a court of chancery to restrain a boycott. The authorities are all the other way. . . . It is idle to talk about the defendants' acts and publications as . . . shielded by constitutional guaranties.

While the court conceded that the claims made by the union in its boycott materials were true, that there was no evidence of force, and that the only coercion employed was that of workers refusing to patronize the boycott target, the union and its supporters were still enjoined.[67]

In *Gompers v. Buck's Stove & Range Co.*, the U.S. Supreme Court held that an injunction against the American Federation of Labor did not constitute prior restraint upon publication in defiance of the actual record quoted in its own opinion.[68] The trial court twice imposed prison sentences against AFL officials for violating the injunction, although those were overturned on appeal on technical grounds.[69]

Even the right to engage in political advocacy unrelated to the workplace was at best tenuous in this era. During the nineteenth century, a handful of states enacted laws restricting employers' right to discipline or terminate workers for voting or campaigning for candidates or political causes.[70] Such restrictions are an exception to the general U.S. doctrine, articulated by the Tennessee Supreme Court in 1884, that employers have the unfettered right to terminate employees for any reason, or for no reason at all.[71] Under this doctrine, courts continue to uphold employers' right to fire workers for off-the-job speech to this day.

Leaving to the side workers' very limited protections in some states against employer retaliation for individually exercising their First Amendment rights of assembly, association, petition,[72] and speech, their unions continue to face restrictions and even outright prohibitions upon the collective exercise of these rights. Thus, courts consistently uphold legislative restrictions on so-called secondary boycotts, jurisdictional picketing, and picketing for union recognition by labor organizations, even while finding that such activities are protected under the First Amendment when exercised by others for what the courts recognize as political activity.[73]

Labor organizations have long responded by lobbying for legal protections, through publicity campaigns aimed at building public support for the right to organize, and through community and workplace mobilizations that challenge these restrictions and seek to constrain the authorities' ability to exercise them. Although these efforts bore substantial fruit in the 1920s and 1930s, those gains have been steadily eroded in recent years.

This discrimination against labor's rights of assembly and expression has deep roots in American jurisprudence. Lacking any theoretical or constitutional rationale, it would appear to be grounded in nothing more than animus against those who must toil to support themselves.

Notes

1. See Fiske v. Kansas, 274 U.S. 380 (1927), for what I long believed to be the first case where the Supreme Court overturned a criminal conviction for free speech activity—in this case an Industrial Workers of the World organizer convicted under Kansas's criminal syndicalism law for distributing IWW newspapers and trying to recruit workers into the union. The decision was based not on the First Amendment but rather on due process grounds. However, a member of the Knights of Labor was released from a much shorter sentence in 1888 when the Court ruled his conspiracy conviction could not stand because he had been denied his right to trial by jury. Callan v. Wilson, 127 U.S. 540 (1888).

2. Jim Hawkins, "Papers, Petitions, and Parades: Free Expression's Pivotal Function in the Early Labor Movement," *Berkeley Journal of Employment and Labor Law* 28, no. 1 (2007): 66. Emphasis in original.

3. David M. Rabban, *Free Speech in Its Forgotten Years* (New York: Cambridge University Press, 1997), 13.

4. John Nerone, *Violence against the Press: Policing the Public Sphere in U.S. History* (Oxford: Oxford University Press), 1994.

5. Cited in Rabban, *Free Speech in Its Forgotten Years*, 135.

6. Some Chicago police were killed by a bomb while attacking a lawful rally protesting police violence against strikers; police gunfire killed at least four workers and wounded scores of others. Murder charges were brought against the editors of three anarchist and labor newspapers and other labor activists, none of whom were involved in the actual bombing. Four of the Haymarket defendants were hanged, a fifth committed suicide while awaiting execution, and three served long prison terms before being pardoned. There is an extensive literature on this case; the most comprehensive account remains Paul Avrich, *The Haymarket Tragedy* (Princeton: Princeton University Press, 1984). More recently, Timothy Messer-Kruse has sought to rehabilitate the prosecution's case in *The Trial of the Haymarket Anarchists: Terrorism and Justice in the Gilded Age* (New York: Palgrave Macmillan, 2011).

7. Quoted in Hawkins, "Papers, Petitions, and Parades," 79.

8. German Central Committee of the United Trades, "Declaration," *New York Tribune*, July 26, 1850. The statement ends by adding the seventeen member associations' endorsement to the resolution of the New York City Industrial Congress denouncing the prosecutions and supporting the tailors' efforts to secure wages adequate to "enable them to live without being dependent upon charity."

9. Adam Tuchinsky, *Horace Greeley's "New-York Tribune": Civil War–Era Socialism and the Crisis of Free Labor* (Ithaca, NY: Cornell University Press, 2009), 10.

10. Ex parte Jackson, 96 U.S. 727 (1877), cited in Rabban, *Free Speech in Its Forgotten Years*, 36. The Heywood prosecutions are discussed on pp. 32–36.

11. Jon Bekken, "'No Weapon So Powerful': Working-Class Newspapers in the United States," *Journal of Communication Inquiry* 12, no. 2 (1988): 104–19.

12. Jon Bekken, "The First Anarchist Daily Newspaper: The *Chicago Arbeiter-Zeitung*," *Anarchist Studies* 3, no. 3 (1995): 3–23.

13. Nerone, *Violence against the Press*, 170.

14. David Montgomery, *Beyond Equality: Labor and the Radical Republicans* (New York: Knopf, 1967).

15. Herbert Gutman, "Joseph P. McDonnell and the Workers' Struggle in Paterson, New Jersey," *Power and Culture: Essays on the American Working Class* (New York: New Press, 1987), 98–100.

16. Rabban, *Free Speech in Its Forgotten Years*, 143–44.

17. David Kairys, "Freedom of Speech," in *The Politics of Law*, ed. David Kairys, rev. ed. (New York: Pantheon Books, 1990), 239. The ruling in Commonwealth v. Davis, 162 Mass. 510 (1895), was upheld on appeal by the U.S. Supreme Court; see Davis v. Massachusetts, 167 U.S. 43 (1897). Four decades later, in Hague v. CIO, 307 U.S. 496 (1939), the Court evaded its earlier holding by noting that Davis had refused to apply for a permit.

18. Although some historians are keen to emphasize that no pre–Civil War prison sentences were imposed by the courts, in many cases union members and officials were held in pretrial detention.

19. Commonwealth v. Hunt, 445 Mass. (4 Met.) 111 (1842).

20. The relevant decisions are gathered in John Commons et al., eds., *A Documentary History of American Industrial Society* (Cleveland: Arthur H. Clark, 1910). Christopher Tomlins offers a detailed analysis of this literature in *Law, Labor, and Ideology in the Early American Republic* (Cambridge: Cambridge University Press, 1993). Although these prosecutions have been addressed by labor historians, and to a lesser extent in the law journals, they have been ignored in the communications literature.

21. Although we are now accustomed to referring to a right of association, the actual text of the First Amendment references the right to "assemble," implying a right to use public space and to act that goes well beyond mere association. John D. Inazu, *Liberty's Refuge: The Forgotten Freedom of Assembly* (New Haven: Yale University Press, 2012), 4–5.

22. "Address of the Working Shoemakers of the City of Philadelphia to the Public," *Philadelphia Aurora*, November 28, 1805, cited in Tomlins, *Law, Labor, and Ideology*, 109–10.

23. This discussion and the quotes are taken from Tomlins, *Law, Labor, and Ideology*, 128–33.

24. Tomlins offers a detailed review of this evolution in ibid., 128–219. In an 1821 case, shoemakers brought a prosecution against a group of master ladies' shoemakers on a charge of conspiracy to reduce wages. The earlier cases had been clear in condemning all combinations to set wages, and the trial judge evidently felt compelled to apply the same standard to employers as to employees. A Pennsylvania Supreme Court justice remanded the case, warning of the danger of "impart[ing] criminality to the most laudable associations" and holding that prosecutions for combination should focus on the object of the conspiracy and whether injury would result from it (146). There is no record of the ultimate outcome, though it seems likely that the employers were released. The precedent served to increase the number of acquittals for members of labor associations.

25. Ibid., 150–51.

26. Hawkins, "Papers, Petitions, and Parades," 103.

27. People v. Faulkner (N.Y. Ct. Oyer & Terminer 1836). This discussion draws upon Hawkins, "Papers, Petitions, and Parades," 92–97, and Tomlins, *Law, Labor, and Ideology*, 160–66.

28. Unionists made an urgent appeal for funds when the verdict was announced and so were able to pay the fine. Otherwise the tailors would have been imprisoned until the funds could be secured. Tomlins, *Law, Labor, and Ideology*, 162–65. Wage data from Marian Henry, "New York State Census Records," 2003, downloaded September 5, 2014, from http://www.americanancestors.org/new-york-state-census-records/.

29. People v. Cooper (1836), cited in Tomlins, *Law, Labor, and Ideology*, 166–67. A Philadelphia jury similarly acquitted unionists on conspiracy charges as they had merely refused to work with a nonunion worker. He continued on the job, and they left. Commonwealth v. Grinder (1836), cited in ibid., 173.

30. Commonwealth v. McConnell (1842), cited in ibid., 175–78. The case was heard by a three-judge panel rather than by jury. The ruling agreed that the defendants had the legal right to strike and to assemble to pursue their common interests. However, they had "confederate[d] to raise the wages beyond the rate the manufacturers were willing to pay," held "hostile demonstrations," and induced other workers to quit work in support of the strike. The three strike leaders were fined $95 and more than $1,000 in costs. Unable to pay, they were committed to prison for two weeks. A public subscription raised the funds to meet the costs of the prosecution.

31. See ibid., 180–219, for an extended discussion of this case, which remained the leading case for decades to come. The indictment arose when the boot makers fined one of their number for violating union rules; he refused to pay and was fired after union members refused to work alongside him. The judge's instructions stressed that workers did have the right to form a society, so long as they did not "injure or control" employers or those who did not join the union. However, the Society of Journeymen Bootmakers "was a new power in the state" whose "secret and unknown tribunals" could lead only to "frightful despotism" (204). In 1842, Massachusetts's Supreme Judicial Court ruled that conspiracy indictments required evidence of either unlawful purpose or unlawful means. The conviction was therefore reversed, as neither had been alleged.

32. Josiah Lambert, *"If the Workers Took a Notion": The Right to Strike and American Political Development* (Ithaca: ILR Press, 2005), 21.

33. See, e.g., ibid., 22. Lambert follows a long line of scholars who contend that in none of these early cases "did strikers serve any jail time." This is not true. Although none resulted in prison sentences, workers were often imprisoned pending trial or held after sentencing until they could pay fines or costs; the latter could be quite substantial.

34. Tomlins, *Law, Labor, and Ideology*, 164n112. However, imprisonment was sometimes ordered in later cases. In *Callan v. Wilson*, Callan was convicted on conspiracy charges and ordered to pay a fine of twenty-five dollars or serve thirty days in jail. Refusing to pay, he was imprisoned until the Supreme Court ordered his release, agreeing with his contention that he was entitled to trial by jury.

35. Bruce Laurie, *Working People of Philadelphia, 1800–1850* (Philadelphia: Temple University Press, 1980), 90–92; Tomlins, *Law, Labor, and Ideology*.

36. Montgomery, *Beyond Equality*, 146–48.

37. State v. Glidden, 55 Conn. 46 (1887). The Supreme Court of Errors' opinion dripped with contempt toward the unionists who proposed through "fear and terror" (no evidence of anything more than "concerted withdrawal of the patronage of the defendants and their associates" was on offer) "to deprive the Carrington Publishing Company of its liberty to carry on its business in its own way." The conspiracy conviction was upheld; the record does not reflect the sentence imposed.

38. Felix Frankfurter and Nathan Greene, *The Labor Injunction* (New York: Macmillan, 1930), 137–38.

39. Lambert, *"If the Workers Took a Notion,"* 22–23.

40. Montgomery, *Beyond Equality*, 100–101.

41. Lambert, *"If the Workers Took a Notion,"* 44.

42. Troy Rondinone, *The Great Industrial War: Framing Class Conflict in the Media, 1865–1950* (New Brunswick: Rutgers University Press, 2009).

43. Lambert, *"If the Workers Took a Notion,"* 53–54.

44. Melvyn Dubofsky, *The State and Labor in Modern America* (Chapel Hill: University of North Carolina Press, 1994), 10–11.

45. Herbert G. Gutman, "The Tompkins Square 'Riot' in New York City on January 13, 1874," *Labor History* 6, no. 1 (1965): 44–70. Forty-six workers were arrested and held on $1,000 bond. Some served several months in prison before being released.

46. Peter Carlson, *Roughneck: The Life and Times of Big Bill Haywood* (New York: W. W. Norton, 1983), 54–56.

47. Ibid., 62.

48. MaryJoy Martin, *The Corpse on Boomerang Road: Telluride's War on Labor, 1899–1908* (Lake City, Colo.: Western Reflections, 2004).

49. Russell Jones, "Secondary Boycotts under the Railway Labor Act after Burlington Northern," *Southern University Law Review* 18, no. 1 (1993): 1.

50. Frankfurter and Greene, *Labor Injunction*, 21. Only for labor disputes were unincorporated unions permitted to sue or be sued as an entity (82).

51. Dubofsky, *State and Labor*, 13–21. See, e.g., Brace Bros. v. Evans, 5 Pa. Co. Ct. Rep. 163 (1888).

52. This requirement was routine. See, e.g., In re Phelan, 62 F. 803 (1894), in which the ruling issuing one of scores of injunctions against the American Railway Union and its officials makes much of F. W. Phelan's evasive answers on the stand as he faced prison time for his role.

53. Justice Caldwell, dissenting, Hopkins et al. v. Oxley Stove Co., 83 F. 912, 939–40 (1897). The majority insisted the enjoined boycott was to be maintained

> through fear. . . . It may be conceded that, when the defendants entered into the combination in question, they had no present intention of resorting to actual violence for the purpose of enforcing their demands; but it is manifest that by concerted action, force of numbers, and by exciting the fears of the timid, they did intend to compel [the employer and his customers] to . . . submit to the dictation of others in the management of their private business affairs.

Boycotts, the justices concluded, are "a species of intimidation which is no less harmful than actual violence." The dissent meticulously demolished their summary of the facts and the law, demonstrating that they were grounded in nothing more than animus against those who must labor for their livelihood.

54. In re Debs, 158 U.S. 564 (1895); Frankfurter and Greene, *Labor Injunction*, 87.

55. *In re Phelan*, 62 F. at 823. The judge conceded he had no right to punish Phelan "for the havoc which he and his associates have wrought to the business of this country" but only to "secure future compliance with the orders of this court."

56. Lambert, *"If the Workers Took a Notion,"* 58.

57. Dubofsky, *State and Labor*, 30.

58. Vegelahn v. Guntner et al., 167 Mass. 92 (1896); Frankfurter and Greene, *Labor Injunction*, 1.

59. *Vegelahn v. Guntner* at 98, emphasis added.

60. The majority reinstated a sweeping preliminary injunction against which the union had successfully appealed, winning a more limited injunction that simply restrained the use of force. As the two dissenters (one of whom objected to an injunction of any sort) noted, there was no evidence of violence or intimidation. Rather, the majority felt that it was unlawful for the union to attempt to persuade other workers to support its efforts to secure higher wages.

61. Sherry v. Perkins, 147 Mass. 212 (1888).

62. Riggs v. Cincinnati Waiters' Alliance, 8 Ohio Dec. 565, 567 (1898), cited in Joseph Tanenhaus, "Picketing as Free Speech: Early Stages in the Growth of the New Law of Picketing," *University of Pittsburgh Law Review* 14 (1952): 397–418. Although some courts were troubled by the prior restraint implications of such injunctions, by the early twentieth century most had come around:

> Courts which in theory at least supported the rule forbidding injunctions against peaceful picketing as violative of freedom of speech approved the restraining of picketing because it was intimidatory, a nuisance, destructive of property rights, an interference with the right to acquire and possess property, part of a scheme or an unlawful conspiracy, or an infringement of the right "to decline to listen." (401)

63. Lambert, *"If the Workers Took a Notion,"* 64–65. By the 1920s one out of four strikes was met with an injunction. In one case, an appellant sought an expanded injunction barring any picketing or parading, outcries, efforts to persuade customers not to patronize the plaintiff, or efforts to "induce" employees to support the union. The appeal was rejected on the grounds that the injunction already covered this. Frankfurter and Greene, *Labor Injunction*, 91. Even someone unconnected to a dispute who posted a "No Scabs Wanted in Here" notice (Taliaferro v. U.S., 290 Fed. 906 [1923]) and a newspaper that characterized strikebreakers as "dirty scabs" (Cohen v. U.S., 295 Fed. 633 [1924]) were held in contempt for violating injunctions. Frankfurter and Greene, *Labor Injunction*, 125.

64. Norman J. Ware, *The Labor Movement in the United States, 1860–1895* (1929; repr., New York: Random House, 1967), 334–45.

65. In a case involving a boycott of their beer garden, five unionists were convicted of extortion and intimidation and sentenced to prison terms. Their sentences were commuted after some weeks, and they were released from prison. Ibid., 344.

66. Barr et al. v. Essex Trades Council et al., 53 N.J. Eq. 101 (1894).

67. Casey v. Cincinnati Typographical Union No. 3, 45 F. 135 (1891). In addition to publishing appeals to boycott the firm that had locked out the typographers and recommending that unionists instead patronize newspapers and printers employing union labor, it was alleged that a union committee threatened advertisers that the boycott would be extended to them unless they withdrew their business. The union disputed this and presented affidavits from the advertisers in question denying that any threats had been made; the judge dismissed this evidence, accepting the complainant's allegations at face value.

68. Gompers v. Buck's Stove & Range Co., 221 U.S. 418 (1911), n. 1. The American Federation of Labor and its officials

> are hereby, restrained and enjoined . . . from declaring or threatening any boycott against the complainant or its business, . . . and from printing, issuing, publishing, or distributing through the mails, or in any other manner, any copy or copies of the American Federationist, or any other printed or written newspapers, magazine, circular, letter, or other document or instrument whatsoever, which shall contain or in any manner refer to the name of the complainant, its business or its product in the "We Don't Patronize," or the "Unfair" list of the defendants, . . . or which contains any reference to the complainant, its business or product, in connection with the term "Unfair" or with the "We Don't Patronize" list, or with any other phrase, word, or words of similar import . . .

69. Gompers v. U.S., 233 U.S. 604 (1914). The Court reversed the conviction on the grounds that the statute of limitations had lapsed.

70. As early as the 1820s, several states enacted legislation prohibiting employers from penalizing or terminating employees as a means of "influencing" their vote. Eugene Volokh, "Private Employees' Speech and Political Activity: Statutory Protection against Employer Retaliation," *Texas Review of Law and Politics* 16 (2012): 297–301. Some states went further (most in the twentieth century), protecting workers from retaliation for political or, in the case of New York, "recreational" activity, protections that the courts typically interpret quite narrowly. Volokh, who believes that this is bad public policy, concludes, "About half of Americans [now] live in jurisdictions that protect some private employee speech or political activity from employer retaliation" (297). Thus, half of Americans can lawfully face employer retaliation for political activity and for other free expression–related activity. See, e.g., Ann C. McGinley and Ryan P. McGinley-Stempel, "Beyond the Water Cooler: Speech and the Workplace in an Era of Social Media," *Hofstra Labor and Employment Law Journal* 30 (2012): 75–119.

Every year, large numbers of U.S. workers are disciplined and fired for union organizing, expressing political or social views their employers find objectionable, and other speech-related offenses. The International Labor Organization regularly finds that the United States fails to adequately protect workers' rights of freedom of association. See, e.g., James Gross, "A Human Rights Perspective on United States Labor Relations Law: A Violation of the Right of Freedom of Association," *Employee Rights and Employment Policy Journal* 3 (1999): 65–103; Steve Charnovitz, "The ILO Convention on Freedom of Association and Its Future in the United States," *American Journal of International Law* 102 (2008): 90–107.

71. Payne v. Western & Atlantic Railway, 81 Tenn. 507 (1884).

72. Some states that withhold union recognition from public sector employees allow unions representing those workers to "meet and confer" with employers, in essence to petition for redress of grievances; other states do not. The courts have seen no violation of the First Amendment protections of the rights of association and petition.

73. See, e.g., Barbara Anderson, "Secondary Boycotts and the First Amendment," *University of Chicago Law Review* 51 (1984): 811–36; "Labor Picketing and Commercial Speech: Free Enterprise Values in the Doctrine of Free Speech," *Yale Law Journal* 91 (1982): 938–60; Mark D. Schneider, "Peaceful Labor Picketing and the First Amendment," *Columbia Law Review* 82 (1982): 1469–97; and Lee Goldman, "The First Amendment and Nonpicketing Labor Publicity under Section 8(b)(4)(ii)(B) of the National Labor Relations Act," *Vanderbilt Law Review* 36 (1983): 1469–1509. These were largely touched off by the *DeBartolo* decision in which the courts flirted with First Amendment reasoning in considering whether provisions of the Taft-Hartley Act prohibited truthful, noncoercive union speech. Since then, the courts have largely ignored the First Amendment when considering labor union activities (except in passing, as in granting unions the same rights to expend unlimited campaign funds as corporations, so long as these are not taken from members' dues, which is restricted by law) outside of commercial speech rulings.

9. FREEDOM OF EXPRESSION FOR WOMEN

THE FIGHT FOR SUFFRAGE AND PERSONAL LIBERTY

LEE JOLLIFFE, PAULETTE D. KILMER,
AND SANDRA DAVIDSON

Centuries of living like bugs stuck in amber, unable to move upward in society, motivated the downtrodden to sail to the New World. There, sheer freedom inspired high ideals and energy in the immigrants who created the early Republic. But along with a quest for personal liberty, these pilgrims also brought with them Great Britain's common law made from judges' decisions, thus saddling themselves with many of the very strictures they sought to escape.

As second and third generations of ostensibly free people developed institutions in their new country, the essential tension between the ideals forged in America and the old social norms that citizens had retained as part of their culture began to pull at the social fabric. For women, the restrictive role of invisible domestic servant—whether as wife or low-paid help—was particularly galling, as men enjoyed social mobility, access to the vast new resources of the Americas, and participation in self-government.

By the nineteenth century, the mythology of paternalism had cemented the disparity between men's and women's opportunities into the social expectation that women were neither strong enough nor smart enough to survive in the public arena. On the other hand, like such well-known figures as Abraham Lincoln and Mark Twain, males in general filled their résumés with a wide range of work as lawyers, riverboat pilots, storekeepers, surveyors, miners, and any other sort of laborer necessary for bringing resources in the newly conquered land to marketplaces. Men pursued these opportunities as a birthright. By contrast, women's destiny was limited to shaping their family's home life in whatever conditions might arise from the men's ambitious pursuit of land and riches. Single women's job prospects revolved around domestic service. For example, early in her life, Civil War reporter Louisa Alcott, who became a famous novelist, worked as a seamstress, nursemaid, lady's companion, and domestic servant.[1]

Perhaps Alcott's adventures in the public arena as a writer grew out of the changes that had begun during the Second Great Awakening. In this atmosphere of social reform and progressive change,[2] the abolitionist movement gradually developed a national following by the 1830s.[3] Moreover, women felt drawn to support the antislavery cause and found in abolitionism a training ground for demanding their own liberty. A group of Quaker women formally launched the woman's rights movement at a national meeting in July 1848 at Seneca Falls, New York.[4] After more than fifty years of American independence for landholding men, women had finally begun to protest their lack of freedom.

This chapter explores the efforts of women suffragists to express their ideas publicly and to achieve what they regarded as the ultimate free expression in a democracy: the vote itself. Of course, groups ranging from mobs of "levee toughs" to members of the clergy and male voters in referenda constantly opposed these efforts. Ultimately the contingent most determined to silence protesters about suffrage, woman's rights, and voting—the liquor interests—considered these progressive reforms dangerous to their business.

The conviction that women, like dogs and children, should remain quiet arose from a meshing of social norms and religious tenets. In the early nineteenth century, opinion leaders defined "womanhood" based on passages from the Bible, most notably on an admonishment attributed to the convert Paul that women ought to obey their husbands.[5] The imported system of British common law and its construct of "coverture" codified this precept of women as passive, submissive pieces of property.

Nancy Cott finds an "outpouring of novels, poems, essays, sermons, and manuals on the family, children, and women's role" in the 1820s and 1830s.[6] The growing notion of women's proper sphere in an idealized "home" relied upon the view of men as animalistic, scarcely controlled beings that only women could civilize. As Reverend Henry Ward Beecher put it in a Woman's Rights Convention speech,

> If I were to take my daughter and my wife, and walk down to the polls with them, and there was a squirming crowd of bloated, loud-mouthed, blattering men, wrangling like so many maggots on cheese, what would take place but

> that, at the moment I appeared with my wife and daughter walking by my side with conscious dignity and veiled modesty, the lane would open, and I should pass through the red sea unharmed. Where is there a mob such that the announcement that a woman is present does not bring down the loudest of them?[7]

First as abolitionists and then as suffragists, women witnessed crowds of "bloated, loud-mouthed, blattering men" only too happy to disrupt the upstart women when they dared to speak in public. These men's notion that women ought to be invisible grew from a legal concept deeply rooted in British and American law: coverture.

WOMEN'S VOICES AND THE "DISABILITY" OF COVERTURE

Coverture simply meant the "condition or state of a married woman."[8] But often the term served as shorthand for all the legal baggage women picked up with marriage. Under the magistrate-made law that U.S. judges adopted from their British counterparts, married women ceased to exist. They had no legal identity of their own. It was as if one organism (the husband) had enveloped another organism (the wife) and produced, as the result, one organism: a husband.

As the U.S. Supreme Court explained, "At the common law the husband and wife were regarded as one. The legal existence of the wife during coverture was merged in that of the husband, and, generally speaking, the wife was incapable of making contracts, of acquiring property or disposing of the same without her husband's consent."[9]

This statute was so problematic that lawyers referred to it as the "disability of coverture."[10] Some judges linked coverture with insanity. For example, the Supreme Court said of poor Hannah Turner that "she was laboring under the disability of coverture, and also of insanity."[11] And it was as disabling as being legally too young to exercise rights. For example, the Supreme Court called a Mrs. O'Hara "a woman, under the double disability of coverture and infancy."[12]

Unless their husbands agreed, married women could not enter into contracts, they could not own or dispose of property, and, of course, they could not engage in any of the occupations that required them to be able to make contracts or buy or sell. This ban effectively silenced women's voices in commerce, the professions, and politics. The right to vote belonged only to men, who could enter into contracts and own property. A drunken or greedy husband could sell his children into lives of servitude as "apprentices" from ages as young as five, and the frequency of such outrages prompted reformers to organize the Women's Christian Temperance Union.

Once a married woman became a widow or was divorced (a rarity), she was freed from coverture. But while unmarried women were freed from the bonds of coverture and could enter into contracts and buy and sell property in many places, they were still hemmed in by the "males only" barricades erected around essentials of community life, such as voting. For a long time, some states required single women to turn over their salaries and property to male kin, usually a father or brother.

While national reform of coverture was slow, states could, and under pressure from woman's rights activists did, pass laws to protect women, at least somewhat. For example, in 1861 Illinois passed "an Act to protect married women in their separate property." Therein, a married woman could claim "separate property" that she owned prior to marriage or acquired through inheritance "or otherwise" from anyone "other than her husband." This property "shall, notwithstanding her marriage, be and remain during coverture her sole and separate property, under her sole control, and be held, owned, possessed, and enjoyed by her the same as though she was sole and unmarried," the law said. Furthermore, that property "shall not be subject to the disposal, control, or interference of her husband, and shall be exempt from . . . attachment for the debts of her husband."[13] So, for example, in Illinois after 1861 a woman did not have to turn over to her husband the silverware she had inherited from her mother to pay her husband's debts.

Women's position in American society, then, was this, ably summed up by Matilda Joslyn Gage for the New York State Woman Suffrage Society:

> (1) Woman is held *politically* to have no existence; (2) *civilly*, she is a minor; (3) in marriage she is a serf; (4) in labor she is made inferior and robbed of her earnings; (5) in public instruction she is sacrificed to man; (6) out of marriage, answers to the faults committed by both; (7) as a mother is deprived of her right to her children; (8) she is only deemed equally responsible, intelligent and answerable in taxes and crimes.[14]

ABOLITION SPEAKING: A TRAINING GROUND FOR SUFFRAGISTS

Crusaders from the abolitionist movement were the earliest change agents to join the woman's rights movement. These women had seen mobs torch churches, homes, and meeting halls as well as assault and occasionally even kill speakers or writers espousing abolitionism. Certainly this battle-toughened coterie scarcely flinched in the face of the annoying but seldom physical threats during their suffrage speeches.

But that lack of violence—not always, but in general—created a problem of its own. Where the broader newspaper press would express outrage at physical attacks on abolition speakers, there was rarely much public interest in the news that jeering and hissing rowdies had disrupted a woman's suffrage meeting.

Some noteworthy incidents did involve mobs and the threat of violence. At Port Byron, New York, an anti–woman suffragist dumped cayenne pepper into the stove, emptying the hall by making the air unbreathable.[15] Abbey Kelley's speaking tours in the antislavery movement led to "scorn, ridicule, violence, and mobs accompanying her, [resulting in her] suffering all kinds of persecutions." For listening to her speak on Sunday, many people were expelled from their churches.[16] Young Paulina Wright helped organize the first Anti-Slavery Convention, held in Utica, New York, on October 21, 1835, but the meeting was "mobbed and violently dispersed. . . . It was a fearful day for Abolitionists . . . as the mob of roughs was backed by leading men." The abolitionists fled to speaker Francis Wright's house, but the thugs pursued them and then tore down fences and piled them against the house, preparatory to burning it with the abolitionists inside. Only the quick thought of the women inside, who knelt to pray within sight of the downstairs windows, prevented their being burned alive.[17] When abolitionist speaker and writer Angelina Grimké attempted to visit her mother in Charleston, South Carolina, the mayor sent police to prevent her landing and announced he could not hold back the mob who wanted to harm her if she came ashore.[18] And Gage told of a suffrage convention in Buffalo where the mayor, chief of police, and fifty police officers hired to quell the expected horde simply took part in the rowdy mob.[19]

Often rowdies employed sheer obstruction and noise to hamper progress in the woman's suffrage cause. At the Woman's Rights Convention in New York City on September 6 and 7, 1853, suffragists met "the first overt exhibition of that public sentiment woman was then combatting. The mob represented more than itself; it evidenced the general masculine opinion of woman, which condensed into law, forges the chains which enslave her."[20] The *New York Tribune* felt that this sort of confrontation helped the suffrage cause: "Nothing is so good for a weak and unpopular movement as this sort of opposition."[21]

As the *Tribune* predicted, hostile behaviors did create sympathy for the movement. For instance, Abigail Scott Duniway, publisher of the suffrage newspaper

New Northwest, faced an angry crowd while on a speaking tour of southern Oregon. In Jacksonville in 1879, shrieking bullies pelted Duniway with eggs and burned her in effigy at sundown. Duniway wrote of this mining town, "Its would-be leading men are old miners and refugees from the bushwhacking district whence they were driven by the civil war. The taint of slavery is yet upon them and the methods of border-ruffians are their hearts' delight." Yet the more civil Oregonians were embarrassed at such a reception. When Duniway arrived back in Portland after citizens there had received word of the attacks, "a perfect ovation" awaited her. "Hundreds of men and women who had not before allied themselves with the movement made haste to do so. The newspapers were filled with severe denunciations of the mob."[22]

Gradually, over decades of women's activism, the tenor of mobs changed. In a reminiscence about Matilda Joslyn Gage, Elizabeth Cady Stanton wrote,

> Our experience [of mobs breaking up suffrage meetings] was the same, varied only by the fertile resources of the actors and their surroundings. Thirty years of education had somewhat changed the character of Northern mobs. They no longer dragged men through the streets with ropes round their necks, nor broke up women's prayer meetings; they no longer threw eggs and brickbats at the apostles of reform, nor dipped them in barrels of tar and feathers; they simply crowded the halls, and with laughing, groaning, clapping, and cheering, effectually disrupted the proceedings.[23]

Proslavery, anti-woman's rights newspapers happily jeered at suffrage speakers, both female and male. One wrote, "The women are coming! They flock in upon us from every quarter, all to hear and talk about Woman's Rights. The blue stockings are as thick as grasshoppers in hay-time, and mighty will be the force of 'jaw-logic' and 'broom-stick ethics' preached by the females of both sexes."[24]

Suffragists may well have been "thick as grasshoppers in hay-time," but since focusing on a multitude is difficult, let us examine how three key figures in the fight for suffrage—speaker and publisher Lucy Stone, legal activist Virginia Minor, and the inimitable Susan B. Anthony—used tactics common among their sisterhood to advance their cause. A fourth section, on the disappointment women faced after the Civil War and the Fourteenth Amendment, shows how suffragists renewed their efforts in the face of this blow.

Lucy Stone focused her efforts on making that necessary cultural "sea change" among the wider populace in order to influence lawmakers, publishing the *Woman's Journal*, a long-lived weekly magazine aimed at middle-class women and their spouses and traveling endlessly advocating full citizenship for African

Americans and for women. Virginia Minor raised eyebrows and won respect when she demanded the "voice" of voting itself in a citizenship rights case that went to the country's highest court. And Susan B. Anthony, publisher of the newspaper the *Revolution*, advocated for an array of social reforms—from reexamining marriage and investigating prostitution to trying to bring about political change through petitioning legislatures and campaigning for state referenda—deserving a place in any consideration of how women's First Amendment rights were violated, even as activists fought for equal citizenship.

EARLY ACTIVISTS AND LUCY STONE, THE "MORNING STAR"

Like many early advocates of woman's rights in the United States, Lucy Stone came to the movement obliquely, from the abolitionist activism of the 1830s. As a leading speaker for the antislavery cause, she experienced many of the more violent methods of suppression of free speech, from being doused with a fire hose in the middle of winter to weathering barrages of firecrackers, cobblestones, and rotten eggs hailed over her during her speeches.[25] And like the abolitionists, early woman's rights advocates expected to invoke the "moral suasion" preached during the revivals of the early nineteenth century to change minds.[26] Indeed, one of her teachers at Oberlin College, Charles Grandison Finney, had served as a leading preacher from the Great Awakening.[27] A key tenet of the revival movement promised that if enough people could be converted to live ethical, moral lives, it might be possible to bring about heaven on earth, the Millennium of Christian beliefs.

To Lucy Stone and others in the social change movements that were born of the Second Great Awakening, a second tenet followed the first. They believed that, in a democracy, the way to create positive change was to change the minds of the people, who would then elect moral leaders. In modern parlance, Stone hoped that diffusion of ideas would create a grassroots demand for fairness toward women.[28]

In the early years of the movement, even Stone's school, the liberal Oberlin College, quashed her desire to speak in public, so she and her friends practiced their oratory outside of classes. Abolition's great leader William Lloyd Garrison appreciated her talent and hired her to join his speakers' circuit. Stone traveled constantly, discoursing on abolition and eventually also on woman's rights. Both her topics and her very presence at the podium generated harsh reactions; she was summoned before the "Ladies Board" of her college and tossed out of her church for living a life "inconsistent" with their notions of Christianity.[29] Late in her life, she said, "I think, with never-ending gratitude, that the young women of today do not and can never know at what price their right to free speech and to speak at all in public has been earned."[30]

After thirty years of service to the equal rights cause, Stone found herself at odds with Susan B. Anthony and Elizabeth Cady Stanton. Anthony and Stanton had allowed a wealthy British gadabout, George Frances Train, into their inner circle, perhaps swayed by his promise to fund a national journal for their cause (which during its brief life would be called the *Revolution*). As was typical of the dilettante, however, he first alienated readers and supporters with his articles espousing free love and socialism; then he decamped to England, where he spent a year in jail, leaving the publication nearly without funds. Woman's rights historian Eleanor Flexner has written that Stanton and Anthony's "catholic attitude toward issues and allies led them into more than one quagmire, similar to the Train episode. The most unfortunate of all was their brief alignment with the notorious Victoria Woodhull and her sister Tennessee Claflin."[31] Woodhull and Claflin had, among other questionable deeds, performed séances in a carnival. Sometimes Anthony and Stanton's misjudgment in choosing allies set the woman's rights movement back in public opinion.

In response, Lucy Stone and a large contingent of other woman's rights activists left the National Woman Suffrage Association and formed the American Woman Suffrage Association in 1869. But much damage had been done. A widely reported sermon was delivered at the Concord Congregational Church, attacking woman's rights as so much "free-love" and debauchery.[32] The *Vermont Watchman* announced that the woman's rights movement had "thrown scorn upon marriage and upon the Divine Word."[33]

Using the power of print media, Lucy Stone set about correcting negative images generated through the alliances with Train and the sisters Woodhull and Claflin. In 1870, reductions in postal rates and printing advances helped launch a positive armada of women's magazines.[34] At this juncture, Stone created the *Woman's Journal*, aimed at well-educated clubwomen, now part of their own national movement,[35] and professionals. She not only covered political and legal issues facing women but also lauded their accomplishments, helping to legitimize women's work outside the home.[36] Her strategy was to engender in the public view a belief that women might remain womanly and yet be citizens and voters.

In an early editorial, Stone's publication addressed attacks like those made from the Congregationalist pulpit and in the *Vermont Watchman*: "Many well-meaning people insist on dragging in their peculiar views on theology, temperance, marriage, race, dress, finance, labor, capital—it matters not what." This "confusion of ideas that have no logical connection" with woman suffrage should not "load . . . the good ship, Woman Suffrage, with a cargo of irrelevant opinions."[37]

Free love advocate Victoria Woodhull reads the delegation of suffragists' demand for enfranchising women based on the Fourteenth and Fifteenth Amendments to the Constitution. The Judiciary Committee of the House of Representatives in Washington, D.C., allowed her to speak but then did nothing. *Frank Leslie's Illustrated Newspaper*, February 4, 1871; Library of Congress Prints and Photographs Division, Washington, D.C.

Unfortunately, the "good ship" of suffrage now had plenty of baggage. Sermons against woman's rights abounded and were published and republished. Reverend Holmes grumbled that a woman suffragist had had the nerve to argue with him and complained that she was meant to be subordinate to his "clerical authority . . . divinely ordained of heaven."[38] Robert Laird Collier, in his sermon "The Folly of the Woman Movement," said women had but one goal, "dissolution of the marriage tie" or "free love."[39] For conservative men, the quick riposte to attempts to gain woman's rights became simply the accusation of "free love."

But direct opposition to Stone's publishing effort came chiefly from the powerful, moneyed liquor interests. Already suspected of paying "grog shop rowdies" to invade Stone's public speaking engagements,[40] the brewers' associations funded an anti-suffrage movement and anti-suffrage publications.[41] The more the Women's Christian Temperance Union grew, the more the liquor interests blocked woman suffrage, fearing correctly, as it turned out, that voting women would outlaw liquor.

The power of this opponent was formidable. Temperance activists reported to their allies in the suffrage movement that liquor's influence extended through all levels of government, to which they paid "billions in revenue," and also held purse-power over the "farmers who find in breweries and distilleries the best market for their grain." This power was so extensive that "they . . . control millions of votes, . . . are among the largest contributors to political campaigns," and are "positively, unanimously and unalterably opposed to woman suffrage."[42]

In their publication *Progress*, the Wisconsin liquor dealers wrote, "The condition is serious. Woman suffrage means prohibition."[43] Whenever state referenda were held on woman suffrage, the liquor dealers wrote to their distributors, barkeepers, hoteliers, and grocers throughout that region. Barkeepers were part of political machines of the day and fielded "voters" who traveled from precinct to precinct on carts loaded with beer barrels, voting in place of anyone who had died since the last election. Suffragists wrote that they had to "exercise the utmost vigilance" at every polling place to see that entries were tallied correctly and to hire private detectives to follow completed ballots to city vaults and guard them against tampering.[44]

Standing strong against such powerful opposition, Lucy Stone's publication *Woman's Journal* was the longest-lived woman's rights publication, spanning from 1870 until 1917. Her early speaking skills and life-long efforts led to her reputation as "the morning star of the women's rights movement."[45]

DISAPPOINTMENT FOR WOMEN AFTER THE CIVIL WAR

During only one period after the Seneca Falls Convention of 1848 did the suffragists stop campaigning for woman's rights: for the duration of the Civil War, they suspended their conventions, publications, and lecturing for woman's rights. The suffragists and the abolitionists, including Frederick Douglass (who participated in the Seneca Falls Convention), always had supported each other's causes.[46] When the founder of the Free-Soil Party, Massachusetts senator Charles Sumner, asked citizens to circulate petitions favoring freedom for black people, Susan B. Anthony and Elizabeth Cady Stanton organized the Woman's National Loyal League with headquarters in New York City's Cooper Hall. Members distributed tracts and corresponded with President Abraham Lincoln. The result of their activities "was a mammoth petition with over three million names presented to Congress."[47]

When the Civil War ended, the suffragists expected political leaders, especially Republicans, to reward their service. Historians Eleanor Flexner and Ellen Fitzpatrick note, "They were still so inexperienced in politics that they failed to estimate the extent and complexity of the forces arrayed against them."[48] When Congress drafted the Fourteenth Amendment, suffragists' hopes were dashed because "for the first time the word 'male' [appeared] in the Constitution. Its three-fold use in the proposed Fourteenth Amendment, always in connection with the term 'citizen,' raised the issue of whether women were actually citizens of the United States."[49]

The U.S. Constitution did not specify "men" anywhere. The creation of state constitutions determined the status of women and their rights in property, inheritance, marriage, divorce, and custody. After the Revolutionary War, before New Jersey adopted a constitution limiting voting to certain male property owners, some women had cast their ballots. But the Fourteenth Amendment limited federal rights to men. The blow meant that the suffragists would have to convince politicians to add an amendment to the Constitution. Stanton predicted that the Fourteenth Amendment would prevent women from voting for another century; actually, the struggle lasted an additional sixty years.[50]

Congress passed the Fourteenth Amendment on July 9, 1868, and on November 3 of that same year, 172 women, black as well as white, voted in Vineland, New Jersey. When male election officials turned away the women because they were not registered, they set up their own table with a box for ballots. At the end of the day, 168 women had voted for Ulysses S. Grant and four for Horatio Seymour.[51] Feminist historian Janet Zollinger Giele notes, "In 1870, the elderly Grimke sisters, veterans of abolition and the early woman's rights movement, set out in a winter storm leading a delegation of 40 women to vote in Hyde Park, Massachusetts."[52] The first female attorney in Pennsylvania, Caroline Burnham Kilgore, broke the election law in 1871. And from 1871 until 1876, protesters in Geauga County, Ohio, demanded suffrage for U.S. women. But the amendment was not to fulfill women's hopes.

Even longtime ally Frederick Douglass retreated from his work for woman suffrage in order to concentrate solely on black suffrage, explaining that black people needed the vote immediately to defend themselves from rampant violence, economic repression, and educational inequities. He said black women suffered the same fate as the men because of their color, not their gender. Like the other abolitionists, he believed the freed slaves needed to be protected.[53]

The U.S. Senate first debated in 1866 whether women should vote when a senator from Pennsylvania suggested removing "male" from a bill to give black people living in the District of Columbia the right to vote. The opponents made the same argument that always arose against woman's rights: the woman's place was in the home, shaping the men to rule; if they entered the public sphere, they would neglect their hallowed role as nurturers and moral decay would destroy society. The senate did not include women in the law.

Progress for black men had not opened the door to citizenship for white or black women, and so woman's rights leaders regrouped. However, the climate for their ideas had improved a bit. The conventions, articles, pamphlets, and speeches prior to the war as well as the expansion of women into some professions and the growth in the numbers of female wage earners had all worked to increase the pool of believers in equality. The suffragists expanded their antebellum tactics for raising consciousness, which consisted of sponsoring conferences where prominent, talented women and men spoke on the issues, and securing press coverage in women's journals and magazines. They also lectured extensively around the nation. As Susan B. Anthony's biographer Ida Husted Harper explained, the goal always involved "agitating the question and creating a favorable public sentiment."[54]

While Anthony and Stone worked to change broad cultural mores, other women challenged interpretations of the Constitution and its amendments in court, hoping to gain leverage for women. And in U.S. law, there was much to challenge, most notably adult women's near-complete invisibility as human beings under the British laws that had crept into the United States and set its standard. Most troubling were the lack of any voice in lawmaking, the lowly jobs open to women who did not wed, and the invisibility of married women.[55]

VIRGINIA MINOR: TAKING WOMEN'S RIGHT TO VOTE TO THE U.S. SUPREME COURT

In Missouri, Virginia Minor, an early proponent of women's right to vote, had served as the first president of the Woman Suffrage Association of Missouri in 1867, two years before Susan B. Anthony and Elizabeth Cady Stanton established the American Woman Suffrage Association.[56] Anthony and Stanton spoke to Minor's organization in the fall of 1867.[57] Minor exercised her freedom of expression to rally others to her cause, and she wanted women to exercise their freedom of expression in the way that truly counted—by voting.

Minor, who was over twenty-one years old, wanted to vote in the national election in 1872, but a St. Louis registrar, Reese Happersett, would not let her register to do so. She sued. Chief Justice Morrison Waite wrote the opinion in her case, *Minor v. Happersett*.[58] Minor's case raises one question: are women "persons"? Yes, the U.S. Supreme Court declared, and that seemed promising. Women are persons, and they are *citizens* (165):[59] "Women have always been considered as citizens the same as men," the Court said (169), and then it spoke of

> the fact that sex has never been made one of the elements of citizenship in the United States. In this respect men have never had an advantage over women. The same laws precisely apply to both. The Fourteenth Amendment did not affect the citizenship of women any more than it did of men. In this particular, therefore, the rights of Mrs. Minor do not depend upon the amendment. She has always been a citizen from her birth, and entitled to all the privileges and immunities of citizenship. (170)

The high court declined to say what advantages come with citizenship, opining that it did not have to do so: "The Constitution does not define the privileges and immunities of citizens. . . . In this case we need not determine what they are, but only whether suffrage is necessarily one of them" (170). So the question boiled down to this point: does citizenship confer the right to vote? The Court answered no. And no law conferred on women the right to vote.

The Court had pointed out at the outset of its opinion that the constitution and laws of Minor's home state, Missouri, limited voting to men. And that led the Court to this question:

> Whether, since the adoption of the Fourteenth Amendment, a woman, who is a citizen of the United States and of the State of Missouri, is a voter in that State, notwithstanding the provision of the constitution and laws of the State, which confine the right of suffrage to men alone. . . . (165)

The Court made clear that it might have decided Minor's case "upon other grounds," but "the case was undoubtedly brought to this court for the sole purpose of having that question decided by us, and . . . we have concluded to waive all other considerations and proceed at once to its determination" (165).

The answer to the question of whether the Fourteenth Amendment conferred on women a right to vote, notwithstanding state law to the contrary, depended on a long-winded exposition that included this less-than-profound insight:

> There is no doubt that *women* may be citizens. They are persons. . . . There cannot be a nation without a people. The very idea of a political community, such as a nation is, implies an association of persons for the promotion of their general welfare. *Each one of the persons* associated becomes a member of the nation formed by the association. *He* owes it allegiance and is entitled to its protection. . . . For convenience it has been found necessary to give a name to this membership. . . . For this purpose the words "subject," "inhabitant," and "citizen" have been used, and the choice between them is sometimes made to depend upon the form of the government. Citizen is now more commonly

employed. . . . When used in this sense it is understood as conveying the idea of membership of a nation, *and nothing more.* (165–66)[60]

The Court made clear that being a *citizen* did not automatically make one a *voter.* "If the right of suffrage is one of the necessary privileges of a citizen of the United States," the Court said, "then the constitution and laws of Missouri confining it to men are in violation of the Constitution of the United States, as amended, and consequently void." So the Court immediately posed what it called the "direct question," namely, "whether all citizens are necessarily voters" (170).

After much textual analysis of the U.S. Constitution and also of laws from states restricting the right to vote to males, the Court hit on perhaps the coup de grace, the Fifteenth Amendment, ratified in 1870: "The right of citizens of the United States to vote shall not be denied or abridged by the United States or by any State on account of race, color, or previous condition of servitude." The Fourteenth Amendment had already provided that no state could make or enforce any law that could abridge the privileges or immunities of citizens of the United States. If suffrage was one of these privileges or immunities, why amend the Constitution to prevent its being denied on account of race? Nothing is more evident than that the greater must include the lesser, and if all were already protected, why go through with the form of amending the Constitution to protect a part (175)?

The Court harbored no uncertainty about its decision against Minor and all other women wishing to vote. Suffrage was not a privilege of citizenship: "Certainly, if the courts can consider any question settled, this is one" (177). But while the Court seemed certain that "the Constitution of the United States does not confer the right of suffrage upon any one," it did not seem so sure that the laws confining suffrage to men were right, saying that "the constitutions and laws of the several States which commit that important trust to men alone *are not necessarily void*" (178).[61]

The Court also wrote that "our province is to decide what the law is, not to declare what it should be. . . . If the law is wrong, it ought to be changed; but the power for that is not with us" (178). The Court seemed to be saying that its collective hands were tied: "No argument as to woman's need of suffrage can be considered. We can only act upon her rights as they exist. It is not for us to look at the hardship of withholding" (178).

Virginia Minor not only lost but lost unanimously. She could still raise her voice and campaign for the right to vote, but she could not exercise the ultimate freedom of expression of a citizen in a democratic society—the freedom to cast her vote.

SUSAN B. ANTHONY AND THE PERSEVERANCE OF THE SUFFRAGISTS

Suffragists celebrated Susan Brownell Anthony's birthday yearly as a national event, starting when she turned fifty in 1870. On her seventieth birthday, newspapers around the country wrote tributes recognizing her courage and wisdom as a leader in the woman's rights movement. And in 1891, the *Warren (Pa.) Ledger* predicted that Anthony, who had turned seventy-one on February 15, would stand out in history with Washington and Lincoln as "one of the bravest and best in the darkest hour of the most unpopular war ever waged for humanity."[62] Anthony embodied a symbol of hope and accomplishment for women and was a ramrod for suffrage publicity in an era when the meaning of that word was just beginning to be understood.

Anthony conducted her seven-decades-long campaigns for suffrage and temperance until her death in 1906. The "unpopular war" she waged often was fought on the psychological battlefield of public opinion as she tried to build political change. She began her reform work collecting signatures as an abolitionist at the age of seventeen, and her Quaker family, who also believed in social justice, supported her. But typical of the experiences of woman suffrage speakers, she was often the target of hecklers and mobs. In 1861, after an angry crowd in Syracuse, New York, had scared away her audience there, the ringleaders burned Anthony in effigy at Hanover Square.[63]

The tensions among leaders—Lucy Stone on the one hand and Susan B. Anthony and Elizabeth Cady Stanton on the other—over appropriate alliances and strategies caused the suffragists to split in 1869 into two groups: the American Woman Suffrage Association and the National Woman Suffrage Association. To avoid alienating potential wealthy or powerful sponsors, Lucy Stone and the American contingent focused chiefly on voting and worked mostly at the state level. The National group, under Anthony and Stanton's leadership, addressed a wider range of issues.

The National contingent used their short-lived journal, the *Revolution*, to candidly examine "the double standard and prostitution" as well as to "[campaign] for women involved in some of the more lurid crimes of the day."[64] Their stands on these explosive issues cost them valuable allies, as did their partnerships with flamboyant nonconformists like Woodhull, who made history as the first woman to run for the U.S. presidency on a free love and equal rights platform, without the suffragists' consent. She named Frederick Douglass her running mate before telling him.[65]

The suffragists' split into two organizations instead of one meant neither coalition could maximize its resources. At first, Anthony maintained ties with the American group, but then Lucy Stone launched the *Woman's Journal*, a powerful competitor for her own paper's readers. Anthony had started publishing the *Revolution* two and a half years earlier, on January 8, 1868, but eventually she could not afford to publish the paper, since advertisers preferred the *Woman's Journal*.

Although the *Revolution* was short-lived, "it gave the movement a forum, focus, and direction."[66] By the 1870s, working women had joined unions and some had entered previously all-male occupations, like medicine, the clergy, and law. They embraced grassroots political ventures and organized women's groups to improve employment conditions through getting the vote.

When the Radical Republicans added the Fifteenth Amendment to make sure that the former slaves would not be denied voting privileges, Anthony and a coterie of other women decided to test the law. In 1872, she and fourteen others were arrested for voting illegally in Rochester, New York.[67] The poll officials who allowed the women to cast their ballots were also indicted. Anthony refused to pay bail and filed habeas corpus, but her attorney paid the fees. The trial was moved from Albany to Canandaigua, New York. The judge asked if she wished to make a statement concerning the sentence, and the *Rochester Union Spy* reported, "Miss Anthony declared that in her trial every principle of justice had been violated; that every right had been denied; that she had had no trial by her peers; that the Court and jurors were her political superiors, and not her peers, and announced her determination to continue her labors until equality was obtained."[68]

The judge ruled that these questions could not be discussed. Anthony then insisted that the "full rigor of the law" be enforced against her. The judge fined her $100 plus court costs but added that she would not be jailed until she paid. She was free and never paid that penalty, but she could not appeal his decision. The government dropped the charges against the other defendants.[69]

Anthony's own experiences as a schoolteacher convinced her that political rights and economic justice were linked. In the *Revolution*, Anthony called for an eight-hour workday as well as equal pay for equal work. From roughly 1875 to 1895, she traveled the country giving her most moving speech, "Woman Wants Bread, Not the Ballot." To thunderous applause, Anthony explained why women would not get "bread" without the "ballot":

> I beseech you to help to lift woman to a place in which she can help herself in the battle of life. She needs the ballot as a protection to help herself in the battle of life; it is a means and not an end. Until she gets it she will not be

satisfied, nor will she be protected. Labor, then, every woman of you, till she gets the right to a voice in making laws that apply to her as well as to me.[70]

Her lectures threatened the status quo, which did not want the law changed to allow women to vote. Even as the avalanche of news items about her generated support for her cause, some editors continued to mock Anthony. For example, in 1878, commenting on a scientific discovery, the editor of the *Atlanta Constitution* declared, "The remains of another mastodon have been found in Ohio. It is supposed that he was a playmate of Colonel Susan B. Anthony, the venerable but sprightly champion of the right of women to swear, chew tobacco and vote."[71] In 1888, Frank Carpenter suggested that if Anthony were a man, then she would serve as Pythias with Elizabeth Cady Stanton playing Damon: "The two have worked together as sisters, and Cady Stanton said, sometime ago, that Susan B. Anthony was her better angel, always pushing and guiding her to work." Stanton had pointed out that neither she nor Anthony could accomplish alone what they did together. Carpenter reported that Anthony and Stanton had worked together "almost like husband and wife" for thirty years.[72]

All comments, even mean-spirited ones, kept Susan B. Anthony's name alive in the public sphere. Moreover, the caustic descriptions aroused curiosity, and when people heard her speak, she often won them over. No wonder she valued newspapers, especially as women entered the newsrooms late in the century. The women's press organizations that emerged around the country between 1881 and 1899 helped their members earn respect as journalists as well as supported suffrage.[73] In fact, in 1897, Anthony praised the work of women in the newspaper industry and demanded fair salaries for them.[74]

From the time she began to lecture for suffrage in 1853, Anthony persevered despite the cruelty of her critics. Eventually her patience, resolve, and intelligence earned her the public's respect. The *Bismarck (N.D.) Tribune* noted in June 1893, "Poor Susan B. Anthony, who has been egged, sneered at, caricatured, etc., is now commencing to reap what she has sown, and the representative women here [at the World's Fair] have gathered from all parts of the world to honor her."[75] Just six years later, on July 8, 1899, Anthony (the newly elected president of the International Congress of Women) and other ICW delegates were presented to Queen Victoria, who ordered her servants to prepare tea for the hundreds of women who had come to see her. "I had never seen the queen before," Anthony reported, "and could not but feel a thrill when, looking into her wonderful face, I saw her, as her life is going out, welcoming the woman's movement, which is the precursor of the twentieth century."[76]

Samuel D. Ehrhart's illustration contrasts the plight of women with the tyranny of men. The women toil in sweatshops or tenements where they care for children (including a new baby every year) with no chance of rising out of poverty. Meantime, the politicians grow rich enough on graft to bribe bums. The artist suggests that voting would empower women to defeat crooked party bosses and secure economic justice. *Puck*, March 31, 1909; Library of Congress Prints and Photographs Division, Washington, D.C.

SUFFRAGE GAINS AT THE END OF THE CENTURY

Suffrage columns in daily newspapers began to appear as the century wore on. For example, in "Suffrage Squibs" for the *Oakland Tribune*, Winifred Warner reported on the meetings of political equity clubs.[77] Clara Bewick Colby, editor of the *Woman's Tribune* in Beatrice, Nebraska, explained: "The spoken word has its power for the day, but for building up a new line of thought in the popular heart, there must be the written word, which shall be quietly digested and made part of the reader's own thought."[78]

The suffragists in the last decades of the nineteenth century developed strategies for raising consciousness at the community level through newspapers, speeches, and political equity groups. In the West, many suffragists worked tirelessly as lecturers, authors, and newspaper publishers to raise consciousness.[79] Their campaigns resulted in Wyoming, Utah, and Idaho franchising women as they attained statehood. Colorado extended the vote to women in an 1893 referendum. But getting the vote via referenda took time and often failed. Giele points out that "between 1890 and 1918, 29 state referenda were lost; only 14 won."[80] Therefore, by 1910 the suffragists put their efforts into amending the federal Constitution. According to Giele, "In the last analysis, greatest support for adoption of the federal suffrage amendment came precisely from those states that had already affirmed woman's right of franchise at the state and local levels."[81]

The suffragists continued their long-used grassroots efforts to build local clubs, write articles and letters for local newspapers, and publish suffrage journals. They gave speeches, lobbied at the state and federal level, and held conventions. They opened doors for women in professions and universities that would spur a militant generation after the turn of the twentieth century. Their century of protest was waged personally with appeals to help women gain fair wages, custody rights of children, divorce options, educational as well as professional opportunities, and the vote, which they argued was essential for making social and economic progress. But only in a newer century would they gain the vote at the national level.[82]

Women would have to wait until the language of the Nineteenth Amendment was ratified on August 26, 1920: "The right of citizens of the United States to vote shall not be denied or abridged by the United States or by any state on account of sex."

Notes

1. Lee Jolliffe, "Louisa May Alcott," in *American Magazine Journalists, 1850–1900*, ed. Sam Riley (Detroit: Gale Research, Bruccoli Clark Layman, 1989), 12–17.
2. Paul E. Johnson, *A Shopkeeper's Millennium: Society and Revivals in Rochester, New York, 1815–1837* (New York: Hill and Wang, 1978).
3. See "A Press Ablaze" within this volume.
4. Eleanor Flexner, *Century of Struggle: The Women's Rights Movement in the United States* (Cambridge, Mass.: Belknap Press of Harvard University Press, 1975).
5. Ephesians 5:22–24.
6. Nancy Cott, *The Bonds of Womanhood: The Woman's Sphere in New England, 1790–1850* (New Haven: Yale University Press, 1977), cited by Howard Zinn, *A People's History of the United States*, chap. 6, http://www.historyisaweapon.com/zinnapeopleshistory.html, unpaginated.
7. Quoted in Elizabeth Cady Stanton, Susan B. Anthony, and Matilda Joslyn Gage, eds., *History of Woman Suffrage*, 6 vols. (Rochester: Susan B. Anthony, 1881–1922), 2:165.
8. The definition continues: "Sometimes used elliptically to describe the legal disability which formerly existed at common law from a state of coverture whereby

the wife could not own property free from the husband's claim or control." *Black's Law Dictionary with Pronunciations*, 6th ed. (St. Paul: West, 1990), 366.

9. Thompson v. Thompson, 218 U.S. 611, 614–15 (1910) (ruling that married women could not sue their husbands for assault and battery).

10. See, e.g., McDonald v. Hovey, 100 U.S. 619, 625 (1884), and Sims v. Everhard, 102 U.S. 300, 309 (1880).

11. Thorp v. Raymond, 57 U.S. 247, 250 (1850).

12. O'Hara v. Macconnell, 93 U.S. 150, 154 (1876).

13. 1861 Ill. Laws 143 (quoted by the U.S. Supreme Court in Kibbe v. Ditto, 93 U.S. 674, 676 [1876]).

14. Stanton, Anthony, and Gage, *History of Woman Suffrage*, 3:420.

15. Ibid., 1:469.

16. Ibid., 1:41.

17. Ibid., 1:285–86.

18. Ibid., 1:405–6.

19. Ibid., 1:468.

20. Ibid., 1:547.

21. *New York Tribune*, September 9, 1853.

22. Stanton, Anthony, and Gage, *History of Woman Suffrage*, 3:776–77.

23. Ibid., 1:467.

24. Ibid., 1: footnote 103. *The Daily Star* referred to in this note appears to be from Syracuse, N.Y.

25. Alice Stone Blackwell, *Lucy Stone: Pioneer of Woman's Rights* (Charlottesville: University of Virginia Press, 1930), 76.

26. Johnson, *Shopkeeper's Millennium*.

27. Noted in Alice Stone Blackwell's biography of her mother, but more readily available at Joelle Million, "Lucy Stone, Woman's Rights Champion," *Unitarian Universalist World Looking Back* 2, no. 4, http://www.uuworld.org/2004/02/lookingback.html.

28. Lee Jolliffe, "Women's Magazines of the 19th Century: Lucy Stone's *Journal* Popularizes Women's Suffrage," *Journal of Popular Culture* 27, no. 4 (Spring 1994): 125–40, and "Diffusion of Ideas by 19th Century Feminists: The Growth of Women's Magazines," paper presented at the Association of Educators in Journalism and Mass Communication annual meeting, Norman, Okla., 1986, ERIC ED271777.

29. Elinor Rice Hays, *Morning Star: A Biography of Lucy Stone, 1818–1893* (New York: Octagon Books, 1978).

30. Ibid., 300.

31. Flexner, *Century of Struggle*, 156.

32. Rev. S. L. Blake, 1871, in Stanton, Anthony, and Gage, *History of Woman Suffrage*, 3:371–72.

33. Quoted in ibid., 3:387–88.

34. Jolliffe, "Women's Magazines of the 19th Century," 129.

35. Jane Cunningham "Jennie Jean" Croly, *The History of the Women's Club Movement in America* (New York: Henry G. Allen, 1898).

36. Jolliffe, "Women's Magazines of the 19th Century."

37. Published letter of Henry B. Blackwell in *The Woman's Journal*, quoted in Stanton, Anthony, and Gage, *History of Woman Suffrage*, 3:387–88.

38. Rev. Mr. Holmes in ibid., 3:393–94.

39. Collier in ibid., 3:394.

40. "Let Them Be Heard!," *New York Tribune*, reprinted in *Liberator*, September 30, 1853.

41. "Brewing and Liquor Interests, and German and Bolshevik Propaganda, Report and Hearings of the Subcommittee on the Judiciary," U.S. Senate, 65 Cong, 1 Sess., vol. 1, 1032, in Flexner, *Century of Struggle*, 307.

42. "Report," in Stanton, Anthony, and Gage, *History of Woman Suffrage*, 4:xx–xxi.

43. Quoted in Carrie Chapman Catt and Nettie Rogers Shuler, *Woman Suffrage and Politics: The Inner Story of the Suffrage Movement* (New York: Scribner's, 1923), 155.

44. Letter from Clara Schlinghyde to C. C. Catt, November 11, 1911, Library of Congress Manuscripts Division, cited by Flexner, *Century of Struggle*, 265, 306–9.

45. Hays, *Morning Star*, 81.

46. Frederick Douglass, "The Rights of Women (1848)," in *Radical Reader: A Documentary History of the American Radical Tradition*, ed. Timothy Patrick and John McMillian (New York: New Press [Norton], 2003), 177. He said, "We hold woman to be justly entitled to all we claim for man. We go farther, and express our conviction that all political rights which it is expedient for man to exercise, it is equally so for woman."

47. "To the Women of the Republic," address from the Women's National Loyal League supporting the abolition of slavery, January 25, 1864, SEN 38A-H20 (Kansas folder), RG 46, Records of the U.S. Senate, National Archives.

48. Eleanor Flexner and Ellen Fitzpatrick, "The Emergence of a Suffrage Movement," *Century of Struggle: The Woman's Right Movement in the United States*, enl. ed. (Cambridge, Mass.: Belknap Press of Harvard University, 1996), 136.

49. Ibid., 137.

50. Ibid.

51. Susan Ditmire, "Why in Vineland?" *All in New Jersey* (blog), http://www.usgennet.org/usa/nj/county/cumberland/VineVote/Why.html. Also see "Legal Strategies of Susan B. Anthony," *Not for Ourselves Alone*, PBS/WETA, http://www.pbs.org/stantonanthony/resources/index.html?body=legal_strategies.html.

52. Janet Zollinger Giele, *Two Paths to Women's Equality: Temperance, Suffrage, and the Origins of Modern Feminism* (New York: Twayne, 1995), 115. The rest of the examples in this paragraph originated in this book.

53. Flexner and Fitzpatrick, "Emergence of a Suffrage Movement," 163.

54. Quoted in Martha Solomon, *A Voice of Their Own: The Woman Suffrage Press, 1840–1910* (Tuscaloosa: University of Alabama Press, 1991), 21.

55. See, e.g., Gwen Hoerr Jordan, "Agents of (Incremental) Change: From Myra Bradwell to Hillary Clinton," *Nevada Law Journal* 9 (Spring 2009): 580, 591 (footnotes omitted).

56. See, e.g., National Park Service, "Virginia Minor and Women's Right to Vote," http://www.nps.gov/jeff/historyculture/the-virginia-minor-case.htm.

57. Mark H. Neill, "The Women's Rights Movement in Missouri," *Journal of the Missouri Bar* 114 (March–April 2011): 115 (reprinted from the March 1973 edition of the *Journal of the Missouri Bar*).

58. 88 U.S. 162 (1875). Parenthetical page numbers in this section are from this case.

59. The court made it clear that women did not need the Fourteenth Amendment to grant them citizenship. Nor did they need the Constitution to make them citizens. Their citizenship was inherent as a part of the "people" constituting the nation. Ibid. at 165–68. See note 51 in this court case and accompanying text.

60. Emphasis added.

61. Emphasis added.

62. "A Woman of the Times. Sketch of Susan B. Anthony, the Noted Leader. Reminiscenses [*sic*] of Her Life Read at Meeting of the Political Equality Club, Warren, June 26th," *Warren (Pa.) Ledger*, July 3, 1891.

63. Daniel Connors of the OHA, "This Week in History," *Syracuse (N.Y.) Post Standard*, January 9, 2014.

64. Flexner and Fitzpatrick, "Emergence of a Suffrage Movement," 145.

65. Mary Gabriel, *Notorious Victoria: The Life of Victoria Woodhull Uncensored* (Chapel Hill, N.C.: Algonquin Books, 1998); Amanda Frisken, *Victoria Woodhull's Sexual Revolution: Political Theater and the Popular Press in Nineteenth-Century America* (Philadelphia: University of Pennsylvania Press, 2004).

66. Flexner and Fitzpatrick, "Emergence of a Suffrage Movement," 145.

67. "Woman's Suffrage: Trial of Miss Susan B. Anthony for Illegal Voting. The Jury Return a Verdict of Guilty—Opinion of Judge Hunt," *Milwaukee Sentinel*, June 19, 1873.

68. "General News Summary: The East," *Rochester Union Spy*, July 3, 1873.

69. "The News . . . Susan B. Anthony Tried, Convicted, and Fined for Illegal Voting," *Decatur (Ind.) News*, June 27, 1873. The story appeared in separate paragraphs in the columns. The outcome of the trial appeared under the subhead "Political."

70. "Brevities," *Milwaukee Sentinel*, March 18, 1876, in *The Selected Papers of Elizabeth Cady Stanton and Susan B. Anthony: National Protection for National Citizens, 1873 to 1880*, ed. Ann D. Gordon (New Brunswick, N.J.: Rutgers University Press, 2003), 219.

71. *Atlanta (Ga.) Constitution*, April 25, 1878.

72. Frank G. Carpenter, "The Women's Congress. The Noted Suffragists Now Assembled in Washington. Susan B. Anthony and Her $100 Fine, Pundita Ramabal and Hindoo [*sic*] Women, Frances Willard, Frank Leslie, Phoebe Cousins, May Sewell and Julia Howe," *Indiana (Pa.) Progress*, April 11, 1888.

73. Elizabeth V. Burt, ed., *Women's Press Organizations, 1881–1999* (Westport, Conn.: Greenwood Press, 2000).

74. "Woman of the Times."

75. "Ladies Dormitory at World's Fair," *Bismarck (N.D.) Daily Tribune*, June 3, 1893.

76. "Women Leaders and the Queen: Mrs. Sewall and Miss Anthony Presented to Her Majesty," *Frederick (Md.) News*, July 8, 1899.

77. Linda Steiner, "Finding Community in Nineteenth Century Suffrage Periodicals," in *Taking Their Place: A Documentary History of Women and Journalism*, ed. Maurine Beasley and Sheila J. Gibbons (Washington, D.C.: American University Press in cooperation with the Women's Institute for Freedom of the Press, Lanham, Md., 1993), 82.

78. Solomon, *Voice of Their Own*, 28. Colby launched the *Woman's Tribune* in 1883 and kept it alive for twenty-six years. In later years, it was published in Washington, D.C., and Portland, Ore. See Carol S. Lomicky, "Frontier Feminism and the *Woman's Tribune*: The Journalism of Clara Bewick Colby," *Journalism History* 28, no. 3 (Fall 2002): 102.

79. Rebecca J. Mead, *How the Vote Was Won: Woman Suffrage in the Western United States, 1868–1914* (New York: New York University Press, 2004), 17.

80. Giele, *Two Paths to Women's Equality*, 116–17.

81. Ibid., 151.

82. For a very able account of the final successful battles for woman's rights, see among others Linda J. Lumsden, *Rampant Women: Suffragists and the Right of Assembly* (Knoxville: University of Tennessee Press, 1997).

10. THE NATIONAL DEFENSE ASSOCIATION

LIBERAL PROTECTOR OF FREE SPEECH

JANICE R. WOOD

Historian James Parton in 1878 applied his considerable writing talents to more than the books that built his reputation as a leading American biographer of his era. He united with other writers and editors against Anthony Comstock, a figure they feared would find a place in history as a hero, and his infamous crusade against obscene materials in the mail. Parton and fellow free speech advocates never defended the distribution of cheap novels or racy pictures, but they dug in their heels trying to stop the suppression of literature stemming from liberal reform issues of the era. Parton made his views clear to other anti-Comstock supporters:

> You know how I hate and loathe the books and papers that circulate among boys, which can have no other than a corrupting effect. I could join, heart and hand[,] in hanging a wretch who, for a little money, would either write, or publish, or sell such works. And yet it seems to me that the espionage of mails by an illiterate person is even a worse evil than that. It menaces the very citadel of liberty.[1]

Parton's colleagues who were particularly sympathetic to individuals seeking to openly discuss sex-related issues or to criticize social institutions such as marriage and religion launched the National Defense Association in 1878 as America's first advocacy organization devoted to free speech. Members hoped to "roll back the wave of intolerance, bigotry, and ignorance which threatens to submerge our cherished liberties," which they identified as the influence of Comstock and his Society for the Suppression of Vice (also known as the Vice Society), according to the group's constitution.[2]

Liberals particularly objected to postal censors' seemingly unreviewable power to dispose of material they deemed obscene.[3] No due process existed for the writers of such literature. Yet the anti-Comstock forces were not always in agreement as to the powers that state and federal officials should have to restrict speech, press, or expression. A minority of the liberals were absolutists where speech and press protections were concerned; however, the majority did support some restrictions on freedom of expression, provided such laws were written in clear language and were narrowly tailored so as not to stop more speech than was absolutely necessary.

Former abolitionist Elizur Wright voiced the liberals' concern that purity reformers' support for vaguely worded laws to stamp out vice only invited the potential for prosecutorial abuse. At a public rally in Boston on August 1, 1878, to protest the conviction of fellow liberal Ezra Heywood—a former Congregationalist minister and critic of Comstock who had been jailed for mailing a pro-feminist, anti-marriage tract he had penned titled *Cupid's Yokes*—Wright stated,

> Nobody here, I think, would object to a law regulating the transmission of literature through the mails, if it could so define obscenity as not to exclude a great part of our most valuable literature, including the Bible, and so as not to violate the true and constitutional liberty of the press.[4]

The work of the National Defense Association, chronicled in this chapter, emerged from the nineteenth-century free thought movement and laid the groundwork for subsequent freedom of expression advocacy groups, including the Free Speech League and the American Civil Liberties Union.[5] Although it was based in New York City, the National Defense Association also sponsored chapters in Boston and Chicago. Congress's passage of federal anti-obscenity legislation (popularly known as the Comstock Act) in 1873[6] set the stage for the association's fight against obscenity laws and its parallel support of freedom of expression rights. The House and Senate took the opportunity to pass morality-related legislation in an attempt to improve Congress's public image in light of an influence-peddling scandal and beefed up earlier laws against mailing and importing obscene materials.[7]

The act did not define obscenity but merely stated that material could be considered obscene if it might corrupt both the minds and morals of the young and impressionable. The same law also categorized birth control information and paraphernalia, including condoms, as obscene. The latter action made it difficult for doctors to provide patients with family planning materials.[8] The act's vague language gave Comstock and other purity crusaders the legal authority to scrutinize a wide range of printed matter, including medical advice; publications produced by feminists, freethinkers, and free love advocates; artwork (including prints that reproduced the works of famous European masters); popular and classic literature; and gambling paraphernalia.

Comstock particularly loathed popular literature, was highly suspicious of reading, and used his authority to prosecute a number of well-known authors and poets, including Walt Whitman and novelist Albert Ross, whose works reflected the new literary realism movement that began emerging in the 1860s. Unlike the writers from the earlier romantic period, the new authors penned works that included such themes as divorce, labor, poverty, woman's rights, and sexuality.[9]

Comstock was not the only backer of obscenity legislation, just the most tenacious; his version of the federal law passed with minimal debate.[10] The act also made Comstock a special agent of the post office with unlimited power to enforce it, which he did zealously until his death in 1915, describing his anti-obscenity efforts as "weeding in the Garden of the Lord."[11]

From 1872 until 1915, Anthony Comstock served as the nation's chief moralist. Given authority as a special inspector of the post office, the vice fighter arrested thousands of individuals and kept books from being published, plays from being performed, and art prints from being exhibited. Public domain, WikiCommons.

At the urging of Comstock, Congress gave postal officials license to remove from the mail materials deemed "obscene, lewd or lascivious" and "of indecent character," as well as items used to prevent conception and to cause abortion or materials used to promote either. Comstock also found support outside of Congress. His fervor had initially impressed a group of kindred spirits at the YMCA in post–Civil War New York City, including prominent financier J. P. Morgan and soap magnate Samuel Colgate, whose association with anti-vice activities lent Comstock respectability.[12]

These wealthy reformers often supported or were influenced by then-popular views that society was constantly improving and, subsequently, that all individuals could be improved as well.[13] They also sought to stabilize society by ridding the nation of vice and by promoting the concept that marriage and family were the cornerstones of civilization, views to which most Victorian-era Americans subscribed.[14] As one historian has noted, purity reformers like Comstock

> emerged to fill a void left by the diminished authority of the nation's clergy who once served as near-absolute voices on behavioral and social matters. Not surprisingly, the wealthy citizens who joined the purity crusade promoted their values, including prudence, sobriety, Protestant morality, and clean living, as correct and respectable.[15]

Most states accordingly followed up the national legislation with their own "little Comstock Laws."[16] By 1900, forty-two states had either enacted such laws or amended existing laws to further crack down on vice and obscene matter.[17] Courts already were hostile to defendants facing obscenity charges in an era regarded as the "forgotten years" for free speech.[18] Vice had become an issue a decade before Comstock's work began in earnest; a variety of purity crusaders had united against obscenity after it became publicly known that military camps were bastions of impure literature.[19]

Token resistance to the Comstock-inspired national and state laws on obscenity arose outside mainstream society with the National Liberal League, which later spawned the National Defense Association. The league had grown out of the free thought movement of liberal-minded individuals who favored science and reason over religious tradition, authoritarianism, and the influence of the Christian church in government and society.[20]

For freethinkers, as well as for most nineteenth-century Americans, associations held a special fascination, as observed by French political philosopher and historian Alexis de Tocqueville in his classic 1835 analysis of society in the United States, *Democracy in America*. He believed that people coming together for a common purpose cultivated a strong sense of community:

> Americans of all ages, all stations of life, and all types of disposition are forever forming associations. . . . If it is proposed to inculcate some truth or to foster some feeling by the encouragement of a great example, they form a society. . . . In democratic countries knowledge of how to combine is the mother of all other forms of knowledge; on its progress depends that of all the others.[21]

Even more lay ahead. By 1897, a writer for the *North American Review* dubbed his era the "Golden Age of fraternity."[22] The forces that modernized, industrialized, urbanized, and secularized the nation gave rise to such fraternities, in part because these forces unsettled many citizens. Writer Henry James, surveying the changing social landscape, voiced upper-class fears when he said that the nation's rapid shifts filled him with "the dreadful chill of change."[23] Immigration and feminization transformed the look of daily life, and joiners clung to those they perceived to be their own kind for a semblance of order.[24] Americans congregated along racial, gender, ethnic, and occupational lines for social, political, and business purposes. This golden age set the stage for twentieth-century organizational life, reflected in social clubs, reform movements, neighborhood action committees, civic improvement leagues, labor unions, trade associations, and special interest groups, and these organizations hired staff members to handle everyday affairs.[25] As never before, corporations and military units developed principles of organizational science to streamline and bring efficiency to operations.[26]

Members of the National Liberal League mobilized after watching Comstock prosecute three of its members on obscenity charges in 1876 and 1877: Dr. E. B. Foote Sr. for selling and promoting birth control materials and pamphlets; free love advocate Heywood for producing a brochure that criticized marriage as detrimental to women; and free thought editor D. M. Bennett for distributing the Heywood brochure and writing another that questioned Christian teachings. Comstock made good on his promise to destroy free thought publications, and league members felt unfairly targeted.[27] To Comstock, freethinkers were merely "infidels" who threated the moral structure of society.[28]

Free speech activists inside the National Liberal League and the later National Defense Association adopted a lobbying model for their associations; while shielding members from perceived danger, they courted public opinion, campaigned for legislation, and monitored government reaction.[29] With a central message that personal liberties were being violated, the liberals hoped to spark public debate and thereby influence legislators and government officials. They launched anti-Comstock grassroots campaigns with speeches, petitions, fund-raisers, and pamphlets.[30]

After being found guilty in 1876 of violating a federal obscenity statute for mailing birth control information and devices, Dr. E. B. Foote Sr. devoted much of his considerable wealth to defending others who ran afoul of the Comstock Act. Public domain, U.S. National Library of Medicine.

Free speech advocates also penned numerous newspaper and magazine articles for popular publications in an attempt to disseminate their views to a wide audience.[31] For example, Elizur Wright, in a letter to the *Boston Evening Herald* published on June 28, 1883, eloquently put forth the liberals' belief that the nation's founding fathers were opposed to most forms of press censorship. "No doubt the liberty of the press has its evils and dangers," he wrote. "But the framers of our constitution and the people who adopted it seem to have emphatically decided that nothing the liberty of the press could do would be so dangerous as any attempt to restrain it." He added that the framers trusted that members of the press would correct their own "moral errors" more safely than any arbitrary censorship could.[32] Similarly, Albert Ross, a popular novelist of the time who fell afoul of the Comstock Act for the content of some of his books, warned that giving police powers to a small number of morality censors had implications beyond stifling writers' speech; such power also would harm democracy by not allowing ideas to flourish.[33]

The National Liberal League's outstanding pro–free speech effort was a petition drive in 1878 that garnered seventy thousand signatures of people who requested that the Comstock Act either be repealed or be modified to prevent the government from using it to violate freedom of the press or of conscience in the guise of religious, moral, political, medical, or commercial purposes.[34] But when several league members presented the huge petition to the House Committee on the Revision of Laws in February 1878, Comstock denounced it and the committee promptly dismissed it.[35] Liberals knew they faced a difficult fight. Dr. E. B. Foote Jr. acknowledged that arguments for free expression garnered little congressional support because Comstock and other vice crusaders always countered that morality was at stake. "It is about as hard to get an egg back after the hen has laid it, as to repeal a law that has for its ostensible object any moral purpose," he said in a letter to two Michigan liberals.[36]

The league's members who were most zealous for the repeal of Comstock legislation established the National Defense Association. On June 11, 1878, several veterans of the league's petition drive gathered in New York City to organize the new group devoted exclusively to anti-Comstock operations. Each contributed ten dollars toward initial operating expenses. They elected as president Albert Rawson, a biblical scholar; as vice president John Jewett, the publisher of Harriet Beecher Stowe's *Uncle Tom's Cabin*; and as secretary Dr. E. B. Foote Jr., the son of the doctor prosecuted for obscenity for selling birth control.[37]

According to Hal D. Sears's history of sex radicals, several "old-line reform types" from the National Liberal League "provided the moral backbone of the organization."[38] Among them were attorney Thaddeus B. Wakeman; Theron C. Leland, known for his eloquent verbal skills, who was a court stenographer and editor of the National Liberal League's publication, *Man*; and two former abolitionists, Stephen Pearl Andrews and Elizur Wright. Andrews had been a noted anarchist and free love advocate who mentored Victoria Woodhull, the first female U.S. presidential candidate, in her work as a newspaper publisher and lecturer. Wright, an actuary, had led life insurance reform. Elected president of the National Defense Association in 1885, Wright died soon thereafter, yet in name he retained the presidency. A resolution stated, "By honoring his name we give strength to our cause, whose watchword in Liberty."[39] An 1885 list of officers also included New Yorkers attorney Edward Chamberlain and journalist M. M. Pomeroy.[40]

NATIONAL DEFENSE ASSOCIATION GOALS

As the only group formed exclusively to combat Comstock and his restrictions on freedom of speech and press, the National Defense Association vowed in its constitution, adopted September 12, 1278,

> to investigate all questionable cases of prosecution, under what are known as the Comstock laws, State and National, and to extend sympathy, moral support, and material aid to those who may be unjustly assailed by the enemies of free speech and free press;
>
> To rescue those who may be convicted and imprisoned for no other crime than exercising the natural right of an American citizen, to think his thought and express it orally or in print;
>
> To defend honest investigators in all departments of science, and to uphold the rights of the people to acquire a thorough knowledge of human physiology;
>
> Finally, to employ all peaceful and honorable means to roll back the wave of intolerance, bigotry, and ignorance which threatens to submerge our cherished liberties.[41]

Enlightening the public became a high priority, which members attempted with a range of publications that displayed the defense association's challenge to Comstock's control over the courts and legislatures. They circulated documents to raise funds, protested court decisions to influence proposed bills, and presented alternative legal opinions to various audiences, ranging from those among the general public to lawmakers on the national and state levels.[42] At least one of the brochures served multiple purposes. Ostensibly it opposed two amendments to the Comstock Act being considered in Congress, but it also included the text of the defense association's constitution and a speech on the constitutional arguments to repeal the original Comstock Act.[43]

NATIONAL DEFENSE ASSOCIATION LITERATURE

Another publication, *The Fable of the Spider and the Bees*, warned readers of the immediate dangers to freedom of the press imposed by the Comstock Act, particularly for literature concerning sex education, and solicited their support of the association. Written by Dr. E. B. Foote Sr., a New York City physician, the story depicted Comstock as a venomous spider casting a dangerous web over an insect community and portrayed lawmakers as bumblebees who did not care about the damage inflicted by the spider, who bore "on his broad dark back a growth of dirty white down, forming for all the world hieroglyphics which could be clearly interpreted as the letters A and C."[44]

Foote Sr. had developed a personal antipathy to Comstock following his 1876 conviction. The nationally known doctor had enjoyed a thriving medical practice on Lexington Avenue in New York City that included a mail-order business (which dispersed medicines and birth control devices) and a publishing company that produced and shipped Foote's popular home medical advice books as well as birth control pamphlets that the doctor penned. Although Foote was opposed to abortion, he was an ardent feminist who supported woman's rights, including the right for women to control their own reproductive systems.[45] Foote's popular work *Medical Common Sense* became a target for Comstock's anti-vice ire because the doctor advised married couples to decide for themselves how often to engage in physical relations based on their own determination as to how pleasurable sex was for them, rather than encouraged sex only for reproductive purposes. Then, too, the book also explained the male and female reproductive systems to readers.[46]

Another Foote publication, *Dr. Foote's Health Monthly*, featured a section called "The Outlook" that was devoted to free speech issues. Both Foote Sr. and Foote Jr. had launched the magazine to impart medical advice to the public as well as to serve as a voice of opposition to the Comstock Act.[47] The publication became the unofficial newsletter for the National Defense Association. It also updated readers on obscenity prosecutions and legislative activities in Washington and in state capitals around the country.

Foote Jr.'s periodic reports as secretary of the association used anti-Comstock rhetoric, such as calling the era of obscenity prosecutions the "American Inquisition"[48] and a "reign of terror,"[49] characteristic of czarist societies. Using colorful language, articles described victims as being "extracted from the jaws of the Comstockian dragon"[50] and the post office as becoming the "streaming tail on Comstock's kite."[51] Comstock, in turn, used his own labeling tactics, referring to liberals and others who opposed the 1873 act as "the great fraternity of smut dealers."[52]

In contrasting its work to that of Comstock's Vice Society, *Dr. Foote's Health Monthly* characterized the National Defense Association in 1879 as follows:

> The association is not doing battle for indecent people, nor has there been so much as a single contribution to the fund from a dealer in or manufacturer of, what can be called obscene matter. Both members, and contributors are

the cleanest people in the land. . . . There is one advantage which the National Defense Association has over the Society for the Suppression of Vice (so-called). It is this; The former is an inexpensive concern comparatively.

All of its officers are unsalaried. It has no secretary or agent to which it pays the handsome sum of $4,000 per year [referring to Comstock]. If the $7,000 to $8,000 required to carry on the Vice Society for one year were to be put into the treasury of the Defense Association just once[,] those phrases of Comstockism which interfere with popularizing physiology and discussing the live social and theological questions of the day would die a natural death.[53]

NATIONAL DEFENSE ASSOCIATION ACTIVITIES

The work of the National Defense Association is best understood through articles in *Dr. Foote's Health Monthly.* The association's executive committee regularly met to plan a concerted response to the actions of Comstock's Vice Society.[54] When funds were available in the treasury, the money was applied to individual Comstock-related cases. For defendants without financial means, the association hired attorneys to represent them.[55] It also appointed one of its own members to serve as a case manager each time an individual faced prosecution.[56]

Raising funds was always a crucial issue. Active members frequently made contributions but never made withdrawals for themselves, despite their own run-ins with Comstock.[57] The association opened a general fund as well as individual defense funds for specific cases. Members compared their coffers to those of Comstock's Vice Society, whose meetings they attended[58] so they could hand out anti-Comstock literature.[59] Comstock's supporters contributed about $10,000 each year, while the National Defense Association had not raised a comparable total in ten years.[60]

HIGH-PROFILE CASES

Some of the association's best-known cases demonstrate the range of the group's activities to support clients. A committee met at the Foote home to plan an elaborate reception for free thought editor D. M. Bennett when he was released from prison in 1881.[61] Bennett, a former Shaker, was a leading proponent of anticlerical free thought and ran afoul of Comstock via his opposition to the 1873 act. Bennett viewed the law as a state-sanctioned action by Christians to impose their beliefs on the public as a whole. He also viewed the Comstock Act as a violation of liberty of conscience. As a result, the aging editor of the free thought publication the *Truth Seeker* helped lead the massive 1878 petition drive that netted the signatures of journalists, editors, minsters, attorneys, and members of the public.[62]

Bennett's efforts on behalf of freedom of speech and conscience so aroused the vice fighter's ire that Comstock personally arrested the editor in November 1877 on charges of blasphemy and obscenity for mailing two publications, a reprint of a scientific tract written by H. B. Bradford for *Popular Science Monthly* titled *How Do Marsupials Propagate?* and a satirical work that Comstock considered blasphemous titled *An Open Letter to Jesus Christ.* The latter pamphlet, penned by Bennett, posed both biblical and uncomfortable personal questions to Jesus.[63] Bennett was arrested again in August 1878 in Watkins Glen, New York, at a meeting of the New York Freethinkers Association for distributing Heywood's free love pamphlet, *Cupid's Yokes.*[64] Despite his arrests, or perhaps because of them, Bennett also became an outspoken critic of Comstock. Like the Footes, Bennett truly believed in the reform causes he espoused. His writings were never meant to titillate. Comstock's willingness to stop discussion of liberal and reform causes led Bennett to pen a particularly harsh attack against Comstock in 1878 that also included a discussion of his interpretation of the meaning and boundary of freedom of expression.[65]

Considered a free speech martyr, Bennett was honored on a medallion the association forged to garner support and raise money for prosecuted editor Moses Harman and his newspaper, *Lucifer, the Light Bearer.*[66] Harman, his son George, and his coeditor Edwin C. Walker were arrested for violating the Comstock Act for publishing and mailing an issue of their magazine that included a letter from a reader who discussed the issue of forced sex during marriage. Although Harman ran the letter because he was an outspoken feminist, he also courted trouble because he was willing to ignore all norms of social propriety if he felt that a frank discussion would help expose or begin solving any social ill.[67]

The National Defense Association also took up the case of Lois Waisbrooker, a woman's rights advocate, who was prosecuted for printing a letter sent to her small publication describing the writer's continuing affair with another woman; Waisbrooker advised him to end his unhappy marriage and wed the other woman.[68] The association also provided help to Kansan John B. Wise, who was convicted of blasphemy for scribbling on a postcard a Bible verse considered in court to be indecent.[69] Another Comstock arrestee, Elmina Slenker, a Virginia woman who faced obscenity charges for the sexual content of personal correspondence,[70] relied heavily on the defense association for financial and moral support after her personal resources had been drained.

Perhaps the most tragic of all of the association's clients was Ida Craddock, a free speech crusader who killed herself at age forty-five rather than face a five-year sentence for penning a pamphlet, *The Wedding Night*, which a judge had declared obscene. Craddock always claimed she had a "calling" to teach the "divine science" of sex, yet even her supporters worried about her sanity. Craddock never married, but an affair with a married minister led her to associate sex with mysticism. Although she had been a patient at the Pennsylvania Hospital for the Insane for three months in 1898, she was never declared mentally ill by a judge.[71]

Craddock came to Comstock's attention in 1893 in Chicago, where she offered lectures and counseling and sold booklets on marital issues. Renowned defense attorney Clarence Darrow successfully defended her in Chicago, while similar obscenity charges related to her lectures and pamphlets were dismissed in Washington, D.C., after a judge requested she leave town.[72] She was again arrested on March 5, 1902, under New York's anti-obscenity law for mailing copies of *The Wedding Night*. Although she was convicted and served a three-month sentence, Craddock was rearrested upon release under the federal Comstock Act and, after refusing her lawyer's advice to plead insanity, drew a five-year sentence.

Dr. E. B. Foote Jr. established a fund for Craddock's defense, penned a pamphlet titled *Comstock versus Craddock*, and even took the personal step of overseeing her apartment and personal belongings while she served her first jail sentence. In his pamphlet to solicit support for Craddock, Foote chastised individuals who were "not entirely in sympathy" with her work while putting forth his own libertarian interpretation of freedom of expression:

> They are only willing to stand for the right of free press when the preachment is just what they think. They are willing to let anything be suppressed that does not fit their notion of what is right. While I am not able to say that everything that Mrs. Craddock says or does is *all right*, I do say that official or other interference is *all wrong*, entirely unnecessary, and of no advantage to public or private morals.[73]

Additional defense association chapters also emerged to help individuals charged under obscenity laws. In Boston, another section of the association was instrumental in getting charges dismissed against poet Walt Whitman when he refused to delete three poems, "To a Common Prostitute," "A Woman Waits for Me," and "A Dalliance of Eagles," from a new edition of *Leaves of Grass* in 1882 after Comstock leaned on Boston officials to pronounce them obscene.[74]

Whitman was no stranger to attacks for his sometimes-frank poetry. In 1860, for example, a reviewer for the *Springfield (Mass.) Daily Republican* opined that the poet's work was "smut." The unnamed writer expressed dismay that a respected and reputable publisher would issue a book that was not "pure." Whitman's frequent appeals to nature, the article's author said, seemed an attack on Christianity.[75]

The Boston and New York chapters collaborated in the defense of noted editor Ezra Heywood, despite the risk to members of being associated with controversial free love doctrines.[76] The right to publish, rather than the specific topic, was central to liberals' arguments. A representative of the defense association successfully lobbied the White House for Heywood's release from prison, although similar attempts on Bennett's behalf failed. The group of freethinkers who pushed for Bennett's release became known as the "James Parton Club," named after the biographer mentioned in the opening of this study.[77] Another chapter, the Chicago Division of the National Defense Association, as it called itself, patterned its constitution after the New York organization's.[78]

LEGISLATIVE ACTIVISM

The National Defense Association also mounted campaigns in Washington, D.C., and state capitals against attempts to strengthen existing Comstock legislation, with varying degrees of success.[79] Members also lobbied government officials for the release and pardon of clients and against any legislation that reinforced the Comstock Act.

Recorded only in *Dr. Foote's Health Monthly*, the defense association in 1881 sponsored a second petition drive demanding changes to the Comstock postal laws. Several separate petitions were merged into one that displayed between fifteen thousand and twenty thousand names. The Footes through the *Health Monthly* served as a collection point where the various portions of the 1881 petition were assembled on the way to Congress. Mounted on canvas, the composite petition was presented to Congress in January 1881.[80] According to the *Congressional Record*, Representative James W. Singleton, a Democrat from Illinois, delivered the petition, where it was referred to the House Committee on the Post-Office and Post-Roads. In the petition, signers requested that postal laws be repealed or modified to prevent the violation of constitutional rights and to keep the government from censoring the mails. They also asked that the fines and imprisonment imposed under the Comstock Act be repaired or relieved.[81]

LEGAL STRATEGY

Many of the legal arguments and defense strategies presented by both the National Liberal League and the National Defense Association were designed by New York attorney Thaddeus Wakeman. He was credited with writing the organizations' speeches and materials that attacked the censorship inherent in the Comstock Act on constitutional grounds.[82] His legal arguments were at the center of many defense association cases, and his speeches were published by the Footes' Murray Hill Publishing Company.

Wakeman's arguments fell into three categories: the Comstock Act was unconstitutional, unnecessary, and mischievous. First, the act violated the "necessary and proper" powers the Constitution granted Congress for the supervision of the postal system. He also asserted that Congress exceeded its bounds by passing a law that regulated content and defined morality.[83] Second, Wakeman said the Comstock Act was unnecessary because state laws sufficiently served its purpose. He advocated that nationalized obscenity laws be decentralized.[84] Last, he argued that the act was malicious and dangerous, partially because it did not sufficiently define the crime with which people would be charged. Wakeman and other defense association members wanted to carve out a meaning for "obscenity" that precluded the work of their colleagues and attempted also to move the courts away from the Hicklin test, which held that a literary work could be considered obscene if any portion of the material had a tendency "to deprave or corrupt those whose minds are open to such immoral influences, and into whose hands a publication of this sort may fall."[85]

FINANCIAL SUPPORT

Sources generally credit Foote Sr. with providing substantial financial support for the defense association and the cases it accepted.[86] In fact, one member cited Foote Sr. and his son as the association's "heart, soul and purse."[87] No records of the association's funds are available to substantiate the large gifts credited to the Footes. Rather, small gifts of five, ten, and fifteen dollars to defense funds for specific individuals were reported in the *Health Monthly*. The Footes often made the first donations to many of the funds.[88]

Diminishing contributions marked the defense association's decline, according to the secretary's reports that Foote Jr. submitted to the *Health Monthly*. In February 1886, the association's presence had so waned that Foote Jr. reported that despite contrary appearances, the group "has not been dead nor sleeping" for the previous two or three years but gave no details. Without much notice, the officers had continued meeting, assisting Comstock defendants and printing literature whenever funds were available. However, financial contributions had dwindled, especially after the death of popular free thought editor D. M. Bennett in 1882, and substantial financial support was needed to carry on the fight against Comstock's force.[89]

By September 1894, the executive committee was meeting only on occasion, and a desperate appeal for funds included the acknowledgment, "Most of our earnest liberal reformers are poor in purse."[90] However, no more information was given on the status of the organization. After October 1894, the National Defense Association was not mentioned again in the *Health Monthly*, which itself folded in 1896.[91]

As the twentieth century dawned, Foote Jr. and a few other defense association members continued the battle for free speech but expanded their work beyond protecting individuals facing obscenity prosecutions to other issues, including the rights of anarchists, labor leaders, and socialists to speak against the government. Such speakers repeatedly found themselves arrested following President William McKinley's assassination.[92] Foote Jr. and his compatriots formed the Free Speech League in 1902 and promoted First Amendment freedom for all individuals, regardless of perspective, in response to Congress's passage of the Alien Immigration Act in 1903.[93]

The younger Foote was an ideal choice to guide the new organization. Not only had he been involved with two decades of free speech battles through the National Defense Association, but Foote Jr. and his physician-wife, Mary, were strong supporters of many liberal social, political, and economic reforms, including feminism and birth control, whose proponents also faced censorship. Leonard D. Abbott, the editor of *Current Opinion*, said of the younger Foote,

> [He] did not ask whether he saw eye to eye with a man before he would help him. He had the large conviction that there could not be real progress in the world unless we each one of us have the undeniable right to express the truth as we see it.[94]

The Free Speech League's major clients included anarchist and feminist Emma Goldman before she was deported from the United States[95] and birth control activist Margaret Sanger. By the time Comstock sought Sanger's prosecution in 1915, his influence had declined and the U.S. public was beginning to accept birth control. The U.S. attorney's office was less willing to risk a spectacular trial that would make Sanger a martyr and dropped the charges.[96]

The Free Speech League, which was led by nationally known attorney Theodore Schroeder after the death of Foote Jr. in 1912,

> became better known than the NDA, in part, because of the work the Association's members had done to popularize free expression rights as well as broaden public acceptance of progressive views. But numerous government attempts to censor the speech of labor unions, socialists, communists, and anarchists also contributed to the group's popularity.[97]

As with the National Defense Association, the Free Speech League's membership boasted a number of nationally known individuals, including the investigative journalists Lincoln Steffens and Hutchins Hapgood, editor Leonard Abbott, and attorneys Clarence Darrow and Gilbert Roe. The group also patterned its public relations tactics on those of the defense association. Members produced vast quantities of printed works, gave speeches, petitioned the president for pardons, and addressed Congress and state legislatures on freedom of speech issues. The league existed for two decades, dissolving only when its members decided that the newly formed and better-organized American Civil Liberties Union could better continue the fight.[98]

What had the National Defense Association accomplished despite the fact that its target (Comstock) continued taking the field? It had harnessed anti-Comstock sentiment when members found thousands of supporters to sign petitions for repeal of the Comstock Act and for the pardon of particular defendants. The group developed a concerted legal argument against the Comstock Act stressing constitutional rights, which it used to defend as many clients as possible before the need for funding gradually overwhelmed the group's modest monetary resources.

Developing the National Defense Association was one of the most practical measures taken by the Comstock opposition in providing relief for defendants, according to Comstock biographer Margaret Leech. It created "no small amount of worry and trouble" for the Society for the Suppression of Vice.[99] Samuel Putnam, who chronicled the free thought movement, was generous in his assessment of the defense association's success: "Many a worthy man, whom this [vice] society has set out to victimize, he owed his freedom to the influence of the Defense Association."[100] Putnam's generalization was more congratulatory than analytical; his supporting statements lauded the group's distribution of literature more than the outcome of specific cases. Ultimately, however, Comstock sympathizers ruled the day.

Through the eyes of the National Defense Association, one can see just how imposing a challenge it was to oppose Comstock. As an anti-Comstock organization, the group focused on just one aspect of free speech—obscenity—for it was a complex issue. Those who advocated free speech and free press rights for free lovers and freethinkers risked being perceived as favoring obscenity and contradicting traditional views on sexuality, marriage, and religion. They faced insurmountable odds in raising money, harnessing public support, waging court battles, and making themselves heard politically. They supported mostly independent and self-published editors and writers who felt the weight of the government and society bearing down upon them without the buffer of corporate ownership, influential voices, and proven legal advice.

Members of both the National Defense Association and the Free Speech League who conducted uphill battles against Comstock might have found comfort in the legacy that researcher Helen Lefkowitz Horowitz has attributed to them. She wrote in 2002 that the organization "kept the idea of freedom of speech alive" in a dark era for free speech.[101] Or as James Parton wrote, it was a time in which the work of Anthony Comstock was perceived as "the espionage of mails by an illiterate person" that "menace[d] the very citadel of liberty."

Notes

1. Quoted in Edward Bliss Foote Sr., *A Fable of the Spider and the Bees* (New York: National Defense Association, 1881), 40.

2. *Brief for Argument for the Repeal of Section 3893, Title XLVI United States* (New York: National Defense Association, undated), 38.

3. Hal D. Sears, *The Sex Radicals: Free Love in High Victorian America* (Lawrence: Regents Press of Kansas, 1977), 71.

4. *Proceedings of the Indignation Meeting Held in Faneuil Hall, Thursday, Evening, August 1, 1878* (New York: Benjamin Tucker, 1878), 6.

5. Helen Lefkowitz Horowitz, *Rereading Sex: Battles over Sexual Knowledge and Suppression in Nineteenth-Century America* (New York: Knopf, 2002), 381.

6. 18 U.S.C. § 1461–1462. Comstock sought to strengthen the existing 1872 federal statute after he became frustrated by the fact that the then-existing statute did not include newspapers or birth control devices and information among the materials considered obscene. Comstock was not able to use the 1872 law to obtain a prosecution of free love advocate Victoria Woodhull, who exposed the affair between nationally known minister Henry Ward Beecher and his parishioner Mrs. Elizabeth Tilton in her magazine, *Woodhull and Claflin's Weekly*. For more on the scandal, see Sally McMillen, *Seneca Falls and the Origins of the Women's Rights Movement* (New York: Oxford University Press, 2009), 193.

7. Margaret A. Blanchard, *Revolutionary Sparks: Freedom of Expression in Modern America* (New York: Oxford University Press, 1992), 16. The scandal in question was the Crédit Mobilier scandal that involved members of Congress, the Union Pacific Railroad, and the Crédit Mobilier of America Company that was hired to build the eastern portion of the nation's first transcontinental railroad. Edward Chancellor, *Devil Takes the Hindmost: A History of Financial Speculation* (New York: Plume, 2000), 175, 184.

8. Many Gilded Age physicians held traditional views about the roles of men and women, the sanctity of the home and family, and birth control and thus supported Comstock's efforts. See John S. Haller and Robin M. Haller, *The Physician and Sexuality in Victorian America* (Urbana: University of Illinois Press, 1974), 47–137. Some states criminalized the dissemination of family planning materials and prosecuted individuals who attempted to distribute such information even before Comstock and other purity crusaders began their work in earnest. See, for example, Commonwealth v. Landis, 1 Leg. Gaz. R. 42 (Pa. 1870); U.S. v. Chesman, 19 F. 497 (1881); and U.S. v. Clarke, 38 F. 500 (E. D. Mo. 1889).

9. David S. Reynolds, *Walt Whitman's America: A Cultural Biography* (New York: Vintage Books, 1996), 213–30.

10. The vice crusader explained his beliefs and his life's work in a series of articles for a magazine called the *Golden Rule*. A complete collection of the articles is available in the Free Speech League Collection, box 17, Morris Library, Southern Illinois University, Carbondale.

11. Anna L. Bates, *Weeder in the Garden of the Lord* (Lanham, Md.: University Press of America, 1995), 3. For more on postal censorship, see Jon Bekken, "These Great and Dangerous Powers: Postal Censorship of the Press," *Journal of Communication Inquiry* 15, no. 1 (1991): 55–71; and Dorothy Fowler, *Unmailable: Congress and the Post Office* (Athens: University of Georgia Press, 1977).

12. Heywood Broun and Margaret Leech, *Anthony Comstock: Roundsman of the Lord* (New York: Albert and Charles Boni, 1928), 228.

13. Sears, *Sex Radicals*, 3.

14. Nicola Beisel, *Imperiled Innocents: Anthony Comstock and Family Reproduction in Victorian America* (Princeton: Princeton University Press, 1997), 76–103.

15. Mary M. Cronin, "The Liberty to Argue Freely: Nineteenth-Century Obscenity Prosecutions and the Emergence of Modern Libertarian Free Speech Discourse," *Journalism and Communication Monographs* 8, no. 3 (2006): 168; Milton Rugoff, *Prudery and Passion* (New York: G. P. Putnam's Sons, 1971), 30.

16. Blanchard, *Revolutionary Sparks*, 18.

17. C. Thomas Dienes, *Law, Politics and Birth Control* (Urbana: University of Illinois Press, 1972), 44.

18. David M. Rabban, *Free Speech in Its Forgotten Years* (New York: Cambridge University Press, 1997), 131.

19. Paul R. Abramson, *With Pleasure: Thoughts on the Nature of Human Sexuality* (New York: Oxford University Press, 2002), 180.
20. Susan Jacoby Yale, *Freethinkers: A History of American Secularism* (New York: Metropolitan Books, 2004), 16–19.
21. Quoted in J. A. Garraty, *The American Nation: A History of the United States* (New York: Harper and Row, 1966), 294.
22. Jason A. Kaufman, *For the Common Good? American Civic Life and the Golden Age of Fraternity* (New York: Oxford University, 2002), 3.
23. Henry James, *The American Scene* (1905; Bloomington: Indiana University Press, 1968), 232.
24. Kaufman, *For the Common Good?*, 33.
25. James Willard Hurst, *Law and the Conditions of Freedom in the Nineteenth-Century United States* (Madison: University of Wisconsin Press, 1984), 85.
26. Rodney Stark, "19th Century Organizations: The Organizational Age," *Sociology*, 3rd ed., http://analytictech.com/mb021/orgage.htm, retrieved August 28, 2014.
27. Sidney Warren, *American Freethought, 1860–1914* (New York: Guardian Press, 1966), 164. Foote Sr. was convicted on obscenity charges in 1876 and fined $3,500. For more on Foote and the impact of the Comstock Act on him and other medical doctors who sought to distribute birth control information and devices, see Janice Wood, "Prescription for a Periodical: Medicine, Sex, and Obscenity in the Nineteenth Century, as Told in *Dr. Foote's Health Monthly*," *American Periodicals* 18, no. 1 (2008): 26–28.
28. Anthony Comstock, *Frauds Exposed* (1880; Montclair, N.J.: Patterson Smith, 1969), 393.
29. Kaufman, *For the Common Good?*, 88.
30. Martin H. Blatt, *Free Love and Anarchism: The Biography of Ezra Heywood* (Urbana: University of Illinois Press, 1989), 128.
31. For a sampling of such articles, see "National Gag Law," *Word*, February 1876, 2; E. B. Foote Jr., "The Case of Moses Harman," *Twentieth Century*, May 31, 1890, 12–13; Hugh O. Pentecost, "A Good Man Sent to Prison," *Twentieth Century*, May 31, 1890, 9; and Edward W. Chamberlain, "In the Midst of Wolves," *Arena*, November 1894, 835–37.
32. Elizur Wright letter to *Boston Evening Herald*, June 28, 1883, Elizur Wright Papers, Library of Congress, Washington, D.C.
33. Albert Ross, "What Is Immoral in Literature," *Arena*, March 1891, 440. Walt Whitman viewed Comstock as a dangerous, uneducated buffoon and defended the literary realism movement that caught the purity crusader's ire. Writing in the *North American Review*, Whitman stated, "It is not the pictures or nude statues or text, with clear aim, that is indecent; it is the beholder's own thought, inference, distorted construction." Walt Whitman, "A Memorandum at a Venture," *North American Review*, June 1882, 546–50.

34. Section 1785, etc. of the Revised Statutes, 45th Cong., 1st Sess. (1878), and 7 *Cong. Rec.* (1878), H140.

35. H.R. Doc. No. 888, *Repeal of Certain Sections of the Revised Statutes*, 45th Cong., 2nd Sess. (1878).

36. E. B. Foote Jr. to W. and E. M. F. Denton, October 20, 1890, Denton Family Papers, Labadie Collection, University of Michigan, Ann Arbor.

37. Samuel Putnam, *400 Years of Freethought* (New York: Truth Seeker, 1894), 538.

38. Sears, *Sex Radicals*, 200.

39. Putnam, *400 Years*, 543.

40. Ibid., 538.

41. *Brief for Argument for the Repeal of Section 3893*, 38.

42. Blatt, *Free Love and Anarchism*, 184.

43. *Brief for Argument for the Repeal of Section 3893*, 3–33.

44. Foote, *Fable of the Spider and the Bees*, 3; Janice Wood, "Physicians and Obscenity: A Struggle for Free Speech, 1872–1915," *American Journalism* 36, no. 1 (2010): 36–44.

45. Wood, "Prescription for a Periodical," 26–27. Foote's first medical advice book for laymen, *Medical Common Sense*, first appeared in 1858 and sold more than 250,000 copies. An expanded version, *Plain Home Talk Embracing Medical Common Sense*, was issued in 1870 and sold more than 500,000 copies.

46. Cronin, "Liberty to Argue Freely," 185; Sears, *Sex Radicals*, 189–91.

47. Wood, "Prescription for a Periodical," 27.

48. "American Inquisition," *Dr. Foote's Health Monthly*, June 1887, 11–12.

49. "Reign of Terror," ibid., February 1882, 7.

50. "Comstock's Last Victim," ibid., March 1881, 13.

51. "The Postal Department and the Health Monthly," ibid., July 1881, 7.

52. Anthony Comstock to Theodore Schroeder, November 11, 1905, Theodore Schroeder Papers, box 5, Morris Library, University of Southern Illinois, Carbondale.

53. Quoted in Blatt, *Free Love and Anarchism*, 128.

54. "Defense Fund," *Dr. Foote's Health Monthly*, February 1885, 12.

55. "Defense Fund," ibid., January and July 1881, 11–12.

56. "Bleeding Kansas," ibid., September 1894, 7.

57. "Mr. Preston and the Health Monthly," ibid., September 1881, 15.

58. "Annual Meeting of the Vice Society," ibid., March 1886. 10.

59. Blatt, *Free Love and Anarchism*, 128.

60. "Comstock and His Annual Meeting," *Dr. Foote's Health Monthly*, March 1888, 12.

61. Thaddeus B. Wakeman, *In Memory of Edward Bliss Foote, M.D.* (New York: Edward Bond Foote, 1906), 53.

62. Cronin, "Liberty to Argue Freely," 195.

63. The pamphlet raised such questions as "Does it afford you any pleasure for man to hate his own blood relations?" and "Have you ever thought that the miracle alluded to [i.e., turning water into wine] was setting a bad example to young people and an encouragement to wine bibers?" D. M. Bennett, *An Open Letter to Jesus Christ* (New York: D. M. Bennett, 1877). For a recent historical account of Bennett that analyzes his place and role in nineteenth-century struggles for freedom of expression, see Roderick Bradford, *D. M. Bennett: The Truth Seeker* (Amherst, N.Y.: Prometheus Books, 2006).

64. Bradford, *D. M. Bennett*, 137–43.

65. That work was titled *The Champions of the Church: Their Crimes and Persecutions.*

66. "Comstockism Out West," *Dr. Foote's Health Monthly*, April 1882, 13.

67. Sears, *Sex Radicals*, 78.

68. "Bleeding Kansas"; "John Brown's Soul Goes Marching On," *Dr. Foote's Health Monthly*, October 1894, 12.

69. "The Death Knell of Our Free Press," *Dr. Foote's Health Monthly*, August 1894, 12.

70. Sears, *Sex Radicals*, 217–19.

71. Ida Craddock Papers, box 1, folder 1, Morris Library, Southern Illinois University, Carbondale.

72. Janice Wood, "Ida Craddock, Free Speech Martyr," in *Seeking a Voice: Images of Race and Gender in the 19th Century Press*, ed. David B. Sachsman, S. Kittrell Rushing, and Roy Morris Jr. (West Lafayette, Ind.: Purdue University Press, 2009), 319.

73. E. B. Foote, *Comstock versus Craddock* (New York: n.p., 1902).

74. Rabban, *Free Speech*, 31.

75. "Leaves of Grass—Smut in Them," *Springfield Daily Republican*, June 16, 1860; Sherry Ceniza, *Walt Whitman and Nineteenth-Century Women Reformers* (Tuscaloosa: University of Alabama Press, 2013), 204.

76. Blatt, *Free Love and Anarchism*, 111.

77. Foote, *Fable of the Spider and the Bees*, 40.

78. A copy of the Chicago chapter's constitution was found in the documents of the Ralph Ginzburg Papers, 1848–1864, Wisconsin Historical Society, Madison.

79. Wakeman, *Edward Bliss Foote*, 54; Sears, *Sex Radicals*, 200.

80. "The Petition for Repeal," *Dr. Foote's Health Monthly*, March 1881, 13.

81. H.R. Doc. No. 1005, *Postal Laws of the United States*, 46th Cong., 3rd Sess., 1881, and 11 *Cong. Rec.* 2 (1881).

82. Theodore Schroeder, *Edward Bond Foote: Biographical Notes and Appreciatives* (New York: Free Speech League, 1913), 14–15.

83. Thaddeus Wakeman, *Liberty and Purity* (New York: Liberal, 1881), 5.

84. Richard O. Curry and Lawrence B. Goodheart, eds., *American Chameleon: Individualism in Trans-national Context* (Kent: Kent State University Press, 1991), 148.

85. Regina v. Hicklin, L.R. 2 Q.B. 360 (1868).

86. Putnam, *400 Years*, 538.

87. Schroeder, *Edward Bond Foote*, 48. The remark was made by Edwin C. Walker, who served as the first president of the Free Speech League.

88. "Heywood Defense Fund," *Dr. Foote's Health Monthly*, January 1891, 11; "Aunt Elmina's Defense Fund," ibid., June 1887, 13; "Harman & Walker," ibid., December 1887, 10; "News of Wise and Waisbrooker," ibid., November 1884, 12.

89. "All Invited," ibid., February 1886, 12–13.

90. "Bleeding Kansas."

91. "Good-bye," *Dr. Foote's Health Monthly*, January 1896, 1.

92. Scott Miller, *The President and the Assassin: McKinley, Terror, and Empire at the Dawn of the American Century* (New York: Random House, 2013), 306, 343.

93. Rabban, *Free Speech*, 64.

94. Quoted in Schroeder, *Edward Bond Foote*, 45.

95. Emma Goldman, *Living My Life* (New York: AMS Press, 1970), 348.

96. David M. Kennedy, *Birth Control in America: The Career of Margaret Sanger* (New Haven: Yale University Press, 1971), 80.

97. Cronin, "Liberty to Argue Freely," 189.

98. Ibid.

99. Broun and Leech, *Anthony Comstock*, 189.

100. Putnam, *400 Years*, 540.

101. Horowitz, *Rereading Sex*, 382.

11. *DAVIS V. MASSACHUSETTS*

EXPRESSIVE CONDUCT AND REGULATED LIBERTY IN THE NINETEENTH CENTURY

MARY M. CRONIN

The Reverend William Franklin Davis was a persistent man. The evangelical Baptist minister from the city of Chelsea, Massachusetts, made regular trips to Boston Common, the nation's oldest city park, during the 1880s and 1890s to preach to passersby. Davis, who ran a mission in Boston's North End, believed he had a religious duty to preach, a duty he said was upheld by natural law rather than by the laws of man.[1] The laws of man regularly intervened, however. Davis was one of several ministers and orators arrested in the late nineteenth century for speaking on the Common without first obtaining a permit from the mayor, as required by a city ordinance.[2] Davis repeatedly returned to preach, always without a permit, and often was arrested for his actions. All of the arrests led to fines, but one arrest, in 1887, also resulted in a year's imprisonment because Davis had repeatedly flouted the ordinance.[3]

Despite his belief that freedom of speech was derived from natural law, Reverend Davis was one of a growing number of individuals who argued that judges should apply the First Amendment's speech and press protections to all citizens, rather than rely on more restrictive state and municipal ordinances.[4] Like a variety of other religious figures and labor leaders, Davis also recognized and argued that the physical place in which expression took place was an important factor in freedom of speech claims.[5] He knew that public oration often reached individuals who would not have heard such speech elsewhere. Then, too, the act of open-air speaking allowed like-minded individuals to come together in a show of unity to the public.[6]

Davis fought his arrests on constitutional grounds, citing the First and Fourteenth Amendments in support of his right to speak in a public park. Two appeals to the Massachusetts Supreme Judicial Court (in 1886 and 1894) and a subsequent appeal in 1897 to the U.S. Supreme Court challenging the ordinance's constitutionality led to a landmark ruling that upheld government officials' police powers, under the auspices of property law, to restrict expressive conduct on city-administered land for almost four decades.[7] As the reverend would discover, the concept of individual rights was rarely part of judicial thinking before the twentieth century.[8] Similarly, the equally important concept of judicial balancing would not be introduced into freedom of speech cases until the 1930s.[9] The *Davis* ruling would not be fully overturned until 1943[10] and was cited as precedent in a number of cases where speakers and assemblies had been stopped by authorities from expressing themselves in parks and on streets and sidewalks.[11]

Although the *Davis* ruling has led some scholars to cite the case as the foundation for modern public forum analysis,[12] a 1939 case, *Hague v. Committee for Industrial Organization*, is a better starting point for such forum analysis since the U.S. Supreme Court in *Hague* acknowledged for the first time that individuals had a right to express themselves on public property.[13] Furthermore, neither the Massachusetts Supreme Judicial Court nor the U.S. Supreme Court decided *Davis* on First Amendment or Fourteenth Amendment grounds. Given the lack of First and Fourteenth Amendment analyses in *Davis*, the case should instead be thought of as the ruling that established the constitutional status of public speaking during the nineteenth century.[14] That ruling—which relied on the principle that if government officials have the "greater power" to decide whether or not individuals can speak on public property, then they also have the "lesser power" to use a licensing system—was used to restrict speech well into the twentieth century.[15]

The Court's ruling in *Davis* is unsurprising, however, given that two decades previously, in 1875, the Court in *U.S. v. Cruikshank* determined that the Bill of Rights does not apply to the states, despite the adoption of the Fourteenth Amendment. Justices took a restrictive view, holding that the U.S. Constitution did not give citizens the right to assemble peacefully. Instead, in a narrow ruling, the Court said the First Amendment merely prohibited Congress from infringing upon the right. Citizens, the justices held, had to look to states for such a right.[16]

Despite the U.S. Supreme Court's use of property law to deny Davis protection for his expressive conduct, the case is important in American legal history because it demonstrates the clash between orthodox, restrictive legal approaches to freedom of expression espoused by many politicians and jurists during the nineteenth century,[17] and the countervailing, growing public demand, as the century progressed, for broad, constitutional protection for speech and press.[18] Furthermore, *Davis* was one of the few nineteenth-century cases involving freedom of expression on public property that was heard by the U.S. Supreme Court, establishing a precedent that government officials could use broad police powers to deny citizens expressive conduct rights in public parks, streets, and sidewalks.

Analysis of the *Davis* case lends support to a growing body of scholarly research that demonstrates that nineteenth-century judges, politicians, and many citizens supported laws that benefited the collective public welfare and social order, often at the expense of individual rights, including where freedom of speech and expression issues were concerned.[19] As will be shown, both the Massachusetts Supreme Judicial Court's ruling banning Davis's expressive conduct on Boston Common and the U.S. Supreme Court's affirmation of that ruling were consistent with laws that linked restrictions on individuals' freedom of speech in public parks to broader concerns about the public's welfare.[20]

NINETEENTH-CENTURY FREEDOM OF EXPRESSION: A RESTRICTIVE LEGAL TRADITION

The intertwined concepts of freedom of speech and its responsible exercise date to the 1700s when it fell to state lawmakers to determine the breadth of civil liberties afforded citizens under state constitutions.[21] As the nation entered the nineteenth century, judges linked the concept of responsibility to the exercise of all rights—not just freedom of expression—in order to achieve the broader goal of furthering the public's welfare. Throughout the nineteenth century, state and federal government officials and jurists did not embrace the concept of laissez-faire constitutionalism when enacting laws and ordinances. Instead, in an era of rapid population growth and national expansion, politicians consistently endorsed a broad range of laws aimed at creating a well-regulated society. Broad acceptance of the concepts of the sovereign state and rights-bearing individuals would not occur until the twentieth century.[22]

Nineteenth-century jurists and politicians instead developed both a rich private tradition and a public tradition of civic virtue and moral rectitude for the public good. Laws aimed at producing a well-regulated society exhibited "powerful anti-individual sentiment."[23] The era's governance "was predicated on the elemental assumption that public interest was superior to private interest."[24]

Eighteenth- and nineteenth-century legal scholars' writings on freedom of expression demonstrate that those scholars often limited the public's speech and press rights for the benefit of the public as a whole. British jurist William Blackstone, whose writings were highly influential in America throughout much of the nineteenth century, strongly supported a state-regulated view of civil liberties, defining civil liberty as follows:

> This liberty, rightly understood, consists in the power of doing whatever the laws permit; which is only to be effected by a general conformity of all orders and degrees to the equitable rules of action, by which the meanest individual is protected from the insults and oppression of the greatest.[25]

Similarly, two of antebellum America's most influential legal thinkers, New York state supreme court justice James Kent and U.S. Supreme Court justice Joseph Story, also linked the concepts of responsibility and the public's welfare to the exercise of free speech and freedom of the press. Kent, in his influential work *Commentaries on American Law*, warned that without checks on the press, "in the hands of evil and designing men, [journalism] would become a most formidable engine, and as mighty for mischief as for good."[26] He legitimated state and federal restrictions on freedom of expression by arguing against libertarian visions of free expression in his 1827 *Commentaries*. "Private interest must be made subservient to the general interest of the community," he stated. "Any reversal of that sentiment—any attempt to subsume public welfare in private interest—was a perversion of republicanism and a reversion to that dark age when governance was captured by private lords and manors."[27]

Story's elucidation of the scope and limits of First Amendment freedoms largely paralleled Kent's views. His views on liberty of speech and press, like Kent's, were formed during the era of the partisan press, when editors engaged in often-caustic criticism.[28] Taking a dim view of the turbulent nature of the American press in the antebellum years, Story put forth a narrow interpretation of speech and press freedoms in his work *Commentaries on the Constitution of the United States*: "That this amendment was intended to secure to every citizen, an absolute right to speak, or write, or print, whatever he might please, without any responsibility, public or private therefore, is a supposition too wild to be indulged by any rational man." He added that if restrictions were not in place for the common good, citizens' reputations, peace, property, and safety could be disturbed or destroyed.[29]

Support for regulated liberty began to wane in the last two decades of the nineteenth century, the era in which Davis began his public preaching. Some legal scholars, citizens, and jurists began putting forth new, libertarian interpretations of civil liberties that encouraged individual autonomy while calling for a subsequent decrease in state police powers.[30]

An influential treatise writer, Michigan supreme court justice Thomas M. Cooley, largely supported a broader interpretation of freedom of expression than did antebellum-era legal scholars, although he remained a conservative libertarian thinker and was a leading promoter, along with treatise writer and law professor Christopher Tiedeman, of laissez-faire constitutionalism.[31] Cooley viewed the common law as an evolutionary force, stating that laws changed steadily in response to social changes, including changing beliefs. Judges, he added, had to modify common law to meet these new conditions and adapt the law to fit them.[32]

In *A Treatise on the Constitutional Limitations*, Cooley turned the public welfare argument around by stating that government officials should be broadening free expression laws rather than restricting them because the free flow of ideas would spur social, political, cultural, and economic advances. Cooley, therefore, supported an open marketplace of ideas several decades before Justice Oliver Wendell Holmes Jr. popularized the metaphor.[33] And in order to let ideas flow in the public arena and thus further political and social progress, Cooley advocated strong protections for speakers, believing only individuals advocating rebellion or civil war should be punished for their speech.[34]

A contemporary of Cooley, Tiedeman also supported broader press freedom and the reining in of government's regulatory abilities. In his *Treatise on the Limitations of Police Power*, Tiedeman argued the proper role of the government was limited to providing for the public's order and personal security by the prevention and punishment of criminal trespass.[35] Tiedeman's concerns with trespasses upon individual rights led him to argue that judges were to construe police regulations in strict fashion.[36] Similarly, his treatise on municipal corporations also supported limitations on government officials' powers. He declared that

> any ordinance, which commits to the will of a single official, unrestrained by charter or otherwise, the practically absolute power of prohibiting the use of some well-known means of commercial or social activity, not a nuisance—as, or for example, a steam engine, or street processions,—is prima facie unreasonable and oppressive and hence unconstitutional and void.[37]

Although Tiedeman's conservative libertarianism led him to argue for limitations on government regulation, including government restrictions on speech, he also believed that popular government would not be possible without freedom of speech and of the press.[38]

John F. Dillon, a law professor at the University of Iowa and a judge in the U.S. Eighth Circuit, also took a more restrictive view of government police powers. In his 1881 work, *Commentaries on the Law of Municipal Corporations*, Dillon argued that officials could craft regulations only for "a limited number of purposes."[39] Affirming a more expansive view of individual rights and liberty under the U.S. Constitution, Dillon broke from the earlier nineteenth-century tradition and supported individuals' right to expressive conduct on public property, stating, "Making a speech in a public street is not a nuisance per se."[40]

Although it is unclear if the Reverend Davis read Cooley, Tiedeman, or Dillon, he clearly used the emerging libertarian political thinking to argue that freedom of both speech and religion were civil liberties guaranteed to all citizens by the First and Fourteenth Amendments.[41] Before examining Davis's history of public speaking, his convictions, and subsequent legal challenges, it is important to take a brief look at the public parks movement in order to understand how and why politicians linked park usage with legal regulation of that space and how the ensuing battles over changing expectations of behaviors and activities on such property eventually forced lawmakers to adjust their ordinances, including those that limited public expression.

THE CREATION AND REGULATION OF PUBLIC PARKS IN THE NINETEENTH CENTURY

American municipal park development occurred in two waves during the 1800s. Although supporters during both periods desired to preserve open, bucolic space from encroaching urban growth, the latter wave's supporters put forth a second reason for park development, namely that pastoral space served as a safety valve of sorts for society's ills. Park space was meant to provide fresh air and refinement for the growing urban masses. Park advocates subsequently sought and obtained legislation that constrained park activities in order to preserve the bucolic ideal.[42]

The first wave of public park creation began in the 1840s as an outgrowth of the garden cemetery movement of the previous decade. Noted landscape gardener Andrew Jackson Downing implored city officials in a number of metropolitan areas during the 1840s to set aside land while it was still available.[43] New York City's politicians were among the urban officials who heeded Downing's call. They dedicated 840 acres in 1856 for what would become Central Park. Construction of that project began in 1858 after Frederick Law Olmsted and Calvert Vaux were awarded the design contract.[44]

The second phase of park creation emerged following the U.S. Civil War. Although the desire to preserve open space was still an important impetus behind urban park creation,[45] nationally known landscape architects, including

Olmsted, Vaux, and H. W. S. Cleveland, along with city officials, urban reformers, physicians, and other concerned individuals began promoting urban parks as a type of safety valve. As expansive, congested slums became common in urban landscapes, municipal parks provided urban residents with fresh air and, ostensibly, wholesome environments.[46] As such, parks were seen as possible deterrents to urban vice and crime in an age of growing disorder and tumult.[47] Officials in San Francisco, Boston, Albany, New York City, Chicago, Cleveland, Milwaukee, Louisville, and other communities began creating urban parks in the years following the Civil War in the hopes that bucolic space would help tame growing urban disorder by promoting personal refinement and moral order.[48]

Politicians and genteel reformers alike hoped (and some fervently believed) that parks would prove to be not only a counterbalance to urban woes but a direct assault on them.[49] Olmsted believed implicitly in the elevating and restorative power of nature. City parks, he argued, would exert a quiet, natural, beneficent influence, even on those citizens most in need of moral reform.[50] Olmsted divided recreational activities into two types: exertive recreation (which included physical sports as well as intellectual ones, like chess) and receptive recreation (which included music and the fine arts). Not surprisingly, since Olmsted promoted the restorative nature of parks, he strongly discouraged exertive recreation within park boundaries.[51]

Landscape architect H. W. S. Cleveland's views on both the purpose and subsequent usage of parks paralleled Olmsted's. "The object of a park is to secure to the dwellers in the cities the opportunity of enjoying the contemplation of such objects of natural beauty as the growth of the city must otherwise destroy," he stated. Parks, Cleveland added, allowed city residents to enjoy an "intimate" relationship with nature. Following this logic, Cleveland argued that parks should not have monuments or formal gardens. They also were not places for militia exercises or organized athletics.[52]

Both Olmsted's and Cleveland's beliefs were rooted in classic nineteenth-century liberalism. This meant that while both men held meetings on park development with various city officials across the nation, neither was willing to include members of the general public in their planning, nor did they listen to the public's desires. Instead, they believed as their fathers did: the well-educated, well-bred members of the upper class "would do things *for* the masses, not *with* them and certainly without communicating with them."[53]

City officials nationwide largely agreed with park architects' narrow visions of acceptable park activities.[54] If parks were to be panaceas for urban ills, officials believed their uses had to be narrowly defined and laws upholding those uses had to be rigorously applied.[55] Prior to the 1880s, metropolitan officials across the nation issued a plethora of laws restricting park activities and regulating the public's behavior on public property.[56] Public speaking, celebratory gun and cannon fire, picnics, organized sports (including baseball games), bicycle riding, and merchandise sales were among many activities banned by ordinances in many municipalities across the country.[57] These laws were part of a broader nineteenth-century tradition that limited individual liberty in favor of extensive regulation and police power, ostensibly for the benefit of the public's welfare and as a means of achieving stability during a period of tremendous urban growth.[58]

By the 1880s, however, many members of the lower and middle classes were pushing back at restrictive ordinances and demanding broader definitions of legally acceptable activities on city-owned and city-administered property.[59] Growing urban density and changing public needs, including the creation of distinct working-class cultural activities, resulted in regular attempts by citizens, religious groups, newspaper editors, and civic reformers to change the laws that governed recreational space. Wealthy citizens had private clubs for sporting and social activities during the late nineteenth century, but the poor and members of the middle class often had nowhere to go but public parks for similar recreational activities.[60] While walking and enjoying nature were still seen as the acceptable types of park activities by park architects and politicians in the 1880s and 1890s, both poor and middle-class urban residents sought a more expansive vision of public park recreation.[61] Picnicking had become a popular pastime in the late nineteenth century among the middle classes.[62] Members of the working class, who often found themselves crowded into slums, often desired open space for more physical, recreational activities, including organized team sports.[63]

Officials across the country had differing reactions to these contested uses of public space. By the mid-1870s, for example, San Francisco city officials wrestled with multipurpose requests for park usage but passed restrictive ordinances to maintain city parks as quiet retreats that offered citizens a proper moral influence.[64] A decade later, city officials in Des Plaines, Illinois, banned picnics and open-air dances on publicly owned land as nuisances, but a citizen successfully challenged the ordinance as an unconstitutional ban on expressive activity.[65]

Officials in Albany also had to contend with often-competing usage requests, including agricultural fairs, ice-skating, military parades, concerts, and prizefights. During the summer of 1870, Albany officials repeatedly revised

Street preachers, baseball players, smokers, and bicyclists, among others, all sought to change Boston's restrictive park usage laws by the 1880s. Officials largely sought to maintain the city's parks as places of nature, solitude, and quiet reflection, as demonstrated by this image of Boston Common's frog pond in the 1890s. Library of Congress Prints and Photographs Division, Washington, D.C.

their laws governing public grounds and parks in an attempt to modify how such space was regulated.[66] While some activities were allowed, ordinances were enacted that banned public speaking, political meetings, picnics, the congregation of large groups, and the posting or distributing of literature within city parks.[67]

Boston officials also faced similar challenges concerning city dwellers' competing recreational interests.[68] The *Boston Globe*'s editors, in a February 13, 1877, editorial, supported an expanded vision of acceptable public park activities. The Common, the newspaper's editors noted, was established "for public uses. To hold that these employments are to consist in walking, playing and breathing upon it would be to greatly restrict its benefit." To back up their claims, the editors noted the Common had been used for many activities, including religious services, throughout the previous century. Open-air evangelist preachers spoke before large crowds in the 1740s during the era of the First Great Awakening, and New England's Methodists traced their origins to a sermon delivered under an elm tree in 1790.[69] Both British troops and opposing colonial forces had used the park for drills at various times during the Revolutionary War era. Cows had grazed on the Common until the early 1800s when accidents between humans and bovines led to the latter's removal. In the early 1850s, Mayor John Bigelow gave into public pressure and allowed pipe and cigar smokers to congregate in the southwestern corner of the Common under a shady expanse of trees in a "smokers' circle" to discuss the day's events while enjoying their tobacco.[70] A decade later, the Common served as a site for military recruiting during the American Civil War.[71]

Following the Civil War, city officials let the Common be used for festivals, fireworks, a deer park, and a display of industrial products. William F. "Buffalo Bill" Cody was allowed to set up his Wild West show on the Common when he came to Boston. A variety of preachers also had delivered Sunday orations on the Common, and the Salvation Army regularly trouped through the Common with drums beating and brass band playing as its members attempted to save souls.[72] On Sunday afternoons, band concerts took place.[73] By the time Davis began preaching on the Common, the park had a lengthy history as a multipurpose space.

Although Boston city officials began restricting public speaking on the Common in 1862, the city's oldest park had a long history as a multipurpose space. This July 9, 1859, engraving from *Ballou's Pictorial* shows a particularly raucous Fourth of July celebration on the Common, complete with children setting off firecrackers. Library of Congress Prints and Photographs Division, Washington, D.C.

THE ARRESTS AND THE MASSACHUSETTS RULINGS

The reverend's legal ordeal began on Sunday, May 17, 1885, when Davis, along with the Reverend A. J. Gordon, the noted pastor of the Clarendon Street Baptist Church; the Reverend H. L. Hastings, the editor of an evangelical publication called the *Christian*; several street preachers; and Captain Anne Shirley and William Dean of the Salvation Army were arrested at the Common following their respective sermons and services on various parts of the Common.[74] All had violated a city ordinance dating to 1862 (which had been revised in 1870) that held, "No person shall, except by permission of the city government committee, deliver a sermon, lecture, address or discourse on the Common or other public grounds."[75] Prior to 1862, Boston city officials had not restricted speech on public property, including the Common. In 1862, however, politicians enacted an ordinance that required individuals who wished to deliver "sermons, lectures, address[es] or discourse[s] on the common or other public grounds" within city limits to seek permission from city officials.[76]

Davis previously had preached on the Common during the spring and summer of 1882 and the summer of 1884 without incident.[77] Before he began preaching in May 1882, Davis had approached the Boston chief of police to ask whether or not he could preach freely on the Common. He noted in his request that the Salvation Army and a number of ministers had already held religious services or preached there. The police chief referred Davis to the police commissioners for an answer, and they, in turn, sent him to the city solicitor. Davis recounted during an 1887 trial that police assured him they would not disturb free, open-air religious services. Davis preached almost every Sunday afternoon from May through August 1882 and then returned to the Common to preach again in 1884.[78]

Davis, like the preachers who came before him, recognized that geography was an important factor in freedom of speech. Ministers who confined themselves to their churches preached largely to their own congregations and the occasional visitors. By contrast, open-air preaching allowed ministers and other religious believers to reach out to the great "unsaved masses."[79] Although the term "public forum" would not be used in legal circles until the twentieth century, the concept certainly was understood. And a public forum was precisely what Davis both wanted and needed.

The 1885 arrests of the ministers shocked the city's Protestant elite who turned out en masse for their arraignment.[80] Reverend Gordon was a notable figure who oversaw one of the city's most important churches. He was, by all accounts, the epitome of a Victorian gentleman.[81] Hastings also was a notable figure. A member of the Advent Christian Church, Hastings was the first president of its Christian Publication Society and a distributor and/or writer for four religious publications: the *Christian*, the *Armory*, the *Common People*, and the *Safeguard*.

Following his arrest, Hastings penned an article for the *Safeguard* to publicize the incident. He portrayed the police action as an attempt by Boston's growing Catholic political forces to dominate Protestants and to reduce the latter group's "Christian liberties."[82] Hastings also wrote a letter to the *Boston Globe*, which the newspaper ran on May 31, 1885, to get his message about perceived Protestant religious discrimination to a wider audience. Hastings claimed in his letter that the three preachers were singled out by police and offered as proof the fact that members of the Salvation Army regularly preached on the Common but were not arrested (although on May 17 they were).[83]

Of the three ministers, Davis was the most unconventional. He was raised in an abolitionist household by a father who was an Oberlin College graduate and a champion of multiple reform causes. Despite the elder Davis's education, the family was not wealthy or prominent, a fact that led William to work in New England's cotton mills beginning at age twelve. A desire to preach led him to borrow money to attend three prestigious schools—Phillips Exeter Academy, Harvard College, and Andover Theological Seminary—to gain the necessary education. Yet, when he finished his studies, Davis refused ordination and turned down an offer to head his own congregation, preferring instead to spend his life serving mainly as an itinerant preacher.[84] Historian Margaret Bendroth notes that Davis "deliberately sought out marginal and difficult opportunities for evangelism, preaching to lumberjacks in the Michigan woods or managing the North End mission in Boston's most densely populated Catholic neighborhood."[85] The activist spirit instilled in Davis from an early age clearly influenced his determination to preach on the Common and to challenge the ordinance when arrested.[86]

Davis and his fellow ministers were found guilty of violating the city ordinance and fined ten dollars cash each.[87] The following Sunday, May 24, Davis and Hastings held another service on the Common. Hastings read a part of the Sermon on the Mount, the parable of the prodigal son, and the twenty-first chapter of the Book of Revelation. Davis read another portion of the Bible and made brief remarks and comments. The two men again were arrested and this time were fined thirty dollars each for their repeat offense. The judge told the ministers that obtaining a permit to speak on the Common was a simple matter. Since the two men had failed to do so, they were "technically culpable."[88]

Davis appealed his conviction to the Suffolk County Superior Court. His attorney, James F. Pickering, argued the ordinance violated Davis's constitutional right to freedom of worship and freedom of speech. Davis and Pickering both believed that freedom of speech was one of the liberties protected by the Fourteenth Amendment—an interpretation Suffolk County Superior Court judge Peleg E. Aldrich would dismiss. Pickering also argued that the ordinance was not valid because it was not recorded in the ledger of the office of the clerk of the Superior Court and because it was not published in the newspaper, as required by state law. The attorney was incorrect in his latter assertion. The ordinances against public speaking, including preaching, passed by the Committee on the Common had been published in the *Boston Transcript* newspaper but was placed in the "City and Suburbs" notices that few people read.[89]

Judge Aldrich overruled all of the exceptions and did not engage in a full analysis of Davis's constitutional claims. He ruled narrowly, exhibiting the orthodox legal views of the time that supported municipal police powers for the public's welfare. Stating the city ordinance was valid, Aldrich held that Boston officials had the legal right to create "all reasonable ordinances regulating the uses of the Common."[90]

The key question, Aldrich said, was whether or not the ordinance banning speeches on city-owned property was reasonable. Answering in the affirmative, the judge also denied that either Davis's freedom of speech or freedom of religion had been violated. "I think this is to be treated purely as a question of law. It is not a question of a right to preach, but precisely a question of the right to deliver an address, as on geology or any other topic of science or art," Aldrich stated. "It is not designed to interfere with the freedom of speech or the right to preach the gospel. It is for the purpose of keeping the peace and good order," he added, affirming city officials' right to use their police power for the public's welfare. Without such an ordinance, Aldrich said, the Common might be "filled" with preachers every Sunday.[91] The implication was clear—the law was needed to preserve the Common's tranquillity and the public's peace.

Davis then appealed to the Supreme Judicial Court of Massachusetts, where his attorney restated his earlier procedural and constitutional arguments. He also argued that the 1862 ordinance had been rendered obsolete because previous violators often faced no prosecution. Pickering further questioned the validity of the 1870 revised city ordinance, again stating that the revision had not been recorded by the Suffolk County Superior Court Clerk's office and was invalid because the revision had not been published for two consecutive weeks in Boston's newspapers, as required by law.[92] In addition, Davis's attorney said his client's actions were part of his inalienable right to religious freedom under both the Massachusetts Constitution and section 11, chapter 37, of the revised ordinances of the city of Boston. The city ordinance assessed a fine or jail time for any individual who interrupted or disturbed a religious gathering, while Article 2 of the Bill of Rights of the Massachusetts Constitution said that the Commonwealth's citizens had both a right and a duty to publicly worship God.[93]

Writing for the Supreme Judicial Court in January 1886, Judge C. J. Morton denied all of Davis's civil liberties claims while upholding the ordinance as necessary to preserve the public's welfare. "Its purpose is to preserve the public peace, and to protect the public grounds from injury, and it is calculated to effect these ends, without violating the just rights of any citizen," Morton stated.[94] The judge also held that Davis had misread the law on the requiring of bylaws of towns to be recorded in the Superior Court Clerk's office, stating Boston's ordinances were not subject to that provision. Morton added that since the law in question was a restatement of a previous ordinance that had already been published in the newspapers, the revised ordinance did not have to be published.[95] Neither the Superior Court nor the Supreme Judicial Court addressed Pickering's constitutional argument that the city ordinance violated Davis's right to freedom of worship.

Despite losing his case, Davis again returned to the Common to preach without obtaining the necessary permit. His persistence led to four more arrests in 1887, turning the "plucky" preacher, as the *Boston Post* called him, into something of a celebrity. Crowds regularly gathered on the Common and were disappointed if bad weather or other circumstances kept him away.[96] In August of that year, Davis found himself in front of Superior Court judge Hamilton B. Staples but without the presence of his legal counsel. The reverend chose to defend himself, again arguing that his preaching was protected by both the First Amendment and the Massachusetts Constitution. But when Davis tried to argue that the city's ordinance was unconstitutional, Staples overruled him, noting that the state's highest court had found the city's ordinance to be both valid and sufficient the previous year during Davis's challenge.[97]

Davis also touted the nation's Enlightenment heritage during his trial, stating that the First Amendment had long given private citizens the right to express their opinions in public.[98] But despite this line of reasoning, Staples did not address the constitutional argument. And Davis did himself no favors when during his trial he announced that he did not recognize the mayor of Boston's authority to enact such laws and claimed that his counsel was "Jehovah, God."

Staples sentenced Davis to twelve months in prison after the reverend refused to pay a fifty-dollar fine. The *New York Times*, which had reported on each of Davis's arrests and trials, noted the judge lectured Davis on the necessity of civil order for the public's welfare, stating, "You know well that liberty is not unrestrained feeling. There must be laws made to govern or we should not have any peace." The anonymous *Times* reporter noted Davis was "determined to become a martyr."[99] Whether the assertion was correct or not, Davis made good use of his time in prison, penning a lengthy, angry tome that Hastings published and distributed in October 1887 titled *Christian Liberties in Boston: A Sketch of Recent Attempts to Destroy Them through the Device of a Gag-by-Law for Gospel Preachers.*

Other Boston-area Protestants concurred that their faith was under fire. The Reverend J. O. Fulton, an outspoken anti-Catholic preacher, denounced Davis's treatment from the pulpit of Tremont Temple in Boston. But while the applause the large crowd gave Fulton seemed to indicate agreement with his denunciations of Catholic city officials and the courts, few were willing to financially help the incarcerated preacher when Fulton followed up his speech with the request.[100]

When Davis appealed to Massachusetts governor Oliver Ames for a pardon, a reporter opined that although Davis's attempts to spread the gospel were well meaning, the minister was a "crank."[101] Because Davis admitted that he would return to preaching on the Common without a permit, if pardoned, the governor declined to take action. Davis subsequently served ten months and was released two months early for good behavior.[102] Ironically, although Davis (and Hastings) directed much of the blame for the ordinance's creation toward Hugh O'Brien, the city's first Irish Catholic mayor, and penned numerous articles arguing that the ordinance was meant to silence Protestant preaching, the democratic O'Brien noted in his January 1888 inaugural address that he supported rescinding the ordinance but lacked the power to do so. He implied that Republicans on the Committee on the Common and the city council kept the ordinance in place as political leverage.[103]

In 1894 the reverend again ran afoul of the law and was arrested on June 10 following another preaching session at the Common. He found himself before the Massachusetts Supreme Judicial Court for a second time and this time challenged the constitutionality of the 1892 revision of the ordinance. The revised city ordinance not only restricted public speaking without a permit but had been broadened by city officials to restrict other activities in city parks. The revised ordinance read:

> No person shall, in or upon any of the public grounds, make any public address, discharge any cannon or firearm, expose for sale any goods, wares, or merchandise, erect or maintain any booth, stand, tent, or apparatus for purposes of public amusement or show, except in accordance with a permit from the mayor.[104]

Although Davis and his supporters previously had argued the city ordinance forbidding public speaking in Boston's parks without a permit was aimed at stopping religious speech, a secular speaker had been convicted in 1892 for violating the same ordinance after delivering a Fourth of July address in a Boston park.[105] In that case, *Commonwealth v. Henry Abrahams*,[106] the Massachusetts Supreme Judicial Court used the 1886 *Davis* ruling as precedent for prosecuting a local labor union secretary as he addressed a crowd in Franklin Park.[107]

Following his 1894 arrest, Davis again argued—through all the levels of the Massachusetts court system—that the revised ordinance denied his constitutionally protected speech as per the First and Fourteenth Amendments, as well as per the Massachusetts Constitution. He also argued that the permit requirement gave the mayor too much power to determine which individuals could engage in expressive conduct. An appeals court dismissed Davis's constitutional arguments and again relied on property law analysis. The ordinance, the court said,

> only concerned the modes of use of the public lands, that the legislature had the authority to close the public lands and the lesser option of limiting its use by permits was equally valid, and that, if the legislature had the authority to enact such legislation, the legislature had the authority to authorize the city to pass such an ordinance.[108]

When Davis went to the Commonwealth's highest court to challenge the law's constitutionality, Justice Holmes, who wrote the decision, refused to address Davis's constitutional arguments, stating instead that neither the right of freedom of speech nor the right of assembly was involved. Instead, Holmes held that the only question before the court was whether or not the municipal ordinance was constitutional. Holmes quickly affirmed the ordinance's constitutionality, citing the previous *Davis* case as precedent. He then said Davis and his attorney had erred in their argument that the ordinance "is directed against free speech generally."[109]

Basing his ruling on property law, Holmes held that the ordinance was a constitutionally permissible example of a state's police powers to control property it owned.[110] The ordinance, Holmes said, was "directed toward the modes in which the Boston Common may be used." He noted that the legislature could and did exercise control over the uses of public property:

> For the Legislature absolutely or conditionally to forbid public speaking in a highway or public park is no more an infringement of the rights of a member of the public than for the owner of a private house to forbid it in his house. When no proprietary right interferes, the Legislature may end the right of the public to enter upon the public place by putting an end to the dedication to public uses. So it may take the lesser step of limiting the public use to certain purposes.[111]

Holmes's ruling demonstrates that his views on First and Fourteenth Amendment protections for speech fit within the prevailing legal thinking of the late 1800s. His decision made clear the court as a whole was unwilling to hold that expressive conduct on public property should be protected against most government restrictions.[112] Holmes cited as precedent an 1891 Massachusetts case, *McAuliffe v. New Bedford*, to deny Davis's civil liberties argument.[113] In that case, a police officer had engaged in political canvassing in violation of police regulations in the city of New Bedford and was fired for his actions. Holmes, who wrote the *McAuliffe* decision, held that the officer had a constitutional right to speak, but he did not have a constitutional right to be a police officer.[114] In both *McAuliffe* and *Davis,* Holmes dismissed the free speech claims of both men, seeing neither case as having properly raised state or federal free expression issues.[115] Holmes's use of *McAuliffe* as precedent demonstrated that he recognized that Davis may have had a constitutional right to preach, but he had no constitutional right to use the Common for the purpose of delivering a sermon.[116] Holmes's interpretation that the ordinance was not a broad prohibition on speech allowed him to avoid the First Amendment concerns expressed in the 1888 *Des Plaines v. Poyer* decision. In that case, an Illinois village council saw its ordinance—which banned public picnics and open-air dances as nuisances—overturned. The appellate court ruled,

> While the right of the people to be free from disturbance and reasonable apprehension of danger to person and property is to be respected and jealously guarded, the equal rights of all to assemble together for health, recreation, or amusement, in the open air, is no less to be respected and jealously guarded. Because a privilege may be abused, is no reason why it shall be denied.[117]

The narrow, property law–based ruling allowed the court to avoid addressing the constitutionality of a related aspect of the ordinance: providing a mayor with the unbridled discretion to determine whether or not to issue permits to speakers. The court's unwillingness to establish standards to regulate the mayor's discretion demonstrated that the Massachusetts justices' ruling fit within mainstream legal thinking of the time. By subsuming speech protection into property rights, the court denied Davis's call for protection of individuals' civil liberties in favor of broader protection of the public's welfare, peace, and good order.[118]

Holmes's decision fits within William J. Novak's finding that nineteenth-century municipal laws often had a "powerful anti-individual sentiment." Public interests trumped and often restrained individuals' private rights and interests during the nineteenth century.[119] While Davis put forth a vision of a sovereign state and rights-bearing individuals, such a libertarian philosophy was at odds with justices' and politicians' visions of a properly regulated society.[120]

THE U.S. SUPREME COURT RULING

On Friday, March 26, 1897, Davis took his case to the U.S. Supreme Court. His argument against the Boston ordinance was fourfold. First, he argued that the law amounted to censorship and that it "violated the rights of free public speech, of free assembly, and of free public religious worship." Second, Davis challenged the city's rationale for creating the ordinance (that is, that it prevented breaches of the peace and prevented damage to public property), stating these were highly improbable. Third, Davis disputed the constitutionality of the mayor's broad discretionary power to issue or deny permits to speakers. Finally, he argued that the ordinance violated the equal protection clause of the Fourteenth Amendment, stating that officials used the law to stop preachers while largely ignoring secular speakers and Salvation Army parades on the Common.[121]

In a relatively brief decision, the Court affirmed the Massachusetts Supreme Judicial Court's ruling while ignoring Davis's First Amendment challenge. Basing its decision on common law, the Court said an outright prohibition on expressive conduct on public property was constitutional. The justices then supported their argument by restating Holmes's analysis that the legislature could forbid public speaking on property it controlled in the same manner in which the owner of a private home could forbid such speech in his house.[122] The Court's ruling made clear that municipalities could regulate the types of activities that citizens could engage in on publicly controlled property and even forbid the use of city property entirely: "When no proprietary rights interfere, the legislature may end the right of the public to enter upon the public place by putting an end to the dedication to public uses," the Court held.[123]

The Court's justices also disagreed with Davis's argument that the ordinance's provision gave the mayor of Boston too much power to determine who could speak and who could not on public property. Far from being a violation of individuals' civil liberties, the Court held that the mayor's power to exclude individuals from city-controlled public property also included the lesser power to include permits for expressive conduct.

The Court's use of property law analysis again demonstrated that nineteenth-century jurisprudence put the public's welfare over the rights of individuals. Denying Davis's Fourteenth Amendment claim, the Court ruled that the Fourteenth Amendment

> does not destroy the power of states to enact police regulations as to the subjects within their control . . . and does not have the effect of creating a particular and personal right in the citizen to use public property in defiance of the constitution and laws of the state.[124]

While denying Davis's First and Fourteenth Amendment claims, the high court also ignored one of Davis's arguments outright—that religious activities had taken place many times previously on the Common and thus should be considered a traditional "usage" of the park. By leaving this assertion of a common-law right of usage unanswered, the Court's justices did not have to rule on whether or not such a right existed or if it had been infringed by city officials.

Even before the U.S. Supreme Court's ruling in *Davis*—and, in some cases, after—a growing number of state court judges began questioning the prevailing, normative legal rules on freedom of expression on publicly owned property. Ordinances restricting individuals' activities on public property were struck down by state courts in Michigan, Kansas, Illinois, Wisconsin, California, and Oklahoma between 1886 through 1897—the same year the U.S. Supreme Court ruled in *Davis*. These state judges who upheld individuals' right of access to public property ruled that restrictive municipal ordinances were either unconstitutionally arbitrary and/or that such laws violated traditional uses of public property.[125]

Taking what Thomas Cooley viewed as an evolutionary approach to the law,[126] these state judges began supporting individuals' rights to express themselves on publicly owned property while reining in politicians' discretionary power to deny speakers permits, even though those politicians held the traditional view that regulation of public property usage fell within the power of municipal corporations. The judges began recognizing that individuals' demands for freedom of speech and assembly in public places were not mere isolated demands by individuals to speak but were part of the broader issue of how to interpret what was allowed and not allowed in a democracy.[127] Yet late nineteenth-century and early twentieth-century officials who applied the *Davis* ruling to deny permits to speakers did not see their police powers as unconstitutionally arbitrary.[128]

An analysis of the *Davis* rulings further demonstrates that nineteenth-century politicians and justices held restrictive interpretations of freedom of speech and expression—views that would not begin to change until the 1920s. Although prior restraints were strongly disliked in the nineteenth century, the *Davis* rulings contributed to an existing series of laws and precedents that narrowly defined freedom of expression and limited its usage, including the place in which individuals could speak, when such expression was seen as detrimental to the public's collective welfare.[129]

Neither the Massachusetts Supreme Judicial Court nor the U.S. Supreme Court were sympathetic to Davis's First Amendment claims. Neither court concurred with Davis that access to public property was necessary for citizens to exercise their right to free expression, as is the case with modern jurisprudence. Prior to the 1925 *Gitlow v. New York* ruling, which incorporated the First Amendment, state and federal courts often used *Davis* to uphold laws that allowed governments to use their police powers to restrict individuals' freedom of expression by restricting the place in which they spoke.[130] The property rights position held in *Davis v. Massachusetts* would not be struck down by the U.S. Supreme Court until 1943, when Justice Hugo Black, writing for the Court, rejected the property rights argument to deny a defendant access to city streets to distribute handbills in *Jamison v. Texas* and held that public parks are traditional public forums that are considered open for expressive conduct.[131]

The U.S. Supreme Court's application of the right-privilege distinction demonstrates that the *Davis* case cannot be considered the legal origin of modern public forum analysis. The case did not reflect the libertarian philosophy that identifies freedom of expression and freedom of public discussion as "paramount values" of the First Amendment.[132]

Scholars interested in nineteenth-century interpretations of freedom of speech also should recognize that a number of important legal terms, including "public forums" and "time, place, and manner restrictions," would not be developed until the twentieth century. Furthermore, a cornerstone of modern time, place, and manner regulations—the legal holding that speakers may not be denied permits to speak based on their views—is also a twentieth-century legal construct.

Despite these facts, the *Davis* case sheds light on how nineteenth-century judges viewed individual civil rights claims where freedom of speech was put forth as paramount. The *Davis* case, like much pre–World War I freedom of speech and press cases, has largely been forgotten, but its restrictive holding and the case's lack of constitutional analysis provide valuable insight on nineteenth-century legal analysis of civil liberties.

Notes

1. "His Right to Serve God," *Boston Globe*, September 24, 1887; "Boston's Sacred Common," *New York Times*, September 24, 1887; "Jehovah His Counsel," *Boston Daily Advertiser*, September 24, 1887; Francis Henry Lincoln, *Harvard College Class of 1867 Secretary's Report*, vol. 9 (Boston: Alfred Mudge and Son, 1892), 57; "God's License Enough," *Boston Globe*, September 14, 1897.

2. Section 66 of the Revised Ordinances of the City of Boston (1893) stated:

> No person shall, in or upon any of the public grounds, make any public address, discharge any cannon or firearm, expose for sale any goods, wares or merchandise, erect or maintain any booth, stand, tent or apparatus for the purposes of public amusement or show, except in accordance with a permit from the mayor.

On prosecutions for speaking in Boston's parks without a permit, see Commonwealth v. Henry Abrahams, 156 Mass. 57 (1892).

3. "Two Guilty Preachers," *Boston Globe*, July 4, 1885; "Boston Common Held Sacred," *New York Times*, January 10, 1886; Commonwealth v. William F. Davis, 140 Mass. 485 (1886); "Boston Common's Preacher," *New York Times*, August 30, 1887; "His Right to Serve God"; "Served Ten Months for Preaching," *New York Times*, September 8, 1888; Commonwealth v. William F. Davis, 162 Mass. 510 (1895).

4. Michael Kent Curtis, *Free Speech, "The People's Darling Privilege": Struggles for Freedom of Expression in American History* (Durham: Duke University Press, 2000), 13–14.

5. James R. Green and Hugh Carter Donahue, *Boston's Workers: A Labor History* (Boston: Trustees of the Public Library, 1979), 36–40. For a detailed look at the ways in which laborers and their leaders had their expression suppressed, see Jon Bekken's chapter in this volume.

6. The Salvation Army also purposely proselytized in the streets and parks to reach individuals who were not regular churchgoers. Rachel Vorspan, "'Freedom of Assembly' and the Right to Passage in Modern English Legal History," *San Diego Law Review* 34 (1997): 943–44. The Salvation Army was a relatively new religious organization at the time Davis was preaching. For its history, including its street preaching struggles, see Edward H. McKinley, *Marching to Glory: The History of*

the Salvation Army in the United States, 1880–1992, 2nd ed. (Grand Rapids, Mich.: William B. Eerdmans).

7. Commonwealth v. William F. Davis, 140 Mass. 485 (1886); Commonwealth v. William F. Davis, 162 Mass. 510 (1895) (the case was heard in 1894, but the decision was rendered in 1895); Davis v. Massachusetts, 167 U.S. 43 (1897).

8. City of Chicago v. Trotter, 26 N.E. 359 (Ill. 1891); William E. Lee, "Modernizing the Law of Open-Air Speech: The Hughes Court and the Birth of Content-Neutral Balancing," *William and Mary Bill of Rights Journal* 13, no. 4 (2005): 1227.

9. Schneider v. State 308 U.S. 147 (1939); Lee, "Modernizing the Law of Open-Air Speech," 1226.

10. Jamison v. Texas, 318 U.S. 413 (1943).

11. The state and federal *Davis* rulings were cited as precedents to affirm as constitutional laws that speakers and musicians must obtain permits from government officials before their orations, meetings, or performances. Such laws were consistently held as reasonable exercises of police power over the public streets for the benefit of the general public's welfare. Judges in these cases also held that the permit requirements did not abridge citizens' rights of free speech or assembly. See Commonwealth v. Plaisted, 148 Mass. 375 (1889); Commonwealth v. Henry Abrahams, 156 Mass. 57 (1892); Love v. Judge of Recorder's Court of Detroit, 128 Mich. 545 (1901); New York v. Pierce, 83 N.Y.S. 79 (1903); Fitts v. City of Atlanta, 121 Ga. 567 (1905); City of Buffalo v. Till, 182 N.Y.S. 418 (1920); Duquesne City v. Fincke, 269 Pa. 112 (1920); The People of the State of New York v. Thomas F. Doyle et al., 232 N.Y. 96 (1921); City of Pineville v. Marshall et al., 222 Ky. 4 (1927); Commonwealth v. Surridge, 265 Mass. 425 (1929); and Coughlin v. Chicago Park District, 364 Ill. 90 (1936).

12. R. Allan Horning, "The First Amendment Right to a Public Forum," *Duke Law Journal* 39 (October 1969): 932; Jason K. Levine, "Defending the Freedom to Be Heard: Where Alternate Avenues Intersect Empty Public Spaces," *University of Memphis Law Review* 36 (Winter 2006): 291; John E. Semonche, *Keeping the Faith: A Cultural History of the U.S. Supreme Court* (Lanham, Md.: Rowman and Littlefield, 2000), 204.

13. Hague v. Committee for Industrial Organization, 307 U.S. 496, 518 (1939). In *Hague*, the Court ruled that a city ban on meetings held on public property was unconstitutional. The term "public forum" is largely attributed to Harry Kalven's 1965 article "The Concept of the Public Forum: Cox v. Louisiana," *Supreme Court Review* 1 (1965): 3. The U.S. Supreme Court used the term for the first time in Police Department of Chicago v. Mosley, 408 U.S. 92, 93 (1972).

14. David M. Rabban, *Free Speech in Its Forgotten Years* (New York: Cambridge University Press, 1997), 165–66.

15. Coughlin v. Chicago Park District, 4 N.E. 2d 1, 9 (Ill. 1936); Thomas v. Casey, 1 A.2d 866, 869 (N.J. 1938).

16. 92 U.S. 542, 552–53 (1875).

17. Samantha Barbas, "Creating the Public Forum," *Akron Law Review* 44 (August 2011): 810; Kenneth Ira Kersch, *Freedom of Speech: Rights and Liberties under the Law* (Santa Barbara: ABC-CLIO, 2003), 84; Mark A. Graber, *Transforming Free Speech: The Ambiguous Legacy of Civil Liberties* (Berkeley: University of California Press, 1991), 17.

18. Rabban, *Free Speech in Its Forgotten Years*, 23–24; Janice Ruth Wood, *The Struggle for Free Speech in the United States, 1872–1915: Edward Bliss Foote, Edward Bond Foote, and Anti-Comstock Operations* (New York: Routledge, 2012); Ford Risley, *Civil War Journalism* (Santa Barbara: Praeger, 2012), 83–106; Amanda Frisken, "Obscenity, Free Speech, and 'Sporting News' in 1870s America," *Journal of American Studies* 42 (December 2008): 537–77; Mary M. Cronin, "The Liberty to Argue Freely: Nineteenth-Century Obscenity Prosecutions and the Emergence of Modern Libertarian Free Speech Discourse," *Journalism and Communication Monographs* 8, no. 3 (September 2006): 163–219; Mark E. Neely Jr. "Odious to Honorable Men: The Press and Its Freedom in the Civil War," in *The Union Divided: Party Conflict in the Civil War North*, ed. Mark E. Neely Jr. (Cambridge, Mass.: Harvard University Press, 2002); Debra Reddin van Tuyll, "The Rebels Yell: Conscription and Freedom of Expression in the Civil War South," *American Journalism* 17, no. 2 (2000): 15–29; Craig R. Smith, *Silencing the Opposition: Government Strategies of Suppression of Freedom of Expression* (Albany: State University of New York Press, 1996); Mark E. Neely Jr., *The Fate of Liberty: Abraham Lincoln and Civil Liberties* (New York: Oxford University Press, 1991); Donna Lee Dickerson, *The Course of Tolerance: Freedom of the Press in Nineteenth-Century America* (New York: Greenwood Press, 1990); Margaret A. Blanchard, "Filling in the Void: Speech and Press in State Courts Prior to *Gitlow*," in *The First Amendment Reconsidered: New Perspectives on the Meaning of Freedom of Speech and Press*, ed. Bill F. Chamberlin and Charlene J. Brown (New York: Longman, 1982), 14–59.

19. Rabban, *Free Speech in Its Forgotten Years*, 14; Wood, *Struggle for Free Speech*; William J. Novak, *The People's Welfare: Law and Regulation in Nineteenth-Century America* (Chapel Hill: University of North Carolina Press, 1996), 6–16; Howard O. Hunter, "Problems in Search of Principles: The First Amendment in the Supreme Court from 1791–1930," *Emory Law Journal* 35 (Winter 1986): 127; David Currie, *The Constitution in the U.S. Supreme Court: The First Hundred Years, 1989–1888* (Chicago: University of Chicago Press, 1992), 116.

20. Public park management in the latter nineteenth century was not yet viewed as traditional government function. Michael T. Gibson, "The Supreme Court and Freedom of Expression from 1791 to 1917," *Fordham Law Review* 55 (December 1986): 316.

21. James R. Parramore, "State Constitutions and the Press: Historical Context and Resurgence of a Libertarian Tradition," *Journalism Quarterly* 69 (Spring 1992): 105–23.

22. Novak, *People's Welfare*, 3–9.

23. Ibid., 6.

24. Ibid., 9.

25. William Blackstone, *Commentaries on the Laws of England: A Facsimile of the First Edition of 1765–1769* (Chicago: University of Chicago Press, 1979), 1:6.

26. James Kent, *Commentaries on American Law*, 2 vols., rev. ed. (Philadelphia: Blackstone, 1889), 2:69.

27. James Kent, *Commentaries on American Law*, vol. 2 (New York, 1827), 265. Twenty-seven years later, attorney Charles B. Goodrich agreed with Kent's vision of regulated liberty as a necessity in civil society. He stated,

> Liberty is a relative term. Some persons regard it as a right in every individual to act in accordance with his own judgment. Such liberty is unknown to, and cannot be found in connection with or as a result of government, or of the law of society. Government and societies are established for the regulation of social intercourse, of social institutions.

See Charles B. Goodrich, *The Science of Government* (Boston: Little, Brown, 1853), 219.

28. For more on the party press, see Si Sheppard, *The Partisan Press: A History of Media Bias in the United States* (Jefferson, N.C.: McFarland, 2007); and Jeffrey L. Pasley, *The Tyranny of Printers: Newspaper Politics in the Early American Republic* (Charlottesville: University of Virginia Press, 2002).

29. Joseph Story, *Commentaries on the Constitution of the United States* (Boston: Little, Brown, 1858), 3rd ed., 667.

30. Rabban, *Free Speech in Its Forgotten Years*, 34; Janice Wood, "Physicians and Obscenity: A Struggle for Free Speech, 1872–1915," *Journalism History* 36, no. 1 (2010): 36–44.

31. Kersch, *Freedom of Speech*, 86, 92; Stephen A. Siegel, "Historism in Late Nineteenth Century Constitutional Thought," *Wisconsin Law Review* 6 (July 1990): 1452.

32. Siegel, "Historism in Late Nineteenth Century Constitutional Thought," 1497; Cooley had worked as a journalist and was a strong supporter of free speech. See David M. Rabban, *Law's History: American Legal Thought and the Transatlantic Turn to History* (New York: Cambridge University Press, 2013), 6, 23, 25.

33. Normal L. Rosenberg, "Thomas M. Cooley, Liberal Jurisprudence, and the Law of Libel, 1868–1884," *Seattle University Law Review* 4 (January 1980): 50–51; Thomas M. Cooley, *The General Principles of Constitutional Law in the United States of America* (Boston: Little, Brown, 1898), 3rd ed., 299–309. On Holmes and the marketplace of ideas, see his dissent in Abrams v. United States, 250 U.S. 616, 619 (1919). The marketplace concept metaphor also was used by a number of other writers, including John Stuart Mill in his 1859 work, *On Liberty*, and even earlier, by Thomas Jefferson during his first inaugural address. See Thomas Jefferson, *Writings*, ed. Merrill D. Peterson (New York: Library of America, 1984).

34. Thomas M. Cooley, *A Treatise on the Constitutional Limitations Which Rest upon the Legislative Power of the States of the American Union* (Boston: Little, Brown, 1868), 428–29; Kersch, *Freedom of Speech*, 92; Graber, *Transforming Free Speech*, 18–20.

35. Christopher Tiedeman, *A Treatise on the Limitations of Police Power in the United States* (St. Louis: F. H. Thomas Law Book Co., 1894), vii–viii. For more on Tiedeman's beliefs on constitutional limitations, see Rabban, *Law's History*, 57–59.

36. David N. Mayer, "Jurisprudence of Christopher G. Tiedeman: A Study in the Failure of Laissez-Faire Constitutionalism," *Missouri Law Review* 55 (Winter 1990): 128, 132.

37. Tiedeman, *Treatise on the Limitations of Police Power*, 268–69.

38. Graber, *Transforming Free Speech*, 21.

39. John F. Dillon, *Commentaries on the Law of Municipal Corporations* (Boston: Little, Brown, 1881), 242n45.

40. Ibid., 657n4.

41. "His Right to Serve God"; "Preaching on the Common," *Boston Daily Advertiser*, June 16, 1885.

42. John S. Pipkin, "The Moral High Ground in Albany: Rhetorics and Practices of an 'Olmstedian' Park, 1855–1875," *Journal of Historical Geography* 31 (October 2005): 667–69; Terence Young, "Modern Urban Parks," *Geographical Review* 85 (October 1995): 536–37; Terence Young, "San Francisco's Golden Gate Park and the Search for a Good Society, 1865–1880," *Forest and Conservation History* 37 (January 1993): 4–6; Stephen Hardy, *How Boston Played: Sport, Recreation, and Community, 1865–1915* (Knoxville: University of Tennessee Press, 2003), 61–62, 66; Alan Trachtenberg, *The Incorporation of America: Culture and Society in the Gilded Age* (New York: Hill and Wang), 109–11.

43. Francis R. Kowsky, *The Best Planned City in the World: Olmsted, Vaux, and the Buffalo Park System* (Amherst: University of Massachusetts Press, 2013), 10.

44. Paul Boyer, *Urban Masses and Moral Order in America, 1820–1920* (Cambridge, Mass.: Harvard University Press), 236.

45. Recognizing the crowded conditions in the city of Boston, municipal officials passed the Park Act in 1875 to bring more land under municipal control and hired Olmsted to design an "Emerald Necklace" of parks that stretched throughout the city to provide fresh air and a natural environment to urban residents. Geoffrey Blodgett, "Frederick Law Olmsted: Landscape Architecture as Conservative Reform," *Journal of American History* 62, no. 4 (1976): 878–84.

46. Karl Haglund, *Inventing the Charles River* (Cambridge, Mass.: MIT Press, 2002), 79; Hardy, *How Boston Played*, 61–62; Witold Rybczynski, *A Clearing in the Distance: Frederick Law Olmsted and America in the Nineteenth Century* (New York: Scribner, 1999), 271–73; Michael Holleran, *Boston's "Changeful Times": Origins of Preservation and Planning in America* (Baltimore: Johns Hopkins University Press, 1998), 111; Boyer, *Urban Masses*, 237–38; Trachtenberg, *Incorporation of America*, 109–10; George L. Scheper, "The Reformist Vision of Frederick Law Olmsted and the Poetics of Park Design," *New England Quarterly* 62 (September 1989): 370.

47. Trachtenberg, *Incorporation of America*, 109–11.

48. Pipkin, "Moral High Ground," 668–71; Scheper, "Reformist Vision of Frederick Law Olmsted," 371–72; *The Papers of Frederick Law Olmsted*, ed. Charles Capen McLaughlin, vol. 3, *Creating Central Park, 1857–1861*, ed. Charles E. Beveridge and David Schuoyer (Baltimore: Johns Hopkins University Press, 1983), 273; Galen Cranz, *The Politics of Park Design: A History of Urban Parks* (Cambridge, Mass.: MIT Press, 1982).

49. Pipkin, "Moral High Ground," 668; Boyer, *Urban Masses*, 236; Trachtenberg, *Incorporation of America*, 107–9.

50. Boyer, *Urban Masses*, 238; Hardy, *How Boston Played*, 53.

51. Hardy, *How Boston Played*, 80; Kowsky, *Best Planned City in the World*, 6.

52. Holleran, *Boston's "Changeful Times,"* 110–11.

53. *Mayor Hugh O'Brien's 1877 Speech on Boston Parks* (Boston: Franklin Park Coalition, 1984), 2–3.

54. Rybczynski, *Clearing in the Distance*, 278–331; Nancy J. Volkman, "Landscape Architecture on the Prairie: The Work of H. W. S. Cleveland," *Kansas History* 10 (June 1987): 89–110; William H. Tishler and Virginia S. Luckhardt, "H. W. S. Cleveland, Pioneer Landscape Architect to the Upper Midwest," *Minnesota History* 49 (October 1985): 281–91.

55. Novak, *People's Welfare*, 115–17; Hardy, *How Boston Played*, 79–81; Pipkin, "Moral High Ground," 678–79.

56. Novak, *The People's Welfare*, 1. Politicians, the public, and clergy also clashed over lower-class desires to spend much of Sunday engaged in recreation rather than view the entire day as a Sabbath day. John S. Gilkeson Jr., "The Rise and Decline of the 'Puritan Sunday' in Providence, R. I., 1810–1926," *New England Quarterly* 59, no. 1 (1986): 75, 77–78.

57. Hardy, *How Boston Played*, 80–84; Trachtenberg, *Incorporation of America*, 146–47; Commonwealth v. William F. Davis, 140 Mass. 485 (1886); American Steel House Co. v. Willcox, 77 N.Y.S. 1010 (1902); Scranton v. Straff, 28 Pa. Super. Ct., 258 (1905); Commonwealth v. Crowninshield, 187 Mass. 221 (1905).

58. Hardy, *How Boston Played*, ix; Oscar Handlin, *Boston's Immigrants* (Cambridge, Mass.: Harvard University Press, 1979), 215.

59. Cynthia Zaitzevsky, *Frederick Law Olmsted and the Boston Park System* (Cambridge, Mass.: Harvard University Press, 1982), 78; Stephen Hardy, "'Parks for the People': Reforming the Boston Park System, 1870–1915," *Journal of Sport History* 7 (1980): 6.

60. Hardy, *How Boston Played*, 81–84; Heiner Gillmeister, *Tennis: Cultural History* (London: Leicester University Press, 1998), 207–22; Kathy Peiss, *Cheap Amusements: Working Women and Leisure in Turn-of-the Century New York* (Philadelphia: Temple University Press, 1986), 11–33.

61. Hardy, *How Boston Played*, 84.

62. Reynolds J. Scott-Childress, "From 'Nature's Nation' to 'Washington's Playground': Marshall Hall, Middle-Class Culture, and the Commercialization of Leisure, 1865–1900," *Maryland Historical Magazine* 105 (Fall 2010): 239–40.

63. Hardy, *How Boston Played*, 79; Trachtenberg, *Incorporation of America*, 115.

64. Young, "San Francisco's Golden Gate Park," 1; Young, "Modern Urban Parks," 539.

65. The Village of Des Plaines v. Benjamin Poyer, 121 Ill. 348, 14 N.E. 677 (1888).

66. Pipkin, "Moral High Ground," 678.

67. Mary P. Ryan, *Civic Wars: Democracy and Public Life in the American City during the Nineteenth Century* (Berkeley: University of California Press, 1998), 207–9; Stuart M. Blumin, *The Emergence of the Middle Class: Social Experience in the American City, 1760–1900* (New York: Cambridge University Press, 1989), xi. For more on class-based recreational activities, see Roy Rosenzweig, *Eight Hours for What We Will: Workers and Leisure in an Industrial City, 1870–1920* (New York: Cambridge University Press, 1983), 136–40.

68. Zaitzevsky, *Frederick Law Olmsted*, 78; Commonwealth v. Henry Abrahams, 156 Mass. 57, 60, 30 N.E. 79, 79 (1892).

69. Quoted in Margaret Bendroth, "Rum, Romanism, and Evangelism: Protestants and Catholics in Late-Nineteenth-Century Boston," *Church History* 68 (September 1999): 631.

70. Marilyn S. Johnson, "Boston Common, Now Cigarette-Free, Was Once a Smoker's Haven," *Boston Globe*, January 5, 2014.

71. Holleran, *Boston's "Changeful Times,"* 116.

72. Ibid.

73. "Clergymen in Court," *Boston Globe*, May 21, 1885. The Common also was the site of puppet shows, open-air dances, and baseball games, although city officials often debated the latter activity's propriety. Children also used the Common as their personal playground, sledding during the winter months and swimming in the park's ponds during the summer. Margaret Lamberts Bendroth, *Fundamentalists in the City: Conflict and Division in Boston's Churches, 1885–1950* (New York: Oxford University Press, 2005), 43.

74. "Preaching on the Common," *Boston Globe*, May 31, 1885, 5; Bendroth, "Rum, Romanism, and Evangelism," 627–30.

75. Commonwealth v. William F. Davis, 140 Mass. 485 (1886). An article in the *Boston Daily Advertiser* on the ministers' arrests made clear that the prohibition against preaching in public parks, especially Boston Common, began with a city ordinance enacted in 1862. "Preaching on the Common," *Boston Daily Advertiser*, June 16, 1885.

76. Commonwealth v. William F. Davis, 140 Mass. 485.

77. Lincoln, *Harvard College Class of 1867 Secretary's Report*, 57. In his personal report to his Harvard classmates, Davis said he was disturbed only twice by police in 1882. He was not arrested either time, even when he refused a policeman's order to stop his oration, a demand Davis ignored. "The Lord," he said, "had commanded him to go on," and he continued his ninety-minute service for five hundred individuals on the Flag-Staff Hill section of Boston Common.

78. "Boston's Sacred Common."

79. Ernest Gordon, *Adoniram Judson Gordon: A Biography* (1896; New York: Garland, 1984), 60, 103.

80. "Preaching on the Common," *Boston Evening Transcript*, May 21, 1885; Bendroth, *Fundamentalists in the City*, 41.

81. Bendroth, "Rum, Romanism, and Evangelism," 628–29. Also see C. Allyn Russell, "Adoniram Judson Gordon: Nineteenth-Century Fundamentalist," *American Baptist Quarterly* 4 (Winter 1985): 61–89; and Gordon, *Adoniram Judson Gordon*.

82. Bendroth, "Rum, Romanism, and Evangelism," 636–37. For more on Davis and the Boston arrests, see Bendroth, *Fundamentalists in the City*, 41–86. Davis made the same argument two years later. Both Hastings and Davis believed that the 1862 municipal ordinance that required speakers to obtain permission from city officials before delivering an oration on public property was created to silence Protestants who denounced the city's growing liquor trade. For Davis's pamphlet, see William F. Davis, *Christian Liberties in Boston: A Sketch of Recent Attempts to Destroy Them through the Device of a Gag-by-Law for Gospel Preachers* (Chelsea, Mass.: self-published, 1887), 9–10.

83. "Preaching on the Common," *Boston Globe*, May 31, 1885. Also see "Dr. Gordon's View," *Boston Daily Advertiser*, May 25, 1885. Davis reiterated this argument in a pamphlet he published following his 1887 arrest. See Davis, *Christian Liberties in Boston*.

84. "William F. Davis. The Story of His Life," *British-American Citizen*, September 15, 1888, 3; "Man with a Conscience," *Boston Globe*, July 29, 1894. The *Globe* portrayed Davis as a kindly, patriarchal figure who rigorously adhered to his religious and ethical beliefs, regardless of the consequences.

85. Bendroth, "Rum, Romanism, and Evangelism," 629.

86. "God's License Enough." Davis also penned a lengthy tome that explained his determination to become a martyr for religious liberty while denouncing Boston city officials for denying what he viewed as Christian liberties. Davis, *Christian Liberties in Boston*.

87 Although it was not mentioned in court, Boston's mayor at the time, Hugh O'Brien, was a strong champion of public parks who supported Olmsted's vision. *Mayor Hugh O'Brien's 1877 Speech on Boston Parks*, 4; Geoffrey Blodgett, "Yankee Leadership in a Divided City, 1860–1919," in *Boston, 1700–1980: The Evolution of Urban Politics*, ed. Ronald P. Formisano and Constance K. Burns (Westport, Conn.: Greenwood Press, 1984), 88, 98, 132.

88. "Worship on the Common," *Boston Daily Advertiser*, May 29, 1885.

89. Bendroth, "Rum, Romanism, and Evangelism," 637.

90. "Two Guilty Preachers," *Boston Globe*, July 4, 1885.

91. Ibid.

92. Commonwealth v. William F. Davis, 140 Mass. 485 (1886).

93. That article added:

> And no subject shall be hurt, molested or restrained in his person, liberty or estate, for worshipping God in the manner and season most agreeable to the dictates of his own conscience, or for his religious profession or sentiments; *provided* he doth not disturb the public peace or obstruct others in their religious worship.

Pickering also cited the Massachusetts Convention Debates of 1820 that advocated public worship for the "good order and happiness of a community," as well as Thomas Cooley's *Treatise on the Constitutional Limitations* that held that it was unlawful for any state to pass laws restraining the free exercise of religious worship or the free expression of religious belief. See Commonwealth v. William F. Davis, 140 Mass. 485 (1886).

94. Commonwealth v. William F. Davis, 140 Mass. 485 (1886).

95. Ibid.

96. "Plucky Preacher Davis," *Boston Post*, October 3, 1887; "On the Common," *Boston Post*, October 10, 1887.

97. "Boston's Sacred Common"; Commonwealth v. William F. Davis, 140 Mass. 485 (1886).

98. "His Right to Serve God."

99. "Boston's Sacred Common."

100. "Dr. Fulton at It Again," *Boston Post*, October 17, 1887.

101. The Man Who Preached on the Common," *New York Times*, December 25, 1887.

102. Ibid.

103. *Inaugural Address of Hugh O'Brien, Mayor of Boston, before the City Council, January 2, 1888* (Boston: Rockwell and Churchill, 1888), 29–32.

104. Commonwealth v. William F. Davis, 162 Mass. 510 (1895).

105. Bendroth, "Rum, Romanism, and Evangelism," 640; Commonwealth v. Henry Abrahams, 156 Mass. 57, 30 N.E. 79 (1892).

106. 156 Mass. 57, 30 N.E. 79 (1892).

107. 140 Mass. 485 (1886).

108. Commonwealth v. William F. Davis, 162 Mass. 510 (1895).

109. Commonwealth v. William F. Davis, 140 Mass. 485 (1886). Holmes cited Des Plaines v. Poyer, 123 Ill. 348 (1888), as an example of a municipal ordinance that was voided for infringing upon freedom of speech rights.

110. Holmes cited Lincoln v. Boston, 148 Mass. 578, 20 N.E. 329 (1889).

111. Commonwealth v. William F. Davis, 162 Mass. 510 (1895) at 511. Also see William W. Van Alstyne, "The Demise of the Right-Privilege Distinction in Constitutional Law," *Harvard Law Review* 81 (1968): 1440.

112. G. Edward White, "Justice Holmes and the Modernization of Free Speech Jurisprudence: The Human Dimension," *California Law Review* 80 (March 1992): 397.

113. 155 Mass. 216 (1892).

114. John J. McAuliffe v. Mayor and Board of Aldermen of New Bedford, 155 Mass. 216, 29 N.E. 517 (1892).
115. White, "Justice Holmes," 397.
116. Van Alstyne, "Demise of the Right-Privilege Distinction," 1440.
117. 123 Ill. 348, 14 N.E. 677, 678 (1888). See also R. Allan Horning, "The First Amendment Right to a Public Forum," *Duke Law Journal* 18, no. 5 (1969): 932.
118. Van Alstyne, "Demise of the Right-Privilege Distinction," 1440–42.
119. Novak, *People's Welfare*, 6.
120. Ibid., 9.
121. Davis v. Massachusetts, 167 U.S. 43, 44 (1897); Rabban, *Free Speech in Its Forgotten Years*, 166.
122. 167 U.S. at 46–48.
123. Ibid. at 47.
124. Ibid.; "Preacher Davis Failed," *Boston Post*, May 11, 1897.
125. Frazee's Case, 42 N.W. 72 (Mich. 1886); Anderson v. City of Wellington, 40 Kan. 173 (1888); City of Chicago v. Trotter, 136 Ill. 430 (1891); Rich. v. City of Naperville, 42 Ill. App. 222 (1891); In re Garrabad, 54 N.W. 1104 (Wisc. 1893); City of Sioux Falls v. Kirby, 6 S.D. 62 (1894); In re Flaherty, 38 P. 981 (Cal. 1895); In re Gribben, 47 P.2d 1074 (Okla. 1897).
126. Siegel, "Historism in Late Nineteenth Century Constitutional Thought," 1497.
127. Curtis notes this argument, stating that in the struggles for freedom of speech in the late 1700s and throughout the 1800s, "Americans had widely divergent ideas about the meaning of freedom of speech and about how literally to take the creed that in the United States 'we the people' rule." Curtis, *Free Speech*, 3.
128. The U.S. Supreme Court would not address the issue of politicians' discretionary power to deny public permits until the early 1950s. In Kunz v. New York, 340 U.S. 290 (1951), Chief Justice Fred Vinson said the New York City ordinance in question included no "appropriate standards" to guide officials' decisions in granting or denying permits to individuals who wanted to speak on religious matters on city streets.
129. Novak, *People's Welfare*, 115, 120.
130. Gitlow v. New York, 268 U.S. 652 (1925). For more on restrictions on place, see Timothy Zick, "Space, Place, and Speech: The Expressive Topography," *George Washington Law Review* 34 (April 2006): 444; and Thomas P. Crocker, "Displacing Dissent: The Role of Place in First Amendment Jurisprudence," *Fordham Law Review* 75 (April 2007): 2595.
131. 318 U.S. 413 (1943).
132. Barbas, "Creating the Public Forum," 810.

CONTRIBUTORS

INDEX

CONTRIBUTORS

Jon Bekken is an associate professor of communications at Albright College. His research focuses on labor journalism. He is the author of two books, numerous book chapters, and more than eighteen journal articles on labor history and the labor press. Bekken was a journalist prior to his academic career.

David W. Bulla is an associate professor of communication and media sciences at Zayed University in the United Arab Emirates. His research centers on nineteenth-century press performance, particularly during the Civil War. He is the author of two books: *Lincoln's Censor* and *Journalism in the Civil War Era*, the latter cowritten with Gregory A. Borchard. Bulla is the adviser of the ZU student chapter of the Society of Professional Journalists and was a sports writer in North Carolina in the 1980s.

Mary M. Cronin is an associate professor of journalism and mass communications at New Mexico State University. She is the coauthor of one textbook, *The Mass Media: Invention, Development, Application and Impact*, with Charles Scholz; one monograph, "The Liberty to Argue Freely: Nineteenth-Century Obscenity Prosecutions and the Emergence of Modern Libertarian Free Speech Discourse"; and numerous scholarly journal articles, most of which focus on nineteenth-century media history issues. Cronin teaches media law, media history, and print journalism courses at NMSU and helps coordinate that university's Constitution Day and Sunshine Week activities. She publishes as Mary M. Cronin, although legally she is Mary M. Lamonica.

Sandra Davidson is a Curators' Teaching Professor at the University of Missouri's School of Journalism and an adjunct professor at the University of Missouri's School of Law. Davidson has won numerous awards for her teaching. Her research has appeared in newspaper articles, book chapters, and scholarly publications, including *William and Mary Bill of Rights Law Journal*, *Hastings Communications and Entertainment Law Journal*, *Saint Louis University Law Journal*, *Jurist*, and the Oxford Round Table's *Forum on Public Policy*. Her international work includes U.S. Information Agency trips to Prague, Bratislava, and Mongolia and working at the *Beijing Review*. She has taught in England at the Missouri School of Journalism's London Program and is the attorney for the *Columbia Missourian*.

Nancy McKenzie Dupont is an associate professor in the Meek School of Journalism and New Media at the University of Mississippi. Before joining the academy, Dupont was a television news reporter and producer for seventeen years. She has authored one writing textbook and seven book chapters on journalism history, but her primary research interest is secession and Civil War journalism of the South. She is currently writing a book on the beginning of the African American press in nineteenth-century New Orleans.

Joseph Hayden is an associate professor of journalism at the University of Memphis. A former broadcast journalist, he is the author of two monographs on recent presidential-press relations: *Covering Clinton: The President and the Press in the 1990s* and *A Dubya in the Headlights: George W. Bush and the Media*. Hayden's third monograph, *Negotiating the Press: American Journalism and Diplomacy, 1918–1919*, discusses journalism and diplomacy after World War I. He is also the author of two books on the craft of writing.

Lee Jolliffe, an associate professor of journalism at Drake University, is an active scholar specializing in antebellum abolitionists. She has written over eighty academic articles, book chapters, papers, and presentations for *American Periodicals*, *Journalism Quarterly*, *Journalism Educator*, *Journal of Popular Culture*, *Journalism History*, and the Symposium on the 19th Century Press, the Civil War, and Free Expression, among others. Prior to her academic career, Jolliffe worked as a manager of the editing department at Battelle Institute and as a freelance magazine writer.

Paulette D. Kilmer is a professor of communications at the University of Toledo, where she teaches media law and print journalism courses. Kilmer helps coordinate the university's Banned Books Week Vigil, works with the student paper, and participates in First Amendment ventures. She is the author of three books and numerous book chapters and scholarly articles. Her main interest is nineteenth-century press history.

Erika J. Pribanic-Smith is past president of the American Journalism Historians Association (2014–15). More than twenty years of experience in newspaper, magazine, and online journalism inform her instruction of undergraduate and graduate students as an assistant professor at the University of Texas–Arlington. She is the author of several scholarly journal articles, book chapters, and award-winning conference papers focusing primarily on the nineteenth-century Southern press and partisan politics.

Debra Reddin van Tuyll is a professor of communications at Augusta University. She is the author or editor of six books, including her most recent, *The Press in the Fallen Confederacy*. Her coauthored (with Patricia G. McNeely and Henry H. Schulte) *Knights of the Quill: Confederate Correspondents and Their Civil War Reporting* was a finalist for the 2010 Tankard Award from the Association for Education in Journalism and Mass Communication.

Janice R. Wood is a writer and editor living in Montgomery, Alabama. Her research focuses on journalistic and free speech issues of the nineteenth century. She is the author of numerous scholarly articles on nineteenth-century press freedom and of one book, *The Struggle for Free Speech in the United States, 1872–1915: Edward Bliss Foote, Edward Bond Foote, and Anti-Comstock Operations*. She previously worked professionally in corporate communication and newspaper journalism.

INDEX